PENGUIN BOOKS

THE BROTHERHOOD IN SAFFRON

WALTER K. ANDERSEN taught comparative politics at the College of Wooster, Ohio, before joining the State Department as a political analyst for South Asia.

SHRIDHAR D. DAMLE is a private consultant and has written extensively on Indian political developments.

THE BROTHERHOOD IN SAFFRON

*The Rashtriya Swayamsevak Sangh
and Hindu Revivalism*

WALTER K. ANDERSEN
& SHRIDHAR D. DAMLE

PENGUIN BOOKS

An imprint of Penguin Random House

PENGUIN BOOKS

USA | Canada | UK | Ireland | Australia
New Zealand | India | South Africa | China | Singapore

Penguin Books is part of the Penguin Random House group of companies
whose addresses can be found at global.penguinrandomhouse.com

Published by Penguin Random House India Pvt. Ltd
4th Floor, Capital Tower 1, MG Road,
Gurugram 122 002, Haryana, India

Penguin
Random House
India

First published in the USA by Westview Press, Inc. 1987
First published in India in Penguin Books by Penguin Random House India 2019

Copyright © Walter Andersen and Shridhar Damle 1987, 2019

ISBN 9780143446132

Typeset in Adobe Caslon Pro by Manipal Digital Systems, Manipal

Printed at Manipal Technologies Limited, India

We dedicate this book to our late parents,
Mildred Korfitz-Andersen

and Dattatraya Chimanrao Damle
and to Shridhar Damle's late father-in-law,
Shankarrao Tambe

Contents

List of Tables

Introduction

Every morning at sunrise groups of men in military-style khaki uniforms gather outdoors before saffron flags in all parts of India to participate in a common set of rituals, physical exercises and lessons. For one hour each day in the year, they are taught to think of themselves as a family—a brotherhood— with a mission to transform Hindu society. They are members of the Rashtriya Swayamsevak Sangh[1] (hereafter referred to as the RSS), the largest and most influential organization in India committed to Hindu revivalism. The message of the daily meetings is the restoration of a sense of community among Hindus.

Organizations like the RSS which advocate the restoration of community have a salience to those who feel rootless. Indeed, the alienation and insecurity brought on by the breakdown of social, moral and political norms have become major political issues in the twentieth century, particularly in the developing countries where new economic and administrative systems have rapidly undermined institutions and moral certitudes which traditionally defined a person's social function and relationship to authority.[2] Dislocations in

xi

primary associations which mediate between the individual and society have weakened the web of relations that provide individuals their self-identity and a sense of belonging. Social, religious and nationalist movements have proliferated to express a deeply felt need for the restoration of community.

The initial expression of this yearning for community often takes the form of religious revivalism.[3] In South Asia, religious revivalism has taken many forms, reflecting the cultural and religious complexity of the subcontinent. Moreover, revivalist groups represented a wide spectrum of ideologies, ranging from defences of traditional orthodoxy to completely new formulations of traditional norms and practices. They mobilized communal support both to reform group behaviour and to strengthen their own group's bargaining position with the political authorities. In the process, they laid the groundwork for larger communal identities and, ultimately, nationalist movements.

In pre-Independence India, the premier nationalist organization was the Indian National Congress, an umbrella organization which accommodated a variety of interests, including the revivalists. The Congress, to retain the support of its diverse membership, adopted a consensual strategy requiring the acceptance of compromise and, by extension, the principle of territorial nationalism. However, it was not entirely successful in accommodating all groups. Many Muslim leaders, for example, felt that the westernized Hindu elite who controlled the Congress did not adequately respond to Muslim interests. Moreover, there were Hindu revivalist leaders who also believed that the interests of the Hindu community were not adequately protected by the Indian National Congress. The founder of the RSS doubted whether the Congress, which included Muslims, could bring about the desired unity of the Hindu community.

The RSS was established in 1925 as a kind of educational body whose objective was to train a group of Hindu men who, on the basis of their character-building experience in the RSS, would work to unite the Hindu community so that India could again become an independent country and a creative society. Its founder was convinced that a fundamental change in social attitudes was a necessary precondition of a revived India, and that a properly trained cadre of nationalists would be the cutting edge of that change. The two leaders of the RSS during the pre-Independence period—its founder, Keshav Baliram Hedgewar (1925–1940) and Madhav Sadashiv Golwalkar (1940–1973)—laid a firm foundation, supervising the training of the full-time workers who spread the organization outward from its original base in eastern Maharashtra.

Linked to the RSS in India are several affiliated organizations (referred to in the RSS literature as the 'family'),[4] working in politics, in social welfare, in the media and among students, labourers and Hindu religious groups. The symbiotic links between the RSS and the 'family' are maintained by the recruitment into the affiliates of swayamsevaks (members) who have already demonstrated organizational skills in the RSS. This process guarantees a high degree of conformity to 'legitimate' behavioural norms among the cadre in all the affiliates. It has also resulted in a high degree of loyalty to the organization on the part of the cadre. The recruitment process employed by the 'family' of organizations around the RSS has enabled the RSS itself to remain insulated from the day-to-day affairs of the affiliates, thus protecting its self-defined role as a disinterested commentator of Indian society.

From its inception, the RSS adopted a cautious non-confrontational approach towards political authority to reduce the chances of government restrictions, but it often failed in this effort. After Independence in 1947, the RSS has on several occasions been the object of official censure, in large part because political leaders feared that it had the potential to develop into a major political force that might threaten their own power and India's secular orientation. The RSS was banned twice (in 1948–49 and in 1975–77), and restrictions have been periodically placed on its activities. These restrictions have not weakened the RSS. Quite the contrary, they have strengthened the commitment of its members and encouraged the RSS to expand the range of its activities. Indeed, such pressures against the RSS led the organization to get involved in politics.

Nonetheless, the controversy surrounding the RSS made it (and to a certain degree its affiliates) an unacceptable partner in joint activities during much of the post-Independence period. Only since the mid-1960s has the RSS been accorded a measure of general public respect. This new respectability owes much to the participation of its political affiliate in state coalition governments during 1967–69, the active part played by the RSS and its 'family' of organizations in a popular anti-corruption movement in 1973–75, the underground movement against restrictions on civil and political liberties during the 1975–77 state of Emergency, as well as to its support for the political alliance that captured power in the March 1977 national elections. Its political affiliate, the Bharatiya Jana Sangh, merged into the new governing party, the Janata Party, and former Jana Sangh leaders were included in the national cabinet and served as chief ministers in several states during the twenty-seven-month period that the Janata Party remained in power. Never before had the RSS worked so closely with such a broad range of groups, many of which had previously demanded restrictions on its activities. As a result, mutual suspicions were significantly diminished, though by no means eliminated.

While the RSS is still the object of much criticism for its Hindu revivalist orientation, it is now far more self-confident about its place in Indian society than at any time since Independence. The unprecedented growth of the RSS and its affiliates in the 1980s may be related to the upsurge of militancy among Hindus following the much-publicized conversion to Islam in 1981 of sane low-caste Hindus in the village of Meenakshipuram in the southern state of Tamil Nadu. The amorphous sense of danger to Hinduism intensified with the subsequent communal disturbances in Punjab and Jammu and Kashmir, two states with non-Hindu majorities, and with the increasing assertiveness of India's non-Hindu groups. Many Hindus are also convinced that government 'pampering' of the minorities hampers their integration in the national mainstream. The government's decision in March 1986 to enact legislation negating a court order that did not adhere to traditional Islamic law on the question of alimony is seen as a sign of such favouritism.

The growing Hindu militancy is reflected in a proliferation of Hindu defence associations, in movements to restore temples now used as mosques, in renewed efforts to convert Christians and Muslims to Hinduism, and in efforts to get a uniform civil code enacted into law. The RSS and its 'family' of organizations have been in the thick of many of these activities. However, the deep regional, linguistic and social divisions among Hindus, as well as the lack of overarching Hindu institutions, continue to hinder the development of Hindu solidarity nationally.

This study focuses on the 'family' of organizations around the RSS, especially its political affiliate.[5] The affiliates all have a highly centralized authority structure very similar to that of the RSS. All of them recruit their cadre largely from the RSS, and the RSS-trained cadre occupy the key organizational positions. We propose that it is this recruitment policy which shapes the ideology and organizational dynamics of all the affiliates. We have given considerable attention to the political affiliate of the RSS, largely because information regarding its recruitment, organization and impact on the public are more easily available. Some of the field research was conducted prior to the 1977 amalgamation of the Jana Sangh into the Janata Party. In 1983, still more field work was carried out in India to reassess those earlier findings. Our initial analysis regarding the organizational dynamics of the RSS 'family' was substantially buttressed by the subsequent research. One significant change, however, is that the political affiliate has a diminished significance in the 'family', in part because the RSS leaders are less concerned about political protection and because they have decided that the RSS can make a greater impact on society through the non-political members of the 'family'.

This shift in orientation can be traced to the Jana Sangh's participation in the Janata Party government (1977–79). The RSS was shocked by the attacks on the organization by the Jana Sangh's partners in the Janata Party. The RSS leaders discovered that close association to political power arouses envy and opposition which hinders their efforts to influence the larger public. Indeed, the attack on the RSS was one of the reasons the Jana Sangh group withdrew from the Janata Party in 1980. Since the re-establishment of the Jana Sangh under its new name, the Bharatiya Janata Party (BJP), the RSS has been maintain to sanction the close association that existed prior to 1977, though almost all in the top leadership of the BJP have an RSS background, and they have recently indicated a growing desire to remain within the 'family' of RSS organizations. But still the RSS now seems reluctant to put all its political eggs in the BJP basket. Indeed, politicians from other parties are seeking its support.

Most of the leadership and the leading activists of the Jana Sangh, as we shall show, underwent a period of training within the RSS. This continues to apply to its successor party, the BJP. This training is carried out in shakhas of the RSS which meet daily to teach character building (behavioural norms and a world view) to the swayamsevaks (participating volunteers). The founders of the RSS devised a training system which was intended to establish a brotherhood which, in the pursuit of a renewed sense of community, could transcend parochial antagonisms and social disorder. It was expected that this 'enlightened' group would work together to restore order and social harmony through reshaping society in a way compatible with the RSS interpretation of Hindu thought. RSS leaders maintain that this remains the organization's raison dêtre.

RSS training ideally starts in pre-adolescence and becomes more ideologically oriented during adolescence. The most explicitly ideological training occurs at a time when youth generally are working out in their own experiences a satisfying relationship between themselves and society. It is a period when the individual is particularly susceptible to ideological appeals.[6] It is a time when, if G. Morris Carstairs is right, Indian youth seek a person or a cause to which they can give their uncompromising support and obedience.[7] The RSS appeals to this impulse by advocating the sacrifice of self for society, organizationally expressed through service in the RSS and by deference to RSS leaders. The society envisaged is not the existing order, but a reformed and revitalized social order, a perception which permits young swayamsevaks to combine loyalty to the 'nation', (represented by the RSS) with rebellion against the various establishments which make harsh demands on the adolescent. The RSS holds out to its participants a cause to which they dedicate themselves and thereby transcend the mundane and ordinary affairs of the world.

The RSS expects of its members something very close to religious zeal, demanding from them strict self-control, disciplined activity and identification with the group. A system of myths, rites and symbols are intended to fuse the individual's identity to the larger Hindu community which the RSS claims to represent. In comparison with this larger community, the individual is only a minor element and he is valued as a part of a group and of a historical continuum. The training offered in the collective environment of shakha teaches the participants to identify private desires with the group and to enjoy cooperation and loyalty for their own sake.

The shakha offers a unifying experience for the participants, providing them with a similarity in speech and outlook. It also creates a certain aura of uniqueness among those who successfully complete the training and induces them to respect each other for what they have become. The intensity of the bonds which are formed may account for the commitment to the ideology of the RSS. This commitment probably has a greater influence on organizational loyalty than the substantive content of the ideology itself.

Members of all castes are welcomed into the RSS and are treated as equals if they conform to behavioural standards considered proper by RSS leaders. Those standards continue to reflect, to a large extent, the Maharashtrian brahmin values of the founders of the RSS. Many brahmins in Maharashtra had a world view that was both 'priestly' and 'kingly' (and this was not unique to Maharashtra).[8] Aspects of both world views have been incorporated into the RSS. Its brahmanical orientation is reflected in its emphasis on a fastidious and ascetic lifestyle, selfless devotion to an ideal, learning and the symbols of the great tradition of Hinduism. The RSS, for its part, conceives of itself as a source of enlightenment and its leaders compare it to the ancient ashrams (traditional religious training centres). Its martial orientation shows up in its glorification of physical strength and bravery, and the use of traditional weapons and drills. The RSS discipline, its uniform and the Sanskritized military terms employed at its meetings convey a martial impression. Those historical figures which it honours tend to be warriors that the RSS associates with nation building (e.g., Shivaji, Rana Pratap, and Guru Govind Singh). Conformity to the accepted behaviour patterns and the expression of loyalty to RSS symbols confer acceptance. However, acceptance is bestowed not because of individual achievement, but rather because of the participant's contribution to the group's collective efforts.

We attended shakhas in several states and were struck by the group loyalty demonstrated by those who participated together in the small sub-units of the shakha. We observed friendships between boys from opposite ends of the economic, social, and ritual hierarchies. Many of those we interviewed claimed that those friendships formed in the RSS were among the strongest and most long lasting. We believe it is this strong group cohesiveness, developed within the shakha, which constitutes the 'cement' which binds the swayamsevaks to the organization. The strong bonds which develop between RSS participants also have an important effect on the cohesiveness of the RSS affiliates. When the RSS swayamsevak transfers to the affiliate, he brings along with him strong loyalties to his RSS comrades, many of whom will be in the affiliate. He also brings ideological and behavioural orientations which enable the organization to adhere to established principles and to an accepted command structure. The organizational skills developed within the RSS make the cadre of its affiliates the envy of other Indian organizations. Our interview data suggests that RSS socialization has a greater effect on the cadre's ideological orientation than such socio-economic variables as age, income, caste and occupation.

We maintain that it is participation first within the RSS and then the affiliate which creates an 'interest', rather than the objective class or social backgrounds of the participants. Organizations, in our view, are the necessary intermediaries through which social conflict takes on an ideological dimension, for it is within organizations that the linkages between norms and behaviour take place.[9]

Regarding the presentation of the material, we analysed in some depth how events and circumstances shaped both the content of the curriculum of the RSS and its organizational structure. Consequently, the first chapter looks at the roots of the Hindu revivalist ideology of the RSS. The second chapter analyses the formation and early development of the RSS. The third chapter considers the ideology of the RSS and the fourth focuses on the establishment of the affiliates and on the symbiotic relationship between them and the RSS. The last two chapters concentrate on the RSS brotherhood in politics.

1

Hindu Revivalism

The origins of the nationalist movement in nineteenth-century India can be traced to the expansion of Western education through the English language during the early part of the century.[1] The English-educated elites were concentrated in Bengal, Bombay and Madras, three coastal presidencies where greater opportunities existed for the new education and for vocations based on it—law, medicine, journalism, education, banking, modern trading and manufacturing. Those attracted to the new education came primarily from caste Hindu groups in all three presidencies.[2] The proponents of social, political and religious reform among Hindus were drawn from this English-educated class.

Until very late in the nineteenth century, most politically articulate Indians were willing to collaborate with the colonial administration. Political action took the form of petitions for greater Indian participation in the bureaucracy and in the legislative councils, protection of indigenous industry, reform of judicial administration and legal procedure to bring them into line with the practices established in England, and

1

reforms of the Hindu social order that would make it more compatible with Western norms.[3]

MODERNISTS AND REVIVALISTS

A shift from collaboration to criticism began in the latter part of the nineteenth century. This approach required new techniques of public protest. As older social, economic and psychological commitments were eroded among those most exposed to the change, newly acquired Western norms were employed to judge society.[4] Two broad movements emerged among Hindus seeking to define their national identity, and we shall refer to them as the modernists and revivalists.[5] The former adopted models of social and political change based upon Western patterns, and the latter looked to Hindu antiquity. Both groups found themselves wanting when judged by the new norms. Within both groups a broad range of ideological perspectives was present. Revivalism included those who wanted to preserve the traditional social order as well as those who sought to reform Hindu society as a way of strengthening Hindu solidarity. The RSS traces its roots to the latter and hence we shall limit our discussion of revivalism to the Hindu reformers.

The Hindu revivalists sought to recover fundamental truth which they felt had been lost since the era of its original revelation. They argued that the loss of national consciousness had created conditions conducive to foreign domination. By appealing to an idealized past, the revivalists reminded the Hindu public of the suffering and degradation experienced under alien rule. The call for independence was a logical corollary, for the degraded present could only be overcome by eliminating the foreign intruders who had disrupted the original blissful society. Muslim rulers and the British were identified as sources of that disruption and many revivalist spokesmen sought to place limits on their political power and on their cultural influence. Consistent with the traditional Indian concept of knowledge, changes within Hindu society were justified by the proposition that the changes were not new at all, but were in fact a revival of older, purer forms of Hindu culture that had degenerated during foreign rule.

The revivalists, unlike their modernist counterparts, spoke to an almost exclusively Hindu audience. The style of the revivalists was more aggressive and tended to reflect a kshatriya (warrior) world view.[6] The identification with the martial tradition of Hinduism enhanced their self-esteem by the same standards used by many British to evaluate the worth of Indians.[7] Research of Western orientalists confirmed the faith of the revivalists in the achievements of Hindu rule and civilization.[8] The romantic nationalism sweeping Europe at the end of the nineteenth century provided additional intellectual justification for reconstructing the present by reaching back to the classical roots of the civilization.[9]

PROTEST AGAINST BRITISH RULE

The English-educated Indian elite organized political associations, located initially in the presidency capitals, primarily to persuade the colonial authorities to increase Indian recruitment into the bureaucracy and the legislative councils, and to legislate reforms of Hindu society. Several of these associations sent representatives to Bombay in 1885 to organize the Indian National Congress.[10] While the Congress included many revivalists who advocated a militant style of protest and greater contact with the masses, it tended to be controlled, at least at the national level, by modernists until 1916 when it passed into the hands of a group associated with Bal Gangadhar Tilak, a Maharashtrian revivalist leader. The mantle of leadership then passed in 1920 to Mohandas Karamchand Gandhi, who, while drawing heavily from Hindu concepts, was bitterly opposed by many revivalists, especially by the followers of Tilak.

Opposition to British rule increased among both modernists and revivalists, as the contradictions between colonial rule and new aspirations became more obvious. Criticism of India's colonial status was buttressed by the perception that the British viewed Indians and Indian culture as inferior. Educated Indians were incensed when the British began to characterize them as feminine, cowardly, and unrepresentative of the indigenous culture.[11] The racial arrogance often expressed by European officials, businessmen and missionaries made a substantial contribution to nationalist sentiment. Constitutional reforms which offered increased Indian participation in legislative bodies and the bureaucracy did not match expectations. The Western-educated Indians believed that they should enjoy the same civil liberties as the English. With the development of new techniques of agitation, the government undermined popular trust by enforcing regulations which curtailed civil liberties. The claim that British economic policies caused a drain of wealth from India further enforced the view that the British were fundamentally unconcerned with the country's well-being.

Developments in the late nineteenth century created conditions conducive to the expansion of revivalism.

Nationalism was beginning to assert itself. The revivalist message, based on traditional Hindu concepts regarding society, was appealing to many Indians. There were few other organizational alternatives for expressing grievances. Technical developments in the fields of transportation and communications provided revivalists opportunities to spread their message quickly to a larger audience.[12]

INFLUENCE OF THE HINDU WORLD VIEW

Revivalism was expressed in new organizations which attempted to blend religion with socio-economic values to foster a revived sense of community and ultimately to espouse nationalism. Hindu society had degenerated, according to many early spokesmen of revivalism, because Hindus had not observed dharma (a code of conduct for various social categories, situations and stages of life). Many revivalists argued that India could not regenerate itself unless dharma was properly observed. Aurobindo Ghose, an influential Bengali revivalist, maintained: 'All great awakenings in India, all her periods of mightiest and most varied vigour have drawn their vitality from the fountain-head of some deep religious awakening.'[13]

The causative relationship between religious observance and socio-political affects represented a general commitment to Hindu metaphysics. Major Indian schools of thought offered a moral conception of existence based on the view that behaviour and natural phenomena are guided by inviolable laws. A good society can exist only when it is rooted on correct principles of dharma.[14] The state's obligation in the classical Hindu texts was to protect the established order so that individuals could perform the duties prescribed by caste and stage of life.[15]

To pursue and legitimize the political task of national integration and self-government, the revivalists selectively drew from a vast mosaic of often conflicting values. They redefined traditional concepts to justify public protest and to rationalize a restructuring of Hindu society. A central concern was to redefine the linked concepts of dharma-karma. Rules of dharma maintained social integration at the local level of Indian life and were enforced by a consensus of the elders of the local castes. The rules encompassed an individual's moral and religious life, and regulated social, political, and economic responsibilities. Karma refers to the willed actions of an individual. These actions have a good or bad effect which determines the quality of life in succeeding incarnations. Hindu practice tended to specify dharma according to the endogamous caste into which a person was born, though many of the Hindu sacred texts do not make this connection.[16] A person was required to observe dharma unselfishly and without interest in the results of the action. At a more advanced stage on the path to moksha (release from the bonds of existence), the devotee subjectively seeks 'realization' of the divinity. These concepts strengthened an identity with the small groups to which an individual belonged by birth and made collective identifications of a larger sort more difficult.[17] According to P. T. Raju, the cumulative effect of Hindu thought is a negative attitude towards the material world.[18] Rajni Kothari proposes that the strains produced by national defeat and humiliation further encouraged other-worldliness, fatalism and pessimism.[19]

Many revivalists, in their reinterpretation of dharma-karma, attempted to substitute the larger Hindu 'nation' for primary group identification and to create a life-affirming orientation. Like millennial movements in Europe, the political character of Indian revivalism derived much of its strength from the importance of preparing for salvation.[20] Three persons prominent in redefining the dharma-karma concept for political purposes were Narendranath Datta (1863–1902), who took the name Swami Vivekananda after he came in contact with Ramakrishna Paramahansa (the Bengali saint who was his spiritual preceptor), Aurobindo Ghose (1872–1950) and Bal Gangadhar Tilak (1856–1920). They all employed the *Bhagavadgita* to legitimate their reformulations. The Gita had obvious advantages for the revivalists. It was both popular devotional literature and a source of Hindu philosophical speculation.[21] Because it discusses the major paths that lead to salvation, the Gita provided an opportunity to speculate on their comparative merits.

Bal Gangadhar Tilak, a leading Maharashtrian publicist of revivalism, sought to create a philosophic justification for 'energism'[22] that would replace a negative attitude towards life.[23] Tilak dismissed the popularly accepted commentaries of the Gita by Shankara (AD 787–838) and Ramanuja (AD 1017–1137?), claiming that these writers were primarily interested in justifying their own interpretation of spiritual realization. He maintained that their commentaries 'twist the meaning of such statements as might be totally inconsistent with their cults...'[24] According to Tilak, the interpretations of Shankara (renunciation combined with knowledge) and Ramanuja (devotionalism) contributed to a negative view of life. Their mistake was the misuse of traditional hermeneutics. He accepted as authoritative Mimansa's rules of interpretation (propositions at the beginning and at the end of a treatise should receive greater importance) to justify his case for *karmayoga*.[25]

The Gita, in its opening passages,[26] focuses on Arjuna, a military leader whose chariot had been driven between his army and that of the enemy. The opposing army is led by his cousins who wrongly occupy his throne. Recognizing friends, teachers and relatives on the other side, Arjuna is overcome by doubt and is not sure whether he should obey his kshatriya dharma and fight the battle. There then follows a dialogue between his charioteer, Lord Krishna (incarnation of the Divine), and Arjuna. Tilak maintains that, in the end, Lord Krishna rejects devotionalism and renunciation, and orders Arjuna to act according to his dharma; in other words, to order his army to fight the epic battle.[27] Rather than teaching that life is a necessary evil, Tilak proposes that the Gita demands action (karmayoga) with the implication that it is a 'great good fortune that one got human birth'.[28] In a departure from conventional Hindu norms, he delinks dharma and caste by claiming that Hinduism teaches that the individual must decide which duty is most suitable.[29] Moreover, action is 'selfless' if it is 'for the public good and not for the enjoyment of pleasure'.[30] The Gita's justification of social involvement and its emphasis on single-mindedness in secular pursuits made it a favourite among revivalists generally.

Bipin Chandra Pal, a Bengali revivalist contemporary of Tilak's, felt that India's decline could be traced to the Hindus' separation of spiritual enlightenment from society's welfare.[31]

Two fellow Bengalis provided a linkage between spiritual enlightenment and society's welfare in theological terms.

Aurobindo Ghose and Swami Vivekananda based their formulations on advaita (non-dualist) philosophy and the doctrine of shakti. Advaita philosophy is a form of monism which postulates the identity of the individual soul, jiva, and the divine soul, jagadishwar. Salvation is achieved when the former merges into the latter by a recognition of their essential unity. By recognizing this unity, the 'true believer' also recognizes the divine component in every person and demonstrates faith 'when the distress of every other man bearing that name Hindu comes to your heart and makes you feel as if your own son were in distress'.[32]

Both men drew on the traditional religious concept of shakti (the kinetic power of the divinity, symbolized by the feminine aspect of the divinity) to argue that every person possesses a vast potential power.[33] Shakti doctrine holds that this power can be tapped by the practice of sadhana (form of worship) that leads to a realization of the unity of the individual soul with the divine soul. Having realized this unity, the worshipper fuses his Self with the Goddess (shakti) and can partake of divine power.

Aurobindo Ghose, in the spirit of such European nationalists as Mazzini, saw a divine expression of God in the nation. Nationalism for him was not merely a form of patriotism, but 'nationalism is a religion that has come from God'.[34] Both Ghose and Vivekananda believed that national rejuvenation would come only when Indians tapped that potential source of power and directed their energies to the 'Mother Goddess' as she manifested herself in the Hindu nation.

EXPRESSION OF GRIEVANCES THROUGH REVIVALIST ORGANIZATIONS

When the Hindu revivalist movement developed in the late nineteenth century, there were few channels for the expression of grievances except through traditional caste structures or religious sects and movements. However, few traditional organizations were suited to mass mobilization, and most were ideologically incompatible with the reformist orientation of the revivalists. Few traditional organizations were capable of advancing the revivalists' desire for an expanded sense of community. New organizational forms and tactics were required.

The nineteenth-century revivalists, unlike their modernist counterparts, sought to create a mass movement, and many expressions of revivalism succeeded in attracting widespread popular support. Revivalists generally spoke in a traditional idiom and utilized philosophic concepts and symbols which were widely understood. Revivalism also offered enlarged communal identities without necessarily demanding a denial of the heritage and culture of its recruits. Revivalist leaders inside the Congress, such as Tilak and Ghose, argued that the activities of the Congress were too narrowly based; each of them turned to traditional symbols to arouse mass support against the British. The Congress itself did not develop a mass base until after Mohandas Karamchand Gandhi took control of it in 1920.

Revivalist activity emerged first in Bengal, Bombay and Punjab. Each presidency had its own distinct problems caused by social and economic change, and in each the revivalists used Hindu symbolism salient to their own region. In the nineteenth century, it would be more accurate to speak of Hindu regional revivalism. Only gradually did revivalist groups develop syncretic symbols capable of arousing support on an all-India level. Not until the twentieth century did revivalist organizations succeed in appealing to an all-India audience.[35]

Organized revivalism had its initial success in mobilizing support in Bengal, headquarters of England's Indian Empire. The Hindu Mela was formed in 1867 to revive a pride in Hindu civilization. At the annual meetings of this group, self-reliance and self-respect were promoted by exhibitions of indigenous arts and crafts, traditional sports, and the performance of patriotic songs and dramas. The widely read novels of Bankim Chandra Chatterjee popularized the concept that Hindus had a divine sanction to struggle for a society in which their dharma could be freely expressed. In his novel, *Anandamath*, he identifies the Goddess Kali (the 'Mother') with Bengal. Hindu revivalists all over India later adopted this symbolism and his poem, 'Bande Mataram', identifying the motherland with the 'Mother', was set to music in 1896 and became a favourite anthem among them.[36] Secret societies were formed to struggle for political emancipation, recruiting primarily young students from the middle-class elements of Bengal. Some of these secret societies evolved into revolutionary groups.[37] Swami Vivekananda founded the Ramakrishna Mission and its Order to teach karmayoga and shakti. Although both the Order and the Mission remained outside politics, they provided the rationale for political activity; and many revivalist activists, including the founders of the RSS, were inspired by Vivekananda's message. The second head of the RSS was himself an ordained member of the Order.

Patriotic folk festivals were organized by Tilak in the Marathi-speaking part of Bombay Presidency to worship the god Ganesh and to honour Shivaji, the seventeenth-century Maratha ruler who successfully challenged Muslim rule. These festivals became extremely popular and were occasions for heightening Hindu group identity and self-esteem through songs, lectures and ritual.[38] The festivals became catalysts for the formation of secret societies pledged to the independence of India.

Among the most active of these secret societies was the Mitra Mela (Friends' Group), later known as the Abhinava Bharat Society (Young India Society) formed in 1899 by Vinayak Damodar Savarkar. Recruiting primarily among college students, the various units of this group promoted traditional forms of exercise, and popularized nationalist ballads and poetry to serve as tools in spreading their message among the masses. The Abhinava Bharat Society advocated armed revolution to throw off the shackles of foreign rule.[39] Links between the Abhinava Bharat Society and its Bengali counterpart, the Anushilan Samiti, were established to coordinate revolutionary activity.

Revolutionary activity increased significantly after 1905 when the partition of Bengal was announced.[40] This activity was most pronounced in Bengal, Bombay and Punjab. Both the Abhinava Bharat Society and the Anushilan Samiti sought mass support to foment a national uprising. However, by addressing themselves almost exclusively to the political issue of independence, the middle-class group could tap the social discontent of neither the lower classes nor the peasantry. The educated youths who led these organizations were virtual strangers among the peasantry, and they appear to have had little comprehension of rural society or how to organize it.

The most popular revivalist group in northern India was the Arya Samaj.[41] Like the earlier reform societies, the Arya Samaj sought to change Hindu religious and social behaviour. It opposed, among other things, the hereditary aspect of the caste system, the ritual supremacy of brahmins, child marriage, and idol worship. It advocated a strict monotheism and a simplified ritual.[42] To counter the proselytizing activities of Christian missionaries, it borrowed many organizational techniques from them. The Arya Samaj relied on printed material to further its cause, sponsored missionary activities to convert Muslims and Christians, and performed ceremonies to raise outcast Hindus to the twice-born status. The desire of the Arya Samaj leadership to establish Hindu nationalism on the foundations of religious and social unity resulted in the formation of shuddhi sabhas (conversion councils) and the formation of the All-India Shuddhi Sabha in 1909.

EXPANDING COMMUNICATIONS FACILITIES

The spread of any movement depends on the existence of facilities for disseminating its message. Modern concepts of nationalism and self-government were introduced from the West at the elite level and filtered down to the population through the educational system and the press. Education, however, was not universal and Western education was limited to a tiny elite segment of the population. Since most Western education was controlled by the Christian missionary societies or by the government, a major goal of many revivalists was to form educational societies that were free from pro-Christian or pro-British influence. Technical advances in printing provided the revivalists with new opportunities for building self-esteem and for communicating with larger audiences. Exposure to Western culture and literature created a demand among the literate for printed material that touched on contemporary problems and regional tomes.

Newspapers espousing the revivalist cause in both English and the vernacular were established in cities all over India. English-language newspapers linked nationalist groups all over the country. Newspapers in the vernacular broadened the nationalist impact among the masses. Vernacular narrative prose often focused on heroic figures and events from a region's past, thus helping to inculcate a pride in things Indian. In addition, the revivalists recognized the mobilization potential of traditional forms of communication. Religious festivals were organized to revive the glory of Hinduism, to praise the exploits of its heroes, and, more importantly, to establish a national identity based on distinctly Hindu symbols.

REVIVALIST RESPONSE TO GANDHI

Mohandas Gandhi, when he emerged publicly on the Indian political scene after World War I as the Mahatma, received widespread revivalist support. Indeed, many believed him to be one of them. Around his style of leadership there developed a charisma which attracted a large number of Indians to the nationalist cause. Lloyd I. Rudolph and Susanne Hoeber Rudolph argue that his charisma had traditional roots; his asceticism in personal and public life convinced many that he was able to realize ideals which many held, but which few could realize.[43] The concept finds ample support in Hindu thought.

Since desire is the root cause of the bonds that chain people to the cycle of rebirths, desire must be quenched.[44] Various Hindu sects practice different forms of ascetic austerities in order to quench desire and teach a path to moksha. Linked to the concept of asceticism is the doctrine that its practitioners can acquire power.[45] Gandhi himself publicly practised tapasya (a form of austerity) to induce changes in Indian life.[46] This saintly style attracted to Gandhi an enormous following who trusted the 'inner voice' that spoke to him and who believed in the potency of his power.

To reach the Indian masses, Gandhi rationalized the Congress organization and involved it with activities that touched on the lives of the masses. The tool that he employed to express protest against British rule and other perceived injustices was satyagraha ('truth force').[47] The technique had been practised in India for centuries. It consisted of resisting injustice through fasting and non-violent protest, to bring moral pressure against the agent of injustice.[48] Gandhi refined the technique to fit it to social, economic and political injustices by employing vast numbers in civil disobedience. He implemented the techniques of satyagraha in a series of non-violent disobedience campaigns that would bring all sides of a dispute together in harmonious recognition of justice (or 'truth').

While Gandhi had much in common with the revivalists, many came to oppose him as they became better acquainted with his ideas. They were disturbed by his ascetic, non-kshatriya style of leadership, his definition of dharma as the non-violent pursuit of 'truth', and his assimilationist conception of the Indian nation, which he saw as a brotherhood or a confederation of communities.

Some opposed his vision of an economy, society and polity based on the self-sufficient village. But it was on the first three objections that they took issue with his leadership, for they felt his views would not sustain the militancy necessary to force the British out of India.

Regarding tactics, many Hindu revivalists questioned Gandhi's assertion that non-violent action was the only morally permissible technique of protest. Perhaps more disturbing to them was their concern that Gandhi's emphasis on ahimsa (nonviolence) discouraged the 'energism' and militancy needed to conduct a prolonged struggle against British imperialism. Tilak justified himsa (violence) in Hindu ethics with the proposition that the sacred canon made self-protection a higher duty than ahimsa.[49] According to him a 'villain' who comes to do harm should be punished, even killed if he 'does not listen to reason'.[50] Means and ends were not convertible terms for him, or for many other revivalists. Consequently, violence, collaboration, or almost any other means was justifiable if it led to the elimination of the British 'villain'. Dr Kurta-koti, *Shankaracharya* (a Hindu spiritual guide) of Karvir Peeth, expressed the views of many revivalists when he wrote in the 1920s that Gandhi's use of ahimsa in the non-cooperation movement would 'uproot the very principle of Hinduism and Aryan philosophy'.[51] He claimed that ahimsa as employed by Gandhi undermined Hindu self-respect and encouraged the Muslims to dominate the Hindus. Moreover, he maintained that 'passive and non-resisting sufferance is a Christian and not-Aryan principle'. He implored Hindus to return to the militancy advocated by Tilak, Vivekananda and Ghose. Many other revivalists were in agreement, and when Gandhi took control of the Congress in the 1920s, the stage was set for a revivalist search for new forms of protest against colonial rule. The issue that triggered their departure from the Congress was Gandhi's conciliatory approach towards Muslims, which they characterized as appeasement.

2

Formation and Development of the Rashtriya Swayamsevak Sangh

The RSS emerged during a wave of Hindu-Muslim riots that swept across India in the early 1920s. Its founder viewed the communal rioting as a symptom of the weakness and divisions within the Hindu community. He argued that independence could be achieved only after the splintered Hindu community—divided by caste, religion, language and sect—coalesced. He believed that the Congress, in which he had been an active participant, had appeased Muslims and was therefore unable to unite the Hindus; and in his view Hindu unity was the necessary precondition for any successful independence struggle.

DETERIORATION OF HINDU–MUSLIM RELATIONS

In 1916, the Indian National Congress and the Muslim League made a major effort at Lucknow to draw Hindus and Muslims together politically at the national level. The leadership of the two organizations agreed, among other things, to support the demand for complete self-government

18

and for the continuation of separate Muslim electorates in the legislative councils.[1] Some revivalists, such as Madan Mohan Malaviya, a political activist from the United Provinces, opposed the Lucknow Pact on the grounds that this approach to Hindu–Muslim unity in fact seriously undermined Hindu interests.

Most revivalists also argued that Gandhi's efforts in the early 1920s to strengthen Hindu–Muslim bonds by lining up the Congress organization behind the Muslim protest against the dismemberment of the Turkish empire, referred to as the Khilafat movement, would encourage Muslim separatism. When he launched his first major non-cooperation movement in India on 1 August 1920, one of the issues was the British unwillingness to satisfy Muslims on the Turkish issue. Gandhi called for a complete boycott of government institutions, while simultaneously including the doctrine of non-violent resistance as an integral part of the movement. A considerable number of Congress members, including many revivalists, opposed both the objectives and tactics of the boycott.[2] Particularly outspoken were those Hindu Congress members who were followers of Tilak. G. S. Kharpade, a Maharashtrian colleague of Tilak, prepared a formal statement which claimed that the non-cooperation movement might 'develop powers of endurance, but cannot breed the energy or resourcefulness and practical wisdom necessary for a political struggle'.[3] This proposition was to become accepted wisdom among Gandhi's revivalist critics. Nevertheless, many Hindu revivalists did support the 1920–21 non-cooperation movement. There was no other viable nationalist organization.

The apparent failure of Gandhi's non-cooperation movement, which was followed by widespread communal rioting, convinced many Hindu revivalists that a different approach was needed. Many believed that the 'weakness' of the Hindu community could be overcome only if Hindus strengthened community bonds and adopted an assertive kshatriya outlook. Accordingly, communal peace, they argued, would result only if Muslims and Hindus both realized that an attack on one community would result in a devastating response by the other. When conflicts developed between members of the two communities, communal allies were often sought through appeals to the most sharply defined cleavage separating Hindus and Muslims, namely, religion.[4] The success of that appeal depended, in large part, on the degree of cultural differentiation in a particular area. Violence frequently erupted over some alleged dishonour to the symbols of the two communities. As a result of violence, a history of communal affronts could be drawn upon to arouse communal tension.[5]

Hindu revivalists were particularly alarmed by the widespread communal rioting which occurred on the Malabar coast of south-western India during August 1921. Events there underscored the revivalist concern about the dangers facing the Hindus of the subcontinent. Muslim resentment against British rule in the Malabar area was coupled with anti-Hindu sentiment, and the rioting grew to such proportions that the civil administration was unable to contain the violence in many places.[6] This uprising, which also was accompanied by forced conversions of Hindus, confirmed the fears of many Hindus that the violence on the Malabar Coast was a covert attempt to enhance the political influence of Muslims at the expense of the Hindu community. Many Hindus feared that similar outbreaks would occur elsewhere, and these apprehensions fuelled revivalist sentiment.

The All-India Congress Committee condemned the events on the Malabar Coast, but not forcefully enough to suit some Hindu congressmen.[7] N. C. Kelkar, a senior Congress y figure from Bombay province, told the Congress Enquiry Commission, which was investigating the rioting, that 'the condemnation by Mahomedans of the forced conversion of Hindus in Malbar [sic] was not as full throated and did not ring as true as it should in these days of Hindu-Muslim unity'.[8] Dr B. S. Munje, a revivalist leader of the Congress in the Central Provinces, suggested that 'we [Hindus] should devise a scheme for encouraging and providing for settlement in Malabar of the martial communities of the Hindus such as Mahratta, Rajputs, and Sikhs'.[9] The Dehra Dun branch of the Hindu Mahasabha warned, 'The Hindu race once so great and glorious is truly speaking "nobody's child" now. The result is that it is usually the Hindus who fall an easy prey to the aggression of those more united and virile.'[10]

HINDU NATIONALISTS ORGANIZE

As a result of the intensification of Hindu–Muslim tension between 1921 and 1923, the dormant Hindu Mahasabha, formed in 1915 as a forum for a variety of Hindu interests (e.g., cow protection, Hindi in the Devanagari script, caste reforms, etc.) was revitalized.[11] Hindus, alarmed at the entry of Muslim ulema into politics, the talk of holy wars, and the pan-Islamic aims of some Muslim leaders, were convinced that they had to create an effective organizational mechanism if they were to contain a revived and aggressive Islam. A large number of new Mahasabha centres were formed in north India, particularly in Punjab, Delhi, the United Provinces and Bihar, areas where communal antagonism had reached alarming proportions. Such centres were also organized in areas where the Mahasabha had previously made very little impact, such as Madras and Bengal.[12]

Hindu leaders called a national meeting at Benares in August 1923 to revive the Hindu Mahasabha, and it was attended by a broad spectrum of the Hindu community. Pandit Madan Mohan Malaviya, a spokesman of Hindu revivalism in the United Provinces, stated that the major objectives of the session were to 'devise means to arrest the deterioration and decline of Hindus and to effect the improvement of the Hindus as a community.[13] Malaviya, in his presidential address to the session, stated: 'If the Hindus made themselves strong and the rowdy section among the Mahomedans were convinced they could not safely rob and dishonor Hindus, unity would be established on a stable basis.'[14] To attain this end, he suggested that caste Hindus accept untouchables as 'true' Hindus, and end their segregation at schools, wells and tenpins. He also suggested that a movement should be launched to reclaim Hindus 'who had been willingly or forcibly converted'.[15] At this session, Hindus were encouraged to form gymnasiums for both men and women. The kshatriya model, combining elements of militancy, vigour and domination, was called upon to overcome the perceived cowardice of Hindus.

The call for greater fraternal unity among Hindus was often frustrated by orthodox Hindu opposition to reforms that could lead to greater social integration. The orthodox members of the Hindu Mahasabha were particularly disturbed by the reformist revivalists' advocacy of interdining between untouchables and caste Hindus, and by their proposal that untouchables wear the sacred thread. Din Dayal Sharma, a leading spokesman of the orthodox group within the Mahasabha, charged that these resolutions ignored traditional theological injunctions.[16] Nevertheless, the Mahasabha's increasing commitment to Hindu solidarity and social reform demonstrated the growing power of its revivalist members. The orthodox were gradually to withdraw from it.

In his presidential address to the eighth Hindu Mahasabha session in 1925, Lajpat Rai proposed that non-violent non-cooperation could seriously weaken Hindu solidarity and thus adversely affect the freedom struggle. 'We cannot afford to be so weak and imbecile as to encourage others to crush us, nor can we be so obsessed by the false ideas of ahimsa but at our peril'.[17] He stated that nonviolence would result in 'laziness', 'fake contentment', 'cowardice', 'lack of spirit', and a 'slave mentality' among Hindus.[18] These charges were similar to those raised earlier by the revivalists in their criticism of Hindu orthodoxy.

This growing belligerency also undermined support for Gandhi. His inability to bring about the premised swaraj and to calm the communal frenzy led many to question his leadership. In late 1924, a Home Department report on a visit of Mahatma Gandhi to Punjab stated 'It is literally true that people who not long ago credited the Mahatma with superhuman and even divine powers, now look upon him as a "spent force", "an extinct volcano", and a person altogether divested of power and capacity'.[19]

The challenge from Islam in the early 1920s was viewed by many Hindus as a threat to their self-esteem. The proliferation of Hindu sabhas and other 'defensive' Hindu associations were reactions to the growing communal violence, the increasing political articulation of Muslims, the cultural 'Islamization' of the Muslim community, and the failure to achieve independence. While these organizations probably had little effect on British policy, they did advance Hindu unity, while simultaneously generating a heightened sense of Muslim political and cultural consciousness. Such organizations provided Hindus with an opportunity to express their hostility towards the 'oppressors' (the Muslims and the British); and, through them, Hindus may have experienced an increased respect for themselves and their co-religionists for having repudiated the impulse of giving in to their 'oppressors'.[20] It is in this setting of Hinduism in danger that the RSS was established.

EARLY DEVELOPMENT OF THE RSS

The roots of the RSS are imbedded in the soil of Maharashtra. Its membership and symbols were almost exclusively Maharashtrian. Its discipline and ideological framework were shaped almost entirely by Dr Keshav Baliram Hedgewar, a medical doctor who had abandoned a potentially lucrative practice to participate in the struggle against colonialism. Hedgewar was born on 1 April 1889 at Nagpur, the capital of the ethnically diverse Central Provinces. According to his most reliable biographer, the Hedgewar family migrated from Hyderabad, a Muslim princely state in south India, and settled in Nagpur around the turn of the nineteenth century.[21]

Hedgewar's father was aware of the advantage that could result from an English education, and he selected his brightest son, Keshav, to attend a modern school.[22] The father's decision not to prepare his son for the traditional role of priest may also have been influenced by Keshav's disinterest in orthodox ritual. In fact, accounts of his youth suggest that he felt much of it was rather silly.[23] The young scholar was keenly interested in history and politics, particularly the life history of Shivaji. Hedgewar's biographer notes that young Keshav dreamed of emulating the seventeenth-century Maratha warrior-king. For example, on the occasion in 1896 of Queen Victoria's sixtieth coronation ceremony at Nagpur, he and a group of young comrades unsuccessfully attempted to replace the Union Jack flying over the British fort with Shivaji's standard.[24]

The young man, who avidly read Tilak's *Kesari* (a nationalist weekly published in Pune) drifted into the nationalist circle of youth which formed around Dr Balkrishna Shivram Munje, a young doctor who had returned to Nagpur from the Boer War.[25] Dr Munje, with whom Hedgewar lived during much of his adolescence, was a major influence in his life. Hedgewar enthusiastically accepted Munje's militant nationalism and was expelled from several schools because of his participation in anti-British activities. According to one source close to both men, Munje sent Keshav to Calcutta in 1910 to study medicine at the National Medical College because he wanted Hedgewar to establish contacts with the revolutionaries in Bengal.[26]

During his six years in Calcutta, Hedgewar joined the Anushilan Samiti, a revolutionary society based in Bengal, and rose to its highest membership category.[27] On his return to Nagpur in 1916, he decided, much to the dismay of his family, neither to marry nor to practise medicine. He resolved to remain in the revolutionary struggle. Very little is known of his revolutionary activities during the war years. The Nagpur District Gazeteer reports that he was 'the brain behind the revolutionary movement in Nagpur'.[28] The Gazeteer also reports that he developed contacts with revolutionary groups in other parts of India, and, indirectly, established contact with England's enemies.[29]

With Germany's defeat in World War I, revolutionary ardour diminished. Public apathy and the lack of commitment on the part of many fellow revolutionaries embittered Hedgewar.[30] It is likely that his political mentor, Dr Munje, persuaded him to join the Indian National Congress. The Rashtriya Mandal (the Congress affiliate in the Central Provinces) was controlled by the followers of Tilak, and Hedgewar was accepted into its inner circles. In 1919, he was asked to organize the distribution of *Sarikalpa*, the Mandal's newly founded newspaper. While working for the newspaper, he established important contacts that were to assist him later in spreading the work of the RSS.[31]

During the early 1920s, Hedgewar became even more deeply engaged in Congress party activities. At the 1920 annual Congress session in Nagpur, he organized a volunteer unit of some 1200 young men to keep order at the meeting.[32] At that session, Gandhi promised freedom within the year through peaceful non-cooperation. Tilak had died the previous August and his supporters were unable to counter Gandhi's programme.[33] Many of Tilak's supporters, including Hedgewar, decided to give the experiment in non-violent disobedience a chance to prove its efficacy. Following a special Congress session at Calcutta in September 1920, which endorsed Gandhi's non-cooperation movement, the Central Provinces Non-cooperation Council asked Hedgewar to mobilize public support for the proposed boycotts.[34] On 14 August 1921 Hedgewar was sentenced to a one-year prison term for defying the ban on political meetings.[35] He was released from prison on 12 July 1922 at a time when the tactics of the Congress appeared incapable either of uniting Indians or loosening the colonial grip on the country. The year 1921 ended without the promised swaraj (freedom). Gandhi called off a much-heralded non-cooperation campaign in early 1922, because a mob had killed a number of policemen in the United Provinces. Gandhi wrote to Motilal Nehru, a leading Congress politician in the United Provinces, that 'our people were becoming aggressive, defiant and threatening ... They were getting out of hand and were not nonviolent in demeanor'.[36] Hedgewar (and others) believed Gandhi had made a serious tactical mistake. Though Hedgewar remained within the Congress and continued to take an active interest in Congress affairs until 1928,[37] he became increasingly disenchanted with Gandhi and with politics.

The outbreak of communal rioting in 1923 caused Hedgewar to question the previously attempted methods used to rid India of colonial rule. The riots, in his view, were the signs of a deeper social problem—disunity among Hindus—that would have to be addressed if India were to be independent. He observed the problem at close quarters since Nagpur was one of the major centres of the rioting. Because of communal tensions, the district collector in September 1923 banned processions during the annual festival honouring the Hindu deity Ganesh, and the Hindu community complied with the order.[38] On 30 October 1923 the collector banned Dindi processions (a musical procession in honour of a Hindu deity),[39] but this time influential Hindu leaders decided to disobey the ban. One newspaper reported that up to 20,000 Hindus marched in defiance of the government order.[40] Hindu leaders were surprised not only by the popular response, but also by the involvement of most segments of the Hindu community. A way had been found to unite the Hindus in a movement 'that identified both the British and the Muslims as "oppressors".' Out of this defiance emerged the Nagpur Hindu Sabha. Dr Munje was chosen the vice-president of the local sabha and Hedgewar became its secretary.[41] The sabha organized more protest marches, and it negotiated a compromise with the government and with leaders of the Muslim community which permitted Hindus to march in religious processions at times and in places that would not interfere with Muslim religious observances.

Hindus in Nagpur were not slow to appreciate the influence they could exert if they organized. The experience established a precedent for their response to communal riots the next year. Hindus reacted by declaring a boycott against Muslim-owned businesses.[42] This was a serious blow to the Muslim craftsmen in the city, whose suppliers and customers were largely Hindu. To restore communal harmony, two well-known national Congress leaders, Motilal Nehru and Abul Kalam Azad, went to Nagpur where they arranged a compromise between leaders of the two communities.[43] Despite this agreement, the situation remained tense.

Hindu revivalists such as Hedgewar saw that organization was a necessity, but they argued that more was needed to protect Hindu interests. They argued for the Hindu community to adopt a more martial kshatriya (warrior) world view. Dr Munje expressed dismay at the alleged cowardice of Hindus, noting that

'Out of 1.5 lakh [150,000] population of Nagpur, Muslims are only 20 thousand. But still we feel insecure. Muslims were never afraid of 1 lakh 30 thousand Hindus. So this question should be regarded hereafter as the question of the Hindus. The Muslims themselves have taught us to behave as Hindus while in the Congress, and as Hindus outside the Congress.'[44]

During this period of escalating Hindu Muslim animosity in Nagpur, Hedgewar began to develop the intellectual foundations of the RSS. A major influence on his thinking was a handwritten manuscript of Vinayak Damodar Savarkar's *Hindutva*, which advanced the thesis that the Hindus were a nation.[45] The central propositions of Savarkar's manuscript are that Hindus are the indigenous people of the subcontinent and that they form a single national group. Considering the obvious linguistic, racial, social and religious cleavages within the Hindu community, Savarkar felt he needed to explain what Hindus had in common that could justify calling then a single national group. British opinion, both official and scholarly, tended to view India as a geographical rather than as a national concept.

Savarkar accepted the notion that the Aryan people and culture had originated in north-western India and had gradually spread out over the subcontinent. He recognized the existence of non-Aryan peoples; however, he proposed that an intermingling of blood and culture took place between the Aryans and non-Aryans of the subcontinent, producing the Hindu nation.[46] He defines a Hindu as a person who feels united by blood ties with all those whose ancestry can be traced to Hindu 'antiquity', and who accepts India—from the Indus river in the north to the Indian Ocean—as his fatherland (pitrubhu). In addition, a person is a Hindu only if he accepts India as a divine or holy land (punyabhu).

While Savarkar's work may have provided Hedgewar with an intellectual justification for the concept of a Hindu nation that embraced all the peoples of the subcontinent, it did not give him a method for uniting the Hindu community. Hedgewar had experimented with revolution, satyagraha and constitutional reform, but each method, he felt, had failed to achieve independence or national rejuvenation. From his youth, he had searched for a reason to explain India's inability to ward off foreign domination. He was disturbed that a small group of colonial administrators could rule a vast country like India with such ease.[47] He believed that independence and national revitalization could be achieved only when the root cause of India's weakness was discovered. Some time in 1924–25, he satisfied himself that he had discovered the cause: The fundamental problem was psychological and what was required was an inner transformation to rekindle a sense of national consciousness and social cohesion. Once having created a cadre of persons committed to national reconstruction, he believed there would be little difficulty in sustaining a movement of revitalization, which, of course, would include independence as one of its objectives.[48] The first task on the road to independence, then, was to formulate a discipline and an organization to train the cadre.

Hedgewar launched his new movement of Hindu revitalization in September 1925 on the Hindu festival of Dussehra, a festival commemorating the victory of Ram (a mythological Hindu god) over the demon king Ravan.[49] The first participants were recruited from a largely brahmin locality in Nagpur.[50] This early group had neither a name nor a developed programme of activities. The participants were expected to attend an akhara (gymnasium) during the week and take part in political classes on Sundays and Thursdays.[51]

During Hedgewar's involvement in the revolutionary movement, gymnasiums had been his most successful source of recruits, and he again relied on them to recruit participants into his new venture. The traditional Hindu gymnasium is closely associated with the kshatriya lifestyle all over India. In Maharashtra, where brahmins served conspicuously as rulers and soldiers, brahmins also actively participated in akharas. During the communal violence of the mid-1920s in the Central Provinces, the number of akharas in Nagpur division increased from 230 to 570.[52]

Traditional Indian gymnasiums have a spiritual purpose as well as an athletic one, and hence, were considered by Hedgewar the ideal places to look for the cadre he was seeking to create. Youths at such gymnasiums were taught that the exercises performed were a form of worship to the god Maruti (or Hanuman). Maruti is among the most demanding gods in the Hindu pantheon, requiring physical strength, subordination, and a strict ascetic commitment from his devotees, most of whom are young men. In Maharashtra, Maruti is associated with the struggle against 'evil' and his incarnations appear when Hindus are 'oppressed'. Ramdas Swami (a seventeenth-century Hindu saint) was himself a devotee of Maruti, and the god's idol was installed in the mutts (monasteries) which he established. The Abhinava Bharat formed by V. D. Savarkar set the poetry of Ramdas to music to arouse a revolutionary fervour among the youth. Hedgewar drew on the writings of Ramdas for the same purpose.[53] During the formative period of the RSS, members took their oath before the saffron-coloured RSS flag and pictures of Maruti and Ramdas.

Hedgewar selected the first mission of the young organization with great care.[54] He wanted to demonstrate the value of discipline to both the volunteers and to the general public, and chose a popular religious occasion—Ramnavami— to do so. The Ramnavami festival (celebrating the birthday of Ram, the seventh avatar of the god Vishnu) was celebrated in April each year at Ramtek, a village near Nagpur. According to Hedgewar's biographer, the chaotic conditions around the temple created great hardships for the worshippers. Moreover, many villagers were reportedly cheated by Muslim fakirs and brahmin pandits. He decided to take his volunteers to the 1926 festival to remedy the situation. For the occasion, he chose both the name and the uniform of the organization.[55] The swayamsevaks, in their new uniforms, marched to the temple singing verses from Ramdas. According to RSS sources, they enforced queues for the worshippers visiting the temple housing the main idol, provided drinking water, and drove off the corrupt priests.[56]

Soon after this dramatic introduction to the public, lathi instruction (a lathi is a five-feet-long bamboo stick used as a weapon) and group prayers were incorporated into the RSS discipline.[57] In the same year, a large open area was acquired and military training was introduced by Martandrao Jog, a former officer in the army of the maharaja of Gwalior, who was to become head of the military section of the RSS. To strengthen their sense of discipline, volunteers were required to wear their uniforms to the RSS meetings, and a bugle corps was formed to accompany the volunteers when they marched through the streets of Nagpur.[58] In 1926, the first daily shakha (branch) was held, and the practice of meeting daily was quickly adopted by other RSS groups. Ninety-nine young men were accepted into RSS membership in 1928 by taking a life oath in a forest close to Nagpur. The oath was administered before the bhagva dhwaj, an ochre-coloured standard associated with Shivaji.[59] In RSS ritual, this standard is a symbol of the unity of all Hindus, and it is the 'guru' to which each swayamsevak commits himself when he joins the organization. Some of the older RSS informants recall that the paramilitary orientation of the RSS at that time was popular among the youth of the Hindu middle class in Nagpur because it was proof to them that Hindu young men were the equal in manliness to the British soldier.

Communal riots which erupted again in Nagpur in September 1927 led the RSS to take steps which captured the attention of Hindus far beyond the city. Anna Sohani, a former revolutionary and close associate of Hedgewar, organized RSS members into sixteen squads to protect various Hindu neighbourhoods in the city. Perhaps because of the publicity generated by this move, the organizers of the December 1927 Hindu Mahasabha national conclave at Ahmedabad in Bombay province invited Hedgewar to send RSS members in uniform to the session.[60]

Hedgewar's revolutionary past and the paramilitary nature of the RSS convinced the Central Provinces Home Department that the RSS could develop into a dangerous revolutionary group,[61] and this suspicion continued throughout the pre-Independence period. In fact, the RSS remained scrupulously non-political and it was not until after Independence that it began seriously to consider political activities. People who knew the RSS well, such as Dr Hardikar, the leader of the Hindustan Seva Dal (the youth unit of the Congress) criticized the RSS for its refusal to get politically involved.[62] V. D. Savarkar, the president of the Hindu Mahasabha after 1937, frequently denounced the RSS for its 'purely cultural' orientation. In his typically frank manner, Savarkar publicly stated, 'The epitaph for the RSS volunteer will be that he was born, he joined the RSS and he died without accomplishing I anything.'[63]

Hedgewar's stress on the educational role of the RSS—referred to as character building—led some of his senior colleagues, who wanted it to take a more activist stance, to leave the organization.[64] Anna Sohani, one of his closest colleagues, withdrew from the RSS in 1928 when Hedgewar vetoed Sohani's proposal to march uniformed RSS members in front of mosques on Friday as an unnecessarily provocative act. Hedgewar in 1931 condemned the RSS general secretary, G. M. Huddar, for participating in an armed robbery, even though the money was intended to fund anti-British activities. Huddar drifted away from the RSS after his release from prison. While Hedgewar permitted RSS members to take part in political activities in their individual capacity, he was careful to keep the RSS aloof from them. For example, during his own participation in the 1931 Congress's civil disobedience movement, Hedgewar handed over his position to Dr L. B. Paranjpe, a member of Dr Munje's political circle, for the duration of his involvement.

Nonetheless, the RSS continued to expand. Because of this growth, Hedgewar called senior RSS figures to Nagpur in November 1929, to evaluate its work and to consider ways to link together the expanding network of shakhas.[65] They decided that the organization should have one supreme guide (sarsanghchalak) who would have absolute decision-making power. He would choose all office-bearers and personally supervise the activities of the RSS. RSS literature compares the position to the head of a family who acts for the well-being of the collective unit.

By a unanimous decision of the senior workers, Hedgewar was acclaimed the first sarsanghchalak. While the term guru is never employed to describe the position, the guru model of authority governs the leadership principle of the RSS.[66] A guru in the traditional sense is a spiritual preceptor who knows a path to realization, and his guidance is required for the seekers after spiritual wisdom. A novitiate is expected to obey the guru in all matters.[67] Despite Hedgewar's injunction that loyalty and veneration be focused on the organization rather than on the individual, a charismatic sanctity does surround the office. Madhav Sadashiv Golwalkar, Hedgewar's successor, referred poetically to Hedgewar as an avatar (an incarnation of the divine).[68] Hedgewar's samadhi (memorial) at Nagpur is a pilgrimage centre for swayamsevaks.

Following his release from prison in 1931 for participating in a civil disobedience campaign, Hedgewar devoted himself full-time to the RSS. Having established the discipline during the formative years (1925–1931), he now set out to make it a national organization.

EXPANSION OF THE RSS: 1931–1939

In the early 1930s, the RSS began to spread beyond its Marathi-speaking base in the Central Provinces. Bhai Parmanand, a leader of the Arya Samaj in Punjab, invited Hedgewar to Karachi in mid-1931 to attend the All-India Young Men's Hindu Association session. Taking advantage of the opportunity, Hedgewar started RSS work in Sind, and soon after launched the RSS in Punjab and the United Provinces.[69] In the United Provinces, RSS students from the Central Provinces began the work. Among them were

Prabhakar Balwant Dani, later general secretary of the RSS, and Bhaurao Deoras, later a senior RSS zonal organizer. The work in north India progressed so well that Hedgewar in 1937 sent ten organizers to expand the organization in Punjab, Delhi, and the United Provinces.[70] RSS informants admit that much of this growth in north India was due to a growing Hindu fear of Muslim paramilitary movements, particularly the Khaskars.[71] Sikh, Hindu, and Muslim paramilitary groups sprang up all over Punjab in the period immediately preceding World War II. A Home Department fortnightly report stated:

> These militant groups continue to multiply. The stock excuse for each successive formation is the alleged certainty of civil war in the Punjab when war is declared in Europe and the necessity for each sect and community to assert itself.[72]

G. D. (alias Babarao) Savarkar, a former revolutionary and the elder brother of Vinayak Damodar Savarkar, helped the RSS expand into western Maharashtra. He merged his own Tarun Hindu Sabha (Hindu Youth) as well as the Mukteshwar Dal (Liberation Organization), associated with Pachalegoankar Maharaj (a Hindu saint), into the RSS. He accompanied Hedgewar on trips to western Maharashtra, introducing him to Hindu nationalists. Some of these contacts (e.g., K. B. Limaye, Vinayak Apte, and Bhaurao Abhyanker) were to become prominent RSS officials in Maharashtra. Pune developed into the centre of RSS activities in western Maharashtra.

Between 1931 and 1933 the number of shakhas increased from 60 to 125, and the membership increased to 12,000.[73]

Work was started in Madras, Bengal and Gujarat in 1938, and by 1939 there were about 500 shakhas, approximately one half in Marathi-speaking areas, and 60,000 participants.[74]

A women's affiliate, the Rashtra Sevika Samiti, the first RSS affiliate, was started in October 1936 in the Central Provinces by Mrs Lakshmi Bai Kelkar, mother of a swayamsevak.[75] She sought RSS assistance to fulfil one of the revivalist goals—training women in the martial arts. During a visit to Hedgewar, she reportedly told him, 'Just as women are an integral part of the household, so they too are a part of the nation. If the ideology of your organization is taught to women, it would also help the Sangh.' However, Hedgewar considered it imprudent for the RSS to accept women. He agreed to assist Mrs Kelkar to establish a separate women's group. The discipline and organization of this group parallel that of the RSS. While there is no formal connection between the two groups, leaders of the Rashtra Sevika Samiti often consult with their RSS counter parts, and they support the other organizations affiliated with the RSS.[76]

Because the RSS kept no membership rolls during the pre-war period, and because it does not officially recognize caste divisions, it is not possible to make any precise description of its membership. However, RSS informants note that it recruited largely in urban areas and from high caste, middle-income groups.[77] Its success in recruiting middle-level government employees and teachers worried the government, and a Central Provinces Government Gazette notification in 1932 prohibited government employees from taking part in the activities of the RSS.[78] Nagpur district officials also ruled that teachers in government schools could not join the RSS. This ruling was a result of a 31 December

1931 memorandum from the Central Provinces Department of Local Self-Government, advising local government units that its employees could not participate in a 'communal' and 'political organization'. Neither of these restrictions seems to have adversely affected the RSS.[79]

Hedgewar maintained close ties with the Hindu Mahasabha leadership, due to his close association with Dr Munje and V. D. Savarkar. Dr Munje presided over the 1927 Hindu Mahasabha annual session at Ahmedabad, and he invited the RSS to perform drills at the session, providing Hedgewar with the opportunity to establish contacts with Mahasabha leaders throughout India.[80] Material at the V. D. Savarkar collection in Bombay suggests that the RSS benefitted more from this relationship than did the Mahasabha. Prominent members of local Hindu sabhas would introduce RSS organizers to potential recruits and donors, provide organizers housing and the RSS with a meeting area. This assistance led many members of the Mahasabha, including Dr Munje, to conclude that the RSS would function as the youth wing of the Mahasabha.[81] Events were to prove them wrong. To emphasize the non-political character to the RSS, Hedgewar refused to sanction RSS support of the Mahasabha's 1938–1939 civil disobedience campaign in the princely state of Hyderabad, though individual RSS members took part in it.[82] Savarkar was trying to turn the Mahasabha into a political party at a time when Hedgewar was seeking to insulate the RSS from politics. The Mahasabha established its own paramilitary youth group, the Ram Sena, in 1939.

The cooling of relations between the Mahasabha and the RSS after Hedgewar's death in 1940 was a continuation of a process that had begun three years earlier when V. D. Savarkar was elected president of the Mahasabha. Savarkar attempted to give the organization a more specifically political orientation. Neither Hedgewar nor his successor wanted the RSS to be closely associated with a group whose political activities would place the RSS in direct opposition to the Congress.

Savarkar's disdain for Golwalkar further soured relations between the two organizations. Both men were apprehensive regarding the other's role in the Hindu unification movement. Savarkar did not appreciate Golwalkar's saintly style, and Golwalkar had reservations about Savarkar's unwillingness to compromise. Savarkar's followers, particularly those in Maharashtra, considered him the driving force behind the Hindu unification movement. For example, Nathuram Godse, in his final statement to the court which tried him for the murder of Gandhi, states, 'Millions of Hindu Sangthanists looked up to him [V. D. Savarkar] as the chosen hero, as the ablest and most faithful advocate of the Hindu cause. I too was one of them.'[83] RSS members were not prepared to accept this. While many RSS members respected Savarkar, they did not consider him the supreme leader of Hindus. The tension between the two organizations shows up in an angry letter which Savarkar's office issued in 1940 with the advice that

> When there is such a serious conflict at a particular locality between any of the branches of the Sangh RSS and the Hindu Sabhaites that actual preaching is carried on against the Hindu Mahasabha ..., then the Hindu Sabhaites should better leave the Sangh ... and start their own Hindu Sabha volunteer corps.[84]

GOLWALKAR CHOSEN TO SUCCEED

After a protracted illness, Hedgewar died on 21 June 1940 in the home of Babasaheb Ghatate, the Nagpur sanghchalak (chief executive of the province). On 3 July the sanghchalak of the Central Provinces, acting as spokesman for five senior state sanghchalaks assembled in Nagpur, announced that Hedgewar had designated Golwalkar his successor on the day before he died.[85] The choice stunned many RSS members, who had expected that Hedgewar would choose an older, more experienced person. Referring to the decision, Balasaheb Deoras, the sarsanghchalak, recalls that many RSS leaders were not sure if Golwalkar could handle his new responsibilities.

> Possibly some of us may have thought at that time, that Guruji Golwalkar was new to the Sangh, and not experienced enough. So we might have been doubtful about how he would discharge his responsibility. Those who were outside the Sangh but had love for it were also apprehensive about the Sangh after Doctor Saheb.[86]

Golwalkar's family background, training and interests made him an unlikely choice to succeed Hedgewar. Golwalkar, unlike Hedgewar, came from a relatively prosperous and close-knit family. His father was a moderately successful civil servant who ended his career as the headmaster of a high school. Golwalkar, who had a youthful interest in sports and music, had a relatively uncomplicated childhood.[87] His father encouraged him to study the sciences, and he dutifully honoured his father's wishes and was an exemplary scholar. While a student, he displayed none of Hedgewar's intense nationalism; indeed, he was remarkably apolitical. During his late adolescence, he developed a deep interest in religion and spiritual meditation. Two years after earning his MSc in biology at Banaras Hindu University, he was selected lecturer in zoology there. Some of Golwalkar's students encouraged him to attend RSS meetings, but there is no indication that Golwalkar took a keen interest in the organization.

Hedgewar first met Golwalkar while visiting Benares in 1931, and according to account of this visit he was attracted to the ascetic twenty-five-year-old teacher.[88] He was soon to have the opportunity to know him much better. Golwalkar's parents requested that their son return to Nagpur to prepare himself for assuming the duties of a householder. This included studying law, then considered a promising avenue to higher status. Meanwhile, Hedgewar appointed him karyavah (secretary) of Nagpur's main shakha, in 1934. In the summer of 1935, shortly after completing his law examinations, Golwalkar was asked to manage the RSS Officers' Training Camp, a clear sign of his high standing with Hedgewar.

Yet, Golwalkar was a reluctant leader. Hedgewar feared that Golwalkar's ascetic temperament could lead him to become a sannyasi (a religious recluse). His fears were justified, for in October 1936 Golwalkar abandoned his legal practice and his RSS activities and, without informing either his parents or Hedgewar, left for Bengal to study yoga under Swami Akhandananda, one of the surviving disciple of Swami Ramakrishna and a colleague of Swami Vivekananda. A RSS pamphlet says of that experience, 'It had also brought to him the realization of "self" which is the sine qua non for knowledge of the eternal and ultimate truth.'[89] His religious guide died on 7 February 1937, and a distraught Golwalkar returned to Nagpur where Hedgewar persuaded him to fulfil his religious duties through the RSS. Golwalkar, the filial junior, must have had a difficult time reaching the decision to work full-time in the RSS as this meant that he had to ignore his parents' wishes. Nevertheless, he threw himself into his new career with the same energy he had devoted to his earlier academic career, and to religion.

Golwalkar, by his own account, was a rather blunt and short-tempered young man, qualities considered inappropriate for an RSS worker. It disturbed Hedgewar. In a rare insight into his own character, Golwalkar recalls:

> I had read a vast number of books on various subjects in those days, and there developed around me a thick intellectual sheath through which Doctor's words could not penetrate. But a process of absorption began slowly. I then met him and my whole life changed. I forgot my self-importance.[90]

One could question whether Golwalkar ever fundamentally changed. For example, when he was negotiating the removal of the ban of the RSS in 1948, the government frequently expressed its irritation with his blunt manner. T. R. V. Shastri, an attorney who served as a mediator between the government and the RSS at the time, commented on his abrasiveness: 'Mr M. S. Golwalkar is a blunt man innocent of the etiquette required in a correspondence with Government. The soft word that turneth away wrath is not among his gifts.'[91]

Despite his apprehensions regarding Golwalkar, Hedgewar recognized that the young Madhav had the qualities of leadership. He placed him in charge of the annual All-India Officers' Training Camp at Nagpur for three consecutive years (1937–39). The position is a key one, and is a sign of the respect accorded a person by the RSS leadership. The RSS conducts a large number of camps each year, but the most important are the Officers' Training Camps.[92] Hedgewar, from all accounts, was pleased by Golwalkar's ability to handle complex details of a large camp. Hedgewar was also impressed by his public speaking and literary abilities. In 1938 Golwalkar prepared the first systematic statement of RSS ideology, 'We or our Nationhood Defined', a text which he later revealed was an abridgment of an essay on nationalism (i.e., 'Rashtra Mimansa') by Babarao Savarkar. During Hedgewar's increasingly frequent illnesses, Golwalkar substituted for him on the speaker's platform. The confirmation of his acceptance into the inner circle of the RSS came at the 1939 Gurudakshina festival (an occasion for honouring the RSS flag and contributing to the RSS treasury) in Nagpur, where Hedgewar announced that he had selected Golwalkar to be the new general secretary, the second most important position in the RSS.[93]

REORIENTATION OF THE RSS UNDER GOLWALKAR

Golwalkar's saintly style and his apparent disinterest in politics convinced some swayamsevaks that the RSS had become more concerned with other-worldly implications of character building than with its national political implications. Links between the Hindu Mahasabha and the RSS were virtually severed: the military department of the RSS was dismantled;[94] the RSS remained aloof from the anti-British agitations during World War II, and it refused to assist the various militarization and paramilitary schemes advocated by many other Hindu nationalists. Golwalkar, unlike Hedgewar, showed no public interest in the movement to enlist Hindus in the armed forces of British India.[95]

A significant part of the RSS establishment in Bombay province, particularly in the Marathi-speaking districts where the Hindu Mahasabha had a firm base, was disturbed by the reorientation of the RSS under Golwalkar. K. B. Limaye, sanghchalak of the province, resigned, underscoring the depth of the discontent there.[96] A number of swayamsevaks defected in 1942, and formed the Hindu Rashtra Dal the next year. Nathuram Godse, the founder of the paramilitary organization, intended to use it to fight against British rule. It received the blessing of Savarkar.[97]

Despite the apprehensions regarding Golwalkar's leadership, there was no large-scale defection. He moved quickly to consolidate his position by creating a new position—provincial pracharak (organizer)—responsible directly to him rather than to the provincial sanghchalaks. He convinced several local Congress figures to preside over RSS functions, which offered convincing public proof that the RSS was not the youth front of the Hindu Mahasabha.

Throughout the war period, RSS policy was influenced by fears regarding the potential adverse effect of the war on the Hindu community. First, the RSS must be prepared to protect Hindu interests should the Japanese invade the subcontinent. Perhaps even more compelling was the fear that communal warfare would erupt in the post-war period, as it had after World War I. Golwalkar believed that the British should not be given any excuse to ban the RSS. When the British banned military drill and the use of uniforms in all non-official organizations, the RSS complied. On 29 April 1943 Golwalkar distributed a circular to senior RSS figures, announcing the termination of the RSS military department. The wording of the circular reveals his apprehensions regarding the possibility of a ban on the RSS:

> We discontinued practices included in the government's early order on military drill and uniforms to keep our work clearly within bounds of law, as every law abiding institution should ... Hoping that circumstances would ease early, we had in a sense only suspended that part of our training. Now, however, we decide to stop it altogether and abolish the department without waiting for the time to change.[98]

Golwalkar was not a revolutionary in the conventional sense of the term. The British understood this. In an official report on RSS activity, prepared in 1943, the Home Department concluded, '... it would be difficult to argue that the RSS constitutes an immediate menace to law and order ...' Commenting on the violence that accompanied the 1942 Quit India movement, the Bombay Home Department observed '... the Sangh has scrupulously kept itself within the law, and in particular, has refrained from taking part in the disturbances that broke out in August, 1942 ...'[99] Another Home Department official compared the leader of the paramilitary Khaskars to Golwalkar and noted that 'while Inayatullah is an unbalanced and blustering megalomaniac, Golwalkar is wary, astute, and therefore by far the more capable leader'.[100]

At the same time, Golwalkar opposed as unpatriotic the effort of some Hindu organizations to encourage the recruitment of Hindus into the military. He was openly critical of the Hindu Mahasabha for engaging in such recruitment activities. The RSS continued to expand rapidly during the war years despite the defection of some members disappointed by its apparent retreat from activism. British sources indicate that in 1944 some 76,000 men regularly attended shakha in British India alone, of whom about one half were in the Central Provinces and the rest mainly in Bombay and Punjab.[101] Between 1945 and 1948, the RSS membership surged. Most of that increase occurred in areas now part of Pakistan (especially Sind and the North-West Frontier Province), Punjab and Delhi. The membership centre shifted from Maharashtra to the Hindi-speaking heartland of India; however, the leadership remained overwhelmingly Maharashtrian, brahmin, and from Nagpur. Whereas a significant proportion of its Maharashtrian membership were from professional or middle-level service backgrounds, the north Indian membership, at least in the early period, tended to come from families engaged in small-scale entrepreneurial activities. These people, religiously oriented and in the process of consolidating their caste membership, may have been attracted by the reliance of the RSS on the symbols of the Great Tradition of Hinduism, and by its use of these symbols to justify social solidarity. The RSS was also more successful in attracting boys from the lower castes in northern India, where the brahmanical orientation of the RSS did not arouse the opposition of non-brahmins as it did in Maharashtra. Indeed, the RSS in north India may be attractive as a possible route to an advanced status.[102]

EXPANSION OF THE RSS IN THE POST-WAR PERIOD

The post-war expansion of the RSS in northern India coincided with deteriorating communal relations between Muslims and Hindus. The Muslim League, campaigning for the creation of a separate Muslim state, declared a Direct Action Day on 16 August 1946. Communal violence erupted in Bengal and north-western India. According to one account of events in Bengal:

> Between dawn on the morning of 16 August and dusk three days later, the people of Calcutta hacked, battered, stabbed or shot 6,000 of each other to death, and raped or maimed another 20,000).[103] Mary Doreen Wainwright, on the bases of an analysis of the papers of the military commander of eastern Punjab, writes:

> From the middle of 1946, ex-INA [Indian National Army] men were busy in Bengal and the Punjab, and in 1947 were helping to train the Congress volunteers, the RSS Sangh, and the Muslim League National Guard, while in August ex-INA Sikhs were active in organizing attacks of their co-religionists on the Muslims in the Punjab.[104]

She further reports:

> Vast quantities of unlicensed arms and ammunition were in the possession of unauthorized persons, and that in Bengal and the Punjab the accumulation was on a scale beyond the power of the executive police forces and the provincial security authorities to check.[105]

Of the two trouble spots, it was in Punjab that the RSS was able to attract considerable Hindu support. In Bengal, in contrast to Punjab, the RSS neither attracted support from prominent Hindu leaders nor devoted much effort to organizing Hindus. During World War II, Punjab has been governed by a coalition including the Unionists (led by Muslim and Hindu landlords), Sikh Akalis, the Congress and independents. The Unionist chief minister, Sir Khizr Hyat Tiwana, no friend of Muhammad Ali Jinnah (the leader of the Muslim League), was expelled from the Muslim League before the 1946 legislative assembly elections. In those elections, the Unionists could win only 21 of the 175 seats; the Muslim League won 79 of the 86 seats reserved for Muslims, emerging as the largest single party.[106] Tiwana assembled a shaky coalition of Unionists, the Congress and Akalis. On 24 January 1947 his government banned the Muslim League's paramilitary affiliate, the Muslim National Guard. According to one Pakistani writer:

> To keep up appearances, Rashtriya Swayamsevak Sangh, a militant Hindu organization, was also declared unlawful, but no action was taken either against the Congress volunteers, or the Sikhs who, as everyone knew, were busy collecting arms.[107]

The Muslim League responded to this challenge by calling for a non-violent mass struggle to protest the 'injustice' of denying the largest party the 'right' to rule. The government rescinded its ban order on 28 January. The lesson was not lost on the other religious communities. The Lahore correspondent for Allahabad's *Leader* wrote:

When the League forced the coalition government to withdraw its ban on the Rashtriya Sevik Sangh [sic] and the Muslim National Guard, the Sikhs realized that private armies had come to stay in the province and that it was high time they had one such army of their own.[108]

Penderel Moon, a British official serving in Bahawalpur state, observed:

The hooligan Muslim elements in the big cities perceived all too clearly the weaknesses of the government; the forces of law and order, not too staunch in any case, became puzzled and doubtful of what was expected of them.[109]

On 3 March the Tiwana ministry resigned and a Muslim League ministry was formed. Sikh and Hindu politicians refused to support it, and they organized demonstrations to protest a Muslim League ministry. Communal riots soon erupted all over Punjab.

On 3 June 1947 Lord Mountbatten, the British viceroy, announced His Majesty's government's decision to partition the subcontinent on a communal basis (including a division of Punjab and Bengal) and to terminate colonial rule on 15 August 1947. To keep law and order during the partition process, the British created a boundary force. Among the British and many Congress leaders, there was the hope that the large minority communities on both sides of the border would continue to live peacefully in the new states.[110] However, the administrative personnel of the minority community in the two Punjabs shifted to the other side. Moreover, the border police was terminated in September. Millions of Hindus and Sikhs were stranded, unprotected in West Punjab; and the same was true for the Muslims in East Punjab.[111] As early as July, acts of violence drove thousands of frightened people towards the other side. The violence reached a peak in September, and subsided when the minority communities of West Pakistan fled to India. The population transfer on both sides of the border was far from smooth. Describing the transfer in Bahawalpur state, Moon reports:

> To kill a Sikh had become almost a duty; to kill a Hindu was hardly a crime. To rob them was innocent pleasure carrying no moral stigma.[112]

It was in this setting of near anarchy that the RSS earned enormous goodwill for itself by assisting Hindu refugees in their flight to India and by providing aid in their readjustment to life in a new country. Chaman Lal, the RSS office secretary in Lahore at the time of Partition, recalls that government officials in eastern Punjab provided assistance to the RSS (including the issuance of weapons) while they were organizing rescue squads to bring refugees to India.[113] Sindhi refugees in Bombay recall that RSS members in Karachi (now in Pakistan) manufactured bombs for the Hindus in Sind. A former RSS member from Punjab, in a series of articles generally critical of the RSS, concedes that many Hindu Congress politicians in his own town approached RSS officials for assistance in defending the Hindu minority. He recalls that swayamsevaks were assigned to guard Hindu homes; they collected weapons to use during the anticipated Muslim attacks; and they manufactured hand grenades. He also admits that the RSS did not itself organize retaliatory activities against the Muslims in his own area, though many swayamsevaks individually engaged in such activities. He recalls that RSS rescue efforts helped to bolster the confidence and pride among the demoralized Hindus of Punjab.[114] With the breakdown of law and order in many parts of India and Pakistan, vigilante law prevailed and observers report that few hands were clean in the affected areas. The RSS was only one of many paramilitary groups operating in Punjab during the exchange of population.[115]

But the RSS was probably the best organized of the paramilitary groups, and it earned the goodwill of the Hindu community of Punjab, Kashmir and elsewhere. The rapid proliferation of shakhas in the north-west, according to government reports, aroused a sense of militancy among Hindus.[116] Many RSS members were arrested for manufacturing bombs and other weapons, though the RSS itself was careful that none of its office-bearers were linked to such activities. Because the RSS was widely perceived to be the most effective organization working on behalf of the refugees, the Government of East Punjab provided support to it, as did the Congress party in the province.

The growing popularity and activism of the RSS led many to speculate that it was a force to reckon with. In a 16 September 1947 visit to a shakha in Delhi, Mahatma Gandhi pleaded with the swayamsevaks to let the government handle law and order in the increasingly tense capital city. Golwalkar reportedly responded that the RSS was purely defensive, though he could not vouch for the actions of every swayamsevak.[117] Hone Minister Vallabhbhai Patel solicited Golwalkar's help in an effort to convince the Hindu maharaja of Kashmir to merge his princely state with India.

Golwalkar met the maharaja in October 1947 and urged him to recruit Punjabi Hindus and Sikhs into his militia.[118] After Indian troops were invited into the state, the Indian military provided arms to volunteers of the RSS as well as to members of Sheikh Abdullah's National Conference.[119] In September 1947 the Delhi region military commander met Golwalkar at least twice to request his help in maintaining law and order.[120]

As 1947 came to a close, senior political figures became increasingly outspoken about the danger of the RSS becoming an independent political force. A massive RSS rally in Delhi on 10 December 1947, attended by several Hindu princes, prominent businessmen, and an array of leaders from various Hindu organizations, seemed to underscore the hold of the RSS on a significant part of the Hindu community. In fact, Golwalkar was adamantly opposed to the RSS getting involved in partisan politics, though many saw him as a potentiallly malevolent actor in the political arena.

As the Hindu refugees from West Pakistan spread out over northern and western India, they took the RSS organization to their new homes, where they formed the membership nucleus for hundreds of new shakhas. Many of the full-time workers of the RSS were recruited from the refugee community. A large number of these refugees were businessmen, and many prospered in India. Because of the widespread sympathy for the RSS among the refugees, even respected non-RSS refugee professionals presided over RSS public functions and contributed funds to both the RSS and to its affiliates.[121] Businessmen from Punjab refugee backgrounds were, and still are, a reliable source for funds, and RSS informants admit that they have been generous.

Thousands of swayamsevaks were recruited to organize rescue squads, to provide food and medicine, and to organize temporary residential quarters for the refugees when they arrived in India. The largest single refugee relief operation was in Delhi, where the RSS operated four large camps.[122] In the accounts of dozens of swayamsevaks who participated in the rescue and relief operations, one common theme was that the experience generated a loyalty to the RSS that enabled them to withstand the trials they had to face in 1948 and 1949 when the RSS was banned. The rescue operations left them convinced that the RSS has been genuinely concerned about the welfare of the Hindus. There is even a certain romantic nostalgia in their reminiscence. As never before (or after, in most cases), they had a sense of actively participating in a great event in which their services were both demanded and appreciated. Many recall the demands put on their talents and ingenuity, and in their recollection, they found themselves equal to the task.

RSS sources claim that there were about 100,000 swayamsevaks attending shakhas at the start of the war. By the beginning of 1948, between 600,000 and 700,000 were attending some 7,000 shakhas. Much of the growth had occurred in Punjab, Delhi and the United Provinces—provinces receiving most of the Punjabi refugees.[123] When the Punjabi refugees began to pour into Delhi, communal rioting erupted in the national capital. Despite the charge that the RSS had precipitated the violence, the organization had built up too large a fund of goodwill for the government to restrict its activities without clear evidence of its direct involvement in the riots. The provincial premiers and home ministers, meeting in Delhi in November 1947, unanimously advised against curbing its activities.[124] In a speech at Lucknow on 6 January 1948, Deputy Prime Minister Vallabhbhai Patel advised Congressmen to draw the RSS cadre into the Congress: 'They are to be won over by Congress with love'.[125]

Gandhi was horrified at the violence in the capital city of independent India, and took the ultimate step to stop it. On 12 January 1948, he began observing fast, and ended it on 18 January only after leaders of Delhi's Sikh and Hindu communities (including Hans Raj Gupta, sanghchalak of Delhi) promised to adhere to his six-point formula designed to end the violence. Maulana Azad, a nationalist Muslim spokesman, recalls that the agreement was opposed by many Sikhs and Hindus.[126]

THE BAN ON THE RSS: 1948–1949

Gandhi was assassinated on Friday evening, 30 January 1948, at 5.30 p.m., by Nathuram Vinayak Godse. Gopal Godse, brother of Nathuram, recalls:

> Our motive was not to achieve control of the government; ... we were simply trying to rid the nation of someone who had done and was doing great harm to it. He had consistently insulted the Hindu nation and had weakened it by his doctrine of ahimsa. On his many fasts, he always attached all sorts of pro-Muslim conditions ... He never did anything about the Muslim fanatics. We wanted to show the Indians that there were Indians who would not suffer humiliation—that there were still men left among the Hindus.[127]

Nathuram Godse had previously been a member of the RSS,[128] and at the time of the assassination, was an editor of a pro–Hindu Mahasabha newspaper in Pune.[129] Because of his background, the government suspected that the Hindu Mahasabha and the RSS had both been involved in a conspiracy to assassinate Gandhi, and to seize control of the government. Leaders of both groups were arrested. On 3 February 1948 Golwalkar was arrested, and the government banned the RSS the next day.

Before his arrest, Golwalkar instructed the RSS leaders temporarily to cease all RSS activities. Despite this instruction and the subsequent ban, a large number of swayamsevaks continued to meet together under the guise of study groups, sports associations, devotional assemblies, etc. They met together at considerable risk, for the government was arresting those suspected of participating in the RSS. RSS officers from all levels of the organization were arrested. RSS records and funds were confiscated, and property and equipment were impounded. With practically the entire leadership imprisoned, the younger RSS members received instant training in leadership, and they constructed and maintained the clandestine apparatus of the RSS. The leadership engaged in 'seminars' while in prison to determine the future orientation of the RSS. The various options for the RSS were exhaustively debated, and from these debates emerged the guidelines that the RSS pursued in the post-ban period.

RSS sources estimate that approximately 20,000 swayamsevaks were arrested for varying lengths of time during the first few months of the ban.[130] The government was not able to show any RSS involvement in Gandhi's murder,[131] nor its involvement in a conspiracy to overthrow the government. By August 1948 most of the detainees were released, and Golwalkar himself was released on 5 August. Nevertheless, the ban on the RSS was not lifted. Golwalkar was required to remain within the municipal limits of Nagpur, to refrain from addressing any public meeting, and to seek prior approval from the Nagpur district magistrate before submitting any material for publication.[132]

Following his release, Golwalkar initiated correspondence with the prime minister and the home minister on the question of lifting the ban on the RSS.[133] On 24 September 1948 Golwalkar wrote to Nehru that no evidence existed to link the RSS with the murder of Gandhi.[134] On the same day, he wrote to Patel:

> If you with Government power and we with organized cultural force combined, we can eliminate this menace [communism]. I am intensely worried at the waves of victory of that foreign 'ism' which are sweeping our neighboring countries.[135]

Nehru wrote back that the government had a 'mass of information' that the RSS was 'anti-national', 'often subversive', and 'violent'.[136] In response, Golwalkar refuted these charges, emphasizing the non-political nature of the RSS.[137] However, the RSS leadership was, in fact, seriously considering the question of a political role for itself.

Correspondence between Home Minister Patel and Golwalkar was concerned primarily with the political intentions of the RSS. On 11 September Patel wrote of his concern that

> Their [RSS] opposition to the Congress, and that too of such virulence, disregarding all considerations of

personality, decency or decorum, created a kind of unrest among the people.

In the same letter, he proposed that

RSS men carry on their patriotic endeavor only by joining the Congress and not by keeping separate and by opposing.[138]

While this exchange of letters was taking place, Patel was canvassing the provincial governments on the ban issue; all the governments responded that the ban should not be lifted. Following this advice, Patel broke off his discussion with Golwalkar.

Golwalkar's travel restrictions had been temporarily lifted in October so that he could confer with government officials in Delhi. When the discussions were terminated, he was again arrested and returned to Nagpur. Soon after, Golwalkar issued two press statements which were addressed primarily to those who wanted to transform the RSS into a political party. In the second, he wrote, 'I believe that cultural work should be entirely free from political scramble and should not be tagged on to any political party.' To those who wanted to transform the RSS into a political party, he warned, 'This position is unbearable and does no credit to those who may hold it.'[139] The Delhi provincial organizer of the RSS issued a press statement on 3 December 1948, which rejected Patel's suggestion that the RSS merge with the Congress. 'The advice [on the merger] was too queer and unreasonable to be termed a proposal for change.'[140] On 13 November 1948, two days before his second arrest, Golwalkar circulated a memorandum to RSS leaders informing them that his 6 February order to comply with the government's ban order was rescinded, and directed P. B. Dani, the general secretary, to resume RSS activities.[141] The decision was not unanimously supported by the RSS karyakari mandal (executive committee). Some of its members felt that the RSS should not oppose the government in such a dramatic fashion when the possibility for renewed negotiations was still an option. The normally cautious Golwalkar lined up with the activists on the issue, and the RSS launched its first civil disobedience campaign against the government.

On 9 December 1948 the civil disobedience campaign (referred to in the RSS as a satyagraha) was launched. RSS informants claim that some 60,000 swayamsevaks took part in the protest, a very significant response considering that the number of protestors represents about one-tenth of the RSS membership before the ban. The protest was suspended on 20 January 1949 when RSS officials were approached by the government to resume negotiations on a written RSS constitution acceptable to the government.[142]

During the ban, Eknath Ranade, a member of the RSS (central executive responsible for negotiating with the government), and Home Minister Patel conferred secretly several times to discuss the terms for lifting the ban and for releasing Golwalkar. Their first meeting took place at Mussoorie, in the home of G. D. Birla, one of India's leading industrialists. According to Ranade, the meeting was a disaster, as Patel continued to insist that the RSS was creating a climate of violence in the country.[143] Patel did not make clear whether he was referring to actual acts of violence or whether he meant that the opposition to the Congress 'created a kind of unrest among the people', as he had earlier written to Golwalkar. Several months after the first meeting, Ranade again met Patel, and according to Ranade, Patel told him that swayamsevaks should join the Congress and help build up the party's organizational base. RSS leaders close to the negotiations claim that Patel, the organizational leader of the Congress diumvirate, wanted to utilize the RSS cadre to oppose some of Nehru's policies.[144]

At the same time that secret negotiations were being held, the government was holding open talks with RSS mediators regarding a lifting of the ban. Ranade and two associates (P. B. Dani and Balasaheb Deoras) prepared a draft RSS constitution at the request of the government. While Golwalkar approved the draft, the home minister raised several objections.[145] The government charged that the draft contained no specific rejection of violence, no statement of allegiance to the Indian constitution and the national flag, no provision for publishing RSS rules and instructions, no provision for a published audit of RSS accounts, and no system for the democratic election of office-bearers, particularly the sarsanghchalak. Golwalkar responded with a detailed response of the criticism on 17 May 1949, emphasizing the democratic nature of the RSS. On the critical point of succession, he wrote that the sarsanghchalak would nominate his successor in consultation with the executive committee of the RSS.[146] In a letter of clarification to Mauli Chandra Sharma on 10 June, Golwalkar noted that 'this nomination [by the previous sarsanghchalak] is a formal declaration of the person elected by the KKM [the karyakari mandal or the executive committee]'. In that same letter, he wrote that he was nominated by Hedgewar 'in consultation with the then KKM'.[147] In fact, neither he nor his successor was nominated formally by the executive committee. There may have been consultations with the members, but certainly no formal vote on the candidate and certainly no opposition candidate—which appears to be what the government had in mind when it talked about greater democracy in the RSS. In any case, the home ministry was not moved by Golwalkar's 17 May explanation, and responded to him that

> The Government of India regrets to note that your attitude in regard to the activities of the RSS organization seems to have undergone no change. Not only do you see nothing wrong in the ideologies and activities of the RSS in the past but you suggest that the organization would be guided by the same ideology and pursue the same methods in the future.[148]

The public negotiations seemed deadlocked; however, the secret negotiations between Patel and the RSS continued. Patel instructed Mauli Chandra Sharma to leave for Nagpur to work with Golwalkar in revising the constitution. Sharma, Ranade, and Deendayal Upadhyaya (a young pracharak who was to play a prominent role in the Jana Sangh) wrote the new draft version. On some fundamental issues, such as participation of pre-adolescents or the selection of the sarsanghchalak, they refused to compromise. The revised constitution, as clarified by Golwalkar in his letter of 10 June, was accepted by Patel, and the ban was lifted on 11 July 1949.

RSS ADOPTS A MORE ACTIVIST ORIENTATION

On his release from prison, Golwalkar was asked in what ways the RSS would be different. He responded that the RSS had 'given up nothing'.[149] At a reception in Nagpur, he stated: 'There is no compromise undertaking of any kind given to the government.'[150] Between August and November 1949 Golwalkar made an extensive tour of India. The large crowds at his rallies suggest that the RSS retained a large following. Despite Golwalkar's disclaimers, the RSS was a different organization. Its leaders were now prepared for it to take on a more activist orientation.

On 7 October 1949, while Nehru was abroad, the Congress party's working committee voted that RSS members could join the Congress as primary members. The decision immediately set off a controversy within the ruling party, with Patel's supporters generally supporting the action and Nehru's supporters opposed to it. A. G. Kher, minister for local self-government in the United Provinces, and a staunch supporter of Patel, responded to the critics of the 7 October decision by predicting that an adverse decision regarding the participation of RSS members in the Congress might force the RSS into politics.

> The members of that organization [RSS] cannot take part in politics unless they join some political organization. The main political parties are the Congress, the Socialists, the Communities, the Hindu Mahasabha, the Muslim League, and the RSPI. Do we desire that RSS youths should join other groups which are opposed to Congress, or should we desire they should join us? Let those who desire that RSS should not be admitted even as primary members of Congress understand the implications of their attitude. They are compelling RSS men to join the opponents of Congress if they have to take part in politics.[151]

Kher's warning to the Congress proved prophetic, as RSS leaders began to consider seriously the question of political involvement. On 17 November 1949 the Congress Working Committee rescinded its earlier decision. It ruled that RSS members could join the Congress as primary members, but only if they first gave up their RSS membership. This decision virtually guaranteed that the RSS would assume some role in the political process.

Even before the ban, RSS leaders were reassessing the organization's role in an independent India.[152] By RSS standards, Hindu society was far from united. A large part of 'Mother India' had been 'lost,' and the RSS was not reconciled to it. Some believed that the leadership of the Congress had neither the commitment nor the capacity to inspire the sacrifices needed for national rejuvenation. Many felt that the new political order rested on foreign concepts which not only undermined India's Hindu identity but also were contrary to India's historical, social and political legacies, and they were not prepared to admit that the ancient wisdom was irrelevant in the contemporary period.

The negotiations between Patel and various RSS leaders during the ban period reveal that Golwalkar, at the beginning of these negotiations, was ready to accept some kind of relationship between the RSS and the Congress in which the RSS would be entrusted with character building and the Congress with politics. The evidence also suggests that Golwalkar did not want the RSS itself to become directly involved in political matters. With the Congress closing all doors to even minimal political involvement, Golwalkar was forced to deal with the RSS activists who wanted the RSS to play a direct role in the political process, and in other areas as well. The RSS experienced an internally divisive debate on the question, which involved fundamental questions of strategy and goals. The end result was a decision to get far more deeply involved in politics than Golwalkar had originally anticipated. Another outcome of the debate was the decision to sanction the establishment of affiliated organizations around the RSS. We shall analyse these developments in Chapter 4.

3

RSS: Ideology, Organization and Training

Belief systems develop in response to cultural, social and psychological strains which develop when existing symbolic models of authority, responsibility and civic purpose do not adequately explain the social situation.[1] They are cognitive road maps that point out the causal forces operating in society,[2] indicate the legitimate authorities,[3] and motivate activity in given circumstances to achieve certain desired ends.[4] They reduce the ambiguity created by the structural strains which gave rise to the belief system, simplifying reality and giving meaning to complex political and social events. They are, to use Ernst Cassirer's terms, a form of myth-making which organizes and expresses deeply rooted instincts, hopes and fears through linguistic metaphors which relate given phenomena to others which are like it, through signs that announce ideas (i.e., a flag), and through ritual that publicly expresses ideas.[5] Because the RSS draws liberally from the Hindu past to construct its belief system, an investigation is necessary of how Hindu thought and practice inform the verbal symbols, signs, and rituals which the RSS employs.

64

BELIEF SYSTEM OF THE RSS

Hedgewar, like all revivalists, believed that the Hindu past possessed the conceptual tools with which to reconstruct society. Also like other revivalists, he was convinced that only Hindu thought would motivate the population to achieve independence and to restructure society. In the early part of the twentieth century, Aurobindo Ghose stated the case in terms that the RSS was later to emphasize:

> If you try other and foreign methods we shall either gain our end of national awakening with tedious slowness, painfully and imperfectly, if at all. Why abandon the plain way which God and the Mother have marked out for you to choose faint and devious paths of your own treading.[6]

The Rig Veda, the oldest Hindu sacred text, pictures human society as evolving from the Supreme Person (Purusha) and compares the four social divisions[7] to the mouth, arms, thighs, and feet of the Supreme Person.[8] The concept of an organic society was a particularly persuasive argument for the purposes of social unity and nationalism; the revivalists employed it to emphasize the interdependence of all members of society and to suggest the necessity of a single political system.[9] The metaphor conveyed the concept that the members of the body politic are bound together by mutual concerns and a common sense of self-preservation.

RSS theoreticians maintain that the social body functions well only when individuals perform their economic, social and religious duties (dharma).[10] The founders of the RSS concluded that the Hindu social body was weak and disorganized because dharma was neither clearly understood nor correctly observed. While the disintegration of Hindu society was perceived as advancing at a rapid pace in the contemporary period, the malady is traced back at least to the Islamic invasions of India (AD approximately 1000) when it is alleged that creative Hindu thought ceased to inform society about new ways to respond to changing conditions.

A recurrent theme in belief systems is the identification of hostile forces which plot against the nation and which are responsible for the 'disruptive' strains in the country. These forces are often identified with particular social groups, which are usually defined as different, united and powerful.[11] RSS writers identify two general types of potentially 'disruptive' forces in contemporary Indian society: (1) Muslims and Christians who propagate values that might result in the denationalization of their adherents, and (2) the westernized elite who propose capitalism, socialism or communism as solutions for Indian development.

Christians consider themselves a community, and it is this community orientation—and not the dogma itself—that is considered a possible impediment to their identification with the larger nation. RSS writers allege that Christian values have tended to distance Christians culturally from the national mainstream in some parts of the country. From this proposition, a sub-proposition is deduced: because some Christians do not consider themselves culturally Indian, they do not experience a sense of community with other Indians. One could phrase the proposition in the more esoteric terms of the belief system: Because Christians are culturally different, they have separated themselves from the 'national soul'. A weekly journal affiliated to the RSS charged that the subjects taught in the Christian schools of a tribal area in north-eastern India 'are typically Western with no relation whatsoever to the Indian environment . . . It is these students who, on coming out of the missionary institutions agitate for the creation of an 'Independent Nagaland'.[12] Another writer noted that Christian converts 'were given not only psychological affinity with the people of Western countries, but were weaned away from the national society—the language, the script, the dress, other modes of life, the festivals, names and nomenclature—all undergo a change'.[13]

The case against Islam is stated in similar terms. However, Islam is viewed as a more serious problem because of the size of the Muslim community, the recent history of communal animosity between Hindus and Muslims, and the existence of Muslim states in the subcontinent. Golwalkar wrote:

> They [Muslims] look to some foreign lands as their holy places. They call themselves 'Sheiks' and 'Syeds'. Sheiks and Syeds are certain clans in Arabia. How then did these people come to feel that they are their descendants? That is because they have cut off all their ancestral national moorings of this land and mentally merged themselves with the aggressors. They still think that they have come here only to conquer and establish their kingdoms.[14]

Democracy, capitalism, and socialism, according to RSS writers, are Western concepts that have failed to improve the human condition. According to a leading RSS publicist:

> democracy and capitalism join hands to give a free reign to exploitation, socialism replaced capitalism and

brought with it an end to democracy and individual freedom.[15]

These concepts are considered contrary to the traditional principles of Hindu thought. The argument is that each of these concepts limits itself to the premise that man is a 'bundle of physical wants'.[16] While not disagreeing with the notion that 'passion' is natural to man,[17] RSS writers argue that these 'foreign' philosophies stimulate the quest for material gratification which results eventually in greed and class antagonism, attitudes that lead to exploitation, social warfare, and anarchy.[18] As an alternative to these socio-economic systems, the RSS offers a social blueprint that minimizes social conflict and functionally links the various social units together into an organic whole.

The transformation of man is of supreme importance, for such a change is, in the RSS belief system, the necessary prerequisite for revitalizing society and for sustaining it. Golwalkar, in his major treatise of the RSS belief system, mentions four virtues that characterize the ideal person.[19] The first is 'invincible physical strength'. By this he does not mean physical strength in the conventional sense. Rather, he is referring to the calm resolve needed for commitment to disciplined activity. The second virtue, which Golwalkar calls 'character', is a personal resolve to commit oneself to a noble cause. These two virtues, however, must be guided by 'intellectual acumen', the third virtue. Lastly, 'fortitude' is a virtue which permits the honourable person to persevere in a virtuous life. To summarize, the virtuous life is, above all, characterized by industriousness combined with a zealous and painstaking adherence to dharma. As with the puritan ethic in the West, the RSS belief system proposes that disciplined activity is the sign of a virtuous life, a view that such revivalists as Tilak would surely have applauded. Life is considered a struggle against disorder and anarchy; and it requires organization, calculation and systematic endeavour. Because disorder and anarchy are presumably strengthened by human 'passion', the individual must diligently tame and discipline his energies.

RSS writers are quite explicit that the new vision will not be brought about by politicians and bureaucrats. According to one writer:

> He [the politician] does not represent the soul of the people or its aspirations. What he does usually represent is all the average pettiness, selfishness, egoism, self-deception that is above him and these he represents well enough, as well as a great deal of mental incompetence and moral conventionality, timidity, and pretense. Great issues often come to him for decision, but he does not deal with them greatly; high words and noble words are on his lips, but they become rapidly the claptrap of a party.[20]

Inspiration for fundamental reform would have to come from a more lofty source, from the RSS itself and through the character-building training which it employs.

Advaita vedanta, a school of classical Hindu philosophy, provided the founders of the RSS with the core concepts around which the solutions for revitalizing society were constructed. There are several sub-schools of vedanta, and all are based on the Upanishads, a set of over two hundred texts which Hindu commentators have traditionally considered divinely inspired wisdom.[21] Upanishadic speculation explores the relationship of the individual soul to the Universal Soul.[22] Advaita (a form of non-dualist monism) was systemically formulated around AD 800 by Shankara, a brahmin vedanta philosopher. The material world, according to advaita doctrine, is created by a spiritual energy (shakti) which emanates from the Universal Soul.[23] The Brahma as God (Isvara) knows that the created world is His object and only Isvara is the true reality. Illusion (maya) is manifested when the impermanent Divine object (the created world) is perceived as the real. The sheaths of maya are removed as the individual increasingly realizes that he is, in reality, the Brahma itself. The reward to this realization is release from the bonds of material existence, the merging of the individual soul with Brahma.

Knowledge (jnana) of the truth, achieved through deep meditation, is necessarily preceded by correct observance of dharma.[24] Moral perfection and religious devotion are acts which enable the seeker after truth to perform his worldly obligations with detachment and humility, the psychic state required for the final stage of the search for enlightenment. This doctrine was developed in the Bhagavadgita. Krishna informs Arjuna, the warrior-king, that an act performed without thought to its consequences (nishkama karma) leaves no karmic bonds that link the soul to a future material existence.[25] The metaphysical foundation on which the lesson was based is the Hindu notion that every act (meritorious or sinful) leaves an impression on the soul and serves to identify it in its next material existence.[26] Krishna informs Arjuna that he must act, but in a way that leaves no karmic bonds. Arjuna, as a seeker of release from earthly bonds, could then proceed to the final stage of enlightenment, confident that his 'acts' will not predestine him to a reincarnation. Krishna reveals to Arjuna that each person has a divinely implanted set of obligations (dharma) which the seeker after truth must honour. To act contrary to them is an egocentric act that is disruptive of the social order ordained by the divinity. While not clearly indicating the way one could determine dharma, he does describe its determinants.[27]

All matter contains a mix of three 'strands'[28] which form a kind of genetic code: sattva (clarity), rajas (activity) and tamas (darkness). The social organism is sustained through the contribution of an individual's talents. The set of talents which any person possesses is determined by this 'genetic code'. In conventional Hindu practice, dharma is that set of obligations observed by the jati (sub-caste) into which a person is born. While there are conflicting opinions among RSS writers, most reject this notion and propose that dharma is something each person must individually discover. RSS writers also emphasize, as we shall discuss below, that this discovery takes place within boundaries set by a nation's 'soul'. As developed in the belief system of the RSS, every individual must locate himself in the social system so that he contributes to the well-being of the social body in a way that does not result in conflict between its constituent parts. Such a person is referred to as a karmayogin. In its most developed form, karmayoga is combined with a form of bhaktiyoga (devotional worship).

While all forms of bhakti are recognized as valid steps on the path to complete realization, one form is considered superior to all others. In his analysis of the RSS belief system Golwalkar writes:

> People go to temples and try to concentrate on the idols taking them as emblems of the Almighty. But all this does not satisfy us who are full of activity i.e., karma-yogins.

We want a 'living' God. What is the use of a God who only hears but does not respond? These emblems neither weep nor smile nor show any reaction, unless of course the persons are devotees of extraordinarily high merit. But for all ordinary persons they are nonfeeling emblems of the Almighty.[29]

The corporate Hindu nation is identified as the 'living God'.[30] The primary goal of the RSS discipline is preparing the mind so that individuals will act in a detached manner for the well-being of the divine object (the Hindu nation). The mental progression involves bursting through a set of circles of attachment. It has achieved its goal when the individual experiences a greater loyalty to the nation than to any other 'lower' form of attachment. It leaves instruction in higher forms of realization to more specifically religious teachers.

RSS practice suggests that metaphysical concerns, as such, are not a major consideration. In its emphasis on a service ministry, open to anyone with proper training and behavioural characteristics, the RSS has undermined not only the concept of a hereditary priesthood but also the mystical activities carried out by traditional priests. In a sense, swayamsevaks are a lay order whose activities are as important, if not more so, than the activities of traditional priests.

The metaphor of the Divine Mother is used to describe both the nation and the 'sacred' geography where the nation resides. Both are material emanations from the shakti. The Goddess may have both benign and negative aspects (creator, sustainer and destroyer). The imagery which the RSS usually employs emphasizes the benign aspects of the Goddess. The metaphor offers RSS publicists emotionally packed imagery to convey their message. The Mother image informs feelings for the homeland, that piece of earth which has nourished and sustained the people though history and is the true setting for the life of the people today; RSS literature is filled with references to historical desecration of this land. The division of the subcontinent in 1947 is described as 'rape'. Those who threaten the nation of the 'sacred' geography are portrayed as lustful masculine figures. In the 1980s, the RSS and its affiliates used the symbol of the Mother Goddess in mass campaigns to inspire loyalty to the country.

The nation has a 'sacred' geography, encompassing an impressive amount of real estate. Golwalkar spoke of it as extending from Iran in the west to the Malay Peninsula in the east, from Tibet in the north to Sri Lanka in the south.[31] One cannot escape the conclusion that many in the RSS consider the whole area an integral part of Bharat Mata (Mother India) which should be brought together into some kind of a political relationship. Golwalkar's successor, for example, talks of a loose federation to achieve the desired unity. Issues of national integration continue to receive top priority in the RSS, though since the early 1970s senior RSS leaders have begun to pay more attention to social and economic problems.

Besides a 'sacred' geography, the nation is said to possess a soul, referred to as 'chiti' by one prominent spokesman.[32] Chiti is a kind of higher law that takes precedence over any political institutions or manmade rules.[33] It determines the social framework within which dharma is worked out. As we shall explain below, a special category of people are the legitimate interpreters of chiti.

The concept of a national soul rests on the assumption that the cultural heritage of India is derived from a common source. With no qualifying statements, Golwalkar wrote:

The same philosophy of life, the same goal, the same supremacy of the inner spirit over the outer gross things of matter, the same faith in rebirth, the same adoration of certain qualities like *brahmacharya*, *sattya*, etc., the same holy samskars [rituals], in short the same life-blood flowed through all these limbs of our society.[34]

He also wrote that 'The people in the South were always considered to be as much Aryan as those in the North,'[35] and that 'the source of inspiration for all these Dravidian languages has been that queen of languages, the language of gods—Sanskrit'.[36]

Few RSS theorists have attempted any precise description of a society conforming to chiti. The only systematic attempt (as per following schema) was prepared by the labour affiliate of the RSS as a part of a memorandum on labour policy submitted to the National Commission on Labour.[37]

Local Occupational Assemblies	A B C D E F etc.	Local Firm Assemblies	A B C D E F etc.
Regional Occupational Assemblies	↓ ↓ ↓ ↓ ↓ ↓	Regional Firm Assemblies	↓ ↓ ↓ ↓ ↓ ↓
National Assembly of Occupations		National Industrial Family	

In their scheme, every worker is guaranteed a job and the job establishes the social, economic and political responsibilities of the worker and his family. The scheme provides for two systems of representation. A worker in a particular craft or skill within a firm belongs to an occupational assembly representing that skill (or occupation). The occupational assemblies at the firm and regional levels would jointly determine work standards, management of job training, research, and advancement within the occupation. All workers within a firm would also elect a firm-wide assembly. The local and regional firm assemblies would jointly determine production, product distribution, wage policy, living and working standards. The corporatist system culminates in a two-house parliament, one representing occupations and the other industries.

The scheme is intended to reduce the opportunities for both social conflict and exploitation. The major purpose of the two sets of assemblies is to establish a set of checks against possible exploitation of the workers in any part of the productive process. The authors of the scheme recommend that the workers themselves own the industries in which they work, to reduce chances for conflicts that arise from the owner–worker dichotomy. The scheme seeks to funnel interest articulation through one organization rather than have interests contend against each other through separate functionally antagonistic organizations.

However, the authors doubt whether even these institutional mechanisms will sufficiently sublimate self-interest and conflict. Consequently, they propose that each assembly must also include a kind of philosopher-king:

Unless any sabha or assembly is attended by a few exponents
of Dharma those who are detached in mind, are faultless
in expression and action and have no allurements to attend
the Assembly the same cannot be declared as properly
constituted or held.[38]

As people with special insight, the sages are considered the
most legitimate interpreters of the 'national soul'; they are
the commentators on the higher law. Ultimately, they are
beyond the laws of men, as they speak for a higher authority.
This does not necessarily mean that they are saintly rebels.
Indeed, theoretically, their major function is to bring human
law and divine will closer together. Of course, they have
the legitimate right to oppose human law and custom when
either offends their enlightened conscience. The notion of
enlightened sages is frequently referred to in RSS literature;
however, this literature neither describes how they should be
selected nor what their precise duties would be. Apparently,
they would be recognized for their wisdom and selflessness
and voluntarily accepted as legitimate interpreters of the
higher law.

The concept of enlightened sages forms a part of the Hindu
tradition.[39] Sages are men or women who have learned to live
with detachment in the world, the first stage of realization.[40]
They have also successfully completed the second stage, which
begins by a deep study of the Upanishads under the direction
of a guru (teacher) and culminates with the recognition of the
unity of self and the Brahma through a form of meditation.
A person who attains this realization while living is known
as a jivan-mukta. Zimmer describes the power traditionally
ascribed to jivan-muktas:

The perfected saint feels himself possessed by an illimited, far-reaching, all-pervading insight, which amounts actually to a faculty of omniscience; for it is indeed a potential omniscience, not a literal, cumbersome, encyclopedic knowledge about every theoretical, so-called scientific detail ... but an infallible intuition about things as they occur in everyday situations, or as they are brought to the attention of the saint, the enlightening teacher, in the questions and problems posed to him by the children of the world.[41]

Both former leaders of the RSS (Hedgewar and Golwalkar) are described in terms that would qualify than as *jivan-muktas*,[42] and the acceptance of their special qualifications helps explain their authority within the organization. However, neither RSS leader described himself in such a way.

The RSS has experienced no major succession crisis probably because swayamsevaks believe that a sarsanghchalak has the right to choose his successor. Golwalkar was announced to be Hedgewar's choice as the next sarsanghchalak; the swayamsevaks were informed that 'Doctorji Hedgewar is still in our midst, in the form of Sri Madhavraoji Golwalkar'.[43] On assuming the position, Golwalkar attributed ex cathedra qualities to the occupant of the position. He reportedly said, 'the office of Sarsanghchalak ... was like the throne of Vikramaditya [a Hindu king renowned for virtue, justice and valour]. Even a shepherd boy sitting on it would say nothing but right, and do nothing but right.'[44] Golwalkar's successor was also accepted with little overt opposition.

As we shall explain in Chapters 4 and 5, a model of the relationship between the enlightened sages and the assemblies is provided by the relationship between the RSS and its affiliated organizations. Enlightenment is acquired through training within the RSS, and the swayamsevaks who participate in the affiliates are the human instruments for the revitalization of society. The swayamsevaks occupy the major administrative positions in the affiliates; they consult with RSS leaders on unresolved internal controversies, on personnel selection, and on major issues which confront the organization. The advice of senior RSS figures is not necessarily accepted, but it is respected as the opinion of 'detached' individuals.

The RSS belief system is often described as conservative and reactionary.[45] There is little doubt that it represents a form of militant Hindu nationalism. However, the belief system and practice of the RSS do not support the aristocratic order, the dominant castes in the varna system, and the landed and industrial magnates. The RSS defence of Hinduism is sometimes interpreted as support for orthodoxy or for the feudal aristocracy; its anti-communism is considered by some as a defence of the higher classes and capitalism. However, few RSS leaders subscribe to such views. Indeed, there is an egalitarian undercurrent to much RSS writing and practice.[46] Speaking of the caste system, Golwalkar writes:

> The feeling of inequality, of high and low, which has crept into the Varna system is comparatively of recent Origin . . . But in its original form, the distinctions in the social order did not imply any discrimination of big or small, high or low, among its constituents. On the other hand, the Gita tells us that the individual who does his assigned duties in life in a spirit of selfless service only worships God through such performance.[47]

Stating the issue in even stronger terms, he wrote 'the work of social consolidation which is truly the realization of Nation-God can be carried on only on the basis of . . . a spirit of identity as will render us capable of seeing a beggar on the street and a great scholar with an equal eye of love and brotherhood.'[48]

Much RSS writing argues that the desired sense of community will be impossible unless class differences are reduced. RSS writers maintain that wide disparities in income are divisive and prevent the full development of a sense of community. The political affiliate of the RSS has proposed that the range of income not exceed the ratio of 1:20,[49] and this ratio is widely used in RSS literature. The RSS and its affiliates have consistently supported the cause of the small entrepreneur and the yeoman farmer.[50] The acquisition and consumption of luxury items is considered contrary to the non-materialist spirit of Hindu philosophy.[51] A populist purpose can be perceived in the negative stance towards the English language. English is associated with the elites of government, business and education. Because English-medium education is expensive, RSS spokesmen maintain that it discriminates against students from poor families.

The revivalist quest for community comes out in the RSS (and revivalist) interpretation of karmayoga as action for others rather than simply as action in conformity to an ascribed set of duties. The ethical norm that underlies the view suggests a variant of the golden rule—do unto others as you would have others do unto you—for the others are you.

The application of the term 'rightist' to the RSS also presents conceptual problems. In placing a higher value on the well-being of the community than of the individual, the RSS belief system does approach the 'right'. However, when it proclaims the essential goodness and perfectability of human nature, it is closer to the 'left'.[52] In advocating that each group possess a sufficient amount of autonomy to work out its own destiny, it even finds some affinity to the 'new left.'

Some critics of the RSS charge that its belief system reveals its fundamental fascist nature. Certain elements of the belief system certainly seem to justify this charge, such as the RSS concept of the nation as an organic unit, the concept of a collective consciousness, the conception of a national soul which reveals a divine purpose, and the primacy of intuitive knowledge.[53] However, there are significant differences with the European expressions of fascism that should caution one to handle the comparison carefully. In its Western expressions, fascism embodied the national will in a leader.[54] The leadership principle is rejected by the RSS as a logical effect of Western ego-centred ideologies. The belief system of the RSS and its practice do impute a higher wisdom to individuals who have attained 'realization'. Yet these same individuals must at least give the appearance of detachment and must not be too involved in the affairs of the world. At Golwalkar's first monthly shraaddh (death rite), his successor praised him 'because he [Golwalkar] was untouched by temptation for anything worldly, his mind was as pure and innocent as that of a child'. The present sarsanghchalak has stated that he personally does not possess such virtues, and that the work of the RSS is sustained by the joint efforts of the RSS cadre.[55] Soon after founding the RSS, Hedgewar cautioned the first recruits that no man, including himself, should be honoured as the embodiment of the RSS. He decided that the flag (the bhagva dhwaj) should be recognized as its 'living' guru.[56]

Despite repeated warnings against showing excessive reverence to leaders, all three RSS chiefs have possessed considerable charismatic influence. The office itself appears to have brought charisma to Golwalkar and Deoras, his successor. Neither demonstrated charisma before assuming office. Golwalkar skilfully assumed a saintly role that brought him moral influence over the swayamsevaks.[57]

European fascism, like other Western forms of totalitarianism, sought to destroy or to seize control of all existing centres of socio-political and economic power.[58] The RSS has not abandoned the Hindu bias towards semi-autonomous social units within which a group discovers its own ethos. Questioned on this issue, Golwalkar said, 'My feeling is that nature abhors excessive uniformity.' He went on to explain that he had 'no quarrel with any class, community or sect wanting to maintain its identity so long as that identity does not detract from its patriotic feeling'. To the surprise of some RSS members, he even applied the principle to Muslims: 'A reformist's attitude is alright. But a mechanical leveller's attitude would not be correct. Let the Muslims evolve their own laws. I will be happy when they arrive at the conclusion that polygamy is not good for them, but I would not like to force my views on them.'[59]

While fascist doctrine traces all power to the political leader, the belief system of the RSS displays a marked distrust of political leadership. Indeed, there is a millennial hope in RSS literature that political power will fade away when dharma becomes the accepted norm of behaviour. However, it could be argued that the leadership principle is incorporated into RSS practice. In its blueprint of the ideal society, political power is held to be illegitimately exercised unless restrained by 'constitutional' sages who interpret *dharma*.

RSS ORGANIZATION

Dr Hedgewar, between 1925 and 1932, experimented with various forms of discipline that would develop 'character', the frame of mind necessary for karmayogins. The RSS has applied the term samskar to these techniques. Samskars are Hindu rites associated with the transitional phases of life. These rites seek to carry the subject successfully over to the next stage of life and to mould the personality according to an approved pattern of behaviour.[60] Another objective is to purify the body to make it a fit dwelling place of the atman (soul). Many RSS leaders compare the organization's activities to the Upanayana Samskar, perhaps the most important cultural samskar. The rite is a sacrament of initiation which is administered prior to a youth's training in his duties as a member of the community.[61] The sacrament symbolizes a cultural and spiritual rebirth that is attained through discipline and learning.

As we shall show, the ideological purpose of the discipline is to create a loyalty to national symbols that supercedes any 'lower' form of attachment. To state the notion in terms of the world view of the RSS: As the student progresses in 'realization', the boundaries of ego identity will crumble until he merges his own ego with the nation. The training programmes foster comradeship by developing close personal bonds between the participants and by inculcating an allegiance to common symbols. Such comradeship then infuses diffuse support for the RSS itself, establishing a commitment to the RSS and to its affiliated organizations.

THE SHAKHA: THE BOTTOM OF THE HIERARCHY

The basic unit of the RSS is the shakha, which the RSS leadership conceives of as the chief instrument for organizing the Hindu community. Membership in a shakha varies between 50–100 male participants. To have more than 100 is considered dysfunctional for group solidarity. By keeping the units small and oriented to a neighbourhood, participants in a single shakha probably come from similar social backgrounds, which increases the chances for social solidarity within the shakha itself.

Each shakha is divided into four age groups: (1) shishu swayamsevaks—6 or 7, to 10 years; (2) bal swayamsevaks—10 to 14 years; (3) taruna swayamsevaks—14 to 28; (4) proudh swayamsevaks—28 or older. J. A. Curran, on the basis of research carried out soon after India's independence, estimated that about 60 per cent of the participants were between 18 and 25.[62] Our observations substantiate Curran's data. Shakha is held seven days a week, in the morning, the early evening, and at night. A participant decides which time is most convenient for him.[63] There are also weekly and monthly shakhas for those who cannot attend on a daily basis.

The age groups are further divided into gatas (groups); a gata rarely exceeds twenty participants. A gata is composed of a common age group, and the participants tend to live in a particular locality. Attached to each gata is a gatanayak (gata leader) and a shikshak (teacher), both appointed by the shakha's chief teacher (the mukhya shikshak). These two functionaries are the first level in the RSS hierarchy and are the initial testing ground for leadership.

A gatanayak is expected to be an 'elder brother' of the other swayamsevaks in his group and a model of ideal behaviour. He is responsible to his superiors for their behaviour and for their loyalty to the RSS; he is also expected to be an ideal swayamsevak whom his gata-mates will emulate. The shikshak teaches the games and exercises which the swayamsevak is expected to master. He may also lead his gata in discussion, a regular feature of the shakha. Gatanayaks and shikshaks usually meet with the local pracharak (full-time worker) every ten to fifteen days to discuss attendance, programmes, the functioning of the shakha, and RSS policy regarding various political and social issues.

The de jure authority of every shakha is the karyavah (secretary), an older and respected member of the locality. De facto authority, however, resides with the mukhya shikshaks, most of whom have advanced through the ranks from the gatanayak/shikshak levels. Most of the mukhya shikshaks we met were young men, typically in their twenties, who looked at their work as a kind of community service. To a large extent, the success of any shakha depends on the leadership ability of a mukhya shikshak.

Most areas will also have a karyalay (office). It is a kind of clubhouse where swayamsevaks come to talk with the pracharak (who may live at the karyalay), to meet with other swayamsevaks from the area, and to visit swayamsevaks from other cities (who can stay at many of the karyalays at no cost).

The attrition rate in the shakha is very high. The initial attraction for many participants is the opportunity to play games, attend camps and listen to interesting stories.[64] The increasing commitment and demands on their time drive many away from the RSS. Therefore, it is quite important for the RSS to recruit mukhya shikshaks who are able to elicit personal loyalty from the participants. The more cohesive the group he leads, the more pressure will the group exert on other participants to conform to the norms of the leader.[65] Perhaps even more importantly, these small groups of shakha participants are likely to enforce peer-group cohesion by rewarding behaviour functional to maintaining group interaction.

The ability of the RSS to sustain a high level of commitment even under the most adverse circumstances suggests that the RSS has had some success in recruiting capable teachers. A former swayamsevak, who could recall little that was favourable about the RSS, very favourably recalled his former RSS teacher: 'I have not known another man [referring to the mukhya shikshak] endowed with his demonic energy for any work he addressed himself to. Whenever he was out of town, the attendance in the shakha would fall. Not a little of my devotion to the RSS was the result of my deep attachment to him.'[66]

MOVING UP THE HIERARCHY

Above the shakha in the pyramid of authority is the mandal committee (composed of representatives from three or four shakhas in a given locality); representatives from ten to twelve mandals form a nagar (city) committee. Above the city committees there may be zilla (district) and vibhag (regional) committees. Most of the day-to-day work in this structure takes place at the city level. The city committee consists of a sanghchalak (who occupies a position analogous to the karyavah in the shakha) and the heads of the RSS departments (physical training, intellectual programmes, recruitment, financial secretary). The committee meets weekly. The decisions (as well as orders from above) are transmitted down to the mandal through a karyavah (secretary), who usually presides over its deliberations. Representatives from each shakha are represented on the mandal committee, and the mukhya shikshak and/or the local pracharak pass on orders and information to the lowest level of the communications circuit. Above this structure, and theoretically exercising supervision over it, are state and national assemblies.

The prantiya pratinidhi sabhas (state assemblies) are deliberative bodies, but exercise no real power. According to the RSS constitution, a sabha consists of one elected delegate for every fifty swayamsevaks entitled to vote.[67] The RSS constitution also specifies that the state sanghchalak will be elected by the state assembly,[68] and he, in consultation with the state pracharak will appoint lower-level-office-bearers.[69] In fact, the sanghchalaks, with few exceptions, exercise very little power over the day-to-day activities of the RSS. They are older influential men who add 'wisdom' to decision making and 'respectability' to the RSS. It is not uncommon for sanghchalaks to have no prior personal experience in RSS activities.

The Akhil Bharatiya pratinidhi sabha (central assembly), like its counterparts at the state level, meets once a year, and it includes delegates chosen by the state assemblies, sanghchalaks and pracharaks, and members of the central executive.[70] Also like the state assemblies, it has no effective power, though the RSS constitution gives it general supervisory power over the whole organization.[71] Rather, administrative power is exercised by the kendriya karyakari mandal (central working committee) and the general secretary.

PRACHARAK: THE MAJOR LINKING POSITION

Real power in the RSS structure resides with the pracharaks, who form a communications network outside the 'constitutional' system outlined above. They are the links between the various levels of the RSS. They have the commitment, expertise, and time to manage RSS activities; and they report to each other on the state of the RSS at periodic conclaves at both the state and all-India levels. While pracharaks bind the RSS structure together, they possess few of the symbols of power. The glitter belongs to the sanghchalaks, and the pracharaks are expected to behave deferentially towards them. There is an analogous situation in all the affiliates of the RSS.

Most pracharaks are recruited by a state pracharak in consultation with local officials who know the applicant. The state units determine their own manpower needs and have considerable discretion in assigning their own pracharaks. However, ultimate power for their placement resides with the *sarkaryavah* (national general secretary) who may shift them to other states, should manpower shortages exist elsewhere or among the affiliates. Pracharaks are on probationary service for one or two years, and during this period they are referred to as vistaraks. According to one prominent RSS official, 'If he can get along with others, inspire, and work hard, we then send him on for longer periods of time and some specific task.'[72]

Should he complete this second probationary assignment successfully, he will probably be integrated into the pracharak system.

Many of the pracharaks are loaned to the affiliates of the RSS. The pracharaks 'on loan' have a dual loyalty—one to the RSS and the other to the affiliated organization. Almost all pracharaks whom we interviewed stated that their primary loyalty was to the RSS, though they were careful to note that the RSS did not dictate policy to them. Should an affiliate develop on a separate path from the RSS, all insisted that they would immediately leave it. The pracharaks retain a close working relationship with the RSS organization in whatever area they are assigned. The RSS karyalay (office) is a place where pracharaks from several affiliates meet on an informal basis with their RSS superiors and discuss ways in which they can be of mutual service to each other. There are also formal meetings of pracharaks at the local and national level.

The 'typical'[73] pracharak is recruited in his early twenties. He is well educated, usually a college graduate. He is fluent in English and Hindi, besides the language of the area in which he works. Most of those we met were science graduates. He tends to come from an urban middle-class, upper-caste background.[74] He has participated in RSS activities since his early adolescence, attended the three Officer's Training Camps as well as a large number of other RSS camps. He has extensive travel experience, either on his own or on RSS-related business. He is a bachelor, and he has no outside employment. The RSS constitution stipulates that he 'will receive no remuneration'.[75] The unit to which he is attached provides him with living expenses, often including a scooter, and expenses for all travel connected with his RSS duties.

His lifestyle is ascetic, his diet vegetarian, and his clothing distinctly Indian (kurta, dhoti, pyjama, etc.).

While the 'calling' is theoretically a lifelong one, about one half of those we met stated that they intended to return to the 'secular' world. Many mentioned that their families were exerting pressure on them to marry, to find a more prestigious job, and to make money. Others claimed that they had become pracharaks out of a sense of 'devotion to the Motherland', and intended to 'sacrifice' several years of their lives for the nation and then fulfill their duties as a householder. Still others expressed a desire to work in one of the affiliates of the RSS, because the RSS did not offer as much prestige and excitement. Balasaheb Deoras, then sarsanghchalak of the RSS, told us that he was aware of this desire, and he considered it a problem.[76]

SARSANGHCHALAK: THE CHIEF

At the apex of the RSS hierarchy is the sarsanghchalak, chosen by his predecessor.[77] He is described in the RSS constitution as the 'Guide and Philosopher of the Rashtriya Swayamsevak Sangh'.[78] In his last years as sarsanghchalak, Golwalkar left the administrative functions to the sarkaryavah (general secretary) and to the kendriya karyakari mandal (central executive committee).[79] He generally did not intervene in the day-to-day operations of the RSS, doing so only when there was a major division of opinion.[80] Balasaheb Deoras, his successor, takes a more active role, but he too leaves most of the administrative work to his general secretary.

Despite the constitutional provision requiring the sarsanghchalak to choose his successor 'with the consent of the Karyakari Samiti', Golwalkar chose Balasaheb Deoras only a few days before his death, and the central executive acquiesced. A competitive election would be considered a disruptive catalyst, resulting in factionalism that would undermine the unity of the organization. Two months before his death, Golwalkar addressed the annual meeting of the Akhil Bharatiya Pratinidhi Sabha (central assembly) and he warned the delegates to avoid factionalism. He advised them to abide by the decisions of the RSS leadership.[81] Several weeks later, the ailing Golwalkar named his successor in his final testament. This document was not made public until shortly before Golwalkar's funeral procession. In it he wrote that he had chosen his successor after consulting with the central executive committee and the prant (state) sanghchalaks. It is highly unlikely that anyone at their level would oppose the choice.

No RSS leader publicly questioned the legitimacy of the selection process, despite the fact that it neither conforms strictly to the RSS constitution nor to the understanding with the government when the ban was lifted in 1949. No formal debate preceded Golwalkar's choice, nor was there a formal vote. For the central executive committee to question the sarsanghchalak's nominee would undermine the leadership principle of the RSS, and this would cause serious internal instability. However, the RSS leadership does have an indirect opportunity to influence the choice. The general secretary is usually acknowledged to be the likely successor. Both Golwalkar and Deoras were general secretaries before taking over the chief executive position. If the general secretary does not perform well, the senior leaders of the RSS can advise the sarsanghchalak to chose a new one.

RSS TRAINING

The shakha's activities form the core of the character-building process. The common participation in rituals and discussions, a common uniform, and the choice of physical activities are all designed to enhance a sense of community. Shakhas are conducted on an open ground. The programme begins with the swayamsevaks arranging themselves in rows before a flagstaff.[82] The rows may have up to twenty people (i.e., a gata), each row limited to a single age group. From left to right, facing the staff, are rows of shishu, bal, taruna, and proudh. At the front is the agresar (leader), usually the gatanayak. At the back is a shikshak. When the rows are assembled, the bhagva dhwaj (swallow-tailed banner of red ocher colour) is raised. This banner, associated with Shivaji, is the sacred image of the RSS and is honoured as the symbol of the 'Nation-God.'

Flag

Mukhya Shikshak			Karyavah
Shishu (row)s	Bal row(s)	Taruna row(s)	Proudh row(s)
0 (Agresar)	0 (Agresar)	0 (Agresar)	0 (Agresar)
0	0	0	0
0 (Shikshak)	0 (Shikshak)	0 (Shikshak)	0 (Shikshak)

Having raised the banner, the swayamsevaks offer *pra*nam (salute) by raising the right hand to the chest, palm parallel to the ground, head bowed. Following roll-call, the swayamsevaks assemble in different areas of the field in gata groups. The shikshaks, assisted by the gatanayaks, teach Indian games and yogic exercises.

The repertoire of games is quite large, and the games are all meant to build a spirit of cooperation. The most popular game is kabaddi (a vigorous kind of team tag). Sometimes 'defensive' skills are taught, such as the use of lathi (a five-feet-long stick made of bamboo) and the sword.[83] After about half an hour, the mukhya shikshak blows a whistle to mark the end of the physical part of the programme. Either in separate gata, combinations of gata, or as a single group, the members assemble in a circle for the discussion period. The themes of the discussion typically relate to attributes of 'good' character (e.g., fidelity, fortitude, honesty, obedience to superiors, hard work, personal discipline), the need for unity in India, or some hero or heroic event in the history of Hindu India. Occasionally, patriotic songs are sung. Most of these songs praise Hindu warriors and heroes or describe the beauty of the Motherland. The following stanzas from two songs were recalled by a swayamsevak long after he had ceased attending a shakha.

> I don't want glory in the world, nor do I yearn for a place in heaven. Only confer on me, O Mother! a single birth that I may end my days wandering around thy lovely expanses like thy devoted lover.
>
> A star is risen: the star of the RSS; come, ye brave, to the field of battle girt with your beloved beautiful sword. The bugle has sounded: on the field.[84]

Finally, the swayamsevaks again assemble in rows before the banner. The Sangh prarthana (RSS prayer) is then recited in Sanskrit by the whole group—*Namaste sada vatsale matribhume* (Salutations to thee oh loving Motherland).

This is followed by the shout, *Bharat Mata ki jai*! (Victory to Mother India!); following the structured part of the shakha, the participants are encouraged to mix informally. They are also encouraged to visit the sick and those absent.

These activities are referred to as sadhana. This is any activity in the pursuit of religious enlightenment. A loyal swayamsevak is expected to practice sadhana in shakha every day of the year. He is excused from attending an RSS camp, if ill, or if visiting another city. If he is visiting another city, he is expected to report to the RSS karyalay there. Most karyalays will provide roam and board for a visiting swayamsevak.

Absence from shakha is considered one of the more serious offences against RSS discipline. A person who misses shakha will be visited by the mukhya shikshak and the gatanayak. They will usually visit the person at the conclusion of the daily activities to find the cause for the absence. One former swayamsevak recalls the approach that was taken when he missed shakha:

> When he [mukhya shikshak] learnt . . . that I had defaulted for no sound reason whatsoever, he gave me an impassioned talking-to, asking me to realize that if I, supposedly an ideal *swayamsevak*, reneged on my obligation or duties towards the RSS and therefore to mother India, how could he expect others to abide by the shakha discipline.[85]

Indiscipline during shakha will often bring same immediate form of punishment, such as running around the shakha ground, doing sit-ups, etc. The mukhya shikshaks we interviewed felt that the punishment created a sense of guilt and the desire to reform behaviour.[86] We suspect that peer-group cohesion effectively limits the frequency of indiscipline, and we witnessed no cases of indiscipline requiring punishment.

Special baudhik[87] (intellectual sessions) are scheduled a few times each month. A single shakha or a group of shakhas will meet, usually in the evening, for a prepared lecture. These are background sessions to acquaint teachers with issues to discuss at shakha. Occasionally, these meetings are utilized to explain policy decisions made at Nagpur, to seek opinions on social and political issues, or to draw the swayamsevaks' attention to major organizational and ideological problems facing the Sangh. We recall a particularly rousing baudhik in Bombay which discussed the merits of playing an 'old-fashioned game' like *kabaddi* in a city where most of the young people prefer cricket or soccer. The participants were not at all reluctant to disagree with the official support of kabaddi, though kabaddi continues as the officially favoured game. Swayamsevaks dine together at communal dinners (chandan) two or three times a year (usually on a full moon day in October and March) to emphasize their fraternal bonds.

Each year the RSS celebrates six festivals (utsav). These festivals not only articulate the experience of those taking part, but like all ritual, they help to shape the spirit of the group. The ritual year begins with the Hindu New Year (Varsh Pratipad). This utsav provides the shakha leadership an opportunity to evaluate the previous year's progress. The date coincides with Hedgewar's birthday and is sometimes celebrated as Founder's Day.

The second utsav is the Coronation Ceremony of Shivaji (Hindu Samrajya Divotsav) which is celebrated to honour the 'Hindu victory' over 'Muslim Mughal' rule. The baudhiks at this festival frequently emphasize the 'virtues' of strength, bravery and courage.

The third is Raksha Bandhan, a north Indian celebration that Hedgewar introduced into the Sangh. The festival provides an opportunity for a sister to reaffirm her brother's obligation of continuing protection. She does this by tying a silk thread around her brother's wrist. In the RSS adaptation of this festival, the mukhya shikshak or karyavah gives each swayamsevak a rakhi (a silk thread bracelet) to tie around the wrist of a fellow swayamsevak. The baudhik will emphasize the ties of kinship that bind the swayamsevaks together. Groups of swayamsevaks will also visit those who have either left the RSS or who only irregularly attend shakha and give then rakhis encouraging them to renew their fraternal ties.

The fourth festival is Gurudakshina. On this occasion, the swayamsevaks offer money to their 'guru'—the bhagva dhwaj (the banner). Most of the RSS funds are raised at this utsav. Each swayamsevak goes before the banner, offers pranam, and throws flowers on the base of the banner staff. On each side of the banner are the pictures of 'heroes' of the Hindu nation, such as Hedgewar, Golwalkar, Ramdas Swami, and Guru Govind Singh. There are also usually pictures of several well-known Hindu warriors, such as Shivaji and Rana Pratap. Flowers are offered to these pictures as well. The member puts his offering (contained in a sealed, unmarked envelope) along with flowers on a thali (a round metal tray) and presents the offering to the banner. This banner is sometimes the topic of the baudhik. It is the image of the divine which swayamsevaks are encouraged to worship. Madhav Sadashiv Golwalkar has written that the banner is

the symbol of our dharma, our culture, our traditions, and ideal. It embodies the colour of the holy sacrificial fire that gives the message of self-immolation in the fire of idealism and the glorious orange hue of the rising sun that dispels darkness and sheds light all-around [sic]. It has been the one guiding star to all our endeavours, material as well as spiritual, the one unfailing witness to every page of our history.[88]

Dussehra, the festival commemorating the victory of Ram over Ravan, is celebrated with more pomp and on a larger scale than any other festival. All shakhas in a geographic division of the RSS combine to perform the rituals. Prior to the formal function, the RSS band will march through the city followed by uniformed participants. The public is invited to the ceremony. A well-known person from the area, often with no RSS affiliation, presides over the function. The swayamsevaks en masse will offer pranam to this person. He and a pracharak begin the festivities by worshipping a set of weapons (shastra puja) traditionally associated with Shivaji.[89] One offers *puja* (worship) by applying sindur (vermilion) and flowers to the weapons. The RSS bands play martial music, and the assembled swayamsevaks sing patriotic songs. En masse, the swayamsevaks demonstrate their skills with the *lathi*, sword, and various exercises.

Concluding the festival year is the celebration of *Sankrant* (the winter solstice). The major themes of the utsav are personal renunciation and service to the nation. One part of the ceremony is meant to teach a behavioural trait considered 'virtuous'. Sweets are distributed with the injunction that the words that come from the mouths of swayamsevaks should be as 'sweet' as the substance going into it. The injunction is (in Marathi): *Tul gul gya ani god god bola* (take the sweet and speak sweetly).

The RSS operates a large number of camps to indoctrinate the swayamsevaks, to offer instruction regarding the teaching of the samskaras, and to develop a sense of solidarity among members. At any given time of the year, one is likely to find an RSS camp operating somewhere in the country.

Camps fall roughly into three categories. The first are the Instructors' Training Camps (referred to as ITC) usually managed by district committees. These camps last about fifteen days, usually during the winter months. Like other camps, they are isolated from outside contacts, conducted within some large institution (e.g., a college or high school), and are totally self-sufficient, containing their own kitchens, clinic, bookstore and laundry, besides the residential and instructional facilities. Everyone is dressed identically, for the RSS uniform must be worn by everyone attending a camp. Even the camp leaders do not wear their insignia to indicate their position. Swayamsevaks pay their own expenses at the camps.[90] RSS funds are used only for those participants whose families cannot afford the fees. ITCs are intended primarily for the older members, and the emphasis is on the intellectual aspects of the RSS programme.

Numerous three-day camps are also conducted throughout the year. These are designed for specific groups (high-school students, college students, businessmen, etc.). These camps are particularly attractive to the younger members of the RSS.

By far the most important camps are the Officers' Training Camps (OTC) which are run to train the workers of the RSS. The selection process and the planning begin several months before the camps are held. These camps are conducted for about one month during the summer season. The central executive of the RSS staggers the timing of the state camps so that the sarsanghchalak and other senior RSS figures can visit all of them. Every pracharak is expected to attend two of these camps; teachers and other office bearers attend at least one; other swayamsevaks may attend if approved by the shakha's mukhya shikshak and the local pracharak. Those who have completed the second year of OTC are encouraged to attend the third-year training camp held at Nagpur.

Most of the trainees at these camps are between fifteen and twenty-five. The youngest we met was fourteen, and the oldest was thirty, though we were told that there were older swayamsevaks in attendance. We met Africans of Indian descent at several OTCs. They had come to India to take instructional training in the RSS discipline and intended to implement the discipline within their overseas RSS affiliates.[91] The Bharatiya Swayamsevak Sangh (the RSS affiliate in Kenya, Tanzania and Uganda) now conducts its own camps, as does the Hindu Swayamsevak Sangh (the British affiliate).[92]

The participants of OTC are assigned to ganas (groups of between fifteen and thirty) which are directed by ganapramukhs (instructors). The instructor stays with this group throughout the month. He is responsible for teaching the physical (sharirik) and intellectual (baudhik) classes which form the camp curriculum. The instructors we met were in the age group of twenty-five and thirty-five. The camps' directors make a deliberate effort to mix different age groups and people from various regions of the state. We were told that this was done to break down feelings of exclusiveness. While we met men from the scheduled castes, their gana mates were either ignorant of the fact or expressed a lack of interest. If pressed on the issue, a typical response was, 'We are all members of ek jati [one group] here.'

The various activities carried out in the camp are designed to develop a sense of solidarity among the participants. The participants are encouraged to call each other by kinship terms. They take turns serving food to each other. To break down feelings of purity/pollution, they are required to take their turn at cleaning the latrines, sweeping, and other so-called 'defiling' activities. Besides this, the seminars and lectures frequently emphasize the unity of all Hindus.

The activities are designed to teach the participants the games, exercises and songs which form the basis of the shakhas' programme. They are required to participate in the seminars which are held every day. Many participants keep notebooks, in which they record the words of patriotic songs, take notes on physical exercises, games and topics of discussion. Below is a list of moral and civic lessons which one swayamsevak recorded in his diary:[93]

1. A swayamsevak should behave like an ideal person in society. He should not commit any antisocial action and damage the image of the Sangh.
2. Non-Hindus must be assimilated with the Hindu way of life. The words 'Muslim' and 'Christian' denote a religious phenomena, while the word 'Hindu' is synonymous with the nation. Even in the United States, it is emphasized that non-Americans should be assimilated into 'Anglo-Saxon' culture.
3. The RSS was organized to prevent the further disintegration of Hindu society.

4. The RSS is a family. The RSS emphasizes the samskaras [inculcation of good values]. The samskaras create the man. We have to create the man by reviving his unknown virtues.

5. The higher authorities within the RSS can be compared to the head of the family.

6. The lack of leadership in India must be eliminated. A gatanayak [group leader] should work in his own field with a specific purpose. A little work will not do. In the past, castes and pilgrimage places provided group leadership. Now the RSS has to fulfil this responsibility. The RSS shakha programmes create and develop such qualities.

7. We purposely avoid taking credit for achievements, though in reality, many things have been done by the RSS. Whatever we have done, we have done for the good of society. We do not want credit. We have to work as a part of society.

8. Those who attend shakha are one, and the remaining are divided by caste and class.

9. Rational arguments separate people from us. It is not necessary to convince people of the need of the RSS. Our arguments should appeal to the heart. To succeed in RSS work, we should attract society with a sweet tongue. We should avoid a hot temper and debate.

10. Inactivity in a swayamsevak is a psychological sickness, but it can be eliminated. Give others work which they are capable of doing. Tell others of his [sic] capacity. Through this, you can increase his capacity.

11. We are all children of this land. So we are one family without any discrimination between us.

12. Our nation should be so powerful that nobody could dare insult us. If we unite, no power in the world can check our progress.

13. Government cannot change the nation; selfless people change it. So we have to create a cadre of workers in different fields and on different levels, and then planning will be successful.

14. Land and people are the body. Government is the clothing, and culture is the soul.

15. The RSS does not want to organize only a part of society, but all of society.

16. In the last one thousand years, the bonds that linked society were broken. This led to selfish caste mentality that divided society. To unite it, the RSS has devised a certain methodology. Meeting together every day is the heart of the system. RSS shakha is our, home for one hour each day, and RSS work is our duty for the other twenty-three hours.

There runs through these notes an emphasis on submerging the self within the 'nation', which tacitly assumes a commitment to the RSS and which involves the conviction that there exists a mutuality of interests between the individual and the RSS.[94] Another theme is the proposition that those who participate in the RSS are unique. The image used is that of the RSS and society as a family. RSS publicists frequently employ this metaphor not only to deepen the commitment to cooperation, but also to provide a rationale for social obligation. Hindus 'owe' something to each other as members of the Hindu nation and as co-citizens in the Indian state. What is 'owed' is something more than willing adherence to legal obligations; it involves personal commitment to the task of revitalizing the corporate nation, and its social and political institutions.

At the conclusion of a camp, each participant is required to demonstrate the physical skills which he will later teach in his individual shakha. The participants are also required to take a written examination. The following is a sample of questions set for those attending a second-year camp:

1. What are the places where Indian culture dominates?
2. After listening to the three baudhik lectures of Guruji [i.e., Madhavrao Golwalkar], what ideas have come in [your mind] about your work?
3. What is the object of 'gata' system in the shakha?
4. Give one illustration of Dr Hedgewar's life which reflects his way of treating people.

There were also questions requiring the students to recall specific facts, such as,

1. When was the RSS founded?
2. When is Hindu Samrajya Diwas celebrated each year?
3. What is the name of the all-India physical instructor of the RSS?[95]

The camp also provides an opportunity for RSS leaders to observe closely the progress of the participants and gives the RSS a rather comprehensive picture of the recruitment pool from which it will draw its leaders. This training is followed by a kind of probationary assignment at the local level of the organization.

Only a small percentage of those who attend shakha become full members of the RSS. The requirements are quite stringent. A prospective member must demonstrate his loyalty to the RSS by regularly attending shakha, baudhik, chandan, the RSS festivals, and the camps. He must conform to the behavioural model of an ideal swayamsevak, and he must demonstrate the ability to work well in groups. If judged fit, a life oath is administered:[96]

Remembering Almighty God and my forebears, I take this oath. For the betterment of my sacred Hindu religion, Hindu culture, and Hindu community, I will devote myself to the prosperity of my Holy Motherland. I swear that I shall serve the Rashtriya Swayamsevak Sangh with my body, my mind, and my money. I will be faithful to this oath throughout my life.

4

The RSS 'Family' Takes Shape

Events in post-war India confronted the RSS with a series of challenges which forced the organization to reassess its objectives and its programme. The RSS had established its organizational structure and had formulated its ideology. The RSS had become a national organization, and its leadership was determined to play a role in the country's development, though there was an internal debate about how to achieve this goal. The deteriorating communal situation and the partition of British India, both considered disasters of the first order, caught the senior RSS leadership off guard and unprepared. This lack of a programme exacerbated the internal debate regarding tactics.

No senior member of the RSS questioned the relevance of character building in an independent India. The debate was over whether character building was sufficient to bring about the Hindu revivalist ideals of the founders. We shall call activists those who believed that the RSS should have a broader agenda. Those who were wary of such moves outside the narrow character-building environment of the shakha we shall refer to as the traditionalists.[1] In the activist category were many young men who had responded to Golwalkar's call in 1942 for additional pracharaks to expand the organizational base of the RSS.[2] Many of these new recruits were college students who had been deeply disappointed by the apparent failure of Mahatma Gandhi's Quit India movement to bring India closer to independence. Some of them previously had been attracted to communism, but were dismayed by the collaboration of Indian communists with the colonial authority during World War II. For these restless young men, the RSS represented an alternative approach to freedom from that of Mahatma Gandhi and of the communists.

The traditionalists for their part were most prominently represented by those *swayamsevaks* who had been attracted to the RSS in the 1930s by Dr Hedgewar. Most were Maharashtrian and in their twenties and thirties when they joined the RSS. They tended to see organization building as still the priority activity and were reluctant to support any programme that might give the political authorities an excuse to place restrictions on the RSS.

The young activists in the RSS for their part did not have a common agenda or a national spokesman. In Maharashtra, many wanted the RSS to support the political activity of the Hindu Mahasabha,[3] while in other states there were members who wanted the RSS to support the Congress. Still other activists were angry that the RSS had not used its paramilitary structure directly either to oppose the British or to struggle against partition of the country. If the RSS meant anything, it surely stood for the territorial integrity of India—referred to as Bharat Mata (Mother India) in the RSS. They argued that the RSS had considerable assets, such as its very high standing among the Hindus in north-western India,[4] which could have been used to resist the partition.

The partition of India came as a shock to many swayamsevaks and shattered their image of the RSS as a bulwark against the creation of Pakistan. The partition, more than any other event, caused many members to question the judgement of the leadership. Another source of discontent sprang from the absence of an RSS programme to organize students, workers, farmers, businessmen, civil servants, etc. Many activists believed the RSS should organize these groups so that the RSS itself could play a leading part in shaping events during a critical period in India's history. Still others wanted the RSS to engage directly in revolutionary acts against the British. They were deeply disappointed that the RSS did not lend its backing to the naval mutiny at Bombay in 1946.

The activists' criticism of the RSS leadership was muted during the partition, when the full-time workers of the RSS were almost totally absorbed in refugee relief, and during the ban on the RSS, when most were engaged in underground work. However, the activist experience during the partition and the ban appears to have strengthened their conviction that the RSS had to become a more dynamic organization. With the leadership imprisoned during the ban, responsibility for managing the RSS devolved to middle-level pracharaks, who thus became more self-confident about speaking out on organizational matters. With the lifting of the ban on the RSS in 1949, their criticism of the leadership surfaced.

The RSS leadership justified its caution during the partition and pre-partition periods by pointing out that militancy would have undermined national unity at a critical time, that aggressive action would have made it much more difficult for the RSS to carry out refugee relief, and that the organization needed to protect itself for future work.[5] In fact, the RSS leadership had failed to anticipate either the partition or the ban, and lacked a coherent policy regarding both developments. The RSS dream of playing a major role in independent India was shattered. Rather, it was on the defensive. The RSS leadership was under attack both from within and without. The RSS was treated as a pariah organization and the leadership was ridiculed in the press and by politicians. Its membership dropped and the number of pracharaks decreased. Morale within the organization was at an all time low.

AFTER THE BAN: RETHINKING GOALS AND TACTICS

But the organization was to revive. Emerging from the ranks were a few highly talented pracharaks, such as Eknath Ranade, Vasantrao Krishna Oke, Deendayal Upadhyaya, and Bhai Mahavir, who had demonstrated managerial skills during the ban which could be used to rebuild the organization. Most were in their thirties; most were college graduates; and most had been associated with the RSS from their childhood. It was this group, most of whom were activists, that managed the reconstruction of the RSS and organized the network of affiliates that grew up around it.

The leadership agreed with its young pracharaks that mass contact work was necessary to demonstrate that the RSS still had support. The first step in this direction was to stage rallies for Golwalkar in late 1949. RSS pracharaks also began to organize various kinds of social welfare activities in order to give a new and less paramilitary orientation to the RSS and to make it more respectable.

Between the lifting of the ban in 1949 and 1953, Golwalkar was confronted by an organization beset by internal divisions. This disunity was in part the result of the unprecedented independence of the pracharaks during the eighteen-month ban. They operated largely on their own, which gave the pracharaks a relatively free hand to experiment. The central leadership in the mid-1950s was alarmed by what this experimentation would do to the organization.

The senior RSS figures, generally traditionalist in orientation, believed that the weakened RSS should concentrate on rebuilding the battered organization. This divergence of views exacerbated tensions within the ranks of the RSS.[6] To restore discipline and a unified sense of purpose, the central leadership made personnel changes designed to place more reliable pracharaks in key state positions. Eknath Ranade, who replaced Prabhakar Balwant Dani as general secretary in 1956, was largely responsible for implementing this policy. Still another significant personnel change was the replacement of Vasantrao Krishna Oke, the Delhi state pracharak by Madhavrao Mule, the Punjab state pracharak associated with the traditionalist school.

Golwalkar also moved to restore a greater measure of unity by re-establishing his own moral authority. In March, 1954 he assembled some 300 pracharak from all over India to spell out 'positive Hinduism' as a philosophic underpinning for their work.[7] Golwalkar argued that Western philosophy, emphasizing materialism, was divisive and thus a dangerous model to follow. Rather, the country should rely on Hindu philosophy, which stressed the unity of man and society. Golwalkar argued that a person worships God through service to society and he advised his audience to carry out its work in this spirit. His presentation, the first systematic statement of the RSS world view after the ban, may have been intended to do more than refurbish Golwalkar's moral standing within the organization. By virtually ignoring the paramilitary background of the RSS, his speech may also have been an attempt to improve the public image of the RSS.

Golwalkar also recognized that he would have to accommodate the activist demand for new programmes to stem a large-scale defection of the remaining pracharaks in the organization. The activist case was buttressed by the need to improve the image of the RSS. But Golwalkar's caution regarding new programmes was influenced by his concern that such programmes not undermine the central position of character building. In addition, Golwalkar was reluctant to act unless he had a consensus acceptable to the traditionalist element in the RSS. With these considerations in mind, Golwalkar in late 1949 assigned several pracharaks to work with Vinoba Bhave, a disciple of Mahatma Gandhi, in a voluntary land donation programme aimed at convincing land owners to give some of their property to landless peasants. The mass migration of Hindus from East Pakistan in early 1950 provided another opportunity for Golwalkar to involve the RSS in a programme that would be acceptable to the traditionalists and the activists, as well as enhance the public image of the RSS. Eknath Ranade organized a relief programme similar to the work the RSS had carried out for the Hindu refugees from West Pakistan in the wake of the partition. Pursuing this new stress on social welfare,

Golwalkar ordered a large-scale RSS involvement in the rehabilitation of the victims of the 1950 earthquake in Assam.

Besides addressing the concerns of those activists who wanted to get the RSS involved in social welfare programmes, Golwalkar clearly believed that he had to respond to the pressure of those activists interested in politics. Despite his apprehensions regarding political involvement, Golwalkar permitted several pracharaks to assist Dr Shyama Prasad Mookerjee—a prominent Bengali politician who had left the cabinet in 1950 over a disagreement with Prime Minister Nehru regarding his policy towards Pakistan—in establishing the Jana Sangh in 1951. While this step might have been calculated to help a political party that would offer protection to the RSS, his willingness to cooperate with Mookerjee probably was also motivated by a desire to accommodate the restive activists. The electoral debacle of the Jana Sangh in the 1951–52 first general elections demoralized the political activists and provided an opportunity for the central RSS leadership to enhance the position of the RSS relative to the party. The young party needed RSS workers; indeed, it depended on them to establish an organizational base. This dependency meant that the party leadership had to pay attention to the views of the RSS.

Still another example of Golwalkar's efforts to accommodate political activists was his support of swayamsevak participation in a move to liberate the Portuguese enclave of Dadra and Nagar Haveli in 1954. His favourable response to a request from Bombay state officials for such support was prompted by his fear that the communists might gain the upper hand in the struggle against Portuguese rule.[8]

Golwalkar also gave those pracharaks seeking to organize workers and students an opportunity to lay the groundwork for affiliated organizations. Two of the more prominent were Dattopant Bapurao Thengadi, in labour, and Datta Devidas Didolkar, among students. Both men began their apprenticeship by working in non-RSS labour and student organizations.

Golwalkar's personal involvement in the late 1952 agitation against cow slaughter gave the RSS a chance to influence the Hindu religious establishment as well as to build up its popular support. At the grass-roots level, the agitation depended heavily on RSS volunteers who were largely responsible for the collection of signatures petitioning the president of India to ban cow slaughter. Like the tour campaign organized for Golwalkar after his release from prison, the involvement in the agitation against cow slaughter boosted RSS morale and demonstrated to the membership that the organization had the capacity for mass action.

Despite these efforts, the RSS remained in bad shape. It continued to lose members and activist pracharaks. Some of the remaining activists even went to the extent of openly challenging Golwalkar's leadership. Moreover, the RSS was unable either to recruit the desired number of pracharaks or to pay off outstanding debts. Regarding finances, Golwalkar was deeply worried over the inability of the RSS to quickly pay off loans arranged during the ban. Golwalkar was so concerned that he gave serious consideration to selling the RSS headquarters in Nagpur to raise the money. It was not until 1956 that the RSS was able to pay off the debt incurred during the ban.

Given the continuing problems in the mid-1950s, the central leadership decided that further consolidation was needed. Eknath Ranade, appointed general secretary in 1956, ruled that the RSS could not afford to loan pracharaks to the affiliates when its own work continued to languish. The RSS would devote its resources almost exclusively to character building. This policy came as a blow to the affiliates and their leaders lobbied against it. Some activist pracharaks, such as the Deoras brothers (Balasaheb and Bhaurao), withdrew from RSS work.

The consolidation phase ended in 1962. Two years earlier, Golwalkar had called an assembly of full-time workers at Indore to review the future orientation of the RSS. For the first time, pracharaks working in the affiliates were participants in such a national conclave. These pracharaks strongly recommended that the RSS again allow some of its own full-time workers to shift to the affiliates. They pointed out that the future of the affiliates would be bleak unless they could get RSS pracharaks. Their arguments made an impression. General Secretary Ranade, assigned to a long-term project aimed at popularizing the revivalist message of Swami Vivekananda, was replaced in 1962 by Prabhakar Balwant Dani, who had held the position between 1946 and 1956, and who was more sympathetic to the activist view. After 1962, RSS workers again were allowed to shift to the affiliates. Some of the pracharaks who had been disillusioned by the retrenchment policy returned to their work. Perhaps most prominent on this score were the Deoras brothers. Balasaheb was appointed assistant general secretary, and Bhaurao was given the position of northern zonal pracharak.

Perhaps the major reason for the change in policy after 1962 was the enhanced respectability of the RSS, most dramatically demonstrated by the government's decision to permit its participation in the 26 January 1963 Republic

Day parade. The RSS clearly benefitted from the upsurge in nationalism sweeping the country in the wake of the 1962 Sino-Indian war.

The growing membership and the successful recruitment of full-time workers were further proof that the organization had again been placed on a firmer foundation and could afford to pursue a more activist orientation without at the same time undermining its core character-building activity. This reorientation was buttressed by the appointment of Balasaheb Deoras as general secretary in 1965 on the death of Dani, following his informal exercise of the position during Dani's illness in 1964. During his nine-year tenure in that office, Deoras stressed the importance of the affiliates, advocated improved coordination between the RSS and the affiliates, and supported their growing assertiveness. While he was general secretary, the affiliates began to take on a more populist orientation, and this was demonstrated by their increasing resort to agitation.

RSS-AFFILIATED NEWSPAPERS AND JOURNALS

One of the first non-traditional areas of work for the RSS was the print media. Given the critical national questions raised in the immediate post-war period, the RSS leadership wanted to communicate its views quickly to a rapidly growing membership and to the larger Hindu community, whose interest the RSS claimed to represent. There was a dilemma over what form this communication should take, for Hedgewar had, on theoretical grounds, discouraged the use of publicity and mass communications. He feared that publicity would undermine the character-building programme of the RSS.

It might be tempted to employ publicity to recruit supporters who, without the disciplined training, would have only the most superficial commitment to the fundamental goals of the organization. Hedgewar believed publicity had been a major factor in undermining the idealism and commitment of almost every other nationalist movement. Throughout his tenure as sarsanghchalak and well into that of his successor, the RSS leadership refused to publicize its activities.

Reluctant to employ publicity or mass communication, the RSS created an informal communications system based on verbal messages carried by RSS leaders, who were almost continually touring the country. The RSS in its formative stage published no newspapers or journals, and it had neither a written constitution nor a set of written rules. When the government of the Central Provinces issued a memorandum in December 1933, charging that the RSS was a communal organization which government employees were prohibited from joining, Hedgewar refused to issue a protest and requested sympathetic organizations to protest on its behalf.[9] When RSS work was begun in Delhi in 1936, Hedgewar wrote to the organizer:

> It is a bad thing ... that the news [concerning RSS work] appeared in the newspapers ... Due to such publicity, many difficulties will be created in our work, so we don't want publicity in the beginning. If we present some work before the people, it will naturally do the publicity and it is useful to organize so no such mistake should be made again [sic].[10]

Soon after the war, activist pracharaks proposed that the RSS begin to use the print media to publicize its position on the question of partition, on the goals of an independent India, and on how Hindus should respond to communal tension. They argued that the RSS message was not reaching most Hindus at a critical period in India's history. While the leaders refused to sanction the establishment of RSS newspapers and journals, they did consent to the creation of trusts which would publish newspapers and journals sympathetic to its goals. In late 1946, swayamsevaks in Punjab and Delhi began selling shares for the Bharat Prakashan Trust.[11] The trust raised approximately 400,000 rupees and it began to publish *Organiser*, an English-language weekly published in the capital city, on 3 July, 1947, one month after Lord Mountbatten announced the British decision to partition the country and to terminate colonial rule in the subcontinent.[12] The first several issues of *Organiser* focused on partition, calling for Hindu resistance to it.

Organiser, which reached a national audience, became the most prominent forum for the activist viewpoint in the RSS. Indeed, the print media affiliated to the RSS employed many activists who were later to play a major role in the establishment of the RSS 'family' of organizations.

The 1948 ban of the RSS, press attacks on it, and the decision of the Congress party to prohibit RSS members from participating in the Congress or its affiliated organizations strengthened the case of the activists advocating a network of newspapers that would present the RSS view on developments. In order to communicate with the vast majority of the population not literate in English, activist swayamsevaks decided to establish newspapers and journals in the vernacular languages. During the ban, swayamsevaks established two vernacular weeklies—*Panchjanya* in Hindi and *Rashtra Shakti* in Marathi.[13] In the following decade, trusts were formed to publish newspapers and journals in twelve vernacular languages.[14] Each of these publications is owned and managed by a trust, most of whose shareholders are swayamsevaks. Their editorial staff and reporters are recruited largely from among RSS cadre. Many of the staff members meet formally together a few times each year, usually at Nagpur, to discuss technical problems and policy stands. Their common membership in the RSS further strengthens the bonds between them.

Activists were responsible for forming the Hindustan Samachar, India's first vernacular news service. In 1970, with a network of over 1,000 correspondents and 24 news centres, it distributed news to newspapers and journals publishing in 9 local languages.[15] Among its reliable customers were the 41 RSS affiliated newspapers and journals. The Hindustan Samachar was an important element in the communications network of the RSS, for it reported RSS activities as well as the activities of the affiliates. This news service also was important for mobilization purposes because most of the subscribers to its services were not members of the RSS 'family'. Hence, it significantly increased the number of readers exposed to the views of the RSS.

During the 1975–1977 Emergency, the government forced the four national news agencies to amalgamate as part of its post-Emergency effort to control the press. The Hindustan Samachar ceased to function as a separate news agency on 1 February 1976, when the four agencies announced to their customers that all news now would be sourced to the Samachar Society, the new unified wire service.

During the Emergency, the RSS-affiliated print media tried to protect itself from government retaliation by strictly following censorship guidelines. In some cases, they even published laudatory pro-government articles. Nonetheless, the government did close several RSS affiliated newspapers and journals, including *Organiser* and *Motherland*.[16]

After the Emergency, the RSS-affiliated newspapers experienced a surge of circulation, though the number of affiliates in the print media remained stable. However, since 1977 there has been a rapid increase in the number of specialized journals published by the 'family' of organizations around the RSS.

The Janata government which came to power in 1977 restored the four original news agencies that had been amalgamated during the Emergency. The Hindustan Samachar for its part experienced severe financial problems, in part due to the 1979 Palekar Award which mandated higher salaries to workers in the print media. The Samachar found it difficult to meet this additional financial burden in part because it had significantly increased the number of correspondents on its payroll. In addition, the United News of India, a large English press service, began to offer its services in the vernaculars. Because the RSS brotherhood refused to bail it out, the Samachar was forced to turn to the government for operating funds, a step which forced the Samachar to accept a government-appointed managing director. This incident underscores the usual RSS practice of demanding that the affiliates pay their own way after a few years of nurturing. Some exceptions have been made, but only if a convincing case could be made that the cause of national integration would suffer unless the affiliate received additional resources.

RSS-AFFILIATED STUDENTS ASSOCIATION

Few organizations excluded swayamsevaks before the 1948–49 ban. The situation changed drastically after the ban, and swayamsevaks found themselves excluded from the politically dominant Congress party, from all its affiliates, and from many other organizations as well. The activists who had been lobbying for the RSS itself to establish new channels of influence had a very good case now. Not only were individual RSS members prevented from participating in the political process, but the very existence of the RSS was threatened. During the ban, swayamsevaks established a wide variety of organizations, such as devotional groups, sports clubs, students associations, etc., to sustain group solidarity, and to provide general support for RSS objectives.[17] The leadership was hardly in a position to oppose these developments, nor was it in the interest of the RSS to do so during that time.

Students were perhaps the most active organizers during the ban period, and many of the front groups were established on campuses. Hedgewar himself had recognized that college students could play a vital role in mobilizing support. They were receptive to its nationalist ideology and were prepared to sacrifice for an ideal. Moreover, he recognized that it was relatively easy to create a substantial movement among students in a short period of time. The first members of the RSS were students, and the young organizations effectively used them to recruit other adherents. The new student recruits were soon to establish RSS units outside of Nagpur. Indeed, they were probably the most effective agents of its early expansion.

Prior to World War II, many student swayamsevaks participated in activities of the All-India Students' Federation (AISF), the largest association of students. RSS informants claim that the AISF itself became a fertile ground for recruits and some of those recruits were later to play a prominent role in the RSS and in the affiliates.[18] In 1940, the AISF split into the pro-communist All-India Students' Federation and the pro-Congress All-India Students' Congress (AISC). Most RSS members, according to RSS informants, opted for the latter. During the 1942 Quit India movement, the AISC sponsored a wide range of anti-British activities, and many RSS members claim to have participated in these activities.

The failure of the 1942 Quit India movement and the inability of the people to sustain a revolutionary movement against British authority disillusioned many students, some of whom began to question Mahatma Gandhi's tactics.[19] Some of those disillusioned by developments during World War II, according to RSS informants, were attracted to the RSS.[20] Many students were seeking a new approach to revitalize the country, and the RSS certainly offered a new approach.[21] While the RSS did not oppose the British openly during the war, it was not stained by any compromises with British authority, and non-violence received no philosophic support from its leaders. Gandhi's espousal of non-violence and the pro-British policy stand of the Communist Party of India which were not popular among many student activists, provided RSS organizers with an opportunity to proselytize among students looking for a nationalist alternative to either the Congress or the CPI. It is likely that few of the college students recruited during World War II fully appreciated the implications of character building. They, like the RSS activists in general, did not accept the traditionalist argument that character building would be effective only if the RSS teachers and its training programme were insulated from the temptations of power, prestige and money. Many wanted the RSS to organize students and to take an open stand on the major political questions of the time.

The 1948–49 ban offered the activists an opportunity to organize students. The first students' group formed during the ban was at Delhi University, and similar groups were established at many other colleges and universities soon after. The swayamsevaks were most active in Punjab were Balraj Madhok, a young RSS pracharak and a college teacher, was particularly successful in recruiting refugee students. Madhok claims that the RSS leadership did not direct his activities.[22] While this is probably true, the RSS in mid-1948 did assign pracharaks to work with RSS student activists.[23] Some student organizers, all RSS members, met in Delhi in July 1948, to draw up a constitution for an all-India organization that would link the scattered groups together. The new national body was the Akhil Bharatiya Vidyarthi Parishad, and it was registered with the government. Fewer than half of the early participants in the Vidyarthi Parishad were RSS members, according to informed estimates, and the percentage of swayamsevaks has declined much more since then.[24] The Vidyarthi Parishad provides the RSS an opportunity to mobilize support among students who might not be attracted to the strict discipline of the shakha.

The Vidyarthi Parishad differs significantly from other students organizations. It is explicitly committed to reconciling the interests of all parts of the academic community. It is opposed to the 'student trade unionism' espoused by other student groups. Teachers and administrators are welcomed into it, and they play a major role in its activities. Most of the Vidyarthi Parishad presidents, at both the state and central levels, are teachers. It has a special ceremony (vyas *puja*) in which students pay homage to their teachers. At the same time, it expects teachers to take an active interest in the well-being of their students.

As late as the mid-1960s, the Vidyarthi Parishad tended to avoid campus politics and student protests. On both matters it has radically altered policy.[25] Had the Vidyarthi Parishad not changed its stand, the group probably would have lost much of its largely lower-middle-class student constituency. Lower-middle-class students have a variety of complaints with the inadequate educational facilities provided them and with the bleak employment prospects which face them upon graduation. As colleges and universities have expanded, bringing in many students from the lower-middle classes, the Vidyarthi Parishad has also grown, and it now claims to be the largest and most active student group in India. Its repeated student union victories on many campuses, particularly in Delhi, Punjab, Uttar Pradesh, Madhya Pradesh and Maharashtra, suggest that the Vidyarthi Parishad has succeeded in developing a loyal student following.[26] Many of its members come from families who respect the symbols of Hinduism and the value of community bonds. An organization like the Vidyarthi Parishad which relies heavily on the symbols of Hinduism and which offers a surrogate family environment has attracted such students.

Few Indian universities and colleges provide students a wide range of extra-curricular opportunities or counselling services. A major attraction of the Vidyarthi Parishad, and one that makes it unique among student as organizations, is that it does both. In contrast to most other students associations, campus politics, though important, has a lower priority than indoctrination. When a student first enrolls, the Vidyarthi Parishad actively seeks to recruit him and expose the student to its ideology. It operates 'Welcome to New Students' programmes, which are a kind of orientation to college life. It operates 'Study Circles', usually presided over by faculty members, at which the Vidyarthi Parishad subtly advances its own ideology,[27] besides introducing the new student to teachers and students.

The Vidyarthi Parishad conducts a wide range of programmes that involve students in spreading the world view of the RSS. At the larger, more cosmopolitan universities, the Vidyarthi Parishad operates Indo-foreign students bureaus to bring Indian and foreign students together and to introduce foreign students to Indian culture. 'My home is India' and 'Students experience in interstate living' are two programmes which both tap students' idealism and have a nation-building purpose.[28] In the first programme, young tribals, boys and girls between eight and twelve, are sponsored to live in the homes of older Vidyarthi Parishad members. One Vidyarthi Parishad brochure describes the programme as 'another humble attempt of ABVP to bring nearer to the main current of nationalism, the smaller currents flowing freely throughout our Motherland'.[29] The Vidyarthi Parishad organizes student tours to the tribal areas during summer vacations so that students may, in the words of a Vidyarthi Parishad pamphlet, 'experience how unity in diversity is the characteristic feature of India'. Students from tribal areas are also invited to live with Parishad members during summer vacations.[30] In addition, it operates clubs for students interested in sports and the natural sciences, vacation employment bureaus, book banks, tutorial centres, and health clinics. Like the other members of the RSS 'family', it also conducts a series of indoctrination camps.

By the early 1970s, the Vidyarthi Parishad had become a significant force on the campus and in students union politics. In 1974, it claimed 160,000 members in 790 branches and 24 full-time workers.[31] It became more willing than before to participate in activities that involved confronting university and political authorities, though the Vidyarthi Parishad opposed the use of violence, which in its view undermined the desired end objective of establishing a consensus that each of the various sides in a dispute could live with.

Perhaps the most dramatic example of the Vidyarthi Parishad's activism was its involvement in the 1974–75 students agitations in Bihar and Gujarat. In both instances, protests addressing purely campus issues grew into a massive campaign against alleged corruption on the part of the state government. Vidyarthi Parishad literature suggests a mix of motives behind its decision to participate in these protest movements: to limit the influence of such radical groups as the Naxalites (revolutionary communists), to mobilize additional support for itself, and to force a perceived unresponsive state government to heed legitimate student demands.

In Bihar, the Vidyarthi Parishad fully backed the student movement's invitation to Jaya Prakash Narayan, the respected leader of a rural reform movement, to shape the tactics and policies of the student campaign. Narayan broadened the scope of the student campaign to include 'total revolution', a kind of participatory democracy. In Gujarat, the Vidyarthi Parishad participated in the *Nav Nirman* (new society) students movement, which eventually forced the Congress party state government there to resign in February 1974. Emboldened by the success of the students movements in Bihar and Gujarat, state leaders of the Vidyarthi Parishad assembled at Nagpur in March 1975, to discuss the possibility of similar movements elsewhere, but the declaration of the Emergency three months later blocked the implementation of such plans.[32]

When the Emergency was declared on 25 June 1975, the Parishad adopted a cautious, wait-and-see attitude. While it was not banned, the leaders of the Vidyarthi Parishad could not be sure that the government would not take this step since it had been deeply involved in students agitations and because of its own links to the RSS. But the arrest of over 4000 Parishad workers,[33] including Arun Jaitley, one of its most prominent student activists,[34] in the first two months of the Emergency prompted it to act. 60 of its 80 full-time workers reportedly went underground.[35] Over 11,000 Vidyarthi Parishad members, according to its own estimates, were arrested during the November 1975–January 1976 protest against the Emergency. At the same time, the Vidyarthi Parishad used its overground activities (debates, concerts, etc.) to preserve its infrastructure and to sustain the morale of members.

After the victory of the Janata Party in 1977, the Vidyarthi Parishad experienced a rush of new members, as did the RSS itself. Over the next five years, it grew from 170,000 members to 250,000; from 950 branches to 1100; and from 80 to 125 full-time workers.[36] As the only pro-Janata Party youth group with a functioning grass-roots structure, it was under considerable pressure to merge with other pro-Janata Party youth groups. The Parishad leadership was initially willing to discuss the idea as long as the objective was a youth organization independent of any political party. It sent delegates[37] to a conclave of pro-Janata Party youth groups on 17 April 1977 at Sarnath (Uttar Pradesh), but the Parishad representatives walked out on the first day when it became clear that other participants wanted to link the united youth group to the governing party.[38]

The same manoeuvring for power that racked the Janata Party between 1977 and 1979 existed among its affiliated youth groups. The Janata Party was never able to establish a unified youth group. Indeed, the delegates that remained at the Sarnath meeting formed two groups. One was the Yuva Janata, which included the Congress (O) youth group and several socialist groups; the other was the Janata Yuva Morcha, a pro-Jana Sangh group. Neither had a cadre or significant membership; and without the Vidyarthi Parishad, these pro-Janata Party groups were unable to build a substantial base of support among students. In the wake of this failure to establish a united pro-Janata youth party affiliate, Prime Minister Morarji Desai drew up a compromise that he hoped would satisfy the Vidyarthi Parishad's demand for independence of political parties while at the same time drawing the various pro-Janata Party youth groups closer together. He suggested the formation of two groups both of which would subscribe to Jaya Prakash Narayan's philosophy. One would be independent and the other linked to the Janata Party. But his efforts failed.

Despite the growing activism of the Vidyarthi Parishad during the 1970s, the leadership refused to permit its members to contest the 1977 state assembly elections, even though the Janata Party had offered tickets to it, as it did to other pro-Janata Party youth groups.[39] The Parishad leadership believed that the students had already become overly politicized and that any deeper involvement in politics would destabilize the campus. They also feared that 'constructive work' and 'nation-building' activities, two vital elements of its programmes, would suffer if the trend towards political involvement continued. Vidyarthi Parishad members even refused to serve on the Janata Party's organizational bodies. Arun Jaitley, for example, turned down an invitation to sit on the party's national council.[40]

The Vidyarthi Parishad, however, did contest students union elections in 1977, and it did very well. In a reversal of policy, the Vidyarthi Parishad's national executive decided in June 1978 that the organization would withdraw even from students union politics, and concentrate on 'constructive work' and 'nation building', justifying the move on the grounds that politics should be removed from the campus.[41] While the Vidyarthi Parishad may genuinely have considered this a step in the direction of insulating the campus from partisan political strife, the rapid turn about regarding students union elections probably had something to do with insulating the Vidyarthi Parishad itself from the internal Janata Party controversy regarding the question of RSS members in the ruling party. While a majority of Vidyarthi Parishad members are from non-RSS backgrounds, the senior organizational level is heavily RSS.[42]

Four years later, the Vidyarthi Parishad again shifted course and decided to contest students union seats. Its leaders were probably under enormous pressure from the ranks to move in this direction because of the prestige that comes from winning students union elections. In addition, the Vidyarthi Parishad's links to the RSS were no longer as salient an issue as in 1978 since the Janata Party lost power in 1979 and the Jana Sangh group left the Janata in 1980.

The Vidyarthi Parishad continued, however, to involve itself in confrontational activities against political authority in situations which were perceived as threatening to national integrity. For example, it supported the agitation of the All-Assam Students Union (AASU), an umbrella organization of mainly student groups in the north-eastern state of Assam, which advocated deleting a large number of Bangladeshi immigrants from the electoral rolls and deporting them on the grounds that they had illegally migrated to India.[43] The decision of the Vidyarthi Parishad to get involved in the 1979–86 Assam agitation was prompted by the Parishad's fear that radical political groups might steer the agitation towards demanding an independent state.

RSS AND THE POLITICAL PROCESS

One of the most difficult issues faced by the RSS in the immediate post-ban period was the kind of political role it would assume. No other issue aroused as much internal disagreement, perhaps because the leadership was forced to rethink the strategy and goals of the RSS. During the ban, Home Minister Vallabhbhai Patel demanded that the RSS avoid political activities. The largely traditionalist leadership agreed with him on this point, and Article 4 (b) of the RSS constitution states that the RSS 'had no politics and is devoted to purely social work'. However, the RSS activists never interpreted Article 4 literally. They argued that it was impossible to separate 'politics' from 'social work', and to force such a separation would undermine the nationalist objectives of the RSS. During the first round of negotiations on lifting the ban, Golwalkar explained his personal opposition to a political role for the RSS:

> After the ban has been lifted and swayamsevaks have an opportunity to meet together, they can if they like, convert the Sangh into a political body. That is the democratic way. I for myself cannot say anything. I am not a dictator. Personally, I am outside politics . . . But why should people drag us into politics? We are happy with them as politicians and ourselves as swayamsevaks.[44]

When the negotiations broke down, Golwalkar issued a press statement coming down even harder against any reorientation of RSS activities:

> At the outset let me make it clear the R.S.S. is not a political party with any ambitions for political power in the country. All these years of its existence it has steered clear of politics with its party rivalry and scramble for power.[45]

This statement was probably issued both to reassure Home Minister Patel that the RSS was not a potential political opponent and to notify the activists inside the RSS that the breakdown of the talks was not sufficient cause to launch a political front.

When the ban was finally lifted in 1949, it appears that Golwalkar expected some kind of agreement with the Congress which would allow individual RSS members to join the Congress and its affiliated front organizations, leaving the RSS free to pursue its more traditional character-building activities. This option was eliminated on 17 November 1949, when the Congress Working Committee decided to exclude RSS members. Several other options now faced the RSS leadership. It could (1) transform itself into a political party, (2) form a political affiliate, (3) make some kind of arrangement with the Hindu Mahasabha or another compatible political group, (4) abstain from any political involvement, (5) continue to negotiate with the Congress. The activists tended to support the first two options, and the traditionalists the last two. The possibility of cooperation with the Hindu Mahasabha was never seriously considered. The Mahasabha had performed very poorly in the post-war Central Legislative Assembly elections; a cloud of suspicion hung over it because of its alleged involvement in a conspiracy to kill Mahatma Gandhi; and, outside of Bengal and Maharashtra, it was controlled by rich landlords and businessmen who were not anxious to see it develop into a mass-based political party. A major problem blocking cooperation, and perhaps the critical one, was Savarkar's bitter feeling towards Golwalkar, who had not supported the Hindu Mahasabha in the 1945–46 central assembly elections.

After excluding the Hindu Mahasabha from consideration, RSS activists, especially Vasantrao Krishna Oke, the Delhi state pracharak, and Balraj Madhok, a young activist pracharak from Kashmir, encouraged Dr Shyama Prasad Mookerjee, minister of industry and supplies in independent India's first cabinet, to form a new nationalist party.[46] The initial contact with Mookerjee was not sanctioned by the RSS leadership which was even somewhat apprehensive about the early contacts with Mookerjee made by some of its pracharaks. Golwalkar, for example, was later to say of Oke that he 'developed a liking for political work to a degree uncommon and undesirable for a *swayamsevak*'.[47] Oke's attraction to politics, however, was shared by many other swayamsevaks, particularly those of refugee origin.

While Mookerjee had only a casual acquaintance with the work of the RSS, he was a logical political mentor for it: He was well known; he had established his Hindu bona fides in his defence of Hindu interests in Bengal; he was Sardar Vallabhbhai Patel's ally in cabinet politics; he was extricating himself from the discredited Hindu Mahasabha; and he was looking for another political forum to express his nationalist viewpoint.

Mookerjee belonged to one of Bengal's most prominent families.[48] His grandfather was one of the first graduates of Calcutta University. His father had served on the Calcutta High Court and had been vice chancellor of Calcutta University. Shyama Prasad graduated from Calcutta's most prestigious college and studied law in England. He was elected to the Bengal Legislative Council in 1929 from the university constituency, and five years later became vice chancellor of Calcutta University, the youngest person ever to have held that position.

Mookerjee began his political career under the Congress label, though he questioned Gandhi's periodic call for boycotts. When Gandhi called for a boycott of assemblies in 1930, Mookerjee resigned his seat and ran for re-election in his former constituency as an independent. He again won the seat as an independent in the 1937 assembly elections and joined the Hindu Mahasabha soon after. His support of the Mahasabha was prompted by his fear that the interests of the Hindu middle class were threatened by the policies of state cabinets dominated by Muslims.[49] During the war, he played a prominent role in Bengal politics and also became a major national figure in the Hindu Mahasabha.

After Independence, Nehru invited Mookerjee, one of three Mahasabha members in Parliament, to join the cabinet. Soon after Mookerjee joined the cabinet, Mahatma Gandhi was assassinated, an event that prompted Mookerjee publicly to express long-standing reservations about the Mahasabha. He proposed that the Mahasabha should either become a cultural organization or change its policy of excluding non-Hindus. He argued that Hindus, who formed over 80 per cent of the population, hardly needed a separate Hindu party to protect their interests. He advised the Mahasabha to terminate its political activities.[50]

The All-India Hindu Mahasabha working committee, meeting in New Delhi two weeks after Gandhi's assassination, adopted Mookerjee's proposal that the Mahasabha withdraw from politics and decided 'to concentrate on real *sanghatan* work, the relief and rehabilitation of refugees and the solution of our diverse social, cultural, and religious problems for the creation of a powerful and well-organized Hindu society'.[51] The decision was clearly a tactical manoeuvre; and at its 8–9 August 1948 meeting, the committee decided to 'resume political activities and function as a political organization open to all citizens of India'.[52] The real controversy was over the criteria for membership, and a reorientation committee was appointed to prepare a report on this issue. The majority report recommended that the Mahasabha continued to exclude non-Hindus, and the working committee, at its 8 November 1948 meeting, accepted the majority report,[53] against the advice of Mookerjee. The Mahasabha' s all-India committee met about six weeks later to resolve the issue.[54] Mookerjee lobbied unsuccessfully to defeat the majority report and resigned from the working committee.

A deterioration in Indo-Pakistani relations was soon to prompt Mookerjee to establish a separate political party. In late 1949, communal violence again erupted in both East Pakistan and West Bengal.[55] Nehru and Home Minister Patel had serious disagreements over how to handle the situation. Mookerjee sided with Patel's stand that India take a hard line against Pakistan. Nehru's support of negotiated settlement prevailed, resulting in talks which led to an agreement with Pakistan on 8 April 1950. On that day, Mookerjee and K. C. Neogy, another Bengali cabinet minister, resigned from office.

At this juncture, the RSS itself began to explore supporting Mookerjee. Dr N. B. Khare, president of the Hindu Mahasabha, met Mookerjee three months after his resignation and was informed that Mookerjee and Golwalkar had already met to discuss a new political party.[56] Appaji Joshi, one of the very few older Maharashtrian leaders in the RSS, who lined up with the activists, recalls arranging three meetings between Golwalkar and Mookerjee in 1950. At those meetings, Golwalkar is reported to have shown little interest in extending RSS support to any political party.[57] We also know that senior RSS leaders such as Prabhakar Balwant Dani, the general secretary, strongly opposed any RSS role in politics, on the grounds that the RSS should concentrate on rebuilding itself.[58]

Almost fourteen months elapsed between Mookerjee's resignation from the cabinet in early 1950 and his decision to form a new nationalist party. The evidence suggests that both Mookerjee and Golwalkar hesitated to make any final plans until the leadership struggle in the Congress was resolved. Should Patel's group have emerged victorious, the record indicates that both Mookerjee and Golwalkar would have extended their support to the Congress.[59] When the All-India Congress Committee elected Nehru party president at its 8 September 1951 meeting, this political option was closed.[60]

In his talks with Mookerjee, Golwalkar was concerned with two issues.[61] He insisted that the RSS remain structurally separate from the new party. Golwalkar also wanted an assurance from Mookerjee that his views regarding Bharatiya rashtravad (Indian nationalism) were compatible with RSS views. Despite basic agreement on these two points, Golwalkar still hesitated. Balraj Madhok writes that Mookerjee was so irritated at Golwalkar's delay that he considered forming a party without formal RSS backing.[62] Golwalkar, however, decided to extend RSS support to Mookerjee's new party in early 1951.[63] In late May 1951 a group of RSS activists met at Jalandhar to form the first state unit of the Bharatiya Jana Sangh (hereafter referred to as the Jana Sangh), and RSS pracharaks were selected to organize the party branches in Punjab as well as in other states.[64] In September, state units were established in Karnataka, Madhya Bharat/Bhopal and Uttar Pradesh; in October, units were formed in Assam, Rajasthan-Ajmer, and Vindhya Pradesh (now incorporated in Madhya Pradesh). A unit was formed in the Gujarat area of Bombay state during November, though none was established in the Marathi-speaking districts of the state.[65] The RSS cadre in Maharashtra, heavily traditionalist, demonstrated little enthusiasm for political work.

While RSS activists took the leading role in organizing the party in most regions, Mookerjee himself mobilized support for it in Bengal, where the RSS was an insignificant force. At the first public meeting of the party in Calcutta in June 1951, Mookerjee stated that this party would soon align itself with like-minded political parties elsewhere, undoubtedly referring to the new state organizations which RSS activists were establishing. In outlining his political programme, Mookerjee focused attention on refugee rehabilitation and economic development. He premised greater government support for the refugees and a harder line towards Pakistan. While supporting some form of public/private partnership to tackle India's developmental problems, he was against large-scale government control of the economy. He advocated a land-to-the-tiller policy, regional self-sufficiency, and industrial decentralization. Finally, his party would be what the Hindu Mahasabha was not—'open to all citizens of India irrespective of caste, creed, or community.'[66]

The organizational structure of the new party bore many similarities to the RSS. A well-known local figure, often without an RSS background, was chosen president of the provincial unit. Many of the secretaries were swayamsevaks, usually pracharaks. These secretaries were responsible for establishing district, city and ward units, and for organizing the campaigns for assembly and parliamentary candidates. Within a few months, these novice politicians established an elaborate campaign machine. No small part of their success was due to the support extended them by local RSS leaders. Madhok notes that a party organization tended to take shape in those areas where there were RSS shakhas.[67] We shall explore the development of the Jana Sangh, and its successor party, the Bharatiya Janata Party, in Chapters 5 and 6.

RSS AND LABOUR UNION ACTIVITY

The RSS activists, having set the precedent regarding affiliates in the late 1940s, planned an even more comprehensive expansion of RSS activities. They were deeply concerned with communist successes in organizing students and workers. The Vidyarthi Parishad would counter communist activities on the campus, but there was no equivalent group to work in the labour field. To remedy this situation, Dattopant Bapurao Thengadi, a pracharak and a labour unionist,[68] called together a group of interested swayamsevaks and representatives from 76 trade unions in July 1955 to lay the groundwork for a new labour movement.[69] They decided to form the Bharatiya Mazdoor Sangh (BMS).

Between 1955 and 1963, the BMS maintained a low profile while its leaders developed an ideology and an organizational structure. The organization began to move into a more activist phase when in August 1963 the BMS cooperated with the Hind Mazdoor Sabha (HMS) (the labour affiliate of the Socialist Party) to organize Bombay's bank workers. After 1963, the BMS expanded rapidly. According to BMS records, it grew from 30,000 members to 425,000 members between 1963 and 1969. Its greatest success was among white collar workers, though it also did well among textile and transportation workers. Like the other RSS affiliates, it was most successful at mobilizing support in Hindi-speaking states.[70]

Like the Vidyarthi Parishad, the Mazdoor Sangh argues that it has an Indian approach to labour union activity.

According to BMS theorists, other labour unions in India are based on a conception of a class struggle which is incompatible with Indian culture.[71] According to Dattopant Thengadi, the most prolific Bharatiya Mazdoor Sangh writer, both capitalism and communism are incapable of bringing about good life in any society. Capitalism exploits workers for the sake of profit and places them at the mercy of the laws of supply and demand. Communism, he argues, places excessive emphasis on material gratification, and it tends to rob man of freedom by placing all economic power in the hands of a few political figures.[72] Both capitalism and communism, according to Thengadi, fail to explain man's fundamental needs because they explain human problems in terms of material conditions rather than in terms of the deeper inner needs of each individual. Consequently, any movement that seeks to change the human condition for the better must concern itself with the psyche of man. Thengadi suggests that an economic system must be devised which makes use of a person's 'natural' aptitudes.[73]

G. S. Gokhale, another BMS theorist, argues that workers with similar aptitudes should be grouped together into occupational 'families', with each 'family' determining the working conditions, occupations, duties and goals of the branch of the productive process with which it is associated.[74] Both Thengadi and Gokhale view society as an organism which functions best when it is able to organize people into socio-economic units which motivate them to contribute their maximum efforts for the well-being of the larger society. They also suggest a more 'natural' political order in which representation is based on the socio-economic 'families' rather than the present system of geographic representation.

The Bharatiya Mazdoor Sangh has consistently opposed the nationalization of industry. In its place, the BMS calls for the 'labourizing' of industry.[75] A 'labourized' industry is one in which the workers control the industry in which they contribute their labour. Placed in the larger theoretical framework, each occupational 'family' owns and manages its own industry. Regarding complex industries involving more than one occupational 'family', each 'family' shares in the ownership and in the decision-making process.[76] Gokhale predicts that the 'labourizing' principle, which combines self-interest and national interest, will result in fewer strikes, greater discipline among workers, and higher productivity.[77] Thengadi advocates extending the 'labourizing' principle to Indian agriculture. He argues that the village-based cooperative is not a revolutionary concept. Indeed, it is based on the traditional agricultural system. He believes that 'labourizing' agriculture would reduce rural conflict and give the landless and tenant farmers a greater stake in rural society. However, this proposal has received little support either from the RSS or from the other affiliates.[78]

Regarding rural India, neither the RSS nor its affiliates have been very successful in mobilizing rural support, though efforts to do so have been made. The BMS organized the Bharatiya Rayat Sangh, an association of farmers, in 1971. This organization attempted to organize the landless, tenants, and small farmers, but with little success. On 4 March 1979 a national body of farmers, the Bharatiya Kisan Sangh, was formed. It claims to have 215,000 members in 14 states, though Thengadi candidly admitted in 1982 that the new organization had not really made much of an impact.[79]

To emphasize its nationalist orientation, the BMS has adopted a set of symbols intended to distinguish it from rival unions, who allegedly derive their theoretical frameworks from foreign sources. The official flag is the bhagva dhwaj, 'the universal flag of Dharma'.[80] May Day observance is regarded as dangerous since it is a 'symbol of class struggle and national disintegration'.[81] It has been replaced by Vishwakarma Jayanti, in memory of Vishwakarma,[82] the mythological god of architects who according to legend was the creator of all arts, handicrafts and industry.

By the early 1970s, the Bharatiya Mazdoor Sangh had become assertive, if not militant. Joining the communists and other trade unions in the successful 1973 strike against the government-controlled Life Insurance Corporation of India, it participated for the first time as an equal partner in a joint union strike. This self-confidence was again demonstrated the next year during the violent nationwide railway strike when it was represented on the trade union team that negotiated with the government.[83]

During the Emergency, many of the BMS cadre participated in the underground movement managed by the Lok Sangarsh Samiti. Indeed, in November 1976, Thengadi, then general secretary of the BMS, resigned to take over as general secretary of the Lok Sangarsh Samiti.[84]

Following the 1977 electoral victory of the Janata Party against Mrs Gandhi's Congress party, the BMS was under pressure to merge with other non-communist labour unions, analogous to the merger of the constituents who established the Janata Party on 1 May 1977. BMS leaders met during 10–11 April 1977, at Delhi to discuss a united trade union with their counterparts in the Hind Mazdoor Sabha and the Hind Mazdoor Panchayat, two socialist unions loosely linked to the socialist group in the Janata Party.[85] The Bharatiya Mazdoor Sangh laid down four conditions for the merger: (1) independence from political parties, (2) rejection of the notion of class struggle, (3) acceptance of Vishwakarma Day as the national workers' day, and (4) refusal to use the red flag as the banner of the union. The negotiators arrived at a consensus on the first three, but were deadlocked on the fourth.[86] However, the BMS ultimately decided against merger probably to avoid getting dragged into the contentious question of RSS members holding office in the Janata Party, which had become one of the most divisive issues within the ruling party. This controversy, which involved the right of RSS members to belong to the Janata Party, would probably have become an issue in any union merger involving the BMS since the socialists were the major advocates of denying RSS members the right to play a significant role in Janata Party affairs.

Table 1: Membership of Central Trade Union Organizations

Central Trade Union	Claimed No. of Unions	Membership	Verified* No. of Unions	Membership
Indian National Trade Union Congress	3,457	3,509,326	1,604	2,236,128
Bharatiya Mazdoor Sangh	1,725	1,879,728	1,333	1,211,345

Central Trade Union	Claimed No. of Unions	Membership	Verified* No. of Unions	Membership
Hind Mazdoor Sabha	1,122	1,848,147	426	762,882
United Trade Union Congress (LS)	154	1,238,891	134	621,359
All-India Trade Union Congress	1,366	1,064,330	1,080	344,746
Centre of Indian Trade Unions	1,737	1,033,434	1,474	331,031
Centre of Indian Trade Unions	618	608,052	175	165,614
National Labour Organisation	249	405,189	172	246,540

*Government verification as of 31 December 1980.

Source: Government of India, Research and Reference Division, Ministry of Information and Broadcasting, *India: 1985* (New Delhi, Allied Publishers, 1986), p. 491.

During the 1977–79 Janata Party period, the BMS expanded rapidly, increasing its membership from 800,000 in 1977[87] to about 1,600,000 in 1980.[88] Indeed, it claimed to be the second largest national trade union after the Indian National Trade Union Congress affiliated to the Congress party.

RSS AND THE HINDU RELIGIOUS ESTABLISHMENT

The divisions within the Hindu ecclesiastical community and its lack of unified purpose, according to RSS analysts, have hampered the effort to create a unified Hindu society. Golwalkar, with this concern in mind, invited a selected group of religious leaders to Bombay in late August 1964, to discuss ways in which the various Hindu sects and movements could work more closely with each other. At that meeting, the delegates established the Vishwa Hindu Parishad (VHP); and Shivram Shankar Apte, an RSS pracharak, was elected its general secretary. The delegates specified three objectives for the new organization: (1) to consolidate and strengthen Hindu society; (2) to protect and spread Hindu values, ethical and spiritual, and to make them relevant in contemporary society; and (3) to establish and strengthen the links among Hindus living in different countries.[89]

While the VHP has had only limited success in uniting the various Hindu religious organizations, and almost none in establishing a common doctrinal corpus, it does give the RSS an opportunity to identify itself with the Hindu ecclesiastical community, thus enabling the RSS to lobby for its views among a larger audience. For example, former general secretary Apte, at the third annual conference of the Andhra Pradesh unit, appealed to the people to 'clean every home of "Suvarna Mrigas"—the evilsome [sic] temptation of foreign "isms": foreign fashions, and ideologies'.[90] Apte also warned the group that if the area along the River Brahmaputra in north-eastern India were culturally alienated from the Hindu mainstream, all Hindu society would be threatened.[91] With this in mind, the Karnataka Conference urged the government 'to expel all foreign missionaries from the country forthwith and not to permit their further entry'. In addition, the conference condemned a proposal that would give members of the Scheduled Castes and other backward Hindu castes the right to receive special concessions after their conversion to Christianity.[92]

The VHP has concentrated its resources since the early 1970s on north-eastern India, a region with a large tribal population. Prompting the VHP is its fear that the various tribal groups are susceptible to 'foreign' ideologies which could trigger the formation of separatist movements. To counter this, the VHP has established schools, orphanages, clinics, temples, etc., in an effort both to block the further expansion of Christianity and to enhance national identity.

In the early 1970s, the number of social welfare projects operating under the VHP umbrella increased dramatically. In large part, this was because it absorbed many projects begun by swayamsevaks, such as the state Kalyan Ashrams (societies working among tribals), the Vivekananda Medical Mission, orphanages, student hostels, etc. This development, sanctioned by the RSS leadership, may have been intended to make the ecclesiastical establishment more sensitive to the social needs of many Indians and to involve it more closely in social welfare work. At the same time, this step gave the RSS pracharaks working in the VHP an enhanced moral standing as they deal with the religious leadership.

During the Emergency, the VHP maintained a low profile regarding political events, despite the seizure of Kalyan Ashram centres and schools in some states. Probably the major reason for its forbearance was the unwillingness of the religious leaders to challenge the government. When the Emergency was lifted in March 1977, the VHP again took control of those projects taken over by the government.[93] By

1981, the VHP claimed to have 3000 branch units in 437 of India's 534 districts, and to have 150 full-time workers. It operated 442 hostels, orphanages and vocational schools, some 150 medical centres, and published ten journals.[94]

The national furore aroused by the conversion of some untouchables to Islam in Tamil Nadu during 1981 prompted the Parishad to embark on one of its most ambitious projects to date. In January 1983 the VHP launched a campaign to collect about 50 million rupees (approximately $5 million) for a missionary order that would work among untouchables, tribals and the rural poor, groups considered especially vulnerable to conversion.[95] Such a religious order was necessary, according to an editorial in the official VHP journal, because 'in Bharat [India] religious conversions pose a grave threat to national security and integrity. A large area of our motherland ... is now foreign land to us, because Hindus in those places were converted to/alien faith on a large scale.'[96] Reconversions of Muslims and Christians became a major objective of the VHP. VHP sources in early 1986 highlighted 'return' of two Muslim sub-castes in Rajasthan as an indication of the programme's success.[97]

The VHP organized a month-long Ekatmata Yagna (national integration procession) from 16 November to 16 December 1983, all over the country to raise additional money for the missionary order.[98] Fund-raising was only one objective of the yagna. It was also intended to strengthen Hindu solidarity. There were three major march routes through various parts of India as well as same ninety shorter processions, totalling in all 85,000 kilometres in one month and involving almost 60 million participants.[99] The various processions converged on Nagpur, the central Indian city that is the headquarters of the RSS. The processions were accompanied by a portrait of Bharat Mata (the representative of the 'holy motherland' portrayed in the form of a female deity) and large urns containing water from the River Ganga (a river considered holy in the sacred geography of Hindu India) and from local rivers. The Ganga water was distributed to Hindu temples for use in the worship of the temple deities, and over 1.5 million bottles were reportedly sold.

Building on the perceived Ekatmata success, the VHP in late 1983 became an active participant in the campaign to restore the birthplace of Lord Ram, a popular Hindu deity, as a temple. The issue was controversial, for the site, Ramjanmabhoomi, located at Ayodhya in Uttar Pradesh, had been used as a Muslim mosque since the sixteenth century, and its conversion to a temple has been a major item on the Hindu revivalist agenda since the late nineteenth century.

The VHP credited itself for playing a major role in the February 1986 court decision permitting the performance of puja (worship) at the Ramjanmabhoomi. In its campaign to get the site converted into a Hindu temple, the VHP received help from the Hindu religious establishment, including all four Shankaracharyas (senior interpreters of Hinduism) who had formerly remained aloof from VHP activities. In addition, the Ramjanmabhoomi Liberation Committee (RLC), which managed the public relations efforts, included politicians from several political parties. The RLC concentrated on rural areas of the Hindi-speaking heartland, and its public relations effort featured processions portraying Lord Ram behind bars. This tactic reportedly succeeded in arousing mass sympathy.[100]

The VHP celebrated the court's decision as a major victory for Hinduism. It established a trust to rebuild the temple and pledged to raise 250 million rupees for the project.[101]

Encouraged by this development, the VHP has demanded the conversion of still two other historic sites in Uttar Pradesh: Krishnajanmabhoomi, birthplace of Krishna at Mathura; and the Kashi Vishwanath Temple at Benares. In addition, the VHP identified 25 other mosques to be converted. While this effort is clearly popular, and may result in enhanced Hindu solidarity, it almost certainly will exacerbate Hindu–Muslim tension. Muslims, who themselves are increasingly assertive, will resist. Indeed, the Ramjanmabhocmi campaign itself triggered a wave of rioting across northern India.[102]

In an effort to establish greater solidarity among the various Hindu sects, the VHP in March 1981 formed the Marga Darshan Mandal, a forum or religious leaders who would advise the Parishad trustees 'on Hindu philosophical thought and a code of conduct'.[103] The Mandal provides the VHP leadership still another link to the religious establishment. In 1982, the Mandal established the Dharma Sansad, a deliberative body of religious figures who would formulate a Hindu perspective on social and political problems. In its first year, the Sansad considered such issues as conversion, Hindu–Sikh tensions in Punjab, and the decline in the percentage of Hindus in Kashmir.[104] Some religious leaders in the Dharma Sansad wanted the VHP to support certain candidates in the 1984 parliamentary elections, prompting the VHP in mid-1985 formally to keep the organization aloof from partisan politics.[105] However, the VHP in mid-1986 may have shifted its stance on partisan politics. Shiva Nath Katju, its president, stated that the VHP would work against candidates considered antagonistic to Hindu interests.[106]

In 1970 several RSS members resident in the United States met in New York City to form the Vishwa Hindu Parishad of the United States of America, and the first annual conference was held in Canton, Ohio.[107] Swayamsevaks who came to the United States are encouraged to support the activities of the American branches of the VHP, which organizes summer camps, celebrates Hindu festivals, and runs classes to teach Indian history, culture and languages. The American and Canadian units jointly publish a bimonthly magazine. The most popular programmes are the summer camps. Camps were held in four different places during the summer of 1984. Senior RSS figures from India regularly tour the US to encourage cooperation among the various RSS-affiliated groups in the US, as well as to strengthen their links with counterparts in India. One sign of the VHP's growth in the US was the large turnout for its tenth session at New York City in 1984, attended by some 5000 delegates, in contrast to the 35 delegates who attended its first session in Canton, Ohio, in 1970. Besides the US and Canada, the VHP has spread to other countries with a large Indian diaspora, especially England and several East African and South-East Asian states.[108] In Great Britain, the VHP now claims 40 branches, its own publication, and camps to train workers. Operating from its British base, the VHP organized a European conference at Copenhagen, in September 1986, as a first step towards establishment of chapters in other European countries with large Indian populations. In Kenya, the East African state with the most active VHP, the organization takes at least partial credit for the declaration of Diwali (Hindu festival of lights) as a national holiday, and for the issuance of a stamp featuring the symbol *Om*, the sacred sound associated with God. Kenya is the base for expanding the VHP elsewhere in Africa.

The foreign branches of the VHP, like the overseas organizations of the RSS itself, provide several important mobilization functions for the RSS. They reinforce RSS socialization in an environment where alternatIive socialization messages might undermine the 'faith'; they recruit new supporters who, on their return to India, might support the RSS; they generate financial support for various projects managed by RSS affiliates. They also place Indian RSS leaders in a position to dispense rewards (e.g., through contacts with foreign swayamsevaks who may offer a range of services to Indians who plan to leave the country).

The direct involvement of the RSS leaders with the VHP became more pronounced in the late 1970s. The RSS leadership may have felt a certain obligation to the VHP out of respect for Golwalkar (who died in 1973), who had a special interest in its activities. In addition, Balasaheb Deoras, who replaced Golwalkar as a trustee of the VHP in 1973, was much more of an activist than his predecessor.[109] Because the VHP is engaged in a kind of character building and is non-political, the RSS leadership could participate actively in its work without losing the aura of disinterest it seeks to portray to the public.

RSS AND A NEW CHARACTER-BUILDING ORGANIZATION

To commemorate Swami Vivekananda's birth centenary in 1963, the RSS leadership decided to bring out a collection of Vivekananda's writings.[110] Eknath Ranade was commissioned to edit the volume. After completing the book, Ranade became intrigued by the idea of further popularizing the views of Vivekananda, and in time decided to establish a secular lay order to do so.[111]

Swami Vivekananda preached a message of revivalism in the late nineteenth century which the RSS finds compatible with its own belief system. He has become an important symbol within the RSS and an inspiration for a Hindu lay order dedicated to strengthening Hindu identity among groups vulnerable to other creeds (e.g., tribals, untouchables). Perhaps only Shivaji receives comparable attention. Vivekananda's picture hangs on the walls of many swayamsevaks' homes; books about him serve as primers on nationalism; his message of self-esteem and national revitalization are the subject of innumerable RSS baudhik sessions.

Ranade did not start out to create a new RSS affiliate. The idea for such an organization took root in the wake of the effort to create a memorial to Vivekananda. As part of the 1963 Vivekananda centenary celebrations, a committee was organized to establish a modest memorial on a small island off the southernmost tip of India, where Vivekananda is reported to have received the inspiration to take his message of advaita vedanta to the West. There was, however, opposition to the memorial from the large Roman Catholic community in Kanyakumari, a mainland village not far from the island.[112] The island is also revered by Christians as the place where Saint Francis Xavier brought his mission to south India. The Government of Tamil Nadu, to forestall communal friction, refused to allow the committee to construct the memorial. The controversy was widely reported in the Indian press, and the Vivekananda Memorial Committee approached the RSS for help. Golwalkar instructed Ranade to contact prominent politicians in New Delhi who could bring pressure on Tamil Nadu to change the order. Three hundred twenty-three members of Parliament, according to RSS sources, signed a petition requesting that the decision be reversed. Ranade's well-orchestrated publicity campaign was successful, and he was asked to take charge of the project.

The original plans called for a simple stone marker; however, Ranade and his colleagues decided that a more impressive monument was needed for the ambitious project they planned to organize around the memorial.[113] It was intended to serve as a catalyst for a lay order that would carry out Vivekananda's teaching. A large plot of ground was acquired not far from Kanyakumari and on it the Memorial Committee has built a complex of buildings where young men and women are trained for a lay order of Hindu missionaries. This order differs from religious orders in that the participants wear no religious garb and their training and duties are primarily educational and humanitarian. They are not required to take vows of celibacy, though they must promise not to marry for three-and-a-half years prior to their initiation into the order. Having completed the six-month training at Kanyakumari, they are then commissioned.[114] At the conclusion of a three-year internship programme, the trainees become full-time workers in the order. In 1984, the Vivekananda Kendra claimed 80 full-time workers.[115]

Not until the early 1980s did the Kendra spell out the areas where it would concentrate its efforts. In a 1982 revision of its constitution, the Kendra decided to emphasize rural development. Accordingly, it selected three target districts in Tamil Nadu. The choice of the state of Tamil Nadu may have been influenced by the close contacts that Ranade had established with senior government figures as head of the organization. Besides this, the Kendra could help the RSS mobilize support in a state where the RSS is relatively weak.

The Kendra continues to operate in north-eastern India, where its earliest projects were located. It manages thirteen schools in Arunachal Pradesh and two in Assam. As in Tamil Nadu, Ranade had established good relations with the political authorities in the north-east and his schools in Arunachal Pradesh receive substantial government assistance.[116]

The Kendra has not experienced the rate of growth of the other RSS affiliates. One reason for this could be the extremely high standards required of the Kendra's full-time workers by Ranade and his successor. Still another reason may have something to do with Ranade's cautious temperament. His neutral stand regarding the Emergency put him out of step with his RSS colleagues. In addition, his long illness, beginning in 1979 and lasting until his death in August 1982, prevented him from lobbying vigorously on behalf of the Kendra. His successor, Dr M. Lakshmi Kumari, is considered a very competent organizer, but she is not a member of the brotherhood.

POST-1977: A TIME OF EXPERIMENTATION

In March 1977, following the lifting of the ban on the RSS, an assertive RSS leadership supported a wide range of new programmes, focusing attention on work among tribals, untouchables and the very poor in both rural and urban areas. These groups are considered vulnerable to ideologies which could undermine national solidarity (e.g., communism, Christianity, Islam, regional nationalism), and therefore, are in need of programmes that strengthen Hindu identity.

Large-scale economic development, as a tool for integrating the poorest parts of society, is a new approach in the RSS 'family' of organizations. Economic development as a tool of national integration is an outgrowth of RSS flood relief efforts begun following the devastating cyclone which struck the south-eastern coast of India on 19 November 1977.[117] The original RSS programme there included the disposal of the dead, the construction of community halls, the reconstruction of housing, and providing educational opportunities for orphans.[118] The Deendayal Research Institute (DRI) took control of the work, underscoring the enhanced role of the relatively new DRI in the 'family' of organizations. The DRI, launched in 1972 at Delhi, was originally intended to be a research facility to provide RSS scholars and researchers with the facilities and time to develop a more sophisticated presentation of the RSS belief system and apply it to specific problems.[119] Nana Deshmukh, one of the most prominent RSS pracharaks, has given it a broader mandate.

Deshmukh vastly expanded the scope of the DRI's activities. Besides the disaster relief work started by the RSS itself, the DRI constructed a model village, named Deendayalpuram, in Andhra Pradesh soon after taking over the relief work from the RSS. With the experience gained from the model village, Deshmukh selected Gonda district, a district in Uttar Pradesh which he then represented in Parliament, as the site for a large-scale development project. His scheme, referred to as integrated rural development, called for irrigation facilities, new agricultural techniques, small-scale industries and craft centres, vocational training institutes, producer cooperatives, schools and medical clinics. Work began in late 1978 with 50 volunteers. Operating on the premise that the very poor will not feel a sense of community with the larger society, Deshmukh declared that the immediate objectives of his development programme were full employment and a minimum income of 2500 rupees per year for every family.[120] The Uttar Pradesh experiment was judged to be so successful that Deshmukh selected three additional model districts in other states. Besides this development work, the DRI is now trying to coordinate and guide similar local projects begun by swayamsevaks.

The RSS, seeking to integrate the tribal population into the Hindu community, has allocated considerable resources to tribal work since the late 1960s. The early work was carried out largely by the VHP. In 1977 the VHP handed over its work among the tribals to the Bharatiya Vanavasi Kalyan Ashram (BVKA), a national organization set up that year to coordinate work among the tribals. The BVKA traces its origins to work begun in Madhya Pradesh in 1952 and expand to other states in 1966. The RSS demonstrated its approval of the BVKA's efforts by giving it the primary role for coordinating work among tribals. One of the most capable RSS pracharaks, Rambhau Godbole, who had previously served as an organizing secretary in the Jana Sangh, was placed in charge of the new national organization. By 1983, the BVKA operated 89 student hostels, 136 primary schools, 137 health centres, 19 agricultural development centers, 26 vocational traning centres, and 83 orphanages.[121] At its national council meeting in September 1984, the Ashram decided on a major expansion of its activities during 1985–1986. Balasaheb Deoras, in his address to the council, gave his blessing to the effort, a sign that council, gave his blessing to the effort, a sign that RSS is likely to provide significant support, both in workers and money, to this effort.[122]

Regarding the Scheduled Castes, Balasaheb Deoras inaugurated the Seva Bharati in 1979 to coordinate work, largely educational, on a national level.[123] This emphasis on education underscores the importance the RSS gives to education as a tool for national integration. Almost all the affiliates of the RSS are engaged in some form of teaching.

Besides this specific educational programme among the Scheduled Castes, RSS members have operated private schools since the late 1940s. In 1978, many of these schools were brought together into a national organization. The Vidya Bharati was established in that year to serve as the coordinating body for over 1000 elementary and secondary schools.[124]

One of the most ambitious initiatives of the post-1977 period is a Hindu missionary programme launched by the Vishwa Hindu Parishad in 1983 to work among tribals, Scheduled Castes and the poor. The project grew out of the national furore that developed after the conversion to Islam of several hundred Scheduled Caste people in a small village in Tamil Nadu. That event touched off a nationwide debate among Hindus regarding ways to enhance Hindu solidarity, and thus diminish the chances for more such conversions. The VHP decided to train 100 pracharaks, as the missionaries are called; and they were assigned to various parts of the country in July 1982. These missionaries were instructed to train a cadre of workers in their own areas of responsibility.[125] By December 1982, the first group of 600 were given their assignments. They were joined by an additional 1400 in December 1983, thus completing the first phase of the training.[126]

With the rapid expansion of the RSS and its affiliates, the RSS itself became increasingly hard-placed to satisfy the demands for full-time workers. In 1983 the general secretary of the RSS reported that in the previous year the RSS had trained 200 new pracharaks and vistaraks (probationers), a number 'not in keeping with the demands of the time'.[127] In the face of such personnel shortages in a rapidly expanding network of organizations, the RSS moved to improve the lines of communication both vertically and horizontally among the pracharak network, so that it would be in a better position to identify priorities and problems, and to provide the brotherhood a more accurate basis for determining the assignment of workers and the allocation of money among the 'family' of organizations. In late 1977 in some places the RSS established forums, called samanvaya samitis (coordination committees), designed to bring together full-time workers from the RSS and from the affiliates at the district and state levels.[128] This step bore the mark of Balasaheb Deoras' activist orientation.

The Jana Sangh group in the Janata Party was not invited to attend the meetings of the samanvaya samitis.[129] Prior to the Emergency, senior Jana Sangh leaders, in their capacity as pracharaks, had attended the annual meeting of the national RSS *pratinidhi sabha* in Nagpur, the only formal occasion for bringing together the 'family' prior to the establishment of the samanvayasamitis.[130]

Why this effort to distance the RSS from the Jana Sangh group? From the Jana Sangh side, tactical considerations were surely an important reason. This Jana Sangh group within the Janata Party was then under attack because many of its seniormost figures were RSS members. These senior Jana Sangh figures were charged with dual loyalties. Attending samanvaya samitis would have provided ammunition to the critics of the Jana Sangh group. The RSS for its part also had good reasons to keep the Jana Sangh group out of the samanvaya samitis. The RSS leadership, then orchestrating an ambitious expansion programme, wanted to insulate the RSS itself from political criticism that could lead to restrictions on its activities.

But even after the Jana Sangh group pulled out of the Janata party in April 1980, no representative of the Bharatiya Janata Party (BJP) attended the samanvaya samiti conclaves. Was the leadership of the new BJP steering the organization away from the 'family'? The answer seems to be both yes and no. Two legacies—that of Jaya Prakash Narayan, the moral guide of the Janata Party, and that of the Jana Sangh—were contesting for the soul of the new party. The former legacy involved a weakening of links with the RSS. Between 1980 and 1984, aspiring to be the national alternative to Mrs Gandhi's Congress party, the BJP emphasized its secular credentials to achieve this objective. Advocating a democratic front until late 1984, the BJP wanted to end the political isolation brought about by the RSS controversy. On the other hand, the BJP clearly wanted to continue recruiting RSS workers into the organization. As long as there was some prospect of the BJP developing into a national alternative, the swayamsevaks grudgingly went along with the leadership's efforts to stress the Jaya Prakash Narayan legacy.

However, following the electoral debacle of the BJP in 1984 the party seems to have been veering back to its Jana Sangh roots. But it is still an open question whether the leadership will be satisfied with a 'little' or with an ideologically oriented party in the Jana Sangh mould. Attending the samanvaya samiti meetings would send a strong signal that the party leaders had opted conclusively for the Jana Sangh legacy and had fully rejoined the 'family'. In mid-1985 the press began to report such BJP participation in a few places.[131] The election to party president in 1986 of Lal Krishna Advani, an advocate of closer RSS–BJP relations, will probably hasten this process.

SYMBIOSIS: A TWO-WAY FLOW OF INFLUENCE

The Vidyarthi Parishad, the Bharatiya Mazdoor Sangh, the BJP, and other affiliates operate as the moral stepchildren of the RSS. Legitimacy flows to the RSS leadership, largely because they are involved in the 'higher calling' of character building. Of all the affiliates, it is only the Vivekananda Lay Order and the VHP which could challenge the RSS monopoly on moral superiority, since they too are engaged primarily in character-building activities. However, full-time RSS workers have certain advantages vis-à-vis those of the Kendra and the VHP. They have a general training which enables the RSS-trained worker to step in as manager in all the affiliates, whereas the Kendra and the VHP give specialized training for specific tasks within their own organizations. The RSS-trained worker also has the advantage of a much longer training period which involves practical experience in managing the activities of others. Finally, the RSS is the parent organization, and its trainees are accorded respect throughout the 'family'. Balasaheb Deoras, the present sarsanghchalak, is him self more of an activist than his two predecessors. He has made it clear that the RSS would pursue a more open and aggressive style under his leadership. He has pledged to involve the RSS more directly in the nation's development and, by implication, to take a greater interest in the affiliates.

Golwalkar worked hard to preserve the moral legitimacy of the RSS, and this required a certain separation from the activities of the affiliates. Should the RSS abandon this detachment, the leadership may discover that it is even less able to influence the affiliates than in the past. As long as the RSS leaders give the impression of remaining outside the struggle for power, prestige and money, they inherit a charisma deriving from their detachment. This factor will undoubtedly continue to preserve a certain amount of autonomy for all the affiliates. The professional skills required to work in the affiliates also serves to insulate them from the generalist RSS leadership who have neither the training nor the experience to qualify than to comment on the wide range of technical issues which the affiliates must confront. The affiliates are tasked to translate the belief system of the RSS into policies specific to their areas of activity. However, the RSS belief system is on too high a level of generality to inform many of the issues which face the affiliates. As a result, the affiliates have influenced the RSS itself (as well as other affiliates) on issues which fall within their own field of responsibility, creating complex flows of influence between the RSS and its affiliates.

The affiliates are left, within certain limits, to their own devices to mobilize support, and they have adopted a range of different strategies. Nevertheless, the network of affiliates operates within broad parameters set by the common socialization of their leaders within the RSS, by their reliance on common symbols, and by the close consultation among their leaders. The RSS would perhaps temper its support for them if these organizations of mass mobilization were to permit any real challenge to the elites trained in character building.

5

The RSS in Politics

Many senior RSS figures had an ambivalent attitude regarding party politics in independent India. The struggle for power among contending interests or persons was alien to the concept of decision making considered legitimate in the RSS. Soliciting votes seemed corrupting, both for the candidates and the voters. Many believed that the use of propaganda and caste considerations would reduce the chances of the voters electing the 'best' candidates. Some were apprehensive that the democratic process would exacerbate the cleavages between already hostile social groups and thus undermine national integration.

Nevertheless, activist pracharaks were demanding some RSS involvement in politics, and the objective situation seemed to demand political protection. The RSS leadership responded by offering support to the new Jana Sangh of Dr Shyama Prasad Mookerjee. While Golwalkar and most other RSS leaders wanted to keep the RSS outside the political process, they did expect to exercise a moral influence over the new party. They sought some voice without institutionalizing any formal linkage between the RSS and the Jana Sangh. The RSS constitution prohibited political activity, and the government might again restrict RSS activities if it were to engage in overt political activity. The problem was resolved by the decision to loan a number of pracharaks, who were thoroughly socialized in the RSS discipline, to the Jana Sangh. As the party organization expanded, a large number of swayamsevaks were attracted to the party and in time dominated the grass-roots structure of the party organization in most places.

In the Jana Sangh's formative stages, neither Mookerjee nor the RSS leadership looked at the Jana Sangh as the political affiliate of the RSS. At its higher levels, Mookerjee had given responsible positions to prominent Hindu Mahasabha and Arya Samaj activists and to some dissident Congressmen. He placed Mauli Chandra Sharma, a non-RSS Delhi lawyer and son of Hindu Mahasabha orthodox leader Din Dayal Sharma, in charge of the party organization. Associated with him was Bhai Mahavir,[1] a young pracharak with little experience in politics. Generally, the swayamsevaks who joined the Jana Sangh were novices at politics and were willing to follow the leadership of experienced politicians like Mookerjee.

At the first national meeting of the Jana Sangh, on 21 October 1951 in Delhi, a committee was selected to draft a campaign manifesto. That manifesto, published on 29 October, focused on national integration:[2] India's unity would be furthered by an educational system reflecting 'bharatiya culture', by one indigenous link language (i.e., Hindi in the Devanagari script), by the full integration of Jammu and Kashmir into the Indian Union, and by a policy denying special rights to any minority.[3] It proposed that the actual tiller of the soil own his farm; it called for the development of the country through private enterprise, except in such 'vital' industries as defence production. The manifesto paid its homage to tradition by asking for the protection of the cow[4] and for the promotion of traditional Ayurvedic medicine. It advocated generous aid to the refugees from Pakistan and a policy of reciprocity towards that country. It also proposed that India withdraw from the British Commonwealth. In short, the first manifesto was an economically conservative document which displayed a greater concern for cultural and political integration than for social and economic problems.

FIRST GENERAL ELECTIONS AND DEVELOPMENT OF PARTY INFRASTRUCTURE

The young Jana Sangh, with assistance from RSS workers loaned to it, established a complex campaign machinery within three months of its founding. Party leaders, anticipating success, selected candidates for 93 of the 489 parliamentary constituencies and for 725 of the 3,383 state assembly constituencies. They discovered how weak their popular support was when the votes of the first general elections were counted. The Congress, which had organizationally penetrated all regions of the country and which possessed the requisite political legitimacy to attract support, won almost 75 per cent of both the parliamentary and assembly seats. The Jana Sangh won only three seats in parliament and 35 assembly seats. There was some gratification that it qualified itself as an all-India party by polling more than 3 per cent of the total votes for parliamentary candidates.[5]

Mookerjee was able to mobilize considerable support in Bengal which gave the party two of its three parliamentary seats and nine of its thirty-five assembly seats.[6] Besides Bengal, the party also did comparatively well in the Hindi-speaking states, where it won its third parliamentary seat and the remaining twenty-six assembly seats. The restrained political enthusiasm of the RSS cadre in Maharashtra and much of south India, coupled with the brahmin orientation of the RSS in those areas, undoubtedly had its effect on the party's poor showing in those few constituencies where it ran candidates. While the results were as much a disappointment to the RSS leadership as they were to Mookerjee, the RSS leadership did not abandon Mookerjee's party because it had performed so far below their expectations. In a post-election pep talk to swayamsevaks at an RSS camp in Punjab, Golwalkar praised the party's ability to organize 'so well within three months. It has given a good fight and gained valuable experience.'[7]

To unify the opposition within parliament, Mookerjee initiated negotiations with members from several opposition parties and with independents. When the Jana Sangh delegates assembled for the party's first annual session at Kanpur in December 1952, Mookerjee had succeeded in recruiting 32 members of parliament into his opposition bloc, the National Democratic Front,[8] and invited them to attend the party's annual session. At that session, Mauli Chandra Sharma was asked to continue as general secretary. The other general secretary selected was Deendayal Upadhyaya,[9] a young RSS pracharak who was loaned to the Jana Sangh to help organize the party in Uttar Pradesh. By selecting both Sharma and an RSS pracharak, Mookerjee attempted to balance the two sets of forces within the party organization.

Mookerjee directed the delegates' attention to two issues: the special relationship of Jammu and Kashmir (J&K) with the Indian Union, and the condition of the Hindu minority in

East Bengal. On the Kashmir question the delegates decided to involve the Jana Sangh directly in an agitation whose objective was the total integration of the Muslim-majority Jammu and Kashmir into India. This agitation, launched by the Praja Parishad, a Hindu political party in Jammu and Kashmir supported by the RSS, also had the enthusiastic backing of the RSS.

Mookerjee organized a committee to mobilize national support for the Kashmir agitation. As part of his effort to focus national attention on Kashmir, he entered J&K on 11 May 1953. He was promptly arrested and detained. His death from a heart attack on 23 June, while a prisoner, was interpreted by many in the Jana Sangh as murder. RSS members then active in the Jana Sangh recollect that they felt that they had lost their political guru (teacher). Since they did not have the political self-confidence to consider one of their own to head the party, their response was to seek another political figure of national stature. This course of action might also have been adopted to ameliorate the growing strains between the RSS cadre and the other party workers.[10]

The party leaders considered N. C. Chatterjee (a close friend of Mookerjee's, a Lok Sabha representative from West Bengal, a leading member of the National Democratic Front, and the president of the Hindu Mahasabha) a possible successor to Mookerjee.[11] Chatterjee recalls that Mauli Chandra Sharma, Balraj Madhok, and Prem Nath Dogra, leader of the Praja Parishad, visited him in Delhi soon after Mookerjee's death and offered the Jana Sangh presidency to him.[12] Chatterjee maintains that Golwalkar was also consulted on the selection and had agreed to accept him as the party's president. That Golwalkar would be consulted, as a matter of course, is understandable. The party had a major RSS commitment in the many full-time workers loaned to it. The swayamsevaks would expect his approval before they made a final decision on the party presidency.

Chatterjee for his part informed the Jana Sangh leaders that he would have to consult the Hindu Mahasabha leadership before making a final decision.[13] If he were to take over the Jana Sangh, some kind of understanding would have to be worked out between the Jana Sangh and the Hindu Mahasabha. But Savarkar, still the most influential figure in the Mahasabha, opposed any type of cooperation with the Jana Sangh. Chatterjee recalls that Savarkar's negative response to the proposal was due in large part to his dislike of Golwalkar and to his lingering distrust of the RSS for not supporting the Hindu Mahasabha either in the 1946 general elections or in 1949 when it resumed operations as a political party. Moreover, Savarkar assumed that the RSS cadre would take control of the Jana Sangh, and in fact probably already had control of the party organization.[14]

Unable to recruit any nationally recognized politician, the general council of the Jana Sangh met at Allahabad in August 1953 to choose an interim president. Mauli Chandra Sharma, one of the two general secretaries, was asked to serve as acting president until a new president was chosen at the party's next annual session in Bombay. Deendayal Upadhyaya now had sole executive authority over the party's organizational structure. Even before Sharma's assumption of the presidency, Upadhyaya had played a more active role in the day-to-day work of the organization than Sharma, who had a family and a law practice in Delhi.

When the annual session met in January 1954 it was clear that the very energetic general secretary, who could rely on the support of the RSS cadre, had a firm control on the levers of power within the party. Because the delegates were unable to find a suitable national leader to serve as president, they had no choice but again to turn to Sharma. However, the evidence suggests that the RSS cadre had deep reservations about him. *Organiser*, in its report of the session, focused attention on 'the thin unassuming Din Dayal Upadhyaya who stood head and shoulders above all others, and who in a way dominated the whole session'. The report expressed the hope that

> Pt Mauli Chandra Sharma who has the difficult task of fitting himself in the place of the late Dr Mookerjee will succeed in securing the willing cooperation of the Swayamsevak Sangh [sic] workers who form the core of the Jana Sangh. Let Pt. Mauli Chandra Sharma carry them with him and build a great edifice on these foundations.[15]

Sharma could not win the confidence of the RSS cadre in the party, in large part because of differences with them regarding the powers of the party president. Sharma expected to function with much the same independence as Mookerjee; however, he had neither Mookerjee's national reputation nor his charismatic appeal among the RSS cadre. Moreover, there was a group of young swayamsevaks, like Upadhyaya, who during the preceding two years of full-time work in politics, had developed greater political self-confidence and expected to have a major voice in decision making.

The tension between Sharma and the RSS cadre surfaced when Sharma refused to accept a draft list of names for the working committee that was drawn up by Upadhyaya. The Jana Sangh constitution gave the president the right to choose his own working committee, and Sharma decided to substitute some of the nominees with his own men.[16] His choice of Vasantrao Krishna Oke infuriated many of the RSS cadre. Oke, a pracharak, had not received permission from the RSS leadership to join the working committee. Indeed, the RSS leadership had ordered him to leave politics entirely and resume his RSS work.[17] According to Eknath Ranade, at that time a member of the RSS executive, Oke not only broke RSS discipline, but he was in revolt against it. According to Ranade, Oke had proposed that the RSS disband on the grounds that the Jana Sangh could carry out the task of national rejuvenation more effectively than a non-political association like the RSS.[18] Sharma later claimed that he was unaware of the RSS high command's decision to remove Oke from politics until several months after the Bombay session.[19] Yet, he did not remove Oke from the working committee, even after discovering the views of the RSS high command.

For the traditionalist RSS leadership, democratic politics was a necessary though somewhat immoral activity. To enjoy it as much as Oke obviously did struck then as rank apostasy. To suggest the dissolution of the RSS confirmed the heresy.[20]

Soon after the 1953 Bombay session, Sharma and Oke tried to recruit a large number of non-RSS party workers, as well as to solicit funds from wealthy businessmen.[21] Sharma claims that he tried to raise money to finance the expansion of the party's organizational base. It is not clear if he meant to displace the organizing secretaries, most of whom were pracharaks, but had he succeeded in raising the money and in recruiting non-RSS workers, this option would have been open to him. In any case, Sharma was unable to diminish the influence of the organizing secretaries.

When the party's general council met at Indore in August 1954 the organizing secretaries knew they had the votes in the general council to determine party policy, and they were not prepared to compromise with Sharma. Sharma also understood their mood, and he did not bother to attend the meeting, although Oke did.[22] Sharma's presidential address was read for him. The delegates were annoyed by his thinly veiled references to the Jana Sangh's losing its commitment to 'secular nationalism' and 'democracy', and by his glowing references to Nehru's policy towards Pakistan. They were particularly irritated by his suggestion that the party become more democratic by eliminating the position of organizing secretary. Sharma was proposing a complete reorientation of party power. The organizing secretaries, most of whom were former RSS pracharaks, constituted the steel frame of the party. They supervised the day-to-day work of the local units; they were the major communications link between the different levels of the party; they played a major role in the choice of officers in the organization and of candidates for party tickets; and they enforced compliance with executive decisions.[23] It was this authority system which prevented Sharma from developing an effective faction within the party and which ultimately forced him to resign.

There were, however, some units in which the non-RSS element was dominant. As the RSS cadre tightened its control over the party organization, the covert distrust between them and the non-RSS participants developed into overt hostility. One prominent example of the dispute was in the Delhi unit of the party: The Delhi general council had a non-RSS majority, and the RSS cadre intended to take control of it. Guru Vaid Dutt, a well-known Hindi writer and the president of the Delhi State Jana Sangh unit, charged the RSS leadership with dictating party policy, and he resigned.[24]

The RSS cadre also moved to take over the national party organization. With this objective in mind, Deendayal

Upadhyaya scheduled a meeting of the working committee at Delhi on 7 November 1954. Sharma hoped to avert the anticipated purge of party 'rebels' by ordering the general council of the party, which had a non-RSS contingent, to meet at Delhi in early November. Upadhyaya countermanded his order on the grounds that the Jana Sangh constitution permitted only the working committee to call a meeting of the general council.[25] Realizing his hopeless position, Sharma resigned several days before the working committee met. To leave no doubt that he was out of the party, the working committee formally expelled him from the party. Organiser informed its readers that Sharma 'suffered from a fatal flaw of an insufferable self-aggrandisement—even at the cost of the party. In this he had no scruples as to the means he employed. Soon it became clear that he was hardly the man to lead a great and growing organisation.'[26] The working committee replaced Sharma with S. A. Sohani, RSS sanghchalak of Berar.[27] With Sohani's accession to the presidency, the RSS cadre had virtually absolute control of the organizational wing of the party. From 1954 to 1967, RSS pracharak Deendayal Upadhyaya was general secretary, and it was the general secretary who exercised executive power in the party.[28] The RSS cadre maintained their control through the network of organizing secretaries who both serve as gatekeepers of admittance into the organization and manage advancement up the party hierarchy. The only possible challenge to this system might have come from Dr Raghu Vira, a renowned linguist from Madhya Pradesh elected party president in 1962. Raghu Vira, a Congress member of the Upper House of parliament when he bolted from the ruling party in 1959 because of differences with

India's China policy, was welcomed into the Jana Sangh as a national political figure who might make the party more respectable. His death in 1963 may have spared the party a possible power struggle.

There is no evidence that the RSS leadership orchestrated the actions of their pracharaks in the new party, though they were surely kept informed about what was happening in the party. The purging of the party dissidents was an attempt to create a decision-making structure more compatible with that of the RSS itself, not to impose the will of the RSS leadership on the party. Indeed, the traditionalist RSS leadership did not want to take responsibility for running the party.

With the purging of the dissidents, the swayamsevaks proceeded to reorient party priorities. Questions of national integration were still primary, but more serious attention was directed at economic and social issues. The 1954 Indore general council session, at which the purge was initiated, voted for a new economic manifesto which significantly shifted the party's orientation on economic issues.[29] The manifesto called for an addition to the Indian constitution to include as a new right the guarantee of a job; it proposed worker participation in the ownership and control of industry; and it supported labour's right to strike. It advocated the immediate implementation of an income policy which would guarantee a minimum salary of 100 rupees per month and a maximum salary of 2,000 rupees per month. It also proposed that the government adopt a set of policies to guarantee that average minimum wages are at least 10 per cent of average maximum wages. It recommended the abolition of large landed estates without compensation. The delegates also approved a resolution proposing that untouchability become a cognizable offence under the penal code.

THE 1957 AND 1962 GENERAL ELECTIONS: DEVELOPING AN ORGANIZATIONAL BASE

The Jana Sangh went into the 1957 general elections with a far clearer grasp of the electoral process and a less conservative set of policy guidelines. A candidate's ability to finance his own campaign was no longer the major criterion for selection, as it had been in 1951–52. The party was able to generate candidates from within, and it was able to assume more of the costs and responsibilities of the electoral campaign.[30] The party leaders also were aware of the Jana Sangh's relatively limited support base. Table 2 shows the performance of the Jana Sangh in various parliamentary and assembly elections from 1952 to 1971–72.

Table 2: Jana Sangh Electoral Performance in Parliamentary and State Assembly Elections

Election Year	Parliament			Assemblies		
	% of Votes	Seats contested	Seats won	% of Votes	Seats contested	Seats won
1952	3.06	92	3	2.76	725	35
1957	5.93	130	4	4.03	606	51
1962	6.44	195	14	6.07	1177	119
1967	9.41	250	35	8.80	1702	257
1971–72	7.35	159	22	8.56	1233	104

Note. See Appendices C and D for statistics for all states and union territories in which the Jana Sangh contested parliamentary seats.

Despite their limited experience in politics, the RSS cadre in the party was able to organize an effective campaign. Indeed, they were able to mobilize even more support for Jana Sangh candidates than in the 1951–52 elections. The party's percentage of the parliamentary vote increased from 3.06 in 1952 to 5.93 in 1957, and to 6.44 in 1962. Its percentage of the assembly vote increased from 2.76 in 1952 to 4.03 in 1957 and 6.07 in 1962. It won 4 of the 487 parliamentary seats in 1957 and 14 of the 494 parliamentary seats in the 1962 elections. Its assembly representation increased from 51 in 1957 to 119 in 1962. Tables 3 and 4 detail the performance of the Jana Sangh in various assembly and parliamentary elections in selected states and Union Territories from 1952 to 1975.

The party's strength continued to be concentrated in the Hindi-speaking states, especially Uttar Pradesh, Madhya Pradesh, the Union territory of Delhi, and the Hindu-majority cities of Punjab, areas in which the RSS had already established a firm base of support in the 1940s. In Uttar Pradesh, the Jana Sangh's percentage of the parliamentary vote doubled from 7.29 to 14.79 between 1952 and 1957. It won two of the state's 86 parliamentary seats and 17 of the 430 assembly seats in 1957, and increased its parliamentary representation to 7 and its assembly representation to 49 in 1962. The party started out from an urban support base in Uttar Pradesh, as it did in most other states, but it made a concerted effort to build up support in rural areas. Voting statistics demonstrate

Table 3: Jana Sangh Performance in State Assembly Elections in Selected States/Union Territories

State/ Territory	Vote %	Seats contested	Seats won	Vote %	Seats contested	Seats won	Vote %	Seats contested	Seats won
		1952			1957			1962	
Bihar	1.15	44	0	1.19	29	0	2.77	75	3
Delhi	21.88	31	5	...	...	...	...	...	...
Haryana	6.12	23	2	12.02	24	4	13.46	34	4
Madhya Pradesh	5.66	126	6	9.88	126	10	16.66	195	41
Punjab	4.01	52	0	7.47	36	5	7.59	41	4
Rajasthan	6.34	65	11	5.42	47	6	9.15	94	15
Uttar Pradesh	6.64	210	2	9.77	235	17	16.46	377	49
		1967			1971–1975				
Bihar	10.42	270	26	11.37	271	26			
Delhi	33.35	96	52	40.70	99	53			
Haryana	14.39	48	12	6.54	19	2			
Madhya Pradesh	28.20	265	78	28.72	261	48			
Punjab	9.84	49	9	4.95	33	0			
Rajasthan	11.69	63	22	12.04	119	8			
Uttar Pradesh	21.67	401	98	17.30	401	61			

Table 4: Jana Sangh Performance in Parliamentary Elections in Selected States/Union Territories

State/Territory	Vote %	Seats contested	Seats won	Vote %	Seats contested	Seats won	Vote %	Seats contested	Seats won
	1952			1957			1962		
Bihar	0.42	2	0	0.08	2	0	2.34	13	0
Delhi	25.93	3	0	19.72	5	0	32.66	5	0
Haryana	7.41	5	0	22.75	6	0	23.42	8	3
Madhya Pradesh	5.92	11	0	13.96	21	0	17.87	28	3
Punjab	3.36	5	0	13.39	10	0	10.30	9	0
Rajasthan	3.67	4	1	11.10	7	0	9.28	11	1
Uttar Pradesh	7.29	41	0	14.79	61	2	17.59	74	7
	1967			1971–1975					
Bihar	11.05	48	1	12.10	28	2			
Delhi	46.72	7	6	29.57	7	0			
Haryana	19.85	7	1	11.19	3	1			
Madhya Pradesh	29.56	32	10	33.56	28	11			
Punjab	12.49	8	1	4.45	5	0			
Rajasthan	9.71	6	3	12.38	7	4			
Uttar Pradesh	22.58	77	12	12.28	40	4			

that it succeeded in attracting considerable rural support.[31] In addition, the 1959 municipal elections in Uttar Pradesh's five largest cities demonstrated that the party was able to mobilize significant urban support.[32] The Jana Sangh won 56 of the 296 seats in those municipal elections, emerging with the largest party representation in Lucknow, the state's capital, and with the second largest party representation in the other four cities.

In Madhya Pradesh, the party won no parliamentary seats in 1957, though it did receive 13.96 per cent of the total popular vote. In 1962, the Jana Sangh increased its percentage of the vote to 17.87 per cent and won three of the state's 36 seats. The party's performance in the state's assembly constituencies was even more impressive. With 9.88 per cent of the total assembly vote in 1957, it won 10 of the 288 seats. In 1962 it received 16.66 per cent of the vote and 41 seats. Most of the Jana Sangh's support came from the western Madhya Bharat region of the state. Approximately half its seats in both 1957 and 1962 were from this region. Madhya Bharat is the most urbanized and industrialized part of the state;[33] it is also in this region that the RSS had its strongest support.[34] In the first general elections, the Hindu Mahasabha was the second largest party in the region, winning 2 or its 11 parliamentary seats and 11 of its 99 assembly seats from there. The Jana Sangh took its place as the major competitor of the Congress party in the Madhya Bharat region.

The Jana Sangh also performed relatively well in Rajasthan in 1957 and 1962.[35] Despite the fact that the party's percentage of the parliamentary vote increased from 3.67 in 1952 to 11.10 in 1957, the Jana Sangh could win no seats there. It did manage to win one parliamentary seat in

1962, though its percentage of the vote declined slightly. After losing many of its 11 assembly representatives between 1952 and 1957 as a result of the party's anti-landlord policy, the Jana Sangh returned to the 176 member assembly in 1957 with 6 representatives. The party's percentage of the assembly vote almost doubled in 1962 and it won 15 seats. In the first two assembly elections, the Ram Rajya Parishad, representing Hindu orthodoxy, performed much better than the Jana Sangh, winning 24 assembly seats in 1952 and 16 in 1957. After the 1962 elections, the Parishad ceased to be a viable political force in the state. Its role as the major opposition party passed in 1962 to another conservative party, the newly formed Swatantra Party. The leadership of both the Parishad and the Swatantra Party rested on the Rajput aristocracy. The Jana Sangh built a stable base of support in the eastern districts,[36] particularly in the south-eastern districts of Kota division, which border on Madhya Bharat. To a certain extent, the Jana Sangh strength in that region derived from the support extended to it by former ruling families; but more importantly, this region had a strong RSS organization which provided the resources required for party building.

Punjab was something of a disappointment to the Jana Sangh. The party started out with a support base among the urban Hindu middle-class voters, but was never able to make an electoral impact among the Sikh majorities in rural areas. The party won no seats in Punjab's state assembly or parliamentary constituencies in 1952.[37] In the 1957 assembly elections, it won five seats, all urban, and increased its percentage of the vote from 4.01 to 7.47 per cent. While the party's percentage of the assembly vote increased slightly in 1962, its representation dropped to four, in an 86 member assembly. Though the Jana Sangh could poll only a very small percentage of the rural—largely Sikh—vote in either election, it was able to poll approximately a quarter of the urban vote.

The RSS had an urban base in Punjab even before partition, and it was further strengthened by the large number of Hindu refugees who poured into the state between 1947 and 1949. Emotional policy issues hampered the Jana Sangh's efforts to expand beyond the Hindu community. The Jana Sangh's opposition to equal status for Punjabi and Hindi strengthened its appeal to the Hindi-speaking voters in the northern districts of the state where the Sikhs outnumbered the Hindus. But this policy alienated the Sikh voters who wanted Punjabi to be placed on at least an equal status with Hindi. The Jana Sangh also supported the creation of a Maha Punjab (greater Punjab) that would include the Hindi-speaking mountain area to the east.[38] On both issues the party's stand coincided with the influential Arya Samaj, a Hindu revivalist group which manages a network of schools, charitable institutions, and temples in the state.[39] However, the RSS leadership, fearful that a Sikh separatist movement would grow if Punjabi were not given some official recognition, adopted a conciliatory policy towards the Punjabi language. For example, while on tour of Punjab in 1960, Golwalkar appealed to the Hindus in the state to accept Punjabi as their mother tongue. He even suggested that the state be declared a unilingual Punjabi-speaking state.[40] Soon after Golwalkar concluded his tour, the state working committee of the Jana Sangh rejected his proposal for a unilingual state. Instead it resolved that both Hindi, in Devanagari script, and Punjabi, in Gurmukhi script, serve as joint official languages.[41] This considerable shift in policy was undoubtedly influenced by the stand of the RSS. The legislative wing of the party, more responsive to the will of its Hindi-speaking constituency, took a far less conciliatory stand and strongly rejected Golwalkar's pleas for Punjabi.[42]

The Jana Sangh performed better in those southern districts of Punjab which in 1966 became part of the new state of Haryana. It won two of the 60 assembly seats in 1952 and received 6.12 per cent of the total vote there. Almost doubling its percentage of the vote in 1957, the Jana Sangh picked up two additional assembly seats. In 1962, it further increased its percentage of the assembly vote and won four seats. While the party received greater rural support in Haryana, it was a largely urban party in both parts of undivided Punjab. In 1962 the party won three of the 20 parliamentary seats from Punjab, all three from the Haryana region. It received almost one-fourth of the total parliamentary vote in the Haryana region, over double the 11.39 per cent the party received in those northern districts which were to remain within Punjab after the division of the state.

The Jana Sangh performed consistently well in Delhi, where it was able to gain the allegiance of a substantial part of the large Hindu refugee population from Pakistan. While it won no parliamentary seats in the first three general elections, the party accumulated between a fifth and a third of the vote in each election.[43] It also did well in the Delhi Municipal elections, and, despite the 1954 party revolt, won about a quarter of the vote in both the 1958 and 1962 municipal Corporation elections. The Congress, its only serious political rival in the Union territory, was weakened by factional strife in 1958, enabling the Jana Sangh to win 25 of the 80 corporation seats. The dominant and dissident Congress factions patched up their disagreements before the 1962 elections, and the Jana Sangh could win only eight municipal corporation seats.[44]

The Praja Parishad continued to operate as a separate Jana Sangh affiliate in Jammu and Kashmir in both 1957 and 1962. The ruling National Conference reached out for support in the Hindu-majority Jammu region after Bakshi Ghulam Muhammad replaced Sheikh Abdullah as the state's prime minister in late 1953. Bakshi gave greater representation to the Jammu region in the National Conference. His popularity was in no small part assisted by the massive flow of financial aid from New Delhi, and by the resulting improvement in the state's standard of living. [45] The Parishad was able to win only five of the 30 assembly seats allotted to Jammu in 1957, and three in 1952. In both elections, the National Conference polled over twice as many votes as the Parishad in Jammu.[46] The Parishad's support base remained largely caste Hindu, and it was unable to win any appreciable following from Muslim backward castes and from the Scheduled Caste Hindu voters.

Bihar was the one Hindi-speaking state where the Jana Sangh performed poorly in the first three general elections. Neither the Arya Samaj nor the RSS, two major support bases for the party in other Hindi-speaking states, had a strong following in Bihar. Moreover, Bihar had a small Hindu refugee population.

After Mookerjee's death, the Jana Sangh was never to attract much support in Bengal. As in Bihar, supporters of the Hindu Mahasabha and the RSS, which had helped party building elsewhere, were weakly represented. The Jana Sangh contested few assembly seats and accumulated less than 1 per cent of the vote in the 1957 and 1962 assembly elections.

Except for the case of Maharashtra in 1957, the Jana Sangh made no significant gains outside the Hindi-speaking states in the 1957 and 1962 elections. Its relatively strong showing in Maharashtra in 1957 owed much to the Jana Sangh's participation in the Samyukta Maharashtra Samiti, an alliance of parties that advocated the division of Bombay into separate Gujarati and Marathi-speaking states. The Congress, which took an ambiguous stand on this emotional issue, lost considerable support, and the Jana Sangh won four of the eighteen Maharashtra assembly seats allotted to it by the Samiti. The Jana Sangh also won two of the seven parliamentary seats which it contested in 1957. The Congress, however, regained its electoral pre-eminence in the 1962 elections; and the Jana Sangh, which by then had left the opposition alliance, won no assembly or parliamentary seats. As in Jammu and Kashmir, the Jana Sangh was unable to mobilize any appreciable support outside caste Hindu groups. Indeed, it was popularly referred to in Maharashtra as the party of brahmins.[47]

The Jana Sangh also participated in the Mahagujarat Janata Parishad, the Gujarat equivalent of the Samyukta Maharashtra Samiti, although the Jana Sangh reaped few benefits.[48] The party won none of the five assembly seats allotted to it in 1957. In Maharashtra the Jana Sangh relied on the RSS to build the party organization and to mobilize support. It was also able to recruit many of the high-caste Hindu voters who had supported the Mahasabha in Maharashtra. However, the Mahasabha and the RSS were both relatively weak in Gujarat, and the Jana Sangh was not able to build a grass roots organization there until much later.

1967 GENERAL ELECTIONS: THE JANA SANGH ASPIRES TO ESTABLISH ITSELF AS AN ALL-INDIA PARTY

Between the 1962 and 1967 elections, a series of events had eroded support from the ruling Congress party. India fought costly wars with China (1962) and Pakistan (1965) which drained resources that could have gone into economic development; it experienced severe droughts and high rates of inflation. Anti-Congress sentiment was fuelled by outbursts of popular agitation over cow protection and the choice of a national link language. The Congress missed the unifying influence of Prime Minister Nehru, who had led the country from Independence until his death in 1964. His daughter, Indira Gandhi, became prime minister in 1966, and found herself under attack from dissident factions on both the left and the right for deviating from her father's policies.[49]

Jana Sangh leaders believed that the public mood might be shifting in ways they could exploit to strengthen the party's support base. They were confident that the party's support of a tough approach towards China and Pakistan would evoke a favourable response. Indeed, the heightened sense of patriotism appeared to generate a favourable response to the 'family' of organizations around the RSS. One sign of respectability was the invitation to the RSS to participate for the first time in the 1963 Republic Day parade in New Delhi; more than 2,000 swayamsevaks in full uniform, as well as the RSS bagpipe and bugle unit, marched in the parade.[50]

As relations with China deteriorated in the early 1960s, the Jana Sangh found itself more acceptable to other non-communist opposition parties, particularly the Swatantra

Party and the Praja Socialist Party. These three favoured a tougher Indian response to the Chinese occupation of the Aksai Chin area of Kashmir. They worked together in 1962 against V. K. Krishna Menon, Nehru's defence minister, considered by them to be a fellow-traveller, by jointly supporting the candidacy of Acharya Kripalani in the Bombay North-east parliamentary constituency. Over the next two years, they worked out electoral alliances in three parliamentary bye-elections, winning two of them. The losing candidate was Deendayal Upadhyaya, who fought his only parliamentary contest from Jaunpur district in Uttar Pradesh.

In 1963 Balraj Madhok, who had served as a Jana Sangh member of parliament from Delhi in 1961–62, even proposed that the Jana Sangh unite with the conservative Swatantra Party to form a new party. While the Swatantra Party may have agreed, General Secretary Upadhyaya did not want the Jana Sangh to become transformed into a party of the right. In his view, anti-communism was not a sufficient justification for the step proposed by Madhok. The Jana Sangh working committee rejected the notion ostensibly because of the ambiguous attitude of the Swatantra towards Indian control of Jammu and Kashmir. Upadhyaya was then seeking to give a more populist orientation to the Jana Sangh, and a union with a political organization representing the interests of private capital and large landholders was unacceptable. Moreover, the RSS brotherhood could not have relished the prospect of a significant diffusion of its power for the uncertain benefits of the new party.

Even prior to the Jana Sangh's electoral understanding of the early 1960s, the party leadership was under some pressure to formulate a set of principles that would distinguish the

Jana Sangh from other political parties.[51] Perhaps prompted by the Jana Sangh's growing collaboration with some of the opposition parties following the deterioration in Sino-Indian relations, Upadhyaya responded to the demand for a distinct ideological statement by drafting a set of principles he referred to as Integral Humanism. He introduced the concept at the January 1965 meeting of the party's working committee, which adopted Integral Humanism as the Jana Sangh's official statement of fundamental principles. Upadhyaya gave greater substance to the notion in a series of lectures later that year in Bombay.[52]

In justifying the need for a separate ideological statement, Upadhyaya argued that Western political philosophies did not provide an acceptable blueprint for the good society because of their preoccupation with materialism while largely overlooking the social well-being of the individual. Capitalism and socialism in his view were flawed because they stimulated greed, class antagonism, exploitation and social anarchy. In their place, he proposes an 'integral' approach that seeks to create a harmonious society by satisfying the needs of the body (hunger, shelter), the mind (traditions), intelligence (reforms), and soul (the common aspirations of a people that shape their unique culture). He argued that each nation creates institutions to satisfy these needs, and that such institutions must be reshaped to sustain group solidarity under changing circumstances. They might even have to be discarded for something new if they undermine the unity of a people. For example, if the caste system divides society, as he argued it did, it should be scrapped and replaced by something else. Indian tradition, he asserted, stresses the social nature of people and obligates them to create institutions designed to enhance social solidarity. Advaita vedanta (recognition of ourselves in all life) provides the philosophic underpinning of this view.

Social solidarity in his view required a political and economic system in which the people affected by the decisions are involved in the decision-making process. On the economic front, he proposed worker control of the means of production and cooperative ownership over larger, more complex industries. In the political arena, he advocated democracy. However, he believed that political democracy is a sham unless accompanied by social and economic democracy, and vice versa. Upadhyaya did not try to describe in any specific detail what an ideal society would look like. Rather, he assumed that it is the obligation of Indian statesmen continually to apply the relatively few general rules of Integral Humanism to practical politics, in an effort to strengthen social solidarity; and, as he was soon to argue, agitation is a legitimate tool in this process.

In his 1967 presidential address, Upadhyaya defended the call to activism alluded to in his exposition of Integral Humanism. He stated

We should also be cautious about people who see in every popular agitation the hidden hand of communism and [who] suggest that agitation must be crushed. In the changing situation at present, public agitations are natural and even essential. In fact, they are the medium of expression of social awakening. It is of course necessary that these agitations should be made instruments of constructive revolution and not allowed to become violent and adventurist. Therefore, we must actively participate in popular movements and try to guide then. Those who are keen to preserve the status quo in economic and social spheres feel threatened by these movements and are wont to create an atmosphere of pessimism. We are sorry we cannot cooperate with them. We think these sections are trying in vain to halt the wheels of progress and avert the destiny of the country.[53]

Upadhyaya thus legitimized agitation as a technique, and the party's increasing resort to it was to drive out some prominent conservative elements.

To prepare for the 1967 elections, the Jana Sangh's working committee met at Vijayawada in early 1965 to establish policy guidelines. Sensing the rising nationalist mood triggered by India's defeat in the 1962 war with China, the leadership concentrated on foreign policy questions. The working committee suggested that India sever diplomatic relations with China and vote against China's entry into the United Nations; it advocated closer relations with those countries in South-East Asia 'which are interested in the containment of Communist China'; it called for the recognition of the Dalai Lama as the legitimate ruler of Tibet, and it demanded that India recover the areas 'occupied' by Pakistan and China. To back up this tough stand, it called for the compulsory military training of all young men and for the development of nuclear weapons.[54] Resolutions were passed opposing India's agreement to withdraw from those parts of Jammu and Kashmir which it had occupied during the 1965 war with Pakistan,[55] encouraging the government to support the separatist movements among the Pakhtoons in West Pakistan and the Bengalis in East Pakistan,[56] and calling for the establishment of military settlements along the ceasefire line in Jammu and Kashmir.[57]

One year before the 1967 general elections, the Jana Sangh elected Balraj Madhok president, breaking the precedent established in 1955 of figurehead presidents. The party anticipated making major gains in the elections and its leaders wanted a well-known figure like Madhok in that position who could make a significant contribution in the campaign.[58]

Madhok immediately set out on the campaign trail to prepare the local units for the forthcoming elections. As part of its pre-election strategy, the party units were instructed to increase significantly the party's enrolled membership. The general secretary reported in April 1966 that the party membership had increased from about 600,000 in 1956 to 1,300,000 in early 1966, and that it had party units in 268 districts.[59]

Corruption, factionalism and economic hardship had undermined the Congress's popularity. It was returned to power at the centre in 1967 but with a much reduced majority. It won 83 fewer seats in the Lower House of parliament, giving it a narrow 25-seat majority. Moreover, the Congress failed to win an absolute majority in eight of the state assemblies.

The Jana Sangh for its part performed far better than even its leaders expected. Its parliamentary representation increased from 14 in 1962 to 35 in 1967, and its percentage of the parliamentary vote increased from 6.44 to 9.41. The party won 261 assembly seats in 1967, over double the 119 it had won in 1962. While the Jana Sangh's support was still concentrated in the Hindi-speaking states, it won 32 assembly seats and 2 parliamentary seats elsewhere. For the first time since 1952, it won an assembly seat in West Bengal, and for the first time it won assembly seats in Andhra Pradesh (3) and in Karnataka (4).

The Jana Sangh's most impressive gains in the 1967 elections were in Bihar and Delhi. In Bihar, the party increased its percentage of the assembly vote from 2.77 to 10.42 and increased its assembly representation from 3 to 26, in a 318-member assembly. The Jana Sangh performance in the parliamentary contests in Bihar was even more impressive. The party increased its percentage of the parliamentary vote from 2.34 in 1962 to 11.05 in 1967. However, the Jana Sangh could win only one of the 53 parliamentary seats in Bihar in 1967. In an attempt to broaden its support base, the party made a special effort to mobilize scheduled-caste and Scheduled Tribe voters. The RSS and its affiliates had already begun a major effort to attract the support of these groups. This work may have helped the Jana Sangh. It won 5 of the 26 assembly seats reserved for the scheduled tribe candidates in 1967.

The Jana Sangh won a major triumph in Delhi, winning 52 of the 100 seats in the Delhi Municipal Corporation, 33 of the 56 seats in the Metropolitan Council, and 6 of Delhi's 7 parliamentary seats, losing only outer Delhi to Brahm Parkash, the leader of the Delhi Congress organization. Delhi has tended towards a two-party system, and the Jana Sangh was able to do well when the Congress was internally divided, as it was in 1967.

Regarding Punjab, the Jana Sangh reconciled itself to the division of Punjab into two states. In his presidential address to the 1966 annual session of the party, Madhok called upon the Hindus in Punjab to learn Punjabi in the Gurmukhi script. Despite this announced shift in policy, the Hindus in Punjab voted for the Jana Sangh in even greater numbers than before. Many Hindus blamed the Congress for the division of the state. For the first time, the Jana Sangh out-polled the Congress in the urban constituencies, winning 7 of the

9 urban seats in the assembly. Yagya Dutt Sharma, a former RSS pracharak, won the Amritsar parliamentary seat, the first Jana Sangh candidate to win a parliamentary seat from the region included in the new Sikh-majority Punjab. The Jana Sangh built on its already strong support base in Haryana, adding 8 assembly seats to the 4 won in 1962. Its support in Haryana was rather widespread, and it won assembly seats in six of the state's seven districts. Its parliamentary candidate in Chandigarh, capital of both Punjab and Haryana, campaigning on a platform to keep the city the joint capital of the two states, won with 48.70 per cent of the vote. The Punjab and Haryana units of the party had each resolved that Chandigarh should go to their own state. The national leadership took no stand on this question and was willing to live with the non-uniform response of the three party units.

In Rajasthan, the Jana Sangh formed an alliance with the conservative Swatantra Party, and the two parties won 70 assembly seats, 48 for the Swatantra and 22 for the Jana Sangh. The two parties polled 33.79 per cent of the vote, only about 7 percentage points less than the Congress, which won 89 seats. The Jana Sangh continued to draw most of its support from the eastern districts, where it won 16 of its 22 assembly seats, 11 of them in the south-eastern Kota division. Two of its 3 parliamentary seats were also in this division. The impressive showing in this area, where it won 11 of the 16 assembly seats and both parliamentary seats, might be attributed in part to the support which the former royal families of Kota and Mewar extended to it during this election. The Jana Sangh also out-polled the Congress in the state's urban assembly constituencies and won 5 of Rajasthan's 9 urban seats.[60]

One commentator of the 1967 elections in Jammu and Kashmir mentions that the elections there generated greater enthusiasm than any prior election because it appeared that the National Conference might, for the first time, be defeated.[61] Fifty-three of the state's 75 assembly seats were contested, more than in any prior election. The Jana Sangh contested 26 of the 31 seats in the Hindu-majority Jammu region and won 3 of them, and it accumulated over one-fourth the vote in that region. It also contested 2 parliamentary seats from Jammu. While the Congress won both Jammu seats, the Jana Sangh received one-third the vote. Even though the party made a special appeal to the Scheduled Caste and backward caste voter and nominated three Muslims (two for assembly seats and one for a parliamentary seat), it was still boxed into its urban caste Hindu constituency.

The party still received its strongest support from Uttar Pradesh and Madhya Pradesh. In the former, the Jana Sangh increased its vote share by about 5 percentage points for both the assembly and parliamentary contests, winning 98 of the 425 assembly seats, and 12 of the 85 parliamentary seats. The Jana Sangh won 17 of the 45 urban constituencies, more than any other party.[62] With the backing of prominent members of the Scindia princely family of Gwalior in Madhya Pradesh, the party was able to increase its strength in the Madhya Bharat region, where it won 40 of its 78 assembly seats and 5 of its 10 parliamentary seats.[63] In both states, the Jana Sangh out-polled the Congress in cities.[64]

SUCCESSES EXACERBATE INTERNAL PARTY TENSIONS

Because of its electoral successes, the Jana Sangh could not be ignored in the formation of United Front governments. It was a participant in United Front governments in Bihar, Haryana,

Madhya Pradesh, Punjab and Uttar Pradesh. By joining coalitions with the Sikh Akali Dal and with the communists in several states, the party reneged on an earlier policy not to associate itself closely with 'communal' and 'anti-national' forces. There was relatively little opposition to cooperation with the Akali Dal; however, alliances with the communists aroused considerable opposition within the party. Golwalkar himself advised the Jana Sangh leadership against working with communists.[65] At the party's general council meeting at Delhi in April 1967 the leadership was sharply questioned for four hours by the delegates on the issue.[66] The delegates eventually voted their approval of United Front governments, but with no great enthusiasm. A few weeks earlier, the RSS central executive had met at Nagpur and had given its approval to the concept of coalition governments, expressing the hope that such political alliances would 'bring about mutual harmony among the various political parties as envisaged by Sangh'.[67]

By September 1967 the Jana Sangh experience in the rough and tumble world of coalition politics, which many in the party saw as unprincipled, resulted in a re-evaluation of United Front ministries. At the party's working committee meeting in Vadodara on 15 September, the organizational wing of the party decided that Jana Sangh ministers could remain within the United Front governments. One month later, this decision was upheld by a meeting of the Jana Sangh ministers. The issue which caused the most debate was Jana Sangh participation in ministries which included communists. Madhok, for example, described the party's decision to remain in governments which included communists a 'grave blunder'.[68] He hinted that the RSS was exerting pressure on the party to keep them in such ministries. He wanted the party to adopt policies that would protect property and free enterprise. Cooperating so closely with various socialist and communist parties was, in his opinion, bad policy and bad politics.

During this debate, Atal Bihari Vajpayee, who had been a party secretary at the national level since 1955 and was the leader of the parliamentary wing, emerged as the spokesman of the 'left' viewpoint in the party. He favoured continued cooperation with the communists and the parties of the 'left'. He also proposed that the party make a more vigorous attempt to mobilize the underprivileged and discontented voters.[69] Upadhyaya, while distrustful of the communists, tended to support Vajpayee. In supporting a shift to the 'left,' Vajpayee was probably closer to the class interests of the RSS cadre than was Madhok.

Madhok eagerly sought the party presidency in late 1957; however, Upadhyaya himself assumed the position and Sunder Singh Bhandari, a former RSS pracharak, was chosen to succeed him as general secretary.[70] The organization, represented by Upadhyaya, intended to keep a tight control on its much expanded legislative wing. Upadhyaya's assumption of the presidency in 1957 signified that the basic organizing phase of the Jana Sangh was completed and that it now intended to become a serious competitor for power on the national level.

This reorientation of the party did not go unchallenged, and the party faced its most severe internal crisis since the 1954–55 purges. Madhok fiercely resisted the party's leftward turn. He adamantly opposed any form of cooperation with the communists and socialists. During the central government employees' strike in 1968, for example, he advised the party leaders not to support the workers on the grounds that the strike was being orchestrated by the communists. The party leadership was forced to respond to public statements about the strike because the Jana Sangh general council had earlier decided to support the workers' cause.[71] Vajpayee publicly informed the party cadre that the Jana Sangh sympathized with the workers' demands.[72] When Madhok filed a writ petition in the Supreme Court with Minoo Masani, a Swatantra Party member of parliament, in 1969, challenging the nationalization of banks that year, the Jana Sangh working committee cautioned him to consult his colleagues before taking any action that would portray the party as a defender of big business. He was told that the Jana Sangh would, in the future, approach social and economic problems from the 'common man's point of view',[73] and the cadre was told that they were to 'steer clear of the prevalent impression that the Sangh is a party of the "Right".'[74] The working committee called upon the government to implement more forcefully the law on rural land ceilings. It decided to survey the cadre on their views regarding urban property ceiling.[75] None of this pleased Madhok and the conservatives in the party. They were irritated by the party leadership's intention to portray the party publicly and aggressively as a political representative of the poor and dispossessed.

The conservatives were also disturbed by the leadership's move to tighten party discipline over the local units. Party membership had grown rapidly since 1965. The party's electoral success brought many non-RSS people into the legislative wing of the party. To prevent the legislative wing—particularly in states where the Jana Sangh was involved in United Front ministries—from acting independently of party directives, the leadership decided to place the legislative members more closely under the direct supervision of the organization. Legislators were required to report to the local party organization and to take their instructions from it. According to Upadhyaya, who announced the policy, this policy was implemented both to ensure that the legislators would not depart 'from norms of propriety' and to enable the organization itself to serve as liaison between the people and their representative within the coalition cabinets.[76] To enforce discipline within the expanding party structure, the party decided to increase the number of full-time organizers.[77] As early as 1960, Upadhyaya had set the goal of placing an organizing secretary in every district; the party's rapid expansion after 1965 prompted the organizational leaders to implement that unfulfilled goal. For those, like Madhok, who sought to open up the party structure, the idea of recruiting more full-time organizers was an unwelcome move.

RETHINKING ALLIANCES

The United Front ministries which had been formed in several states lacked a common set of policy objectives and an effective system of mediation among the participants. They all disintegrated. After brief periods of president's rule, mid-term elections were held in Bihar, Haryana, Punjab, Uttar Pradesh, and West Bengal. The Jana Sangh leadership was disappointed with the United Front experience and opted to fight alone in most places. The Jana Sangh generally performed less well in the mid-term elections than in 1967.

Some senior figures in the Jana Sangh believed that the party could have done better had it worked out electoral agreements. The conservatives, who wanted the Jana Sangh to work more closely with parties of the 'right', put pressure on the party leadership to reconsider the Jana Sangh's alliance strategy. Though the senior leaders remained apprehensive about alliances, they did agree to talks with other non-communist opposition parties to consider some kind of united front for the forthcoming general elections. Unofficial talks took place in March and April 1969 between leaders of the Jana Sangh, the Bharatiya Kranti Dal, the Swatantra Party, and the Praja Socialist party, at a meeting convened by Prakash Vir Shastri, a member of parliament from Uttar Pradesh. In those talks, Vajpayee, who had become party president following Upadhyaya's death in early 1968, insisted that any merger or electoral alliance must be preceded by a commonly accepted set of principles.[78] The mysterious circumstances surrounding Upadhyaya's death on 11 February 1968 led many Jana Sanghis to conclude that he had been murdered. The wave of sympathy aroused by his death probably helped establish among the cadre the legitimacy of Atal Bihari Vajpayee, Upadhyaya's protege and member of parliament since 1957. Vajpayee had already become the party's parliamentary leader and its most articulate orator and public spokesman. Following Upadhyaya's death, he had considerable freedom to formulate policy and, as the opposition parties manoeuvred for alliance partners in the late 1960s, Vajpayee's preference was to avoid a relationship unless there had been a prior agreement on principles.

After the Jana Sangh's 1969 annual session at Bombay, the leaders of the Jana Sangh, Swatantra Party, and Bharatiya Kranti Dal resumed their talks. Because the Jana Sangh representatives ruled out the option of merger, and because they continued to insist on a consensus regarding principles, the Swatantra Party and the Bharatiya Kranti Dal leaders decided to continue their talks without the Jana Sangh.[79] While Vajpayee and most of the working committee members were moving away from participation in any 'grand alliances', Madhok and his supporters argued for a merger with other conservative parties. Political polarization was, in their view, the wave of the future. The Jana Sangh, being neither 'fish nor fowl', would became isolated from the voters unless it committed itself to one or the other of the developing ideological configurations. They pressed for a merger between the Jana Sangh and the Swatantra Party, and even coined a name for the projected party—the Nationalist Democratic Conservative Party. Madhok was infuriated by the leadership's refusal to heed his advice. In public speeches, he insinuated that the leftward tilt was due to some kind of collusion between the leadership and Prime Minister Indira Gandhi. He compared his differences inside the Jana Sangh to the disagreements between Jawaharlal Nehru and Vallabhbhai Patel. Madhok identified himself with the 'nationalist', 'democratic', and 'conservative' Patel; and he compared his opponents to Nehru. The Jana Sangh parliamentary board met in Delhi in September 1969 and censured Madhok for his remarks.[80]

Despite pressure from the right, Vajpayee was reluctant to change the ground rules for negotiations on political alliances. However, the situation changed drastically when on 27 December 1970 leaders of the Congress (0), Swatantra Party, and the Jana Sangh met in Delhi to consider an electoral alliance. On 3 January party leaders announced that they were considering a national electoral alliance. About a week later the Samyukta Socialist party (SSP) joined the discussions. The state units of the four parties were instructed to set up committees to allocate the seats among candidates of the four parties. On 25 January the coordinating committee of the 'grand alliance', as it was called in the press, reached an agreement on 300 of the 520 parliamentary seats.[81] Despite the public show of harmony, the allies were still deeply divided; the one issue on which they all agreed was their opposition to Prime Minister Gandhi.

THE JANA SANGH IN THE 1970S: THE PARTY TURNS TO POPULISM

The Jana Sangh leadership, having established a firm organizational base, was also laying a programmatic groundwork for a 'party of the common man', a phrase used by some advocates of the new approach. This approach was opposed by a conservative section led by Balraj Madhok. However, it was more in tune with the world view of the RSS, with the pracharak network and probably with the class background of most swayamsevaks. This approach also offered greater prospects for expanding the party's mass support base, and party leaders already envisaged the Jana Sangh becoming a major all-India party.

The Jana Sangh went into the 1971 general elections linked to the 'grand alliance', There was considerable grass-roots apprehension regarding this alliance and its ability to put up a viable contest against a prime minister whose slogan was 'the elimination of poverty', Many of the cadre were dismayed both by what they considered to be the blatant opportunism among the ranks of the alliance partners and by the rightist image of the 'grand alliance'.

The results of the 1971 parliamentary election seemed to add substance to the fears of the cadre, though the Jana Sangh did make some scattered gains. In Bihar, it continued to do well and won one additional parliamentary seat. In Madhya Pradesh, the Jana Sangh, with the help of the former rulers of Gwalior,[82] increased its parliamentary representative from 10 to 11 and polled over one-third of the vote. The Jana Sangh and a Jana Sangh-supported SSP candidate won all but one of the parliamentary seats in the Madhya Bharat region of Madhya Pradesh. The party also managed to win 4 seats from Rajasthan, one more than in 1967. Maharajkumar Brij Raj Singh and Raja Homendra Singh, members of the Kota and Udaipur princely families respectively, won 2 of the party's 4 seats in Udaipur division. The party also did quite well in Rajasthan's city elections which were held several months before the general elections. It ran 803 candidates in 103 towns where it won 252 seats, not counting the 33 independents backed by the Jana Sangh. It won a majority of the seats in 12 towns and emerged as the largest single party in Jaipur, the state's capital city.[83]

Everywhere else, the results were a disappointment. The Jana Sangh lost its seats in Punjab and Chandigarh, and barely managed to retain one seat in Haryana. It lost every parliamentary contest in Delhi by substantial margins,[84] and its representation from Uttar Pradesh dropped from 11 to 4. With 22 seats in the parliament, the Jana Sangh still remained one of the larger opposition parties. Among the opposition parties, only the Congress (0) with 10.42 per cent of the popular vote out-polled its 7.35 per cent. Only the Jana Sangh and the Communist Party of India (Marxist) managed to maintain their 1967–69 voting strengths, perhaps indicating greater partisanship among supporters of these two ideological parties.

When the general council of the Jana Sangh met at Jaipur, the leadership came in for severe criticism from the party cadre. Many delegates blamed the losses on the party's unreliable coalition partners and on the rightist tarring it received from its association with the 'grand alliance'. They demanded that the party stay out of future national electoral alliances, and proposed that the party contest the 1972 state assembly elections on its own. The party leadership was forced to reverse its alliance policy in the face of mass discontent from the cadre.[85]

Such open friction between the leadership and the cadre was rare, because the Jana Sangh leadership usually solicited the opinion of the cadre at the local level before reaching a final decision. The local units met at least once a month and were required to discuss issues brought to them by a higher unit. In the case of an electoral alliance to fight the 1971 elections, the Jana Sangh leadership did not have much time to canvass the local units, and it made a decision that the cadre strongly opposed. In the face of the criticism, Vajpayee concurred with the majority opinion that the party must more effectively portray itself as committed to social and economic justice.[86]

The Jana Sangh's performance in the 1972 state assembly elections was also disappointing. For the first time, the party did not improve upon its performance in previous elections. Prime Minister Gandhi's Congress party strengthened its position in the sixteen states and two Union territories in which assembly elections were held. In Madhya Pradesh, the Jana Sangh won only 48 of the 296 assembly seats, though it received almost one-third of the popular vote. In Punjab, without the support from the Akali Dal, the Jana Sangh lost every assembly seat. It also drew a blank in Andhra Pradesh, Karnataka, and West Bengal. Its representation dropped from 12 to 2 in Haryana, 33 to 5 in Delhi Metropolitan Council, and 22 to 8 in the Rajasthan assembly. The Congress had reached an agreement with the former ruler of Kota, and it won all 16 seats in Kota division, a region which had given the Jana Sangh 11 seats in 1967.[87] However, the Jana Sangh was only 1 seat down in the Bihar assembly. It won 2 additional seats in Gujarat and one additional seat in Maharashtra; it retained 3 seats in the Jammu and Kashmir assembly.

The leadership called the general council together to discuss the elections, and the delegates' criticism of the leadership matched that of the Jaipur meeting the previous year. While party leaders blamed the defeat on the Congress 'misuse' of the government machinery and on the 'credit' it took for the military victory over Pakistan in late 1971, the delegates were not prepared to let the leadership escape at least part of the blame.[88] Vajpayee admitted 'full responsibility' and asked Dr Bhai Mahavir, a Jana Sangh vice-president and member of the Rajya Sabha,[89] to chair the meeting in his place so that the delegates could freely criticize him. Their criticism centred on the party's conservative image and its weak support base among the poor. Many delegates charged that the leadership had done little to dispel the popular conception of the Jana Sangh as a party of the rich. To cite a specific example, they blamed the leadership for not formulating a clear land ceiling policy. They passed a resolution proposing that rural land holdings should not exceed a size which could provide a Rs 1500 per month income for a family of five. They also passed a resolution limiting a family's expendable income to Rs 2000 per month, with the excess income invested to generate greater production and higher employment. To mobilize additional support, they decided to establish front organizations among youth, women and the Scheduled Castes. They also decided to step up efforts among Sikhs and Muslims.[90]

The party leadership did not take much convincing to make the Jana Sangh a party 'of the common man'. At the party's 1972 session at Bhagalpur, Vajpayee reported to the party delegates that the Jana Sangh would launch a campaign to mobilize the support of 'landless labour, small peasants, Harijans, workers, and employees in mills and offices, youths— particularly students, artisans, and small-scale entrepreneurs'. In line with Upadhyaya's earlier justification of agitation as a tactic, Vajpayee informed the delegates that 'we extend Jana Sangh's activities beyond the confines of parliamentary politics. It is essential that our approach should not be merely reformist. Jana Sangh has to organize popular discontent and exert itself as a militant and dynamic party.'[91]

The leadership prepared the party cadre for a major leftward thrust at its eighteenth annual session in Kanpur in early 1973. At that session, Lal Krishna Advani, former Jana Sangh speaker in the Delhi Metropolitan Council, was selected to replace Vajpayee, who was placed in charge of the campaign for the important 1974 assembly elections in Uttar Pradesh.[92] Advani's presidential address to the delegates focused on the nation's economy. It included attacks on 'monopoly houses'; it advocated a policy of enforced austerity through strict controls of imports and a consumption tax on family expenditures above Rs 2500 per month. He advocated an income policy which would permit the highest salaries to be no more than 20 times the lowest.[93] Resolutions were passed directing the party leadership to speak out publicly for the dispossessed and to organize mass demonstrations on their behalf.

Conferences of women, farmers, and youth met concurrently with the eighteenth annual session. The women's conference proposed that men and women receive equal pay for comparable work and that nurseries be established for the children of working mothers. The farmers' conference demanded a massive public works programmes in rural areas, rural drought relief, and a need-based wage policy for the rural labourer. The youth conference proposed the reduction of the voting age from 21 to 18, as well as a government-funded unemployment benefit scheme, joint participation of teachers and students in university policy-making bodies, and a termination of imported technology, foreign investment and aid. Vajpayee, in his address to the youth conference, advocated a two-year compulsory national service scheme for every sixteen-year-old man and woman. He suggested that the service include job-oriented instruction suited to the 'aptitude' of the participants as well as military training for both men and women.[94]

After 1972, the Jana Sangh embarked on a much more activist strategy, and party volunteers in several places participated in demonstrations against the rise in prices and against the government's handling of the severe drought situation. In a speech in Bombay on 23 April 1973 Vajpayee told his audience that the party would not hesitate to encourage people to break those laws which, in its view, tended to keep basic commodities scarce. He even expressed sympathy for those who looted government fair price shops to get food for their families.[95] The party had now officially adopted agitation as a tactic to express its dissatisfaction, and agitation provided the party with new opportunities to mobilize support.[96]

REVOLT ON THE RIGHT

The party's rapid shift in policies and tactics left Madhok and other conservatives an isolated minority. Following the working committee's deliberations at Kanpur in February 1972, Madhok left for Delhi without participating in the plenary session of the party. The working committee had discussed and rejected a twenty-two page list of recommendations from Madhok, in which he recommended a new set of party policies and a restructuring of the party organization. Regarding party rules, he advocated changes which would give more power to the lower units of the party hierarchy. Besides proposing the abolition of the position of organizing secretary, Madhok suggested that the delegates to the plenary session themselves elect half of the party's working committee and that they nominate presidential candidates. Under Jana Sangh rules, the president selected the working committee, and the state working committees nominated presidential candidates. The intent of his proposals was to transfer power from the secretarial network to the grass-roots level of the party.[97]

With the firm backing of the secretarial network and the RSS leadership, Advani dealt firmly with Madhok. In a letter to Madhok, Advani detailed Madhok's 'indiscipline'. He pointed out that Madhok had opposed the Central government employees' strike even when the party had officially backed the workers' demands. He reminded Madhok of his circulation of a pamphlet at the 1969 Patna plenary session which criticized the party's policies. He pointed out that Madhok had bestowed respectability on groups of expelled Jana Sangh members in Bihar and Madhya Pradesh by addressing their meetings. To demonstrate how isolated he was from the other party leaders, Advani reminded Madhok that the general council was unanimous in its opposition to his activities.

Not only did Advani question Madhok's 'character', but he refused to submit Madhok's case to Golwalkar, as Madhok had earlier suggested. He informed Madhok that Golwalkar 'would also emphasize the importance of discipline and collective functioning in any organization'. On a matter as important as this, Advani very likely had already conferred with Golwalkar before writing to Madhok.

Madhok refused to apologize for his 'indiscipline' and asked for the 'trust' and 'confidence' of his colleagues. Advani expelled him from primary membership in the party for three years.

Madhok informed the press that his expulsion was another sign of a 'fascist attitude' within the Jana Sangh.[98] In a letter which he circulated among the party cadre, he wrote that the Jana Sangh had developed into an RSS front organization and, while not personally opposed to the RSS, he was against its 'dominating' influence in the party.[99] He wrote that the Jana Sangh was not able to mobilize additional support because of RSS influence. He identified Vajpayee as the leader of the forces which were subverting the party's traditional ideological orientation. Madhok wrote that Vajpayee's affiliation with the pro-communist Students' Federation during his youth could explain his 'leftist' ideology and his 'softness' for the Nehru family.[100] Madhok left the Jana Sangh to establish his own political party.[101]

The Madhok episode did not deter the Jana Sangh's efforts to make itself a 'party of the common man'. In early November 1973 the Jana Sangh leadership called upon its members to agitate against mounting inflation. The party resorted to its new agitational approach by loaning cadre to Jaya Prakash Narayan's movement of 'Total Revolution' in Bihar.[102] That campaign grew into a national political challenge directed against the prime minister, and the Jana Sangh became one of the constituent units in the National Coordination Committee, established by the leadership of the Jana Sangh, the Samyukta Socialist Party, the Congress (0), and the Bharatiya Lok Dal in late 1974 to assist Narayan's movement.[103]

The closer links among the opposition parties were to pay rich electoral dividends. In March 1975 the four opposition parties participating in the National Coordination Committee formed the Janata Morcha to contest the June state assembly elections in Gujarat. In those elections, the Congress party won a higher percentage of the vote (41 per cent compared to 38 per cent for the opposition party alliance), though it won fewer seats (75 compared to 86).[104] The four opposition parties formed a United Front ministry in the 182 member assembly, with the support of the twelve-member Kisan Mazdoor Lok Paksha, a party representing the interests of rural landlords. The Jana Sangh itself won 18 of the 40 seats it contested.

The revolts against the Jana Sangh leadership between 1972 and 1974 could not elicit much support from the organizational cadre. The party, by recruiting a majority of its cadre from the RSS, was guaranteed a high degree of organizational stability. The party organization gave its organizing secretaries sufficient power to enforce compliance with party directives. Most of the organizing secretaries were swayamsevaks; many were pracharaks. For them to break loose from the party would mean separating themselves from comrades with whom they had worked for many years.

When interviewing Vasantrao Krishna Oke, who had rebelled against both the RSS and the Jana Sangh, it was obvious that his most painful recollection was the memory of separation from former RSS colleagues who ignored him during his 'fall from grace.' It was equally obvious that their acceptance of him was perceived as a kind of personal redemption. These men believe in the value of organized effort and are loathe to tolerate any person who threatens to splinter either the RSS or its affiliates.

The organizing secretaries, many without families or other social or economic commitments, orchestrated the party's more populist orientation, as Madhok and other dissident conservatives recognized. By and large, pracharaks appeared to take seriously the social and economic implications of reformist advaita vedanta. As gatekeepers to party recruitment and advancement, the organizing secretaries and senior-level secretaries established the boundaries within which party policy was set. Those who sought to influence Jana Sangh policy had first to convince them that the proposed policy was consistent with the Hindu-oriented integrationist belief system of the RSS. The organizers, in turn, also had to translate the belief system into strategies and policies capable of mobilizing support.

THE SWAYAMSEVAKS IN POLITICS

Our initial fieldwork suggested to us that the secretarial network of the Jana Sangh, drawn almost exclusively from the RSS and guided by the full-time pracharaks, enforced commitment both to the world view of the RSS and to acceptable patterns of organizational behaviour by recruiting other swayamsevaks to fill party positions. To test this, we interviewed a sample of cadre at all levels of the party organization in three parliamentary constituencies (Allahabad City in Uttar Pradesh, Sadar in Delhi, and Bombay North-east in Maharashtra) between 1968 and 1971. The 190 interviews were taken starting at the bottom of the party hierarchy from officers serving in committees at the sthaniya (block, level I), the mandal (neighbourhood, level II), zilla (district, level III), the nagar (city, level IV), as well as in the state (level V) and national working committees (level VI).[105]

Table 5 shows that 90 per cent of the office-bearers in the sample had an RSS background. Notice that no non-RSS members were in the two highest party categories, and that non-RSS members were weakly represented at the district level (6.7 per cent), the most important decision-making body for the day-to-day activities of the party.

Table 5: RSS Membership by Jana Sangh Position Level

Jana Sangh	RSS (%)	Non-RSS (%)	Total (%)
Level I	32 (86.5)	5 (13.5)	37 (100.0)
Level II	68 (87.2)	10 (12.8)	78 (100.0)
Level III	28 (93.3)	2 (6.7)	30 (100.0)
Level IV	12 (85.7)	2 (14.3)	14 (100.0)
Level V	13 (100.0)	0 (0.0)	13 (100.0)
Level VI	18 (100.0)	0 (0.0)	18 (100.0)
Total	171 (90.0)	19 (10.0)	190 (100.0)

Similarly, we expected the secretarial gatekeepers of the party to select for higher party positions those who had already proved themselves in the RSS. Table 6 strongly backs the proposition that advancement in the Jana Sangh is related to prior advancement in the RSS. The swayamsevak who had already done well in the RSS, we assumed, had developed those organizational skills and behavioural values which gave him an advantage over others in the party. If socialization in the RSS provides the skills and attitudes required for holding a high party position, as Table 6 suggests, it follows that such socialization would also influence the rank at which swayamsevaks entered the party. This proposition is strongly supported by Table 7. Those given greater responsibilities in the RSS tended to enter the party at a higher rank than those who had not been given such responsibilities. Indeed, none of the other variables tested (see Appendix B) with party position gave as high a correlation as that between prior advancement in the RSS and party position.

The data in Tables 6 and 7 helps to explain the high degree of cohesion in the Jana Sangh (and in the other members of the 'family' which have a comparable recruitment policy). Group commitment is one of the most highly valued, of RSS norms, and one that lends itself to organizational cohesion. Consequently, the advancement of those swayamsevaks who have demonstrated leadership capacity is conducive to maintaining support for the goals of the party. A substantial body of research has shown that commitment to leaders tends to generate support for the leaders' norms and the norms of the organizations they represent.[106] Recruitment of local RSS achievers strengthened group cohesion in the party since many RSS members worked under their former RSS teachers within local party units. The deliberate recruitment of local RSS leaders strengthened not only compliance not only within the local party unit but also cohesion horizontally (between units on the same level) and vertically (between units at different levels). This could explain the comparatively low degree of factionalism within the party's organizational wing, even in those cases where the local leadership was instructed to support unpopular decisions (e.g., official language in Punjab). It could also explain the comparative lack of factionalism in the other members of the RSS 'family'.

Yet RSS informants admit that there is a rather heavy attrition rate from the RSS, particularly during late adolescence and early adulthood. Among the reasons are the concern of swayamsevaks (or their parents) that RSS membership will hinder their career possibilities or undermine their social status. Also, their commitment to the RSS might be weakened by new, and possibly conflicting, socialization experiences. Nevertheless, many members continue their participation—despite possible family opposition, various objective liabilities and counter-socialization. The extensive peer group contacts which the RSS provides for its members clearly has induced sufficiently strong consensual norms among a large number of swayamsevaks to resist pressures to leave it.[107] Those who remained had developed strong cohesive bonds in the RSS prior to membership in the Jana Sangh. It is likely that peer group cohesiveness was transferred to the Jana Sangh when the RSS member shifted to the party, since many shakha colleagues worked together in the party. Cohesiveness was also reinforced by continued participation in RSS activities after joining the Jana Sangh.

Table 6: RSS Position by Party Level

	Swayamsevak/Gatnaik/Shikshak/ Mukhya Shikshak/Karyavah Mandal/ Nagar/Zilla/Pracharak						
Level I	17	5	1	5	1	3	0
(%)	(53.2)	(15.6)	(3.1)	(15.6)	(3.1)	(9.4)	(0.0)
Level II	28	12	3	13	6	3	2
(%)	(41.8)	(17.9)	(4.5)	(19.3)	(9.0)	(4.5)	(3.0)
Level III	10	0	0	4	7	3	4
(%)	(35.7)	(0.0)	(0.0)	(14.3)	(25.0)	(10.7)	(14.3)
Level IV	4	0	1	1	3	2	1
(%)	(33.3)	(0.0)	(8.3)	(8.3)	(25.0)	(16.7)	(8.4)
Level V	3	0	0	2	0	4	4
(%)	(23.1)	(0.0)	(0.0)	(15.3)	(0.0)	(30.8)	(30.8)
Level VI	2	0	0	2	2	1	11
(%)	(11.1)	(0.0)	(0.0)	(11.1)	(11.1)	(5.6)	(61.1)
TOTAL	64 (37.6)	17 (10.0)	5 (2.9)	27 (15.9)	19 (11.3)	16 (9.4)	22 12.9)
Pearson correlation coefficient = 0.4871; Significance = 0.000							

Table 7: RSS Position by First Party Position

	Swayamsevak/Gatnaik/Shikshak/ Mukhya Shikshak/Karyavah Mandal/ Nagar/Zilla/Pracharak						
Level I	10	1	1	1	3	3	0
(%)	(52.5)	(5.3)	(5.3)	(5.3)	(15.8)	(15.8)	(0.0)
Level II	10	10	3	11	2	3	1
(%)	(25.0)	(25.0)	(7.5)	(27.5)	(5.0)	(7.5)	(2.5)
Level III	8	1	0	3	7	4	3
(%)	(30.9)	(3.8)	(0.0)	(11.5)	(26.9)	(15.4)	(11.5)
Level IV	4	0	0	2	3	1	1
(%)	(36.4)	(0.0)	(0.0)	(18.1)	(27.3)	(9.1)	(9.1)
Level V	3	0	0	0	1	0	11
(%)	(20.0)	(0.0)	(0.0)	(0.0)	(6.7)	(0.0)	(73.3)
Level VI	1	0	0	0	0	0	1
(%)	(50.0)	(0.0)	(0.0)	(0.0)	(0.0)	(0.0)	(50.0)
TOTAL	36 (31.9)	12 (10.6)	4 (3.5)	17 (15.0)	16 (14.3)	11 (9.7)	17 (15.0)
Pearson correlation coefficient = 0.3680; Significance = 0.001							

Long association with colleagues in the Jana Sangh also strengthened group bonds. At all levels of the party, the cadre commented that they were content to remain mere 'soldiers' in the cause, satisfied to serve in whatever capacity party leaders deemed them best suited. Whatever the accuracy of such statements, the data reveals that the cadre tended to hold their positions for rather long periods of time. Over half of the sample held only one position in the party. Almost 60 per cent held their current position for at least four years,[108] and slightly more than 40 per cent for at least six years. Given the extended time the Jana Sangh members remained in their positions and interacted with a common peer group, it was likely that the cadre in an organization unit had a high degree of loyalty to each other. Research on groups with a low turnover among group members suggests that the members of the group are likely to be committed to those norms which encourage continued participation in the group.[109] This might explain the apparent lack of ambition for higher position among many RSS participants.

Universal suffrage in a system of single members constituencies[110] forced the Jana Sangh leadership to mobilize support on a larger scale than any of the other RSS affiliates, thus causing a higher degree of tension between the sometimes conflicting urges for ideological consistency and group solidarity on the one hand and electoral support on the other. Selective recruitment of the cadre promoted organizational cohesion, but it also placed limits on the party's mobilizing capacity. The belief system on which the party was grounded threatened the world view of a substantial part of the population—Muslims, Christians and those committed to Western models of modernization, among others. The relatively controlled recruitment system made the Jana Sangh a less attractive political instrument for local notables than those political parties which enabled group and factional leaders to exert exogamous influence on party policy. The centralized decision-making system managed by the organizing secretaries of the Jana Sangh sometimes resulted in situations where the cadre was required to support policies which, while ideologically 'correct,' resulted in widespread loss of electoral support (e.g., advocating Punjabi as an official language in Punjab).

We asked the interviewees a set of questions regarding their opinions on a set of political issues to determine how closely their personal views coincided with what we considered to be the RSS position. The interviewees were asked to state their reaction (agreement or disagreement) to a series of normative statements. Each statement in Table 8 is a paraphrase of the situational statement used in the interview schedule.

Table 8: Value Orientations of Jana Sangh Cadre

Value Statement	% Agree	% Disagree
1. Income variations should be narrowed.	97	3
2. Cow slaughter must be prohibited.	94	6
3. Class identification weakens national loyalty.	83	17
4. The state has responsibility for maintaining minimum living standards.	79	21
5. Workers should share in ownership and management of industry.	76	24
6. Strike is a legitimate technique for workers to employ.	72	28
7. Foreign aid and assistance would help India to overcome its economic problems.	71	29
8. The powers of the Central government should be strengthened.	71	29

Value Statement	% Agree	% Disagree
9. Religious leaders provide valuable services to preserve national well-being.	43	57
10. Caste loyalty should disappear.	41	59
11. The major industries should be nationalized.	39	61
12. The government should take control of all educational and social welfare activities.	28	72
13. A democratic form of government cannot generate the strong leadership required for national progress.	28	72
14. Agriculture should be organized on cooperative basis.	24	76
15. It is socially wrong to permit inter-caste marriages.	22	78
16. English should be retained as a link language.	14	86
17. Since creation of Pakistan, Muslims have been loyal to India.	10	90

A central theme of the RSS belief system is the restoration of social harmony by more equitably distributing access to economic and political power. Relating to this theme are statements referring to collapsing income differences (Table 8: No. 1), eliminating class and caste exclusiveness (Nos 3,10,15), and entrusting ownership of the productive process to the workers (No. 5). On all these statements, we compared the answers with RSS position and party position, and discovered that those in the higher ranks of the party and/ or the RSS were more likely to give answers that conformed to the RSS belief system than those in the lower ranks. On the question of the patriotism of India's Muslims (No. 17), those who had held a higher position in the RSS and in the party also indicated a greater willingness to accommodate Muslims, perhaps reflecting their greater commitment to eliminating those social and cultural barriers which separate Indians from each other.

On some issues, the responses appear inconsistent with the RSS belief system. Two examples are the high degree of support for the right to strike (No. 6), and the opposition to agriculture organized on a cooperative basis (No. 14). The former assumes a certain measure of class consciousness, and the latter goes against the corporatist nature of the belief system. Strike was considered one of the more effective forms of protest against entrenched interest and an unresponsive government. Cooperative agriculture was opposed on the grounds that it would provide bureaucrats and politicians more opportunities to exploit the farmer. The labour affiliates of the RSS had on occasion expressed support for cooperative agriculture; however, the Jana Sangh had consistently opposed the idea. Rather, it had advocated stricter enforcement of land ceiling legislation and the distribution of land to the actual tiller of the soil.

Distrust of the government and the bureaucracy among the respondents in this sample showed up in the negative response regarding the nationalization of industry (No. 11), and regarding exclusive government control of education and social welfare (No. 11 and No. 12). However, there is a certain degree of ambiguity in the world view of the RSS regarding the government. On the one hand, there is support for a unitary state strong enough to defend the country from external foes and from internal challenges. On the other, there is a pervasive suspicion that bureaucrats and politicians are self-centred and corrupt. Nonetheless, the Jana Sangh cadre did not oppose government interference in the economy or society generally. Indeed, the answers suggest that Myron Weiner's proposition—that Indians expect the government to satisfy their economic and social aspirations—applies to most in this sample.[111]

Yet support for strengthening the power of the central government (No. 8) appears inconsistent with the populist, anti-establishment mood of the cadre. Two considerations might explain the favourable response to the issue. One is the fear that centrifugal forces are a real threat to the unity of India and that Central government must have more police power to deal with the growing politicization of regional and linguistic demands and sectarian loyalties. The other consideration is the view that the government should use its powers to improve the economy generally and the well-being of individuals specifically. Note the strong support for the fourth item (i.e., No. 4; Table 8), which addresses this point. However, the respondents were quite clear that a stronger Central government does not imply an authoritarian form of government (No. 13). Many of the respondents, in answering No. 13, commented that a democratic form of government, whatever its faults, provided more opportunities to reorient government policy 'in favour of the little man' than an authoritarian system, which many assumed would serve the interests of the powerful elite.

The cadre in this sample, on the whole, supported substantial changes in India's social and economic systems.

While they backed proposals that would result in a wider dispersal of economic and political power, they did not, in principle, support a more restricted role for the government in the country's development. The RSS belief system legitimizes protest against India's economic and political systems and hence, justifies the Jana Sangh's efforts to mobilize the discontented.

According to the interview data, those most likely to agree with the belief system of the RSS were the cadre who had demonstrated successful RSS socialization, as measured by prior advancement through the ranks of the RSS. The RSS belief system, however, is on a very high level of generality, and thus, it is not a precise blueprint for action on specific issues. The affiliates are responsible for applying the broad ideological principles to their own specific areas of interest, and they have considerable freedom of manoeuvre on this matter. Indeed, they have often influenced the views of the RSS regarding a wide range of issues. They have on occasion even acted contrary to the wishes of RSS leaders or the official policy set by the central assembly and the central executive committee of the RSS.

Despite the obvious limits to the Jana Sangh's mobilizing capacity imposed by the symbiotic linkage to the RSS, the cadre demonstrated considerable skill at party building and mobilizing support. They used political campaigns to mobilize electoral support. Party spokesmen promised benefits to potential support groups (e.g., higher pay to schoolteachers, higher procurement prices for farm commodities, more physical amenities to slum dwellers, etc.). The party appealed to diffuse nationalist and communal sentiments; party cadre and legislators also mobilized support through services they could render, such as providing citizens access to government officials, helping to unravel the maze of government regulations, and mediating community disputes. Starting in the 1970s, the party began to employ agitation on a wide scale to tap the discontent against inadequate government performance.

The RSS leaders, for their part, were initially hesitant to accept the legitimacy of the political system established in the immediate post-Independence period, but over time they began to take a more instrumental view of the political process. No Jana Sangh official proposed any fundamental change in India's constitutional system, and RSS theorists have advanced such proposals more as a theoretical exercise than as a real call for change. Undoubtedly, at least part of this support for democracy comes from the recognition that the RSS cluster of organizations has a better opportunity to carry out its work under a democratic system than under some authoritarian form of government.

6

The Triumph of Activism

The RSS in the 1970s confronted a series of political Challenges that pushed it and its affiliates towards a significantly higher level of activism. These challenges buttressed the position of activist leaders who wanted to make their organizations more relevant to the practical problems faced by the people, and who were more willing to employ confrontational tactics to do so. While there are many senior figures who still see the RSS role in the limited context of character building, the need for political protection in the 1970s tilted the scales, perhaps decisively, towards the activist side though the RSS continued to shun a political role for itself.[1] Direct political action would undermine the role the RSS defined for itself as a moral guide above partisan strife. Direct involvement in politics would also again make it a likely target of political attack.

By the mid-1970s, when a state of Emergency was declared and the RSS was banned, the RSS was prepared to cooperate closely with a wide range of groups, many of whom had previously demanded restrictions on its activities. Mutual suspicions were significantly reduced during the 1975–77 Emergency when the RSS cadre worked closely with a wide variety of groups to oppose the restrictions on civil liberties. The 'family' of RSS organizations adopted a more liberal interpretation of Hindu nationalism. While the RSS (and its affiliates) is still criticized for its Hindu orientation, the RSS is no longer the pariah organization that it was for most of the period since India's independence in 1947.

POLITICAL ASSERTIVENESS OF THE RSS

By the mid-1960s, the RSS was beginning to regain its self-confidence. The organization began to add new shakhas, members, and full-time workers, which enabled it to breathe renewed life into the affiliates. Signs of the renewed assertiveness were Golwalkar's acceptance in 1964 of an invitation to address RSS-affiliated groups in Burma (now Myanmar) and the organization's offer in 1965 to King Mahendra of Nepal to address a Makar Sankrant (winter solstice) festival. The Government of India, probably reflecting the still deep suspicions of the RSS, refused to allow the visit of the Nepalese king or to permit Golwalkar to leave the country. Still another indication of a more assertive RSS was the address of General Secretary Deoras to Jana Sangh delegates attending the 1965 annual session at Gwalior, the first time a national RSS official had done so.[2]

Suspicions of the political influence of the RSS, stoked by the success of the Jana Sangh in the 1967 national elections and subsequent state elections (attributed in part to the help given it by the RSS), made the RSS a political target. The split of the Congress party in late 1969, raising the possibility of a non-Congress coalition government at the Centre with Jana Sangh participation, further stoked the fires of concern regarding the political intentions of the RSS. In addition, apprehensions regarding the RSS were exacerbated by a series of communal riots in the late 1960s. The Jana Sangh for its part was branded as communal because of its links with the RSS, and those opposition parties which cooperated with the Jana Sangh were tarred with a similar communal brush. Some senior figures in the Congress party even sought to discredit their factional opponents by charging them with being RSS sympathizers.

The mounting criticism of the RSS in the late 1960s, including demands at very high levels of the governing Congress party that it be banned, alarmed the RSS leadership. The need for political protection again become salient. Against this backdrop, the RSS leadership supported a united front among the non-communist opposition parties to place a brake on the power of the Congress party. The central policymaking body of the RSS—the Akhil Bharatiya Pratinidhi Sabha (the central assembly)—gave its blessing to United Front governments which had been formed in several states.[3] Balasaheb Deoras, general secretary of the RSS between 1965 and 1973, encouraged the increasing activism of the student and labour affiliates (the Vidyarthi Parishad and Bharatiya Mazdoor Sangh, respectively). The RSS also launched its own mass public relations campaign in the late 1970s to counter charges regarding its alleged role in communal riots.

In the political field, the perceived need of the RSS for protection strengthened the activist stance associated with Atal Bihari Vajpayee, president of the Jana Sangh during the late 1960s and early 1970s. He advocated an alliance strategy among opposition parties; he orchestrated the party's leftward move on economic issues; and he involved the party in agitation. The party's more populist stance was resisted by a vocal conservative element led by Balraj Madhok, party president during 1966–1967.[4] Madhok tried unsuccessfully to get the RSS to back him in his dispute with Vajpayee. Bitterly criticizing the RSS, he left the Jana Sangh in 1972.

The poor performance in the 1971 parliamentary elections of the so-called 'grand alliance' of opposition parties which included the Jana Sangh, followed by the mediocre performance of the Jana Sangh in 1972 state assembly elections, forced the RSS to look for protection beyond traditional party structures. The RSS condoned the increasing militancy of its student and labour affiliates between 1973 and 1975. The most dramatic example of such militancy was the increasing politicization of the Vidyarthi Parishad, which became involved in movements directed against the Congress party governments of Bihar and Gujarat during this period. In Bihar, the Vidyarthi Parishad participated in a statewide protest that accepted the Total Revolution concept of Jaya Prakash Narayan, a respected social reformer. Narayan advocated the replacement of a political system dominated by professional politicians with a form of participatory democracy. He initially directed his criticism at the Bihar state government, but in late 1974 concluded that no fundamental changes could take place unless the Total Revolution was broadened to include the centre on the grounds that Prime Minister Indira Gandhi controlled the policies of the state governments dominated by her Congress party. Thus the stage was set for a confrontation between the RSS, which supported Narayan's Total Revolution, and Prime Minister Indira Gandhi.

The Government of India in 1975 charged that the RSS 'family' of organizations was a force in the movement supporting

Total Revolution, and with some justification.[5] From late 1974, the Jana Sangh was closely involved in Narayan's activities. On 25 and 26 November 1974, Jana Sangh leaders met in Delhi with their counterparts from other opposition parties to establish a national coordination committee that would back Narayan's movement of Total Revolution. *Organiser*, the unofficial mouthpiece of the RSS, reported that the Jana Sangh leaders were considering a 'prolonged war of attrition in which civil disobedience and no-tax campaigns would play their due role'.[6] Balasaheb Deoras, at a 1 December 1974 rally in Delhi, called Narayan a 'saint' who had 'come to rescue society in dark and critical times'.[7] The Vidyarthi Parishad was already deeply and directly associated with Total Revolution.

While the central assembly of the RSS took the unusual step of supporting Narayan's Total Revolution, the RSS leadership did not deviate from the organization's traditional policy of keeping the RSS itself aloof from political activities, and it continued to do so until after the July 1975 ban on the RSS. However, RSS leaders certainly encouraged swayamsevaks 'in their individual capacity' to get involved.[8]

Narayan for his part publicly praised the RSS (and other members of the 'family'). At the annual Jana Sangh session in March 1975, he dismissed charges that the Jana Sangh was 'fascist'.[9] At an RSS camp two months later, he complimented the RSS for its efforts to reduce economic inequality and corruption.[10] Such praise from a respected national figure like Narayan was a major achievement for the RSS as it reached out for public acceptance and for political protection.

Events during the first half of 1975 placed the RSS on a collision course with the government.[11] Following several months of student-led demonstrations in which the

Vidyarthi Parishad played an active role, the Congress party government of Gujarat resigned in March 1975. Several opposition parties, including the Jana Sangh, formed the Janata Morcha, an electoral alliance, which won a majority in the June assembly elections there. On 5 June, the Allahabad High Court declared Prime Minister Gandhi's 1971 election to parliament invalid due to violations of the election law. The opposition immediately called for her resignation. On 25 June opposition party leaders met with Narayan in Delhi to form the Lok Sangharsh Samiti (LSS), a coordinating body to direct the activities of the Total Revolution. Nana Deshmukh, the organizing secretary of the Jana Sangh and a former RSS pracharak, was named its general secretary. On the evening of 25 June, Narayan gave a speech in New Delhi appealing to the military not to obey an 'illegal order'. The next morning, Prime Minister Gandhi declared a state of Emergency, ordered the arrest of political opponents and imposed a censorship on the press. On 30 June Balasaheb Deoras was arrested,[12] and on 4 July the RSS and 23 other organizations were banned.[13]

The initial reaction of the RSS leadership was to take a cautious wait-and-see approach. When the government began to arrest RSS workers on a large scale, the RSS committed itself to working closely with the LSS, thus breaking the RSS tradition of keeping the organization aloof from political movements. This decision was taken at a meeting of leading pracharaks at Bombay in late July, after consultation with the incarcerated Balasaheb Deoras.[14] Holding primary responsibility for coordinating RSS work with the LSS were four zonal pracharaks: Yadavrao Joshi (south), Moropant Pingale (west), Bhaurao Deoras (east), and Rajendra Singh (north). In addition, Rambhau Godbole, the Jana Sangh's organizing secretary for Bihar and West Bengal, was instructed to establish contact with opposition party leaders; Moropant Pingale to coordinate activities with the LSS and to organize a nationwide satyagraha; Eknath Ranade, head of the Vivekananda Kendra, to handle discussions with the government.[15]

The July meeting in Bombay established a set of goals for the underground RSS organization: It would (1) maintain the morale of the swayamsevaks by providing them opportunities to meet together (e.g., prayer meetings, sporting events, etc.); (2) establish an underground press and distribution system for it; (3) prepare for a nationwide satyagraha, establishing contact with significant non-political figures and with prominent representatives of the minority communities; and (4) solicit overseas Indian support for the RSS in the underground activities of the LSS. Regarding this last goal, the RSS made use of the Indians for Democracy, an organization established in the US immediately after the Emergency. In November 1976 the Friends of India Society, International, was formed in England to mobilize overseas swayamsevaks for the same purpose.

The grass-roots structure of the LSS included many RSS workers, which presented the RSS cadre with an unprecedented opportunity to gain political experience and to establish a working relationship with political leaders. This RSS activism promoted the careers of dynamic pracharaks, such as Rajendra Singh (now the RSS general secretary) and H. V. Sheshadri (now zonal *pracharak* for the southern states, where the RSS has recently experienced its most rapid growth).

RSS activism reached a high point during the 1975–77 Emergency and set the stage for a more dynamic organization in the post-1977 period. Regarding the Emergency period itself, RSS publications claim that the swayamsevaks played the key role in the underground movement, constituting the 'backbone' of the LSS, according to one senior RSS official.[16] The RSS had also mobilized its extensive support network among overseas Indians to publicize the anti-Emergency effort internationally and to smuggle literature into the country. Whatever the extent of the cadre's role, no one doubts that it was significant. Even Prime Minister Indira Gandhi admitted in late 1975 that 'there has been no let up in its [RSS] activity. They are now functioning in an organized underground manner. Even in a region like Kerala, the RSS has established a foothold.'[17] RSS sources claim that over 25,000 of its members were arrested under the Defence of India rules and an equal number under the Maintenance of Internal Security Act, many of them during the November 1975–January 1976 satyagraha organized by the underground RSS.[18] Nana Deshmukh, a former RSS pracharak with close ties to the top RSS leadership, was asked by Narayan to assume 'full powers' of the LSS when Narayan was arrested.[19] Deshmukh had earlier been selected by Narayan to be the secretary of the LSS, perhaps because of the major involvement of the RSS 'family' of organizations in the movement of Total Revolution. Following Deshmukh's arrest in October 1975, Ravindra Varma, a Congress (O) politician, took charge. He was succeeded in November 1976 by D. B. Thengadi, a former RSS pracharak who was then general secretary of the Bharatiya Mazdoor Sangh.

The RSS also contributed directly to the opposition Janata alliance campaign prior to the March 1977 general elections. So worried was the government by its support to the Janata alliance, according to M. V. Moghe (RSS *baudhik pramukh*, the official in charge of propaganda), that Prime Minister Gandhi instructed a 'high official' to meet underground RSS leaders two weeks prior to the polling to discuss an offer to lift the ban if the RSS would withdraw its support from the Janata alliance.[20] The ban on the JRSS, however, was not lifted until 21 March 1977, after the victory of the Janata alliance.

SUCCESSES AND CHALLENGES:1977–1980

The RSS emerged from its 21-month ban (4 July 1975–21 March 1977) far more self-confident about its role in Indian society than at any time since Independence. The cadre had developed a sense of mission (as they had during the first ban in 1948–1949) that envisaged a programme far more ambitious than character building. And this time—unlike 1949—there was a sarsanghchalak, Balasaheb Deoras, who was inclined in that direction himself.

Regarding politics, the RSS—whose cadre had campaigned vigorously for the Janata alliance candidates—took at least partial credit for the defeat of Prime Minister Gandhi in the 16–20 March 1977 national elections. That defeat was most dramatically registered in the seven Hindi-speaking states, where Gandhi's Congress party won only 2 of the 237 parliamentary seats. The Janata Party, in contrast, swept this area and won 298 out of 542 seats nationally. The share of the Jana Sangh group, whose support base was in the Hindi-speaking states, was 93 seats, making it the largest element in the Janata alliance.[21]

The Janata alliance, which became the Janata Party on 1 May 1977, formed India's first non-Congress national government, and Prime Minister Morarji Desai's cabinet included three Jana Sangh members (all RSS members): Atal Bihari Vajpayee, Minister of Foreign Affairs; Lal Krishna Advani, Minister of Information and Broadcasting; and Brij Lal Varma, Minister of Industry. After the 20 June 1977 assembly elections, Jana Sangh chief ministers (all RSS members) presided over three state governments (Himachal Pradesh, Madhya Pradesh and Rajasthan) and one Union Territory (Delhi), and members of the Jana Sangh group were included in the cabinets of other states where the Janata Party won majorities.

The Janata Party from the start was a fragile coalition. Party leaders battled against each other to improve their own standing and that of their group. The RSS, closely identified in the popular mind with the Jana Sangh group, inevitably became an issue as the groups manoeuvres for influence. In addition, the RSS had taken a direct political role during the Emergency and during the 1977 campaign, and many wondered about its long-range political intentions.

The RSS for its part continued to reject publicly a direct role for itself in politics. A direct political role would have undermined the RSS self-conception as a moral guide above the mundane conflict of personalities. Its leaders probably realized that direct involvement in politics would again make the RSS the object of intense political attack, which would lead to renewed demands for restrictions on its activities. However, the RSS leadership did envisage some kind of cooperative relationship with the government. Indeed, the RSS probably expected favourable treatment from the government. Deoras, for example, told newsmen on 11 May 1977 that the RSS and the government could cooperate in such areas as education, social welfare, youth affairs, but 'the Swayamsevaks of the Sangh are not volunteers who will spread the durries and fix the mike for some leaders to come and make speeches'.[22] But the political situation was so radically different from the past that the RSS leadership probably did not know how it would work out the anticipated cooperation. Moreover, the Jana Sangh ceased to exist as a separate party, and its own members had to work out a relationship with the other constituents of the Janata Party, some of whom were deeply suspicious of the RSS.

Outside the political arena, the RSS leaders must have been pleased by the post-1977 experience. The RSS (and its affiliates) experienced a surge in membership. Its general secretary reported in early 1978 that the number of shakhas had increased from 8500 in 1975 to 11,000 in 1977.[23] One year later, the RSS announced the addition of another 2000 shakhas.[24] Assuming 50–100 participants per shakha, this represents an additional participation rate of 225,000 to 450,000 within two years, the fastest growth of the RSS to that date. (It was to grow even faster during the next several years.) The general secretary reported that the number of shakhas had increased to 17,000 by 1981, an increase of 3000 over the previous year.[25] He reported still another 3000 new shakhas during 1981.[26] The most rapid expansion was in the four southern states in which the RSS previously was weakly represented.[27] According to one survey, by the mid-1980s the RSS had shakhas in nearly all the 5000 villages of Kerala, undoubtedly because of Hindu apprehensions over growing assertiveness of the state's communists and Muslims.[28] A Government of India, Ministry of Home Affairs, report claimed that regular attendance nationally in 1981 was nearly one million, and that the financial contributions at Gurudakshina were over 10 million rupees (about $1.1 million at that time).[29]

The RSS affiliates also expanded rapidly. For example, the Bharatiya Mazdoor Sangh, its labour affiliate, claimed that it had grown from about 1.2 million members in 1977 to about 1.8 million in 1980, making it the second largest national union after the Indian National Trade Union Congress.[30] The Vidyarthi Parishad, its student affiliate, grew from 170,000 to 250,000 members between 1977 and 1982,[31] further strengthening the Vidyarthi Parishad's position as the largest student group in India.

But this apparent success had its costs. It aroused suspicions within the Janata Party that the RSS would use its impressive organizational resources to strengthen the position of the Jana Sangh group, already the largest single element within the Janata Party. Suspicions of the Jana Sangh group's links to the RSS were fuelled by the participation of many of its members in RSS activities. In addition, Jana Sangh members continued to meet with RSS leaders, as they had done in the past, to talk about mutual problems.[32] Fearing that the RSS would act as a parallel political cadre not subject to party discipline, a growing number of Janata Party figures called for the RSS to merge with one of the Janata Party's affiliated organizations. Initially, the demand was restricted largely to members of the Socialist Party's faction, though Charan Singh's Bharatiya Lok Dal (BLD) adopted a very critical approach to the RSS in 1978 when the Jana Sangh group stood in the way of Singh's national ambitions by its steadfast backing of Prime Minister Morarji Desai.

Not surprisingly, the RSS leadership fiercely resisted the merger proposal as did the leaders of the various affiliates.

On 23 August 1977 the general secretary of the RSS stated, 'It should be clearly understood that we are nobody's Boys [sic] Scouts.'[33] He doubted that the labour or student affiliates of the RSS would merge with their Janata Party counterparts. They did not.

THE DUAL-MEMBERSHIP CONTROVERSY

When it became clear that the RSS leadership would not consider the merger proposition, its critics shifted tactics. They demanded that all Janata members sever their ties with the RSS as a condition for membership in the party. They argued that the Janata Party's interim constitution had an exclusionary clause denying membership to anyone belonging to another 'political party, communal or other, which has a separate membership, constitution and programme [sic]'.[34] The Jana Sangh group dismissed this argument on the grounds that the RSS is not a political party. The critics of the RSS then proposed an amendment to the exclusionary clause that would remove the word 'political'; but the Janata Party working committee at its 21 December 1977 meeting, facing stiff Jana Sangh resistance, took no action.[35]

But the dual-membership issue, as the question came to be called, refused to go away. Indeed, it became an even more strident and divisive problem. The controversy was one of the proximate causes for the break-up of the Janata Party in mid-July 1979, when Charan Singh and his Bharatiya Lok Dal group (as well as others) walked out of the party. The persistence of the issue underscored the fragile nature of the Janata Party, more a governing coalition than a party. The dual-membership issue re-emerged with each major jolt to the balance of power within the party. It was used both to gain leverage against the Jana Sangh group and to damage the Jana Sangh group's capacity to mobilize additional support within the party. The issue reflected the fear that the relatively cohesive Jana Sangh group would use its organizational strength to take over the party. This fear was a major reason the Janata Party was never able to hold organizational elections, forcing the party to function on an ad hoc basis at all levels.

The dual-membership question could be contained as long as the two largest groups in the Janata Party—the Jana Sangh and the BLD—cooperated, and they did work together rather amicably for about a year. For example, after the June 1977 state assembly elections, the two groups were able to arrange for a distribution of power in the six Hindi-speaking states captured by the Janata Party (Bihar, Haryana and Uttar Pradesh to the BLD group; and Himachal Pradesh, Madhya Pradesh and Rajasthan to the Jana Sangh). This state-level cooperation, however, could not be insulated from the jockeying for power between party barons at the national level. The Jana Sangh group's steadfast support of Prime Minister Morarji Desai, against whom Charan Singh was engaged in a struggle for power, eventually earned it the enmity of the BLD group. This development at the national level in turn exacerbated the relations of the two groups at the state level. The BLD by mid-1978 had become one of the major advocates for barring RSS members from joining the Janata party.[36]

Jana Sangh leaders for their part publicly resisted any move to deny RSS members the right to participate in Janata Party activities.[37] Atal Bihari Vajpayee, during the height of the controversy in early 1979, warned that the Jana Sangh group might pull out of the government and the party if the critics of the RSS had their way on this question.[38] Leaders of the Jana Sangh group could not accept an exclusion of RSS members and still expect to retain their strong bargaining position within the Janata Party. Their bargaining position was based on the size of the Jana Sangh group, and many Jana Sangh legislators, if forced to choose between loyalty to the Janata Party and continued membership in the RSS, would have chosen the latter. The only way out of this impasse would be for the RSS itself to bar its members from holding elective offices. Not surprisingly, Janata Party leaders, seeking to preserve party unity, began to make overtures to the RSS to do just this. Balasaheb Deoras, for his part, made a public announcement in early July that the RSS would stay aloof from the next general elections, a statement that could well have been intended as a warning that the Janata Party could lose a valuable resource if the attack continued.[39]

A fundamental problem between the Jana Sangh group and its opponents on the dual-membership issue was their differing interpretation over what is political. Charan Singh (and others) defined politics broadly to mean influence, while the Jana Sangh group (and the RSS) defined it narrowly to mean direct organizational involvement in elections and in governing. The RSS leadership clearly intended to keep the RSS outside the formal structure of politics, but the critics of the RSS insisted that its potential to influence Jana Sangh politicians also had to be limited.

When the Janata Party finally began to unravel in mid-July 1979, many of those who left the party mentioned, to justify their action, both the unresolved dual-membership controversy and the exclusively Hindu nature of the RSS. On 9 July Raj Narain, perhaps the most outspoken critic of the RSS, left the Janata Party to form the Janata Party (Secular) to distinguish his party from the 'unsecular' Janata party, and his exit was followed soon after by Charan Singh and others. Manoeuvring began immediately inside the Janata Party to excise the RSS issue in a way that would stem the flow from the party, while not alienating the large Jana Sangh group. Senior party leaders, including Vajpayee, worked out for party consideration a formula barring the membership of anyone who espoused a theocratic state.[40] However, the Jana Sangh group issued a statement on 13 July announcing that its members had not altered their stance towards the RSS.[41] Many Jana Sangh legislators pointed out that the RSS did not define Hindu rashtra, the RSS term for the ideal state, as a theocratic state. Indeed, Balasaheb Deoras issued a statement on 16 July stating that the RSS supported a secular state and respected all religions.[42]

By 15 July, Prime Minister Desai had lost his parliamentary majority and was forced to resign, though it was still possible that the Janata Party (with some 200 members still the largest group in parliament) might regain power by working out an alliance with one or more of the other party leaders. As part of their strategy, the Jana Sangh and the socialist groups unsuccessfully requested Desai to step down in favour of Jagjivan Ram, a respected Scheduled Caste politician who might have brought support from other parties. By this move, the Jana Sangh group could also erode the popular image of itself as a representative of the interests of traders and brahmins. Besides such tactics, defusing the RSS issue remained a high priority item as the various party barons tried to put together a parliamentary majority.

The Janata Party could not specifically exclude RSS members from holding party office since such a step would drive most of the Jana Sangh group out of the party at a time when their votes were desperately needed. The only feasible option was to convince the RSS itself to bar those swayamsevaks holding party office or an elected position from taking part in activities of the RSS. With this objective in mind, Chandra Sekhar, the president of the Janata Party, met with both Balasaheb Deoras and Rajendra Singh (and other RSS leaders) to get their backing for this step. On 24 July Chandra Sekhar told newsmen that Deoras had given him a 'positive' response on the question of barring Janata Party office-bearers and elected officials from the RSS. Complimenting the RSS leadership for their help on this thorny problem, he stated that 'for all practical purposes the Janata Party stands delinked from the RSS, if there was any link'.[43] Rajendra Singh issued a statement on the same day pointing out that the proposal would have to be placed before the central assembly of the RSS, its highest policymaking body, since only it could revise the RSS constitution.[44] Chandra Sekhar in his statement said that he expected the RSS to act quickly on the matter, though the RSS general secretary gave no such public assurances. In fact, he gave no assurance that the central assembly of the RSS would back the proposal—only that it would consider the question.

In all this flurry of activity on the RSS issue, the apparent objective of the party leaders was to give the impression that the party was secular and thus a legitimate contestant for power. Symbolism was very important. For example, the ban on membership to those who supported a theocratic state had proved to be a non-starter, but the party would continue to use this formulation for propaganda purposes. Accordingly, the Janata Party national executive on 29 July unanimously amended the party constitution by adding a provision specifying that 'no member of any organisation having faith in a theocratic state can be a member of the party'.[45] General Secretary Ramkrishna Hegde stated, incorrectly, that from 29 July no Janata party member remained a member of the RSS.[46] When two senior Jana Sangh figures announced the next day that the restriction did not apply to them, Chandra Sekhar criticized them for damaging the reputation of the Janata Party.[47]

One of the more dramatic examples of this public relations campaign was an article critical of the RSS written by Vajpayee and appearing on 2 August 1979 in *Indian Express* (Delhi). Vajpayee argued that the political activities of the RSS affiliates (e.g., attacks on senior political figures in the RSS-affiliated media) 'do not help an organization [the RSS] to establish its apolitical credentials'.[48] He further argued: 'It is possible that some people genuinely feel apprehensive about the RSS. A certain onus accordingly devolved on the RSS, an onus that has not been discharged effectively by the RSS.' Elaborating on this theme, he wrote

> Its [the RSS] repudiation of the theocratic state was welcomed. Yet the question could legitimately be asked—why does it not open its doors to Muslims? Recent statements of the RSS chief, Mr Deoras, indicate that non-Hindus are being encouraged to join the organization. A natural corollary of this process would be clear enunciation by the RSS that by 'Hindu rashtra' it means the Indian nation which includes non-Hindus as equal members.

Many critics of the RSS praised Vajpayee's published views and concluded that the members of the Jana Sangh group were not necessarily pawns of the RSS, a conclusion which both the

Janata leadership and Vajpayee must surely have wanted them to draw.[49] Vajpayee might also have been prompted to write the article to prod the RSS into taking quick action on the dual-membership question.

However, the central assembly of the RSS did not meet until its regularly scheduled sessions in March 1980. Why did the senior-most RSS figures in July 1979 agree to consider the dual-membership issue, and then wait so long to act? It is very likely that the RSS leaders, like their Janata Party counterparts, intended the 24 July 1979 announcement to be largely a public relations gesture to buttress the position of the Janata Party as it sought to retain power. But there may have been other compulsions driving the RSS leadership at that time to consider placing such unprecedented restrictions on its members. The leaders were perhaps under considerable pressure from the traditional elements in the RSS, always apprehensive that any activities that involve the RSS in politics would undermine its character-building mission, to insulate the organization from the political arena. They had a good case. Restrictions had been placed on RSS activities in some places (e.g., the denial of public grounds to RSS shakhas by a Janata Party government in Uttar Pradesh), largely for political reasons. Many in the activist school were also prepared to pull away from politics since their own high expectations regarding cooperation with the new government had been dashed.

But over the short run even the remedies envisaged by Rajendra Singh and Chandra Sekhar to defuse the dual-membership question would probably not have reduced the apprehensions regarding the Jana Sangh group. Jana Sangh cohesiveness, not RSS manipulation, was the problem. The Jana Sangh group acted as a unit,[50] and this capability enhanced its potential to assert power because the other groups were not nearly so united. The Jana Sangh group's cohesiveness was largely a function of its recruitment policies—drafting RSS cadre who were socialized to work together as a unit. Many of the critics of the Jana Sangh group mistakenly attributed its cohesiveness to RSS manipulation and believed that by delinking the RSS and the Jana Sangh group, the Jana Sangh group would become more like the other elements of the Janata.

Internal party elections might have reduced group loyalties over time by encouraging inter-group alliances. But proposals to hold organizational elections were continually shelved because the various partners, with the prominent exception of the Jana Sangh group, feared that their relative standing would suffer. Moreover, the Jana Sangh's opponents could not be certain that the RSS would not instruct its cadre and those in such powerful affiliates as the Bharatiya Mazdoor Sangh and the Vidyarthi Parishad, to work on behalf of the Jana Sangh in organizational elections. There was historical precedent. Thirty years earlier, the swayamsevaks in the young Jana Sangh worked together with tacit RSS blessing to remove senior non-RSS figures from the party.

A Jana Sangh bid to take over the Janata Party, however, would have been much more difficult than the earlier bid to take over the young Jana Sangh. The Janata Party, unlike the Jana Sangh after Dr Mookerjee's death, had powerful political figures like Morarji Desai and Charan Singh who had strong political bases of their own. The RSS element in the Janata Party was comparatively much smaller than was the case in the young Jana Sangh. It is highly unlikely that the RSS leadership would have sanctioned a takeover bid, even in the improbable event that the Jana Sangh group had tried to do so. Such an effort would have earned the RSS the enmity of powerful political forces who might well have ganged up to impose crippling restrictions on its activities. A consistent feature of RSS behaviour since its founding has been to avoid, whenever possible, actions which invite political retribution. Finally, such a move would have undermined the Jana Sangh group's efforts to achieve political respectability. This could be accomplished only by proving that it was a reliable—and non-assertive—partner. Consequently, the Jana Sangh group did not push for representation in government and party bodies commensurate with its position as the largest element within the Janata party.[51]

RSS ACCEPTS NON-HINDUS

Besides the dual-membership issue, the exclusively Hindu membership of the RSS was still another issue which was used to attack the RSS and its affiliates, including the Jana Sangh group in the Janata Party. The issue was linked to the dual-membership question in two ways: RSS members in the Janata Party, it was argued, would alienate minority groups, especially Muslims. Second, membership in the RSS was sufficient cause to deny membership in the Janata Party because the RSS was defined as a communal organization.

Admitting Muslims (and other non-Hindus) to the RSS had been considered, if not very seriously, by senior RSS figures even before the Emergency. The Emergency experience may have encouraged the RSS to open its doors to non-Hindus. RSS cadre worked closely with non-Hindus in Jaya Prakash Narayan's LSS. RSS leaders shared prison cells with non-Hindus. There is some evidence that the question of accepting non-Hindus was discussed at a rather high level during the Emergency.[52] Soon after the ban was lifted, Balasaheb Deoras wrote that he personally had not yet given much thought to the question, though he added: 'We have accepted in principle that in spite of separate modes of worship all of us are Indian nationals . . .'[53] However, he did note that the question of Muslim membership 'had cropped up in jail', but the swayamsevaks discovered the problems in doing so because their Jama'at-i-Islami jailmates, members of another organization banned during the Emergency, 'were the most orthodox Muslims in India'.[54]

Nonetheless, the RSS leadership was under great pressure, including pressure from Jana Sangh leaders, to act quickly to open the RSS to non-Hindus. The question was closely tied to the dual-membership debate in the Janata Party. Such respected national figures as Jaya Prakash Narayan advised the RSS to disband if it did not accept minority members.[55] The RSS wanted to preserve the respectability gained during the Emergency; and many important figures, like Narayan, were not prepared to accord legitimacy to the RSS unless it adopted more inclusive membership policies.

Among the earliest indications of serious consideration of altering the RSS membership rules was a statement by the RSS general secretary in August 1977 that, 'We are in contact with non-Hindu workers in different parts of the country' on the question of closer Hindu–Muslim ties.[56] He noted that as an initial step the RSS was considering programmes such as inter-dining and joint celebrations of religious festivals. However, he also cautioned that the membership issue 'is a delicate matter which merits careful handling'. One important reason for the caution must have been apprehensions within the ranks that a more inclusive membership might undermine the Hindu revivalist orientation of the RSS. Still another reason for caution was the likely lukewarm response from Muslims. Addressing the latter concern, an editorial in *Organiser* stated

> Muslims have no doubt developed love and respect for the RSS. But how many of them will respond to the morning whistle in khaki shorts, lathi in hand? Probably not many. And perhaps the only Hindus who would like to join the Jama'at-i-Islami [whose leaders were being consulted] would be intelligence men.[57]

Nonetheless, Deoras in the fall of 1977 announced that the RSS had opened its door to non-Hindus and that some were already participating in its activities,[58] though there is no evidence of a formal decision taken on this matter.

While opening its doors to minority membership, the RSS did not change its traditional revivalist goals, which Balasaheb Deoras described in his 1979 Vijaya Dashami speech (a day when Hindus celebrate the triumph of good over evil) as uniting the Hindu community and removing from it such practices as untouchability, the caste system and dowry.[59] The RSS leadership was clearly reluctant to take any action which might undermine the brotherhood's commitment to each other and to the RSS. A significant change in membership or ritual might have done just that.[60]

THE RSS AND POLITICS: A DILEMMA

The frantic efforts to remove the RSS question from politics had no appreciable effect on political developments in mid- and late 1979. Indeed, the RSS question, like the efforts to excise the issue, was a political theatre intended to gain support in parliament. None of the jealous groups in parliament were able to put together a majority after Morarji Desai's 15 June 1979 resignation. After a number of unsuccessful attempts to do so, President Sanjiva Reddy on 22 August 1979 asked Charan Singh, the last politician to be given a chance to mobilize a majority, to serve as caretaker prime minister until the next general elections in early January 1980. The rump Janata Party selected Jagjivan Ram as its standard-bearer. During the long parliamentary campaign, the dual-membership issue was relatively dormant within the Janata Party, though its opponents used the issue to attack its secular credentials.

The seventh general elections in early January 1980 were a disaster for the Janata party. It won only 31 seats, compared to the 203 it had when Desai resigned.[61] The Jana Sangh group won 16 of these seats, compared to the 93 it had won in 1977, but closer to the 22 it had won on its own in the 1971 elections. Charan Singh's BLD,[62] with concentrated support in a few Hindi-speaking regions, did better with 41 seats. Mrs Gandhi's Congress party won 351 seats, compared to the 153 her party had won in 1977. The code words she had employed—'law and order', 'discipline', 'a government that works'—had a resonance with many voters disgusted with the interminable bickering among senior figures in the Janata Party government.

Janata Party politicians looked around for reasons to explain the defeat, and the dual-membership issue became one of the commonly cited causes. Jagjivan Ram wrote to Chandra Sekhar, still the party president, on 25 February 1980, demanding a discussion of the dual-membership question.

The Jana Sangh group was now prepared to fight back. Two of its senior figures, Lal Krishna Advani and Sunder Singh Bhandari, had toured the country to test opinion at the grass-roots level and had discovered a groundswell of resentment among Jana Sangh activists regarding their 'second class' treatment in the Janata Party.[63] The cadre was disappointed by the number of parliamentary seats allocated to their group (about one-fourth the nominees) and were apprehensive about the number they would get for the forthcoming state assembly elections in May. The press speculated that traditional Jana Sangh supporters refused to support the Jana Sangh group's candidates because of their shoddy treatment within the Janata Party. (This is another way of saying that many RSS workers sat on their hands during the election, and there is apparent substance to this speculation.)

Jagjivan Ram for his part blamed the party's poor showing on the 'hostile activities of the RSS', even charging that a 'secret' agreement existed between the RSS and Mrs Gandhi's Congress party.[64] It is likely that the RSS cadre was lukewarm towards many of the Janata Party's non-Jana Sangh candidates. Reporters covering the March 1980 meeting of the central assembly of the RSS wrote that some delegates asserted that RSS workers did not support Janata Party candidates.[65] An editorial in *Organiser* reminded Ram that the 'RSS as such does not work in elections—and that swayamsevaks in their individual capacity are free to support candidates and causes of their choice'.[66] *Organiser*'s 'Political Correspondent' warned that the persisting dual-membership controversy alienated 'not only a chunk of its [Janata Party's] own sincere workers, but also a large number of supporters outside',—a thinly veiled reference to the RSS.[67]

Still other critics of the Jana Sangh group argued that the presence of RSS members in the Janata Party tarred the party with the brush of communalism. Presumably, the party had done poorly in the general elections, and would continue to do so in the future because of this association with the RSS. However, the available evidence of voting in 1980 is ambiguous on this proposition. The swing back to Mrs Gandhi's Congress party was as great in non-Muslim constituencies as in those with a large Muslim population.[68] Whatever the causes for the Janata Party's poor showing, many Janata Party's politicians believed that the communal issue had damaged the party.

Prime Minister Indira Gandhi's decision to hold state assembly elections in May 1980 forced the Janata Party to act on the dual-membership question. Senior party figures on both sides of the controversy believed that a decision one way or the other was necessary if the party were to put together a viable strategy. But there was no consensus regarding who should make the decision regarding restrictions on RSS members. The Jana Sangh leadership insisted that the central assembly of the RSS, which was scheduled to consider the question at its annual 21–23 March 1980 meeting should make the decision, whereas Chandra Sekhar (and others) maintained that the party had the right to act on a question involving its own membership requirements.

The Jana Sangh's decision to leave the matter to the RSS was the only real option it had. The Jana Sangh leadership risked being on the wrong side of the RSS if it were to come down on either side of the dual-membership question. The central assembly of the RSS had not yet acted, and it could conceivably go either way. Deoras and Singh in their discussion with Chandra Sekhar in 1979 seem to have tilted towards restrictions, but the political circumstances which had then influenced their stand had changed. In fact, press reports note considerable confusion among the Jana Sangh cadre regarding the question, suggesting that the RSS leadership did not arrive at a decision on the question until the very last minute.[69] But the Janata RSS critics did not wait for the RSS to act. The parliamentary board of the party, against strong Jana Sangh group objections, proposed on 18 March 1980 a formula for the consideration of the national executive that would bar legislators and office-bearers from participating in RSS activities.[70]

The central assembly of the RSS at its 21–23 March meeting decided to take no action, ostensibly on the grounds that the Janata Party's parliamentary board had pre-empted the issue by its vote on 18 March,[71] even though the parliamentary board's decision was only an advisory one for the party's national executive, which was to meet on 4 April. The RSS leadership clearly decided to back away from the question, and the Janata parliamentary board's decision provided a convenient excuse not to act.

What led Singh and Deoras between July 1979 and March 1980 to make what appears to be a shift in stand on the dual-membership question? It could not have been only the considerable opposition within the RSS ranks (and within the Jana Sangh group as well) to the proposition that RSS members not hold elective offices.[72] If the RSS leaders had insisted on such exclusion, the central assembly of the RSS would have gone along with their decision, whatever the degree of discontent. What had changed were the political circumstances. In mid-1979 the Janata Party, weakened by defections, still had some prospect of returning to power. After Indira Gandhi's 1980 parliamentary victory, the Janata

Party was reduced to a small group of 31 members in the Lok Sabha. The RSS now ran the risk of earning the enmity of the ruling party if it tried to preserve the unity of one of the Congress party's major political opponents. Furthermore, the Janata Party itself could not be relied upon to be friendly towards the RSS. The party contained a large element (a majority of its officers, as events were to reveal) who were implacably opposed to the RSS. Indeed, the RSS may well have wanted the Jana Sangh group to leave the Janata Party. Its non-action line on the dual-membership question placed the ball in the court of the Jana Sangh group, and the RSS thus preserved its apolitical credentials.

Within a few days of the RSS central assembly's adoption of a no-action line, the Jana Sangh group announced plans for a national convention to be held on 5 April, one day after the Janata Party's national executive was scheduled to decide on the dual-membership question. Despite a flurry of last-minute efforts by Morarji Desai (and others) to work out a compromise acceptable to both sides, the Janata Party's national executive rejected by a vote of 17 to 14 Desai's compromise, and opted for the hard-line stand earlier recommended by its parliamentary board.[73]

On 5 April over 3500 'delegates' (including 15 of the remaining 28 Janata Party members of the Lok Sabha), representing both the Jana Sangh group and some others who had also walked out of the Janata Party, met to form a new party. The conveners portrayed the new party—named the Bharatiya Janata Party—as the 'real' representative of Jaya Prakash Narayan, as well as that of Deendayal Upadhyaya, a choice clearly intended to underscore the philosophic orientation of the new party. The choice was also perhaps intended to demonstrate that this new party was not simply a resurrected Jana Sangh, but that it was a party which aspired to a much broader following. Vajpayee, who was selected the new party's president, chose several non-Jana Sangh figures to serve on his working committee. One of the general secretaries, Sikander Bakht, was a Muslim.[74]

The leaders of the Bharatiya Janata Party (BJP) had to determine what kind of party they wanted. First of all, they clearly wanted the RSS cadre. With this in mind, the dual-membership issue was formally resolved with an explicit reference in the BJP's Basic Policy statement: 'The Party reiterates that the members of all those social or cultural organisations which are working for the social or cultural uplift of the masses and are not engaged in any political activity are welcome to join the BJP . . .'[75]

But the recruiting of talented RSS cadre might be a problem. The disenchantment of the RSS with politics was deep. Rajendra Singh noted in mid-1983 that 'many [RSS members] have left politics because it is considered a dirty business'.[76] The depth of the alienation with politics was suggested in an article written by Nana Deshmukh when the Jana Sangh group withdrew from the Janata Party.[77] He questioned the legitimacy of the political vocation. He wrote that those engaged in politics had to ask some hard questions regarding the efficacy of politics, given the experience of the prior three years: 'Did the leaders corrupt the political process or did the political process corrupt them? Will it be possible to defeat the present immoral dictatorial tendencies in Indian politics through a resort to the power-oriented opportunistic and vote-getting politics? If not, what is the alternative to see that grass roots people's [sic] power comes into being?'

Besides seeking RSS cadre (for organizational purposes), the party leadership also wanted to portray the BJP as the legitimate successor of Jaya Prakash Narayan's idealism (for mobilization purposes). Accordingly, the Jana Sangh leadership retained the word 'Janata' in the new party's name; it adopted Gandhian socialism rather than Deendayal Upadhyaya's Integral Humanism as the party's statement of first principles, although the party gave an honoured place to Upadhyaya's ideological statement. It chose a different flag, a more 'secular' green and saffron similar to that of the Janata Party rather than the solid saffron flag of the Jana Sangh; and it adopted a new symbol, the lotus rather than the lamp. It also did not restore the office of the organizing secretary, the position that had constituted the iron frame of the Jana Sangh. Rather it adopted the looser organizational model of the Janata Party.

But there is a certain tension between its two legacies, and the party would have problems working out a synthesis between the two. For example, Jaya Prakash Narayan's organizational model was a decentralized structure based on participatory democracy, but the RSS cadre are socialized to accept democratic centralism. A massive infusion of non-RSS activists would undermine the sense of community that had attracted swayamsevaks to the Jana Sangh. In general, the symbols adopted by the BJP were not those of the brotherhood, which would create a certain psychological distance between it and the new party. They worried that the new party would be characterized by the factionalism which they regarded as the bane of Indian institutions.

Generally optimistic about the party's future, the delegates to the BJP's first plenary session (held at Bombay in December

1980) expressed considerable discomfort with the new party's symbols. The party's adoption of Gandhian socialism, though defined to sound like Deendayal Upadhyaya's Integral Humanism, aroused the most outspoken criticism. What bothered the delegates was the use of the term socialism, which many identified with Marxism, long identified as a 'foreign' ideology by the RSS. Vijaya Raje Scindia, the BJP's vice-president, circulated a note to the working committee charging that the adoption of Gandhian socialism as the party's ideology would make the BJP look like a 'photocopy' of Mrs Gandhi's Congress party, and thus cause the party to lose its 'originality'.[78] She later withdrew her objections when, according to press reports, the party leadership convinced her that the BJP's 'socialism' had an 'Indian content'.[79]

Vajpayee, in his address to the delegates, took pains to distinguish Gandhian socialism from Marxism. He claimed that Gandhian socialism rejected (a) the notion that all ideas are grounded in 'material conditions', (b) violence as an instrument of policy, and (c) the concentration of political and economic power.[80] Yet doubts continued to be expressed. One delegate, objecting to the use of socialism in the party's economic statement, suggested that the statement be discussed in local units; still another delegate proposed that the word socialism be replaced by Ram Rajya (ideal state).[81] The debate was not over substance. Gandhian socialism was defined in a way that kept the BJP well within the centrist economic orientation of the Jana Sangh. The problem was with symbols.

The party also had to work out the thorny question of what approach it would take towards the opposition parties. The RSS cadre, given their unpleasant experience over the previous three years, was wary of working too closely with other parties. Another merger was clearly out of the question. But this was not an immediate prospect since the party leaders were optimistic that the BJP could on its own develop into a national alternative to Prime Minister Gandhi's Congress party. The party decided that any arrangements with the opposition would be temporary electoral adjustments. However, if the BJP's electoral performance sagged, some difficult decisions regarding broader cooperation would have to be made.

The early electoral tests sustained the BJP's initial optimism regarding its future. The first test came almost immediately after the Jana Sangh group walked out of the Janata Party. Prime Minister Gandhi had called for assembly elections in late May 1980 in nine states where her party had done well in the general elections. The BJP had only a few weeks in which to nominate candidates, raise money and conduct a campaign. The results demonstrate that it was able to reclaim much of the old Jana Sangh's support base.

The greatest gains were in Rajasthan and Madhya Pradesh, two states with Jana Sangh chief ministers during the Janata period. The largest losses occurred in Uttar Pradesh, where Charan Singh's Lok Dal was a major force, and in Punjab, where the BJP campaigned without the backing of the Alkali Dal, whose earlier support to the Jana Sangh was responsible for its good showing.

The party's electoral good fortune continued. In late 1981 the BJP won two assembly bye-election contests, and in January 1982 it wrested the Sagar (in Madhya Pradesh) parliamentary seat from Prime Minister Gandhi's Congress party. This parliamentary victory was considered significant because Sagar is outside the traditional area of Jana Sangh strength in the north-western part of the state. On 19 May 1982 four more states (Haryana, Himachal Pradesh, West Bengal, and Kerala) went to the polls. The BJP worked out electoral arrangements with Charan Singh's Lok Dal in Haryana and Himachal Pradesh, though the two parties admitted that the understanding in Himachal Pradesh broke down largely because many Lok Dal candidates refused to withdraw from seats which had been assigned to the BJP. Nonetheless, the BJP improved its representation in Himachal Pradesh from 24 to 29 in a house of 68 seats, making it the largest single party there.[82] In Haryana the BJP representation dropped from 11 to 6 of the ninety-member house. In Kerala and West Bengal, the BJP fought alone in the hope of laying the groundwork for a third alternative (between communist and Congress-led alliances in the two states). While it won no seats in either state, party leaders justified the go-it-alone strategy as a tactic intended to acquaint voters with the party. In seven scattered parliamentary contests conducted at the same time, the BJP added one new seat (Jabalpur in Madhya Pradesh), and it retained the Thane seat, which adjoins Bombay.

With this string of electoral good fortune, party leaders were optimistic that the BJP could become the national alternative to the Congress party. This optimism prompted the party's national executive in February 1982 to reject the concept of a National Front, then being actively considered by other opposition parties, to concentrate on an electoral strategy for the forthcoming elections rather than 'carrying out unending talks about unity which create more disunity than unity'.[83] The national executive prepared a statement governing the BJP's relations with other opposition parties. The BJP would 'retain its separate identity'; would support 'concerted action by opposition parties ... on specific issues relating to people's welfare and democracy'; and would participate in 'electoral arrangements with other parties aimed at ensuring the defeat of Congress (I) candidates'.[84]

In an effort to provide a more precise programmatic content to the BJP, its national executive in August 1983 drew up a set of economic priorities. These were presented as the party's 'five demands': (1) the reduction of rural poverty, (2) the expansion of the public distribution system to cover the 'entire' rural population, (3) the revival of the food-for-work programme, (4) the establishment of employment generation as a criteria for evaluating industrial performance, and (5) the expansion of credit for small-scale industry.[85]

The RSS for its part appears to have softened its anti-politics line. A 10 October 1982 editorial in *Organiser* was full of praise for the BJP, noting among other things that 'where most other parties have no membership and no party elections, ad hoc committees and presidents for life, the Bharatiya Janata Party brings a whiff of fresh air of party democracy'. It predicted that 'the BJP is poised to take off—and take a great leap forward'. However, it also expressed mild criticism about the lack of new initiatives that would distinguish the BJP from other parties.[86] Balasaheb Deoras, in a late 1982 discussion with swayamsevaks, stated that 'maybe, among political parties, BJP is closer to RSS'.[87] The Vidyarthi Parishad in mid-1982 revoked its 1977 policy against participating in student union elections.[88]

But the BJP did not experience the anticipated take-off, which forced its leadership to rethink the question of cooperation with other opposition parties. Sunder Singh Bhandari, the BJP vice-president, lost a prestigious parliamentary contest in June 1982 to a Congress party opponent. The BJP, with a traditional base of support in the Hindi-majority Jammu area of J&K, lost every seat it contested in the 1983 J&K assembly election. Mrs Gandhi's criticism of Chief Minister Sheikh Abdullah helped to polarize the electorate on communal lines, which resulted in a shift of Hindu BJP supporters to the Congress. The results from the 5 January 1983 assembly elections (which the BJP fought alone) in the two southern states of Karnataka and Andhra Pradesh, did not live up to the party's hope of establishing a firm base for itself in the south, and thus cast doubt on its aspirations of becoming the national alternative to the Congress party. In Karnataka it won only 18 of 225 seats, and in Andhra Pradesh only 4 of 294 seats. While the RSS had experienced a spectacular growth in the south since 1977, this expansion did not seen to have an appreciable effect on the BJP, though it could be argued that the expanded RSS presence provided the BJP with the cadre necessary to establish an organizational framework that could be used to mobilize support in future elections.

But the major shock was the February 1983 elections for Delhi's two legislative bodies. The Jana Sangh had traditionally performed very well in Delhi; the BJP anticipated a victory that would revive its electoral momentum. However, it won only 19 of 56 Metropolitan Council seats and 37 of 100 Delhi Municipal Corporation seats. The Congress had traditionally been the Jana Sangh's major competitor in the capital city; it won majorities in both the Council and the Corporation. The press reported that the RSS cadre maintained a neutral stance in these elections.[89] Despite widespread press speculation of an understanding between the Congress and the RSS, we have no reliable information that an arrangement was arrived at in Delhi or elsewhere offering RSS support to the Congress. More swayamsevaks were clearly voting for the Congress, but not because of any RSS appeal to do so. However, the lukewarm support of the RSS to the BJP in Delhi probably had a significant influence on how many of the RSS cadre worked and voted for the BJP. Vajpayee accepted responsibility for the loss and submitted his resignation, though the party refused to accept it, and he was elected unopposed in March 1983 to serve a second term as president.

The BJP played a negligible role in the politics of Punjab and Assam, two states where inter-ethnic tension aroused demands for increased autonomy by the majority community in each state—demands that were at odds with the RSS conception of an integrated Indian nation. In Punjab, the BJP lost the support of its traditional urban Hindu constituency to the Congress as Hindus and Sikhs polarized politically in the wake of the militant Sikh movement for greater autonomy led by Jarnail Singh Bhindranwale. Indeed the Hindus may have held the BJP responsible for the earlier cooperation between the Jana Sangh and the Alkali Dal, the political arm of the Sikh community. The RSS for its part tried to diminish the tension between two groups it defined as Hindu, and in the process alienated much of its Hindu support base. The RSS did, however, support military action in June 1984 to expel Sikh militants from the Golden Temple in Amritsar. For many Hindus, both the RSS and the BJP had lost their aura as protectors of Hindu interests, and many flocked to various Hindu defensive organizations that formed in response to the communal tensions in the state. The Hindu voters almost totally abandoned the BJP in the September 1985 Punjab assembly elections.

In Assam, a state where the Hindu Assamese were protesting the migration of Bangladeshis into India, the RSS bypassed the BJP and gave responsibility to the Vidyarthi Parishad to project solutions to the anti-foreigner protest movement led by a regional student association—the All-Assam Students' Union (AASU). The BJP, with a minuscule base, played virtually no role in the politics of the state and mobilized little support in either the 1983 or the 1985 assembly elections.

Indications began to appear in early 1983 that many in the brotherhood were disappointed with the BJP. On 10 April 1983, for example, an article critical of the BJP appeared in *Organiser* under the pseudonym of 'Sindu'. The writer argued that the BJP had failed to develop into a movement with a distinctive programme capable of attracting mass support. Rather, the BJP appeared to follow the lead set by other parties. 'Sindu' also criticized the BJP for playing down its Hindu orientation, arguing that 'nobody need quarrel with its efforts to attract non-Hindus. But many may also view it as a certain weakening of character.'

The series of electoral setbacks resulted in a controversial shift in tactics. In April 1983. Vajpayee advised the party's national council to support a United-Front line intended to bring together all 'nationalist democratic forces', barring the communists and the Muslim League in order to improve the opposition's chances in the anticipated mid-term polls. Vajpayee may have feared the political isolation of the BJP. To reduce concerns about another united opposition party, Vajpayee emphasized that his proposal did not include a merger of opposition parties.[90] The proposal aroused such resistance that the council avoided a formal decision, leaving the matter to the national executive, which at its 7–9 May meeting in Bombay adopted Vajpayee's proposal.[91] But the national council also decided to tighten up the party structure. Of the four general secretaries, only Lal Krishna Advani was retained—a step which was probably intended to give the general secretary the broad powers once performed by the organizing secretary in the Jana Sangh, and which was another step away from the Janata model. Complaints about 'indiscipline' in local units may have prompted the national council to tighten control over both recruitment and promotion. The step may also have been influenced by Vajpayee's National Front Scheme. Vajpayee might try to broaden the party's support base with his National Front strategy, but the party at the same time would be better prepared to ensure that this move did not undermine organizational cohesiveness.

With the imprimatur on the notion of a National Front, Advani met with the leaders of thirteen other opposition parties, including the communists, at a 28 May 1983 conclave called by Chief Minister N. T. Rama Rao of Andhra Pradesh to discuss common approaches to national problems. There were several other such meetings, but differences over policies and personalities blocked the formation of the overarching National Front envisaged by Vajpayee. Rather, three different groups emerged. The BJP for its part joined with Charan Singh's Lok Dal to form the National Democratic Alliance (NDA). But even this partial front shattered when Singh arranged for the merger of his Lok Dal with several other opposition parties in November 1984 to form the Dalit Mazdoor Kisan Party without consulting with his BJP alliance partners. Thus Vajpayee's experiment proved a failure. The BJP went into the 24–27 December general elections with no national allies, though it did arrange for adjustments with a variety of parties in several states.

The results of the national elections were a disaster for the BJP, as they were for the opposition generally. The Congress party, under Rajiv Gandhi's leadership, won a landslide victory, capturing 401 of 508 contested parliamentary seats, and 49.16 per cent of the vote. Campaigning under the slogan, 'Continuity that gives the country unity', the Congress received its greatest victory since India's Independence. This slogan is rooted in fears that Indira Gandhi's assassination on 31 October 1984 by two Sikh bodyguards underscored the dangers to national unity, apprehensions that RSS leaders shared.

In the December 1984 national elections, the BJP won 2 seats (out of 221 contested), one in Gujarat and one in Andhra Pradesh,[92] 14 less than in the outgoing Lok Sabha. Vajpayee and the entire BJP establishment lost their contests, and the party was totally decimated in the Hindi-speaking states that had provided most of its seats in the past. There is widespread speculation that many RSS cadre backed the Congress party, and that they were pleased by Prime Minister Indira Gandhi's tough policy against Sikh militants in Punjab and against alleged softness of the Abdullah government towards pro-Pakistani elements in Jammu and Kashmir. The pervasive view that a solid victory for Rajiv Gandhi was necessary to keep in check the forces of disintegration probably had a compelling appeal for many RSS members, as it must have had for a large part of the BJP's traditional constituency.

Still another factor which may have convinced many RSS members to vote for the Congress was the refusal of the ruling party to make the RSS an issue, in contrast to the 1980 campaign.[93] The prospect of the fractious opposition leaders forming a coalition government must also have struck many as disquieting. A replay of the unstable Janata Party government in such dangerous times could undermine national unity.

The BJP recouped its losses somewhat in the subsequent eleven state assembly elections (see Table 9). However, its showing did not remove the questions regarding the party's strategy. Vajpayee's National Front strategy was one of the victims of the electoral debacle. The national executive at its 3–6 January 1985 review of the national elections specifically ruled out any National Fronts and announced that the party would contest the forthcoming assembly elections alone whenever possible, though any decision on seat adjustments was left to state units.[94] The national elections also forced the party leadership to reconsider which of its political legacies—the Janata or the Jana Sangh—would shape

Table 9: BJP Performance in March 1985
State Assembly Elections

State	Total Seats	BJP Victories	Previous BJP Showing*
Andhra Pradesh	294	8	4
Bihar	324	12	21
Gujarat	182	11	9
Himachal Pradesh	68	7	29
Karnataka	224	2	18
Madhya Pradesh	320	58	60
Maharashtra	288	16	14
Orissa	147	1	0

State	Total Seats	BJP Victories	Previous BJP Showing*
Rajasthan	200	38	32
Sikkim	32	0	0
Uttar Pradesh	425	16	11
	TOTAL	169	198

*Figures calculated from elections after April 1960.

its future. Early indications—tighter party discipline, stress on an ideological consensus, the continued recruitment of RSS pracharaks,[95] and a suspicion of alliances—suggest a tilt towards the Jana Sangh legacy. Still another sign of movement towards the Jana Sangh legacy is the BJP's adoption of controversial Jana Sangh policies which the Janata Party had not accepted. The most prominent examples of such policies are the national council's decisions advocating the repeal of Article 370 of the Indian constitution, which gives a special status to Jammu and Kashmir, and its backing of an Indian nuclear weapons capability.

Even the symbols are being altered in ways more consistent with the Jana Sangh background of the BJP. At the party's July 1985 national executive session, Integral Humanism replaced Gandhian socialism as the BJP's philosophy, though substantively the party's economic policy remained the same.[96] As a follow-up to this decision, the party held a six-day conference beginning 8 October 1985 to discuss the report of a working group set up by party president Vajpayee to review the functioning of the BJP since 1980.[97] The working group rejected the proposal to revive the BJP in the mould of the Jana Sangh, though it supported the July 1985 executive committee decision to restore Integral Humanism as the BJP's philosophy. The executive committee, as expected, agreed. The executive committee also adopted a 'Gandhian approach' to socio-economic problems, rather than Gandhian socialism as a guiding principle for the party. The national council, however, meeting after the executive committee, restored the phrase Gandhian socialism, while retaining Integral Humanisn as the basic party philosophy. The debate in the national council lasted for several hours, and it was not about substance, but about symbols. Without totally rejecting its Janata past, the BJP moved significantly back to the symbolism of the Jana Sangh, thus underscoring the membership's desire to restore greater cohesiveness while at the same time recognizing that 'socialism' as a symbol reflected the populist course which the BJP, like the Jana Sangh, had accepted.

A principal proponent of strengthening party cohesiveness is party president Advani, elected to his position in May 1986. More outspoken in defence of his own RSS ties and of RSS norms than former party president Vajpayee, Advani seems to be emerging as the most powerful figure in the party. Having the support of organizational leaders, he can be expected to reorient the party in the Jana Sangh image.

In his presidential address at the 9–11 May 1986 annual party session, Advani emphasized the BJP's Jana Sangh roots.[98] Barely concealing his appeal for the support of the RSS cadre, he demanded the scrapping of Article 370 of the constitution, which gives Jammu and Kashmir a special status; and he called for a common civil code while denouncing Prime Minister Rajiv Gandhi's government for enacting legislation forcing the courts to apply traditional Islamic law—rather than a common civil code—to alimony cases involving

Muslim women. In addition, Advani's warnings about the threats to national unity may have been intended to convince the RSS cadre that the BJP would be a better manager of national interests than Rajiv Gandhi's Congress party.

Besides the appeal to the RSS cadre, his message seems to have been calculated to regain Hindu support in anticipation of the May 1987 state elections in Haryana, Himachal Pradesh, Kerala, Mizoram and West Bengal, as well as possible mid-term polls in Punjab and Jammu and Kashmir. The BJP's performance in those state elections may well determine whether the party retains the confidence of the RSS cadre. If the BJP repeats its earlier dismal electoral performance, the RSS may decide that it has more to gain by expending resources to strengthen other affiliates like the Vishwa Hindu Parishad, the Bharatiya Mazdoor Sangh, and the Vidyarthi Parishad.

While the May 1986 national conference underscored the BJP's Jana Sangh legacy, the party leadership did not totally sever its links with the Janata past. Gandhian Socialism was retained as a party principle, though of course not on a par with Integral Humanism, and some non-Jana Sangh/RSS officers were retained. But the party continued to move away from its Janata association. This was most clearly reflected in the appointment of men from RSS backgrounds to staff the four general secretary positions: Kidar Nath Sahani (Delhi), Murli Manohar Joshi (Uttar Pradesh), Krishan Lal Sharma (Punjab), and Pramod Mahajan (Maharashtra). It is likely that the centralized structure of the BJP will eventually accord one of these men major responsibility for organizational work. Indeed, Advani may be testing the four to determine who would be best suited for a position so central to all the constituents of the RSS 'family'.

The post-1977 experience of the Jana Sangh group underscores the political dilemmas created by the symbiotic linkages between the RSS and a political party. The RSS wants a representative in the political arena which will speak out on behalf of its Hindu nationalist ideology, if only to provide protection to the RSS and its affiliates. But the more successful such a party becomes, the more obvious it is that the links between the RSS and the party could harm both organizations. The political enemies of the party might well gang up against the RSS, identified as the source of the party's strength.

RSS: A SHIFT IN FOCUS

The fall of the Janata Party government in 1979 and the subsequent fragmentation of the party was a setback for the RSS activists, and these events forced the RSS to rethink its tactics. The traditional element in the RSS had always demanded a distancing from the political arena. After 1980 their activist colleagues were inclined to agree that political activities might play a much reduced role in bringing about the desired unity of Hindus, and that other affiliates might be more important for achieving this goal. Moreover, the increasing respectability of the RSS in the 1980s reduces the compulsions for it to be closely linked to a political party. After 1980 the RSS shifted its focus to the affiliates, especially the Vishwa Hindu Parishad (VHP).

In late 1982 the conversion of some low-caste Hindus to Islam at Meenakshipuram (Tamil Nadu) set off alarm bells, raising fears of Hinduism in danger. The RSS felt ccmpelled to assist the VHP, the affiliate which could play the major role in meeting the perceived threat. The RSS supported the VHP's fund-raising efforts, its Ekmata Yatra (unity pilgrimage) campaign, which sought to create all-India Hindu symbols, its effort to unify the Hindu religious establishment, and its social welfare activities aimed at insulating vulnerable groups from conversion. The other affiliates were also encouraged to take a more active interest on questions relating to national unity. In Assam, for example, the Vidyarthi Parishad was the most assertive 'family' participant in the anti-foreigner agitation. In Punjab the RSS itself took the lead in trying to diffuse Hindu–Sikh communal tensions, sending pracharaks from all over the country to the state. In addition, Sikh swayamsevaks were dispatched to Punjab to demonstrate that the RSS considered Sikhs a part of the Hindu community. However, this non-political approach may not help to solve the complex problems in Punjab.

The RSS shift away from politics is at least partly the result of its uncertainty regarding the electoral future of the BJP. If the BJP cannot develop into a major national political party, close identification with it could antagonize other parties. The Janata Party experience had demonstrated the dangers of even a perceived close relationship. Even if the BJP achieved significant electoral gains, the RSS interest might still be better served by keeping the party at arm's length, thus providing incentive to other parties to woo the RSS. The rapid growth of the RSS and of its affiliates enhances the potential political value of the RSS if it does not put all its political eggs in one basket. Indeed, the RSS cadre already seem to be dividing their votes. There will be even greater incentive for them to do so if the BJP demonstrates that it cannot develop into a viable national party.

The BJP for its part will try to develop into a national political force, but it is questionable whether it can do so with a cadre drawn largely from the RSS. Within the party's organizational structure, the cadre has been reluctant to share power with politically prominent figures from non-RSS backgrounds who could mobilize mass support for the party. The RSS training, emphasizing the sacrifice of self for the larger good, and the apolitical orientation of the RSS ideology make it unlikely that politically charismatic figures will emerge from within its own ranks.[99] On the other hand, it is questionable if the BJP could survive politically without the RSS cadre, and the cadre will not stay unless the leadership of the party stays firmly in the hands of the 'brotherhood'.

Conclusion

The founders of the RSS assumed that India would not become a strong and independent country until there had been first a cultural revolution. The training process they constructed emphasized discipline, work and a desire for order. They assumed that those men who had gone through the training would on their own take a leading role in reshaping Indian society.

The urge towards personal purification as a prerequisite to political action is a motivating factor behind much of contemporary radical politics.[1] Such movements are now most widespread in the new states of Asia and Africa, for it is in these states that the most rapid social and moral dislocations have occurred. Independence, the emergence of new social forces, the displacement of traditional elites, and the rationalization of public administration have undermined existing images of responsibility and civic purpose. These dislocations have resulted in a search for new symbolic frameworks to make the new social environment meaningful and to create conditions for people to act purposefully in society.

The Hindu revivalists of the 1920s believed the divisions in Hindu society rendered the Hindus incapable of overcoming foreign political and cultural domination. Hindus were separated by traditional commitments to specific occupations and religious observances, by rules of endogamy and commensality, and by linguistic and regional loyalties. Dr Keshav Baliram Hedgewar, who organized the RSS during a period of widespread Hindu–Muslim rioting in the mid-1920s, saw in the riots a fundamental sociological problem of the Hindu 'nation'. Even though Hindus were the majority community, the revivalists considered then a suppressed majority, robbed of vigour and purpose. A thousand years of foreign domination were the testimony to that weakness. The revivalists had a deep sense of anguish over the vast tracts (e.g., Afghanistan, Tibet) which were culturally 'lost'. They feared that Hindu influence would continue to be eroded through conversion to other faiths or through a lower birth rate. They also feared that Hindus, because they lacked a sense of community, lacked the will to resist either the Muslims or the British, both of whom were regarded as foreign. The revivalists held that any attempt to mobilize Hindus against foreign domination was bound to fail unless Hindus overcame their pessimistic fatalism and came to look at themselves as a community. Hedgewar proposed a psychological remedy to the problem of Hindu disunity. He devoted his life to the construction of a programme that would bring about the desired psychological reorientation of those men who would lead the movement for a new and more integrated society.

Hedgewar incorporated into the RSS a training process which came to be called character building, stressing discipline, work and commitment. The process is based on the Hindu conception that disciplined training under an enlightened teacher results in an introspective recognition of truth. The truth was a secularized version of advaita vedanta; it took the metaphysical position that all men are basically one and applied it to Hindu society. Hedgewar's search for a nationalist programme of action arose from a deeply felt need to restore among Hindus a sense of self-respect rooted in Indian culture. In the face of orthodox resistance, he found justification in Indian history and culture for modern technology, scientific knowledge and economic development.

The RSS was conceived of as a school that would teach this new truth. Commitment to it was highly personal and ideological, often requiring the member to abandon his ties to his family. Ideological zeal bound the swayamsevaks together in a brotherhood whose goal was to reshape the country's social and political institutions.

Since its formation in 1925 the RSS has attracted support almost exclusively in urban areas, and largely from the salaried lower-middle-class and small-scale shopkeepers. These are groups whose social and economic aspirations are undermined by inflation, by scarcity of job opportunities, and by their relative inability to influence the political process. The RSS has had little success among the peasantry, whose religious beliefs, practices and sense of community have been less affected by the changes brought on by modernity. However, as change comes to affect increasingly large numbers of Indians, the revivalist appeals offered by the RSS (and by other groups as well) are likely to become more popular, and there are now signs that the RSS is making some headway in certain rural areas. The 1982 Meenakshipuram conversion incident and the demand for the reopening of Hindu temples now used as mosques, were issues that had a resonance in rural India, and both events helped the RSS to build its credibility there.

The RSS, which places very stringent requirements on its members, is not likely to become a mass membership organization. The continuous testing of the members' zeal and self-discipline tends to turn away all but the most ardent supporters. However, the RSS was never meant to mobilize on a mass scale. Hedgewar speculated that it needed to train only 1 to 3 per cent of Hindu men to achieve the cultural revolution. The cadre were to be the leading social group who—endowed with organizing capacity, social respect and strong determination—would eventually assume the leadership role in the revival of the Hindu 'nation'. The RSS expected each member to be a disciplined Hindu activist whose activity would carry him outside the RSS.

Hedgewar and his associates in the young RSS believed that character building was, in itself, sufficient to achieve the desired social and political transformation of India. Those who became virtuous through self-discipline would be moved individually to revitalize society. In the pre-independence period the RSS established no newspapers; it organized no student groups, trade unions, or political groups; the cadre engaged in no underground revolutionary activities (at least not in the name of the RSS). Indeed, full-time RSS workers were discouraged from engaging in politics. Many militant Hindu revivalists, such as Vinayak Damodar Savarkar, ridiculed the apolitical orientation of the RSS. Militant activists, such as Nathuram Godse, left the RSS. Many RSS activists wanted the RSS itself to take a more assertive role in the transformation of Indian society, and some prominent office-bearers resigned when it did not.

At the end of World War II, many RSS members, particularly in north India, began to lobby for a change in

RSS tactics. Their sense of urgency increased as independence drew closer. The RSS defence of Hindus in pre-partition Punjab and its refugee relief operations earned it considerable popularity and established activism in the RSS repertoire of programmes. The urgency to broaden its activities intensified following the ban placed on the RSS at the time of Mahatma Gandhi's assassination, which threatened the survival of the RSS. In addition, the decision of the Congress party to exclude RSS members both from the party and from its affiliated organizations, effectively blocked the political ambitions of its members. The decision to form affiliates was a compromise between those activists lobbying for the RSS to transform itself into a political party and the traditionalist element fearful that political and social activism would undermine the character-building programme.

The formation of the Jana Sangh and the other affiliates mobilized new groups into the 'family'. The decision to establish labour and agricultural affiliates, for example, represented attempts to enhance the influence of the world view of the RSS among a much larger part of the population. This move also influenced the RSS itself. The RSS cadre tended to espouse the interests of the groups among whom they worked, and they in turn shaped the views of the RSS. As the cadre assumed a more activist orientation, they began to relate questions concerning national integration with social and economic issues. This activism inevitably led the RSS and its affiliates to take a more direct role in political events, and to confront political authorities (as demonstrated by their support for Jaya Prakash Narayan's Total Revolution in the mid-1970s). However, the RSS continues to display a reluctance to maintain a sustained opposition to the government. Indeed, it has done so only when government action seemed to threaten its continued survival.

The Hindu symbol system of the RSS is used increasingly to justify the mobilization of groups who consider themselves economically and socially disadvantaged. Hence, the support for indigenous languages versus English, for the small-scale entrepreneur versus big business and nationalized industry, for increasing the influence of the worker in the work place, and for collapsing the distinctions which clothing, entertainment, sport and income make between the powerful and the 'common man.' This shift has caused internal tensions inside the Jana Sangh and the BJP, which showed up in Balraj Madhok's conservative rebellion against the Jana Sangh leadership.

The Jana Sangh and the BJP—the most mobilization-oriented affiliates—have been most successful electorally among Hindu groups undergoing rapid social change and moving towards more intensive internal communication and sharper external boundary definition (e.g., Hindu refugees from Pakistan, urban Hindus in Punjab, non-Christian tribals in Bihar, brahmins in Maharashtra). The Hindu symbol system of the RSS could be used to justify the integrative process among such groups. The Jana Sangh and BJP have been able to mobilize substantial support from such groups when there was a perceived social and political disadvantage in relation to other groups.

The RSS leadership has always tried to avoid day-to-day involvement in the activities of its affiliates. Had the RSS leadership been drawn directly into politics, or into the work of the other affiliates, they would have lost the aura of detachment which provides them their legitimacy as teachers, 'cultural' commentators and arbitrators. Moreover, they genuinely fear that the central values of the RSS would be seriously compromised by the compulsions of bargaining in the political arena.

This fear of involvement in politics brings to mind Max Weber's discussion of an ethics of ultimate ends and an ethics of responsibility.[2] RSS theorists argue that politics, as presently practised, involves morally questionable means and therefore should be kept at a certain distance.[3] Those swayamsevaks who 'work in the world', by participating in the affiliates or other organizations, are required to wrestle with ethical paradoxes forced on them by an imperfect world. This tension between the ethical absolutism of the RSS and the relative ethics of the affiliates has resulted in a sense of moral superiority among RSS leaders, when compared to those who work in the affiliates, for the latter are required to assume responsibility for the potentially 'evil' consequences of their actions. There are RSS leaders who do not see the two ethical standards as moral opposites, but as supplementary to each other. They supported the formation of the affiliates, against the opinion of ethical absolutists like Golwalkar, who agreed reluctantly and out of expediency to sanction them. Nevertheless, ethical absolutism remains a powerful force among the leaders of the RSS and its affiliates. Many of the Jana Sangh and BJP cadre who were interviewed expressed misgivings about the strategies and policies employed to mobilize support, and there existed among them a certain ambiguity regarding the legitimacy of their political vocation.

However, the RSS—the major socializing agency for the cadre in the Jana Sangh and the BJP (as well as for other RSS affiliates)—has exerted influence over both policy and personnel selection without abandoning its apolitical orientation. Full-time RSS workers (i.e., the pracharaks) delegated to the affiliates maintain effective control by determining who will be recruited and advanced up the ranks. As the gatekeepers in the recruitment process, they ensure that the cadre reflect and reinforce the core values of the RSS. The growth of the affiliates has forced them to begin training their own full-time workers, a trend encouraged by the RSS. The RSS, itself experiencing an unprecedented expansion, is now reluctant to loan out pracharaks. This development has probably not undermined the bonds which link these organizers since available evidence suggests that those full-time workers trained by the affiliates tend to come from an RSS background.

The socialization process for many of the affiliates' recruits starts during adolescence when they join the RSS. Young swayamsevaks who do not respond to the nationalist belief system of the RSS or exhibit the requisite leadership characteristics either leave it or are not given greater responsibility. Those that do remain during this sifting process develop strong bonds with their fellow swayamsevaks. Other members of the RSS become, to borrow a phrase from George H. Mead, the 'significant audiences' whose opinions are valued, whose appreciation is sought, and who are important sources for duty and pride.[4] To remove oneself from colleagues (or to be removed from them), as Vasantrao Krishna Oke discovered, is to risk losing a part of one's self-identity. The cement which binds the swayamsevak to the affiliate is, we believe, the emotional ties he has developed with other RSS colleagues who have shifted to the affiliate. Indeed, we believe that these personal bonds play a much greater role in tying the RSS member to the affiliate than any ideological or policy issues. This relationship is further strengthened by continued association with them in the affiliate's work and in RSS activities.

The swayamsevaks included in the survey, as noted in Chapter 5, tended to perceive political participation as an extension of their former RSS activities. For the more committed, participation was gratifying not necessarily for the material rewards or the power that are potentially theirs, nor even the policy positions espoused by the party. The political task, like the 'cultural' task in the RSS, was to mobilize people to support the belief system of the RSS. But perhaps most gratifying was the opportunity to continue association with colleagues who had gone through RSS training. Indeed, if this were not so, the Jana Sangh, which was seldom able to distribute patronage and power, could not have elicited such sustained commitment on the part of its cadre.

Clearly, there were many in the organizational and parliamentary wings of the Jana Sangh—and BJP—whose motivations were not based on ideological commitment or personal bonds to old comrades, a fact which party leaders acknowledged and which concerned them. They attempted to keep such people in check by elevating the most committed (i.e., the full-time pracharaks) to the more important decision-making positions, and especially to the critical position of organizing secretary. These former full-time RSS workers monitored party activities and formed the steel frame of the party bureaucracy. They collectively served as the gatekeepers for recruitment and advancement, the formulators of party consensus, and the key communicators between different levels of the party, and between the party and the RSS.

The affiliates, because they depend on the RSS to train organizational workers, often have to depend on the RSS to begin work in new areas and among new groups. For example, Jana Sangh leaders pressured the RSS to take a more active role among the Scheduled Castes and the tribals, and in rural areas. There was even some pressure to open its ranks to Christians and Muslims. During the 1977–80 Janata period, some of the senior Jana Sangh figures at the centre, in an effort to protect the Jana Sangh group's secular credentials (and thus make it more acceptable to its alliance partners), openly put pressure on the RSS to adopt a more liberal attitude towards non-Hindus. The BJP, as it seeks to build an organizational structure, is trying to prove its good standing in the 'family' of affiliates in order to insure the availability of skilled party workers.

When neither the RSS nor the affiliate can supply a member of the 'family' with cadre in sufficient numbers, it is forced to turn to other sources. Its first preference is likely to be other RSS affiliates. When even that is not sufficient, it must look further afield; that happened on a large scale during the early years of the BJP. But that accommodation to 'outsiders' aroused complaints regarding 'indiscipline' among party leaders, which was the proximate cause for tightening up the party structure in 1983. Accordingly, the party decided to regulate organizational recruitment and advancement more closely to ensure greater conformity with what were considered legitimate behavioural and ideological norms. In short, preference is likely to be given to *swayamsevaks*. But the dilemma facing all the affiliates is that organizational cohesiveness may get in the way of mobilization objectives. So far, no affiliate has been willing to weaken the symbiotic links between it and the RSS in any substantial way.

The reluctance of the brotherhood of pracharaks to weaken the symbiotic links been the RSS and the affiliates can be traced, in our view, to two objectives of prime importance to them: (1) A sense of community must be maintained among the pracharaks, and (2) the affiliates' commitment to their 'mission' (i.e., applying the world view of the RSS to their area of work) must be sustained. The RSS training and its ideology pay special attention to the importance of group solidarity. Those swayamsevaks who become pracharaks have demonstrated the greatest commitment to each other and to the ideology. The pracharaks' sense of community is sustained by working together on a 'mission' in the affiliates. The RSS itself provides frequent occasions to reinforce interpersonal bonds (e.g., daily shakha programmes, camps, periodic meetings of pracharaks from all affiliates, rituals). In addition, the sacrifices demanded of pracharaks enhance the value of the brotherhood. Most are bachelors who have opted to live under austere physical conditions.[5] Many have also severed virtually all their ties with their own families. Recruiting a substantial number of 'outsiders into the key positions of the affiliates would dilute the distinctiveness that makes the organizational cadre a community, as well as undermine the organization's commitment to the 'mission' of the brotherhood.[6] To reduce the chances of this occurring, the brotherhood has constructed highly centralized structures and kept key positions in their own hands, enabling them to regulate entry and promotion throughout the organization. Increasingly, as the affiliates are forced to train their own full-time workers, they have tried to sustain their sense of community in the RSS brotherhood by giving preference to other swayamsevaks.

Regarding its 'mission', the RSS brotherhood considers itself the vanguard of a movement to restructure the domestic order in authentically indigenous terms and without the help of external legitimizing agents or ideologies. It has ideological comrades in many other Third World countries where similar movements have become very attractive as symbols of the reassertion of the dignity of people who feel they have been exploited. Like these comparable movements, the Hindu revivalism advocated by the RSS has a populist orientation which opposes concentrations of power and wealth as disruptive of the social solidarity required to sustain the political and cultural autonomy of India. Moreover, such concentrations of power and wealth are viewed as advancing the cause of such 'foreign' ideologies as capitalism and communism. With the continued challenge to traditional norms and social structures, the RSS message is likely to remain a potent competitor for the loyalty of people seeking a new ordering principle in their lives that does not require a complete rejection of indigenous symbols and beliefs.

Appendix A

RSS ORGANIZATIONAL CHART

I. Sarsanghchalak
II. Kendriya Karyakari Mandal (Central Working Committee)
   A. General secretary
      1. Assistant general secretary
   B. Karyalaya Pramukh (office secretary)—responsible for correspondence and expenditure of funds.
   C. Zonal joint secretaries
   D. Programme chairmen
      1. Prachar Pramukh—responsible for recruitment and placement of pracharaks.
      2. Sharirik Shikshan—arranges physical exercises at shakha and camps.
      3. Baudhik Pramukh—determines songs to learn, books to be read, topics at shakha and baudhik.
      4. Nidhi Pramukh—arranges for collection of funds at Gurudakshina*
      5. Vyavastha Pramukh—coordinator of activities.

275

III. Akhil Bharatiya Pratinidhi Sabha (All-India Representative Assembly). This meets once a year in Nagpur but for the last few years they have been meeting in different towns where the Sangh Parivar provides boarding and lodging facilities to 1500-plus delegates. Resolutions are discussed and voted by the Sabha. Members are elected by swayamsevaks over eighteen.

IV. Kshetra (Zone)

    A. Pracharak

V. Prant (State)

    A. Sanghchalak

    B. Karyavah

    C. Pracharak

    D. Committee

    E. Pratinidhi Sabha

VI. Vibhag (Division)

    A. Sanghchalak

    B. Karyavah

    C. Pracharak

    D. Committee

VII. Zila (District)

    A. Sanghchalak

    B. Karyavah

    C. Pracharak

    D. Committee

VIII. Nagar (City)

    A. Sanghchalak

    B. Karyavah

    C. Pracharak

    D. Committee

IX. Mandal (Neighbourhood)
- A. Karyavah
- B. Committee
- X. Shakha
- A. Karyavah
- B. Mukhya Shikshak
- C. Shikshak
- D. Gatanayak

*Subsequent to a decision to tax gurudakshina (offerings), the RSS constitution was amended to redefine the role of Nidhi Pramukh. Shakhas themselves were vested with individual responsibility in collecting donations to enable the RSS to operate with limits of tax exemption.

Appendix B

STEPWISE MULTIPLE REGRESSION ON VARIABLES INFLUENCING ADVANCEMENT IN THE JANA SANGH

	Multiple R	R^2	Change in R^2
RSS position	.54	.29	.29
Education	.61	.38	.09
Age	.66	.43	.05
Income	.69	.47	.04
Religious observation	.71	.50	.03
Marital status	.72	.52	.02
Year when joining Jana Sangh	.73	.53	.01
Caste	.73	.54	.01

	Multiple R	R^2	Change in R^2
Age when joining RSS	.74	.54	.01
Age at active political	.74	.54	.00
Interest			

Note: Only RSS members from the sample were included in this stepwise multiple regression in order to test if RSS participation was only an intervening variable. The results suggest that RSS participation is itself an independent variable, and that it is a far more influential factor than the other variables included here.

Appendix C

JANA SANGH PERFORMANCE IN ASSEMBLY ELECTIONS

(In the following tables, 'S' stands for Seats, 'C' for Contested, 'W' for Won, and 'V' for Vote Percentage)

	1952 Elections				1957 Elections			
	S	C	W	V	S	C	W	V
Andhra Pradesh	..	..	..	..	301	8	0	0.11
Assam	105	3	0	0.29	..	..	..	..
Bihar	318	44	0	1.15	318	29	0	1.19
Chandigarh**	1	1	0	2.81	..	..	..	..
Delhi**	48	31	5	21.88	..	..	..	..
Goa**	..	..	..	..	..	..	..	..
Gujarat	188	4	0	0.10	132	5	0	0.55
Haryana	60	23	2	6.12	55	24	4	12.02
Himachal Pradesh	50	19	0	6.80	..	..	..	..
Jammu and Kashmir***	..	..	..	..	75	22	5	24.63
Karnataka	211	25	0	1.21	208	20	0	1.34

	1952 Elections				1957 Elections			
	S	C	W	V	S	C	W	V
Kerala****	117	1	0	0.01	126	3	0	0.06
Madhya Pradesh	339	126	6	5.66	288	126	10	9.88
Maharashtra	301	36	0	1.28	264	18	4	2.01
Manipur	..	..	..	..	..	..	..	..
Orissa	..	..	..	..	..	..	..	..
Punjab	111	52	0	4.01	86	36	5	7.47
Rajasthan	189	65	11	6.34	176	47	6	5.42
Tamil Nadu	..	..	..	..	..	..	..	..
Tripura	..	..	..	..	..	..	..	..
Uttar Pradesh	430	210	2	6.64	430	235	17	9.77
West Bengal	250	85	9	5.31	252	33	0	0.98
Total	2,718	725	35	2.76	2,711	606	51	3.36

	1962 Elections				1967 Elections			
	S	C	W	V	S	C	W	V
Andhra Pradesh	301	70	0	1.04	287	80	3	2.11
Assam	105	4	0	0.45	126	20	0	1.84
Bihar	318	75	3	2.77	318	270	26	10.42
Chandigarh	1	1	0	12.18	..	..	..	..
Delhi	..	..	..	..	100	96	52	33.35
Goa	..	..	..	..	56	..	33	..
Gujarat	154	26	0	1.33	168	16	1	1.88
Haryana	54	34	4	13.46	81	48	12	14.39
Himachal Pradesh	..	..	..	..	60	33	7	13.87
Jammu and Kashmir	75	25	3	17.47	75	29	3	16.45
Karnataka	208	63	0	2.27	216	37	4	2.82

	1962 Elections				1967 Elections			
	S	C	W	V	S	C	W	V
Kerala	133	16	0	0.52	133	24	0	0.85
Madhya Pradesh	288	195	41	16.66	296	265	78	28.20
Maharashtra	264	127	0	5.00	270	165	4	8.18
Manipur	..	..	..	..	..	..	..	..
Orissa	..	..	..	..	140	19	0	0.54
Punjab	86	41	4	7.59	109	49	9	9.84
Rajasthan	176	94	15	9.15	184	63	22	11.69
Tamil Nadu	206	4	0	0.08	234	24	0	0.00
Tripura	..	..	..	..	30	5	0	0.35
Uttar Pradesh	430	377	49	16.46	425	401	98	21.67
West Bengal	252	25	0	0.45	280	58	1	1.53
Total	3,051	1,177	119	6.07	3,588	1,702	257	8.80

	1968–69 Mid-term Elections				1972–74 Elections			
	S	C	W	V	S	C	W	V
Andhra Pradesh	..	..	..	..	287	56	0	1.87
Assam	..	..	..	..	114	3	0	0.27
Bihar	318	303	34	15.63	318	271	26	11.37
Chandigarh	..	..	..	..	..	..	..	..
Delhi****	..	..	..	..	100	99	53	40.70
Goa	..	..	..	..	30	9	0	0.03
Gujarat	..	..	..	18.45	168	99	3	8.29
Haryana	81	44	7	..	81	19	2	6.54
Himachal Pradesh	..	..	..	..	68	31	5	7.76
Jammu and Kashmir	..	..	..	..	75	32	3	10.03
Karnataka	..	..	..	..	216	102	0	4.25

	1968–69 Mid-term Elections				1972–74 Elections			
	S	C	W	V	S	C	W	V
Kerala	..	..	..	..	..	..	..	..
Madhya Pradesh	..	..	..	..	296	261	48	28.72
Maharashtra	..	..	..	..	270	122	5	6.44
Manipur	..	..	..	..	60	1	0	0.22
Orissa	..	..	..	..	..	..	..	..
Punjab	104	30	8	9.01	104	33	0	4.95
Rajasthan	..	..	..	..	184	119	8	12.04
Tamil Nadu	..	..	..	..	..	..	..	..
Tripura	..	..	..	..	60	3	0	0.07
Uttar Pradesh	425	397	49	17.93	425	401	61	17.12
West Bengal	280	50	0	0.89	16	16	0	0.26
Total	1,208	824	98		1,677	1,677	214	..

	1975 Elections			
	S	C	W	V
Andhra Pradesh	..	..	..	..
Assam	..	..	..	..
Bihar	..	..	..	..
Chandigarh	..	..	..	..
Delhi	..	..	..	..
Goa	..	..	..	..
Gujarat	182	40	18	9.49
Haryana	..	..	..	..
Himachal Pradesh	..	..	..	..
Jammu and Kashmir	..	..	..	..
Karnataka	..	..	..	..
Kerala	..	..	..	..

	1975 Elections			
	S	C	W	V
Madhya Pradesh	..	..	..	..
Maharashtra	..	..	..	..
Manipur	..	..	..	..
Orissa	..	..	..	..
Punjab	..	..	..	..
Rajasthan	..	..	..	..
Tamil Nadu	..	..	..	..
Tripura	..	..	..	..
Uttar Pradesh	..	..	..	..
West Bengal	..	..	..	..

Sources. The 1952–67 figures are taken from Craig Baxter, *The Jana Sangh: A Biography of an Indian Political Party* (Philadelphia: University of Pennsylvania Press, 1969), and Appendix II, Craig Baxter, *District Voting Trends in India: A Research Tool* (New York: Columbia University Press, 1969). Subsequent election results are taken from the Election Commission of India's statistical reports. No total percentages are given in 1968–69 midterm elections or the 1972–74 elections because of the staggered dates for those elections.

Notes. *Includes elections only in the states and Union territories in which the Jana Sangh had candidates. We have calculated the results on the basis of states as presently constituted.

**The Jana Sangh participated in an electoral alliance in the 1975 state assembly elections in Gujarat. This alliance won a majority of the seats (i.e., 86 seats) to form the state government.

***Figures for 1957 and 1962 are for the Praja Parishad.

****The Kerala assembly elections were held in 1954, 1960, 1965 and 1967.

*****Figures for 1972–74 elections were taken from the 1971 election in Delhi.

Appendix D

JANA SANGH PERFORMANCE IN PARLIAMENTARY ELECTIONS

(In the following tables, 'S' stands for Seats, 'C' for Contested, 'W' for Won, and 'V' for Vote Percentage)

	1952 Elections				1957 Elections			
	S	C	W	V	S	C	W	V
Andhra Pradesh	..	..	..	..	43	1	0	0.04
Assam	12	2	0	3.64	..	..	..	..
Bihar	53	2	0	0.42	53	2	0	0.08
Chandigarh**	..	..	..	..	..	..	..	..
Delhi**	4	3	0	25.93	5	5	0	19.72
Dadra/Nagar Haveli**	..	..	..	..	..	..	..	..
Gujarat	..	..	..	..	..	..	..	..
Haryana	9	5	0	7.41	8	6	0	22.75
Himachal Pradesh	5	3	0	13.66	..	..	..	..

	1952 Elections				1957 Elections			
	S	C	W	V	S	C	W	V
Jammu and Kashmir	..	..	..	..	..	..	..	..
Karnataka	25	4	0	2.22	26	5	0	2.48
Kerala	..	..	..	..	..	..	..	..
Madhya Pradesh	38	11	0	5.92	36	21	0	13.96
Maharashtra	42	4	0	2.00	44	7	2	4.73
Manipur	..	..	..	..	..	..	..	..
Orissa	..	..	..	..	..	..	..	..
Punjab	13	5	0	3.36	12	10	0	13.39
Rajasthan	22	4	1	3.67	11	7	0	11.10
Tamil Nadu	..	..	..	..	..	..	..	..
Tripura	2	2	0	6.14	..	..	..	..
Uttar Pradesh	86	41	0	7.29	86	61	2	14.79
West Bengal	36	6	2	5.59	36	5	0	1.43
Totals	347	92	3	3.06	371	130	4	5.93

	1962 Elections				1967 Elections			
	S	C	W	V	S	C	W	V
Andhra Pradesh	43	8	0	1.17	41	6	0	1.44
Assam	..	..	..	..	14	3	0	5.48
Bihar	53	13	0	2.34	53	48	1	11.05

	1962 Elections				1967 Elections			
	S	C	W	V	S	C	W	V
Chandigarh**	..	..	..	..	1	1	1	48.70
Delhi**	5	5	0	32.66	7	7	6	46.72
Dadra/Nagar Haveli**	..	..	..	..	1	1	0	4.00
Gujarat	22	5	0	1.44	..	..	..	..
Haryana	8	8	3	23.42	9	7	1	19.85
Himachal Pradesh	6	2	0	0.94	6	3	0	19.06
Jammu and Kashmir	..	..	..	..	6	3	0	18.83
Karnataka	26	7	0	2.68	27	5	0	2.25
Kerala	18	4	0	0.68	19	4	0	1.39
Madhya Pradesh	36	28	3	17.87	37	32	10	29.56
Maharashtra	44	17	0	4.40	45	26	0	7.36
Manipur	..	..	..	..	..	..	..	..
Orissa	20	..	..	..	20	2	0	0.55
Punjab	12	9	0	10.30	13	8	1	12.49
Rajasthan	22	11	1	9.28	23	6	3	9.71
Tamil Nadu	..	..	..	..	39	4	0	0.22
Tripura	..	..	..	..	..	..	..	..
Uttar Pradesh	86	74	7	17.57	85	77	12	22.58
West Bengal	36	4	0	1.05	40	7	0	1.39
Totals	437	195	14	6.44	486	250	35	9.41

	1971 Elections			
	S	C	W	V
Andhra Pradesh	41	5	0	1.57
Assam	14	1	0	2.46
Bihar	53	28	2	12.10
Chandigarh**	1	1	0	23.31
Delhi	7	7	0	29.57
Dadra/Nagar Haveli**	..	..	..	..
Gujarat	24	5	0	2.22
Haryana	9	3	1	11.19
Himachal Pradesh	4	2	0	10.64
Jammu and Kashmir	6	3	0	12.23
Karnataka	27	2	0	1.90
Kerala	19	3	11	1.40
Madhya Pradesh	37	28	0	33.56
Maharashtra	45	12	0	5.23
Manipur	..	..	..	..
Orissa	20	1	0	1.00
Punjab	13	5	0	4.45
Rajasthan	23	7	4	12.38
Tamil Nadu	39	1	0	0.02
Tripura	2	1	0	0.49
Uttar Pradesh	85	40	4	12.28

	1971 Elections			
	S	C	W	V
West Bengal	40	4	0	0.85
Total	509	159	22	7.35

Sources. The 1952–67 election statistics are taken from Baxter, *Jana Sangh*; and Baxter, *District Voting Trends in India*; subsequent election results are taken from Election Commission of India's statistical reports.

Notes. *This table includes only those states or Union territories in which the Jana Sangh ran candidates. We have calculated the results on the basis of states as presently constituted.

**Union territories as presently constituted.

Bibliography

PRIMARY SOURCES
Manuscripts

Keshav Baliram Hedgewar, by courtesy of Madhav Sadashiv Golwalkar. Letters at Hedgewar Bhavan, RSS headquarters in Nagpur.

Minutes of the Hindu Mahasabha Working Committee Meetings, 1947–49. Hindu Mahasabha Bhavan, Delhi.

Madan Mohan Malaviya Papers, by courtesy of Padam Kant Malaviya. These papers are now deposited at the National Archives in Delhi.

Vinayak Damodar Savarkar Papers, Savarkar correspondents by courtesy of S. S. Savarkar (no relation, but primary secretary). This collection is now at Savarkar Sadan in Bombay. The Nehru Memorial Museum and Library (NMML)<https://protect-eu.mimecast.com/s/aDOIC2x8NSEB9MOHnBFF5?domain=nehrumemorial.nic.in>, New Delhi, microfilmed by Savarkar correspondents.

Official Records and Reports

Government of Bombay. *Source Material for a History of the Freedom Movement in India (collected from Bombay government records). Vol. 1: 1881–1885*. Bombay: Government Central Press, 1957.

291

Government of Bombay. *Source Material for a History of the Freedom Movement in India (collected from Bombay government records). Vol. 2: 1885–1920.* Bombay: Government Central Press, 1958.

Government of the Central Provinces. *Central Provinces District Gazeteers: Nagpur District*, ed. R. V. Russell. Bombay: Times Press, 1908.

Government of India, Election Commission of India. *Bye-Election Brochure: House of the People and Legislative Assemblies (1 March 1967 to 31 December 1969), Council of States and Legislative Councils (1 March 1964 to 31 December 1969), An Analysis.* Simla: Government of India Press, 1971.

Government of India, Election Commission of India. *Bye-Elections Brochure (1972): An Analysis: House of the People and Legislative Assemblies, Council of States and Legislative Councils (1 January 1971 to 31 December 1972).* Simla: Government of India Press, 1973.

Government of India, Election Commission of India. *Report on the Fifth General Elections in India, 1971–1972. Vol. 1: Narrative and Reflective Part.* New Delhi: Government of India Press, 1973.

Government of India, Election Commission of India. *Report on the Fifth General Elections to the House of the People in India, 1971. Vol. 2: Statistical.* New Delhi: Government of India Press, 1973.

Government of India, Election Commission of India. *Report on the First General Elections in India, 1951–1952. Vol. 1: General.* New Delhi: Government of India Press, 1955.

Government of India, Election Commission of India. *Report on the First General Elections in India, 1951–1952. Vol. 2: Statistical.* New Delhi: Government of India Press, 1955.

Government of India, Election Commission of India. *Report on the Fourth General Elections in India, 1967. Vol. 2: Statistical.* New Delhi: Government of India Press, 1967.

Government of India, Election Commission of India. *Report on the General Elections to the Legislative Assemblies of Andhra Pradesh, Bihar, Haryana, Himachal Pradesh, Jammu and Kashmir, Madhya Pradesh, Maharashtra, Punjab, Uttar Pradesh and West Bengal, 1980.* New Delhi: Government of India Press, 1981.

Government of India, Election Commission of India. *Report on the General Elections to the Legislative Assemblies of Bihar, Haryana, Himachal Pradesh, Jammu and Kashmir, Rajasthan, Madhya Pradesh, West Bengal, Kerala, Maharashtra, Council of Delhi, 1977. Statistical.* New Delhi: Government of India Press, 1978.

Government of India, Election Commission of India. *Report on the General Elections to the Legislative Assemblies of Manipur, Nagaland, Orissa, Uttar Pradesh and Pondicherry, 1974.* New Delhi: Government of India Press, 1975.

Government of India, Election Commission of India. *Report on the Mid-Term General Elections in India (1968–1969). Vol. 2: Statistical.* New Delhi: Government of India Press, 1970.

Government of India, Election Commission of India. *Report on the Second General Elections in India, 1957. Vol. 1: General.* Faridabad: Government of India Press, 1959.

Government of India, Election Commission of India. *Report on the Second General Elections in India, 1957. Vol. 2: Statistical.* New Delhi: Government of India Press, 1959

Government of India, Election Commission of India. *Report on the Seventh General Elections to the House of the People in India, 1980. Vol. 2: Statistical.* New Delhi: Government of India Press, 1981.

Government of India, Election Commission of India. *Report on the Sixth General Elections to the House of the People in India, 1977. Vol. 2: Statistical.* New Delhi: Government of India Press, 1978.

Government of India, Election Commission of India. *Report on the Third General Elections in India, 1962. Vol. 1: General.* Faridabad: Government of India Press, 1966.

Government of India, Home Department. *Political Proceedings and Files, 1925–1945.*

Government of India, Home Ministry. *Why Emergency?* New Delhi: Government of India Press, 1976.

Government of India, Ministry of Information and Broadcasting. *Fourth General Elections: An Analysis.* Faridabad: Thompson Press, 1967.

Government of Madhya Pradesh. *The History of the Freedom Movement in Madhya Pradesh.* Nagpur: Government Printing, 1956.

Government of Punjab, Pakistan. *R.S.S. in Punjab*. Lahore: Government Printing Press, 1948.

Government of Maharashtra. *Maharashtra State Gazeteers: Nagpur District*. Bombay: Government Central Press, 1966.

Newspapers and Periodicals

Hindu (Madras).
Hindustan Times (Delhi)
Hindu Vishwa (Delhi).
India Abroad (New York City).
Indian Express (Delhi).
India Today (Delhi).
Leader (Allahabad).
Link (Delhi).
Mahratta (Pune).
Northern India Patrika (Allahabad).
Organiser (Delhi).
Sangh Sandesh (Birmingham, England).
Secular Democracy (Delhi).
Statesman (Delhi).
Tarun Bharat (Nagpur and Pune).
Times of India (Bombay).
Times of India (Delhi).
Vivek (Bombay).
Ekata (Pune) Hindu, Marathi weekly (Bombay) Kesari (Pune)
Panchajanya (Delhi)

Interviews

A. Interviews with 190 members of the Jana Sangh party organization in three parliamentary districts (i.e., Allahabad City, Bombay North-east and Delhi Sadar), as well as members of Maharashtra and Delhi state committees, and members of the All-India Working Committee. These interviews were conducted between 1968 and 1971, and involved a standardized questionnaire.

B. Other Interviews

Aagi, Om Prakash. National secretary of the Bharatiya Mazdoor Sangh, on 23 June 1983 at Delhi.

Acharya, Govindan. RSS pracharak in Bihar, on 31 July 1983 at New Delhi.

Adil, Mohammed. Muslim politician in Sadar, on 25 March 1969 at Delhi.

Advani, Lal Krishna. General secretary of the Bharatiya Janata Party, on 15 September 1985 at Potomac, Maryland.

Agarwal, Devendra Swaroop. Director of the Deendayal Research Institute, on 26 June 1983 at Delhi.

Agrawal, Kameshwar Prasad. Communist Party of India labour union leader, on 10 May 1970 at Allahabad.

Aher, N. K. Leader of Peasants and Workers' Party group in Kalyan Municipal Council, on 1 April 1970 at Kalyan.

Ahmad, Bashir. Member of Allahabad District Congress (0) Committee, on 8 May 1970.

Apte, Shivram Shankar. Founder and general secretary of Vishwa Hindu Parishad and of the Hindustan Samachar, on 12 January 1969 at Bombay; officer in Bombay office of Hindustan Samachar, on 11 January 1969 at Bombay.

Bahadur, Krishna. RSS member and early organizer of Vidyarthi Parishad in Allahabad, during 25–26 January 1970 at Allahabad.

Bakht, Sikander. Vice-president of the Bharatiya Janata Party, on 8 May 1983 at Bombay.

Bakshi, Sadar. Joint Secretary of Bombay Pradesh Congress (0) Committee, on 20 April 1970 at Bombay.

Bansal, D. C. President of the Delhi Sadar District Congress (R) Committee, on 15 April 1970 at Delhi.

Behere, G. V. Editor of Marathi-language *Sobat*, on 8 April 1983 at Pune.

Bhagwat, Vasant. Secretary of the Maharashtra state unit of the Bharatiya Janata Party, on 6 June 1983 at New Delhi.

Bhandari, S. S. Member of the Bharatiya Janata Party National Executive Committee, on 26 July 1983 at New Delhi.

Bhargava, M. L. Son of founder of Jana Sangh in Allahabad, on 13 February 1969 at Allahabad.

Bhaskarrao, K. Former state pracharak of Kerala, on 24 April 1983 at Bombay.

Bhide, L. S. RSS liaison officer responsible for overseas activities, on 7 September 1983 at Chicago.

Bhishikar, C. P. Former editor of *Tarun Bharat* (Pune), on 28 April 1983 at Pune.

Bodhe, Narayan. Shiv Sena member of Bombay Municipal Corporation, on 31 October 1969 at Bombay.

Banatwala, M. A. Muslim League member of Maharashtra Legislative Assembly from Bombay, on 5 November 1969 at Bombay.

Chandra, Lokesh. Prominent activist in Vishwa Hindu Parishad, on 12 June 1970 at New Delhi.

Chatterjee, N. C. Former president of the Hindu Mahasabha, on 29 May 1969 at Calcutta.

Dandawate, Madhu. Joint secretary of the All-India Praja Socialist Party, on 17 March 1970 at Bombay.

Deshmukh, Nana. Chairman of the Deendayal Research Institute, on 16 April 1983 at Pune.

Deoras, Madhukar Dattatreya (popularly known as Balasaheb). RSS general secretary and present sarsanghchalak, on 21 April 1969 and 30 July 1983 at Nagpur.

Deoras, Murlidhar (aka Bhaurao). Assistant general secretary of the RSS, on 27 June 1983 at Delhi.

Desai, Morarji. Former prime minister of India, on 12 May 1985 at Chicago.

Deval, Madhukar. Former RSS pracharak, on 12 July 1983 at Pune.

Dharia, Mohan. Socialist leader, on 6 July 1983 at Pune.

Dharmadhikar, S. T. (aka Dada). A contemporary and friend of Dr K. B. Hedgewar, on 20 May 1983 at Bombay.

Didolkar, Datta Devidas. An early activist in Vidyarthi Parishad, on 20 April 1969 at Nagpur.

Digvekar, Rajabhau. A secretary of the Vishwa Hindu Parishad, on 14 May 1983 at Pune.

Godbole, Rambhau. Organizing secretary of the Vanavasi Kalyan Ashram, on 7 June 1983 at Bombay.

Godse, Gopal. Brother of Nathuram Godse, on 13 May 1969 at Pune. Gokhale, D. V. News editor of *Maharashtra Times* (Bombay), on 26 May 1983 at Bombay.

Gokhale, Gajanan S. Former leader of the Bharatiya Mazdoor Sangh, on 14 January 1969 and 22 November 1969 at Bombay, and 25–26 April 1983 at Pune.

Gokhale, S. P. Trusteee of the Savarkar National Memorial, on 15 April 1983 at Pune.

Golwalkar, Madhav Sadashiv. Sarsanghchalak of the RSS, on 26 February 1969 at Delhi and 15–18 April 1969 at Nagpur.

Goray, N. G. Socialist leader, on 26 May 1983 at Pune.

Gupta, Shiv Charan. Congress (R) leader in Delhi, on 6 April 1970 at Delhi.

Hafizka, A. K. President of the Bombay Pradesh Congress (0) Committee, on 23 December 1969 at Bombay.

Harmohan, Lala. General secretary of the Vishwa Hindu Parishad, on 23 May at Delhi.

Inamdar, Laxmanrao. RSS zonal pracharak for west India, on 24 May 1983.

Indurkar, G. S. Journalist, on 8 August 1983 at Delhi.

Jaiswal, Saligram. A founding member of the Socialist Party in Allahabad, on 28 September 1969 at Allahabad.

Jajoria, Khuba Ram. Scheduled Caste leader in Sadar, on 6 April 1970 at Delhi.

Jogalkar, J. D. Author of works on Hindu nationalism, on 25 May 1983 at Bombay.

Joshi, Appaji. Prominent RSS worker who was a close colleague of K. B. Hedgewar, on 29 December 1968 at Chandrapur.

Joshi, Jagannathrao. Member of the Bharatiya Janata Party National Executive Committee, on 7 May 1983 at Bombay.

Joshi, Murli Manohar. Secretary of the Bharatiya Janata Party, on 9 August 1983 at Delhi.

Joshi, S. M. Samyukta Socialist Party member of parliament, on 7 December 1968 at New Delhi.

Kadam, Anna. Bharatiya Kisan Sangh official, on 12 May 1983 at Pune.

Kalambekar, Dilip. Editor of *Vivek*, on 7 May 1983 at Bombay. Kale, Malharrao. General Secretary of the RSS from 1940 to 1943, on 30 June 1983 at Nagpur.

Kamath, M. V. Journalist, on 26 April 1983 at Bombay.

Kamble, N. M. Leader Scheduled Caste community in Bombay, on 5 November 1969 at Bombay.

Kelkar, B. K. Former RSS pracharak, author, and journalist, on 2 August 1983 at Delhi.

Kelkar, Yeshwantrao. President of the Vidyarthi Parishad, on 14 January 1969 and 14 July 1983 at Bombay.

Khanna, Jugal Kishor. Prominent Congress worker in Delhi between 1925 and 1945, on 15 April 1970 at Delhi.

Kishore, Giriraj. Organizing secretary of Vidyarthi Parishad, on 31 July 1969 at Delhi.

Kohli, Om Prakash. President of the Vidyarthi Parishad, on 7 May 1983 at Bombay.

Kolhatkar, S. Y. Communist Party of India (Marxist) labour leader, on 1 May 1970 at Bombay.

Kotwal, M. Labour leader in Dock and Port Workers Union, on 5 November 1959 at Bombay.

Krishan, Guru Radha. Communist Party of India activist, member of Delhi's Metropolitan Council, on 10 April 1970 at Delhi.

Lal, A. B. Vice chancellor of Allahabad University, on 27 January 1970 at Allahabad.

Lal, Chuni. Republican party activist in Allahabad, on 6 October 1959 at Allahabad.

Lele, N. B. Former journalist with *Hindustan Samachar*, on 9 August 1983 at Delhi.

Limaye, Madhukar. Former RSS pracharak in Assam, on 12 July 1983 at Pune.

Mahajan, Madhukar. Former Jana Sangh organizing secretary for Bombay, during 21–22 May 1983 at Bombay.

Majgoankar, S. G. Editor of *Manoos*, on 25 April 1983 at Pune.

Majumdar, J. M. Close friend of Dr S. P. Mookerjee, on 30 May 1969 at Calcutta.

Malaviya, Padma Kant. Grandnephew of Madan Mohan Malaviya, on 20 January 1970 at Allahabad.

Malkani, K. M. Editor of *Organiser*, on 24 June 1983 at Delhi.

Marathe, V. N. Shiv Sena worker in Thane, on 8 November 1969 at Thana.

Mathur, J. P. Bharatiya Janata Party member of the Rajya Sabha, on 26 July 1983 at Delhi.

Mehta, Mahesh. General secretary of the Vishwa Hindu Parishad of America, on 10 September 1985 at Chicago.

Mital, Surendra Nath. Former RSS pracharak, on 16 December 1972 at Allahabad.

Moghe, M. B. (aka Bapurao). Member of the central executive committee of the RSS, on 26 June 1983 at Delhi.

Mule, Madhavrao. RSS organizing secretary of Delhi, Haryana, Himachal Pradesh and Punjab, and later RSS general secretary; on 3 and 31 July 1969 at Delhi.

Nanda, Ved Prakash. Founding member of Vidyarthi Parishad, on 7 September 1969 at Delhi.

Nande, Harikar. RSS pracharak in Assam, on 12 July 1983 at Pune.

Narain, Raj. Socialist leader, on 16 April 1983 at Pune.

Nene, Dayanand. Editor of *Chatra Sakti*, on 27 April 1983 at Bombay.

Nene, D. V. Journalist, on 21 April 1983 at Bombay.

Oke, Vasantrao Krishna. First RSS organizer in Delhi, on 4 and 5 September 1969 at Delhi.

Pande, Bishamber Nath. Prominent Congress worker in Allahabad prior to independence, on 5 October 1969 in Allahabad.

Pande, Hari Shanker. Congress (R) worker in Allahabad, on 25 January 1970 at Allahabad.

Pandey, R. N. Member of the Bharatiya Janata Party from Maharashtra, on 8 May 1983 at Bombay.

Patel, Nanabhai. MLA of the Bharatiya Janata Party from Maharashtra, on 8 May 1983 at Bombay.

Pradhan, Datta. Leader of Shiv Sena labour affiliate, on 24 November 1969 at Bombay.

Prakash, Brahm. Prominent Congress party leader in Delhi between 1948 and 1969, on 23 November 1968 at Delhi.

Ranade, Eknath. RSS pracharak and organizer of Swami Vivekananda Mission, 29 December 1969 to 1 January 1970 at Kanyakumari, and 28 February 1970 at Delhi.

Saksena, Laxmi. Joint secretary of Uttar Pradesh Samyukta Socialist Party, on 14 and 26 May 1970 at Allahabad.

Samant, D. M. Samyukta Socialist Party member of the legislative assembly from Bombay, on 2 November 1969 at Bombay.

Saraswat, Ashok. President of the Allahabad University Students Union, on 3 February 1970 at Allahabad.

Sarbadhikary, Manoj Chandra. Hindu Mahasabha worker in Calcutta, on 12 June 1969 at Calcutta.

Sastry, Sripathy. Assistant prant pracharak for Maharashtra, on 3 May 1983 at Pune.

Sharma, Deep Chand. Member of the Delhi Pradesh Congress (R) Committee, on 27 April 1970 at Delhi.

Sharma, Mauli Chandra. Former president of the Jana Sangh, on 18 August 1969 at Delhi.

Sheshadri, H. V. Assistant organizing secretary of the RSS, on 11 July 1983 at Pune.

Singh, Jai. Sikh activist, on 10 April 1970 at Delhi.

Singh, Kartar. Sikh political leader in Sadar, on 12 April 1970 at Delhi.

Singh, Rajendra. General secretary of the RSS, on 16 July 1982 at Chicago, 25 July 1982 at Bethesda, Maryland, and 15 May 1983 at Bombay.

Singh, Ram Naresh. General secretary of the Bharatiya Mazdoor Sangh, on 27 July 1983 at Delhi.

Sudarshan, K. P. RSS baudhik pramukh, on 7 May 1983 at Pune. Telang, Shivrai. Pracharak in an RSS-affiliated cooperative workers' union, on 12 May 1983 at Bombay.

Thackeray, Bal. Founder and leader of the Shiv Sena, on 17 January 1969 at Bombay.

Thatte, Yadunath. Worker for the Rashtra Seva Dal (socialist youth organization), on 24 April 1983 at Pune.

Thengadi, Dattopant Bapurao. Chief theoretician of the RSS, on 10 September 1979 at Chicago, 10 April at Pune, and 26 June 1983 at Delhi.

Tomar, Lajjaram. Organizing secretary of Vidya Bharati, on 23 July 1983 at Delhi.

Vasudevan, G. Organizing secretary of the Vivekananda Kendra, on 27 June 1983 at Delhi.

Vishnuji, Shri. Leader of the Seva Bharati in Delhi, on 25 July 1983 at Delhi.

Wandrekar, W. G. Leader of the Congress (R) Municipal Party in Bombay, on 5 April 1970 at Bombay.

Zulfiqarullah, Sheikh Mohammed. Social worker, on 19 February 1969 at Allahabad.

Jana Sangh Resolutions and Addresses

Election Manifestos for 1957, 1962, 1967, 1971

Jana Sangh Resolutions, 1951–1974. 5 vols. New Delhi: Bharatiya Jana Sangh, 1975.

Resolutions passed by All-India Working Committee, 1953–1974.
Resolutions passed by all-India sessions, 1953–1974.

Publications of the RSS, Its Writers, and Writers Associated with Them

A. English

Advani, Lal Krishna. *Prisoners Scrapbook*. Delhi: Hind Pocket Books, 1979.

Akhil Bharatiya Vidyarthi Parishad. *Why and How*. Delhi: Nav Laxmi Press, New Delhi.

Apte, Bal. *Educational Challenge*. Delhi: ABVP, 1977.

Bharatiya Jana Sangh. *Bharatiya Jana Sangh: Principles and Policy*. Bombay: Excel Printers, 1965.

Bharatiya Jana Sangh. *'Garibi Badhao': Budget 1971–1972*. Delhi: Navchetan Press, 1972.

Bharatiya Jana Sangh. *The Jana Sangh Approach*. Delhi: Navchetan Press, 1968.

Bharatiya Jana Sangh. *Jana Sangh on Bank Nationalisation*. Delhi: Navchetan Press, New Delhi.

Bharatiya Jana Sangh. *A New Civic Deal for Delhi: Brief Report of Jana Sangh Achievements in Municipal Corporation*. Delhi: Navchetan Press, 1970.

Bharatiya Jana Sangh. *Recent Communal Riots: A Report*. Delhi: Navchetan Press, New Delhi.

Bharatiya Mazdoor Sangh. *BMS Souvenir*. New Delhi: BMS, 1980. Bharatiya Vanavasi Kalyan Ashram. Bombay: Kalyan Ashram, 1984.

Bhatnagar, Brij Bhusan. *Who Are Communal: A Treatise Which Tells Who Are Responsible for Partition and Communalism*. New Delhi: Suruchi Sahitya, 1974.

Chandra, Lokesh, et al. *India's Contribution to World Thought and Culture*. Faridabad: Thompson Press, 1970.

Deshmukh, Nana. *R.S.S.: Victim of Slander*. New Delhi: Vision Books, 1979.

Golwalkar, Madhav Sadashiv. *Bunch of Thoughts*. Bangalore: Vikrama Prakashan, 1966.

Golwalkar, Madhav Sadashiv. *From Red Fort Grounds*: 14th November 1965. Delhi: Asia Press, New Delhi.

Golwalkar, Madhav Sadashiv. *Homage to the Mahatma*. Bangalore: Navbharath Press, 1960.

Golwalkar, Madhav Sadashiv. *Spotlight*. Bangalore: Sahitya Sindhu, 1974.

Golwalkar, Madhav Sadashiv. *The War and After*. Bangalore: Rashtrotthana Mudranalaya, 1972.

Golwalkar, Madhav Sadashiv. *We or Our Nationhood Defined*, 4th ed. Nagpur: M. N. Kale, 1947.

Golwalkar, Madhav Sadashiv. *We and Our Students*. Bangalore: Prakashan Vibhag, 1966.

Koka, Subba Rao. *The Verdict*. Bangalore: Kesari Press, 1968.

Malkani, K. R. *India Tomorrow*. Lucknow: Eagle Printing Press, 1972.

Malkani, K. R. *The RSS Story*. New Delhi: Impex India, 1980.

Mathur, J. P., ed. *Jana Deep Souvenir*. Delhi: Rakesh Press, 1971. Mookerjee, Shyama Prasad. *Why B.J.S.?* Delhi: Bharat Mundranalaya, 1951.

Rashtriya Swayamsevak Sangh. *The Answer to All Questions*. Delhi: Bharat Mudranalaya, New Delhi.

Rashtriya Swayamsevak Sangh. *High Courts on R.S.S*. Bangalore: Sriranganidhi Printers, 1972.

Rashtriya Swayamsevak Sangh. *Hindu Rashtra and Minorities*. Bangalore: Navbharath Press, 1969.

Rashtriya Swayamsevak Sangh. *Justice on Trial: A Collection of the Historic Letters Between Sri Guruji and the Government*, 4th ed. Bangalore: Sharada Press, 1968.

Rashtriya Swayamsevak Sangh. *Mysore High Court on RSS: A Historic Judgment*. Bangalore: Kesari Press, 1966.

Rashtriya Swayamsevak Sangh. *Nation at War*. Bangalore: Printersall, 1966.

Rashtriya Swayamsevak Sangh. *Not Socialism, But Hindu Rashtra*. Bangalore: Kesari Press, 1964.

Rashtriya Swayamsevak Sangh. *Our Babasaheb*. Bangalore: Eastern Press, 1972.

Rashtriya Swayamsevak Sangh. *Rashtriya Swayamsevak Sangh: A Brief Introduction*. Delhi: Navchetan Press, New Delhi.

Rashtriya Swayamsevak Sangh. *Sangha Darshan: Sangh at a Glance*. Bangalore: Printersall, 1964.

Rashtriya Swayamsevak Sangh. *Shri Guruji*. Delhi: Punjab National Press, New Delhi.

Rashtriya Swayamsevak Sangh. *Shri Guruji Meets Delhi Newsmen*. New Delhi: Suruchi Sahitya, 1970.

Rashtriya Swayamsevak Sangh. *Shri Guruji, the Man and His Mission: On the Occasion of His 51st Birthday*. New Delhi: Bharat Prakashan, 1956.

Rashtriya Swayamsevak Sangh. *Sixty Years of the RSS*. Delhi: Suruchi Prakashan, 1985.

Rashtriya Swayamsevak Sangh. *Truth and Travesty—RSS vis-à-vis Gandhi Murder. A Myth Exploded*. Bangalore: Jagaran Prakashan, 1973.

Rashtriya Swayamsevak Sangh. *Spearheading National Renaissance*. Bangalore: Prakashan Vibhag, 1985.

Sastry, Shripaty. *A Retrospective, Christianity in India (An Exposition of the RSS Views on the Relevance of Christianity in India Today)*. Pune: Bharatiya Vichar Sadhana, 1948.

Seshadri, H. V., ed. Dr Hedgewar, the Epoch-Maker, comp. B. V. Despande and S. R. Ramaswamy, Bangalore: Sahitya Sindhu, 1981.

Seshadri, H. V. *Hindu Renaissance*. Bombay: Sahitya Sindhu, 1982.

Seshadri, H. V. *The Tragic Story of Partition*. Bombay: Jagran Prakashan, 1982.

Sandhi, M. L. Wanted: *A National Foreign Policy*. Delhi: Navchetan Press, 1968.

Swamy, Subramanian. *Nuclear Policy for India*. Delhi: Navchetan Press, 1968.

Swamy, Subramanian. *Plan for Full Employment*. Delhi: Navchetan Press, 1970.

Thengadi, D. B. *Focus on the Socio-Economic Problems*. New Delhi: Suruchi Sahitya, 1972.

Thengadi, D. B. *Why Bharatiya Sangh?* Pune: V. R. Shingre, 1959.

Upadhyaya, Deendayal. *Integral Humanism*. Delhi: Navchetan Press, 1968.

Upadhyaya, Deendayal. *Political Diary*. Bombay: Jaico Books, 1969.

Upadhyaya, Deendayal. *The Two Plans: Promises, Performance, Prospects*. Lucknow: Rashtradharma Prakashan, 1958.

Vidya Bharati. *Vidya Bharati National Academic Council: Delhi, 19–20 July 1980*. Gwalior: Vidya Bharati Publications, 1980.

Vishwa Hindu Parishad. *Dharma Sansad*. New Delhi: Vishwa Hindu Parishad, 1982.

Vishwa Hindu Parishad. *Hindu Sammelan*. New Delhi: Virat Hindu Samaj, 1982.

B. Hindi

Apte, Umarkant Keshav. *Doctor Hedgewar*. Nagpur: Mudranalaya, 1967.

Bhatia, Ved Prakash. *RSS: Loktantra Ka Prahari*. New Delhi: Suruchi Sahitya, 1977.

Bhatia, Ved Prakash. *RSS: Ek Jhalak, Balasaheb Deoras Sandhan*. New Delhi: Suruchi Sahitya, 1984.

Deoras, Balasaheb. *Hindu Bharatiya*. Jalandhar: Apana Sahitya, 1981.

Deoras, Balasaheb. *Hindutva, Tatva aur Vyavahar*. New Delhi: Suruchi Sahitya, 1981.

Deoras, Balasaheb. *Punjab Samasya aur Samadhan*. New Delhi: Suruchi Sahitya, 1984.

Deoras, Balasaheb. *Rashtra Jivan ki Agni Pariksha*. New Delhi: Suruchi Sahitya, 1981.

Deoras, Balasaheb. *Sadhya aur Sadhan*. Lucknow: Swadesh Press, New Delhi.

Deoras, Balasaheb. *Sangh Shakha*. Jalandhar: Apana Sahitya, 1981.

Deoras, Balasaheb. *Vardhaman Chunaut aur Sangha*. New Delhi: Suruchi Sahitya, 1975.

Golwalkar, Madhav Sadashiv. *Dishabodha*. Pune: Bharatiya Vichar Sadhana, 1982.

Golwalkar, Madhav Sadashiv. *Rashtra Bhakti Le Hriday me*. Patna: Sangh-Sandesh Mudranalaya, 1970.

Golwalkar, Madhav Sadashiv. *Rashtra ki Ekta aur Suraksha ki Adharbhut Manyataye*. Delhi: Navchetna Press, New Delhi.

Golwalkar, Madhav Sadashiv. *Vipatti me Sangh aur Swayamsevak*. Indore: Modern Printer, New Delhi.

Joshi, Yadavrao. *Bhavya atit Ujjval Bhavishya*. Udaipur: Swarashtra Prakashan, 1980.

Kohli, Om Prakash. *Rashtriya Suraksha ke Morcha Par*. New Delhi: Suruchi Sahitya, New Delhi.

Moghe, Madhusudan Vaman. *Bharatiyakaran*. Lucknow: Rashtra Dharma Pustak Prakashan, n.d.

Ranade, Eknath. *Hindu Rashtra ka Jivan-Lakshya*. Lucknow: Swadesh Press, New Delhi.

Rashtriya Swayamsevak Sangh. *Guruji: Rashtriya Swayamsevak ke Sarsanghchalak*. Delhi: Navchetna Press, New Delhi.

Rashtriya Swayamsevak Sangh. *Hamare Adarsh*. Nagpur: Nag Mudranalaya, New Delhi.

Rashtriya Swayamsevak Sangh. *Hamare Hedgewar*. Lucknow: Rashtradharm, Pustak Prakashan, New Delhi.

Rashtriya Swayamsevak Sangh. *Hindu Chintan*, Chunautiya. Lucknow: Lokhit Prakashan, 1982.

Rashtriya Swayamsevak Sangh. *Charcha ke Vishaya—Mukhya Sutra*. Delhi: Mudranalaya, New Delhi.

Rashtriya Swayamsevak Sangh. *Punjab Prant Baudhik 1972–1974*. Delhi: RSS Punjab Prant, 1974.

Rashtriya Swayamsevak Sangh. *Shri Guruji ki Dille me Patrakar Vartta*. Delhi: Bharat Mudranalaya, New Delhi.

Singh, Rajendra. *Sajjan Shakti ka Jagaran*. Nagpur: Bharatiya Vichar Sadhana, 1978.

Thengadi, D. B. *Bharatiya Kisan Dhyeya Path Par*. New Delhi: Suruchi Sahitya, 1984.

Thengadi, D. B. Kommunism: *Appi hi Kasauti par*. Lucknow: Swadesh Press, New Delhi.

Thengadi, D. B. *Loktantra*. Lucknow: Lokhit Prakashan, 1982.

Thengadi, D. B. Railway Karmachariyon di Hartal. Nagpur: Bharatiya Mazdoor Sangh, 1974.

Thengadi, D. B. *Upekshit Pahlu*. Kanpur: Tip Top Printers, 1965.

Thengadi, D. B. *Vichar Sutra*. Pune: BMS Research Institute, 1980.

Upadhyaya, Deendayal. *Amar Shahid*. Delhi: Hindi Pustak Books, New Delhi.

C. Marathi

Adhikari, G. G., ed. *Savarkarachya Athavani*. Pune: Adhikari, 1967.

Bapat, N. S. *Smruti Pushpe*. Pune: N. S. Bapat, 1984.

Bhishikar, C. P. *Babasaheb Apte*. Pune: Bharatiya Vichar Sadhana, 1983.

Bhishikar, C. P. *Bhayyaji Dani*. Pune: Bharatiya Vichar Sadhana, 1983.

Bhishikar, C. P. *Dada Parmartha*. Pune: Bharatiya Vichar Sadhana, 1983.

Bhishikar, C. P. *Ekatmetecha Marga*. Pune: Bharatiya Vichar Sadhana, 1977. Bhishikar, C. P. *Keshav, Sanghanirmata*. Pune: Bharatiya Vichar Sadhana, 1979.

Bhishikar, C. P. *Sri Guruji*. Pune: Bharatiya Vichar Sadhana, 1982.

Bhishikar, Swarnlata. Samarpit ek Adyam Utkat Chaitanya, Dr V. V. Pende. Pune: n.p., n.d.

Bundale, Rambhau. *Vidarbhacha Muktisangarsha*. Nagpur: Bharatiya Vichar Sadhana, 1978.

Damle, M. V. *Savarkar Smruti*. Ratnagiri: S. M. Desai, 1982.

Deshpande, S. H. *Sanghatale Divas*. Pune: Supama Prakashan, 1983.

Dhobale, Nana. *Samaj Talatale Moti*. Pune: Ekta Prakashan,

1981. Godbole, Arvind. *Savarkar Vichar Darshan*. Bombay: Popular Prakashan, 1983.

Gokhale, D. N. *Krantiveer Babarao Savarkar*. Pune: Sri Vidya Prakashan, 1979.

Gokhale, S. P. *Savarkaranchi Sukhasanvad*. Bombay: Magestic, 1983. Hardas, Balsastri. *Bhagwan Sri Krishna*. Pune: Kal Prakashan, 1952. *Hardas, Balsastri. Bharatiya Swatantrasamar 1957 te Subhash*. Pune: Kal Prakashan, 1957.

Hardas, Balsastri. Dharmaveer Dr Munje Yanche Charitra, 2 vols. Pune: Kal Prakashan, 1966 and 1981.

Hardas, Balsastri. *Mahabharatavaril Vyakhyane*. Pune: Kal Prakashan, 1951.

Hardas, Balsastri. *Vahiuki Ramayana*. Pune: Kal Prakashan, 1950. *Hardas, Balsastri. Vedatil Rashtradarshan, 2 vols. Pune: Kal* Prakashan, 1955–1956.

Hardikar, Vinay. *Janancha Pravah Chalala*. Pune: Rajhansa Prakashan, 1978.

Indurkar, Gangadhar. *Dilli Dinank*. Pune: Sri Vidya Prakashan, 1982.

Indurkar, Gangadhar. Rashtriya Swayamsevak Sangh: Kal, Raj, Aani Udya. Pune: Sri Vidya Prakashan, 1983.

Modak, Ashok. *Sanghache Awhan*. Satara: Ajinkya Prakashan, 1984. Majgoanker, S. G. *Balashali Bharat*. Pune: Rajhansa Prakashan, 1987.

Nene, V. V., ed. *Pandit Deendayal Upadhyaya Vichar Darshan*, 7 vols. Pune: Bharatiya Vichar Sadhana, 1986.

Palkar, N. H. *M. S. Golwalkar, Vyakti Ani Karya*. Pune: Hindustan Sahitya, 1956.

Palkar, N. H. *Dr K. B. Hedgewar*. Pune: Hari Vinayak Datye, 1964. Palkar, N. H. *Patraroop Vyaktidarshan—Dr Hedgewar*. Pune: Hindustan Sahitya, 1964.

Pendse, S. D. *Ramdas, Vyakti Ani Vangmaya*. Pune: Kesari Prakashan, 1973.

Rashtriya Punaruttanchya Aghadivar, RSS. Pune: Bharatiya Vichar Sadhana, 1985.

Savarkar, S. S. *Savarkar, Ratnagiri Parva. Bombay*: Veer Savarkar Prakashan, 1983.

Savarkar, S. S. *Hindusabha Parva*, 2 vols. Bombay: Veer Savarkar Prakashan, 1975 and 1977.

Shri Guruji Samagra Darshan, 7 vols. Nagpur: Bharatiya Vichar Sadhana, 1974–1981.

Thengadi, Dattopant Bapurao. *Chintan Samagri*. Pune: Bharatiya Vichar Sadhana.

Thengadi, Dattopant Bapurao. *Dr Babasaheb Ambedkar*. Pune: Bharatiya Vichar Sadhana, 1977.

Thengadi, Dattopant Bapurao. *Hindu Rashtra Sankalpana*. Pune: Bharatiya Vichar Sadhana, 1980.

Thengadi, Dattopant Bapurao. *Rashtrapurusha, Chatrapati Shivarai*. Pune: Bharatiya Vichar Sadhana, 1979.

Thengadi, Dattopant Bapurao. *Sangha Shakhanche Samarthya*. Pune: Bharatiya Vichar Sadhana, 1979.

Secondary Sources

Books, Articles, Unpublished Theses and Papers

Abbott, Justin E., trans. *The Poet Saints of Maharashtra*. Pune: Scottish Mission Industries, 1926.

Adhav, Baba. *Sanghachi Dhongabaji*. Pune: M. Phule Samata Prathistan Prakashan, 1977.

Adhav, Baba. *Sanghapasun Saradha*. Pune: M. Phule Samata Pratisthan Prakashan, 1978.

Ahmad, Aziz. *Studies in Islamic Culture in the Indian Environment*. Oxford: Clarendon Press, 1964.

Ahmad, Imtiaz. 'General Elections of 1967 in a Rural Constituency'. *Economic and Political Weekly* 6 (4 September 1971), pp. 1915–26.

Ahmad, Imtiaz. *Secularism and Communalism. Economic and Political Weekly 4*, special issue (July 1969), pp. 1137–58.

Ali, Chaudhri Muhammed. *The Emergence of Pakistan*. New York: Columbia University Press, 1967.

Almond, Gabriel A. and Powell, G. Bingham. *Comparative Politics: A Developmental Approach*. Boston: Little Brown, 1966.

Altbach, Philip. *Student Politics in Bombay*. Claude A. Eggertsen, ed. Bombay: Asia Publishing House, 1968.

Ambedkar, B. R. *Thoughts on Pakistan*. Bombay: Manektala, 1947. Andersen, Walter K. 'The Jana Sangh: Ideology and Organization in Party Behavior'. Unpublished PhD dissertation, University of Chicago, 1975.

Andersen, Walter K. 'The Rashtriya *Swayarasevak Sangh*'. *Economic and Political Weekly*, 11, 18, 25 March and 1 April 1972.

Andersen, Walter K. 'Political Philosophy of Deendayal Upadhyaya'. In *Destination*, ed. Raje Sudhakar, pp. 43–48. Delhi: Deendayal Research Institute, 1978.

Andersen, Walter K. and Saini, Mahender K. 'The Basti Julahan Bye-Election'. *Indian Journal of Political Science* 30 (July–September 1969), pp. 260–276.

Andersen, Walter K. 'The Congress Split in Delhi: The Effect of Factionalism on Organizational Performance and System-Level Interaction'. *Asian Survey* 11 (November 1971), pp. 1084–1110.

Andrian, Charles F. *Children and Civic Awareness*. Columbus, OH: Charles E. Merrill, 1971.

Apter, David. *The Politics of Modernization*. Chicago: University of Chicago Press, 1965.

Apter, David, ed. *Ideology and Discontent*. New York: Free Press of Glencoe, 1964.

Arendt, Hannah. *The Origins of Totalitarianism*. Cleveland: Meridian Books, 1962.

Auspitz, Reuben. 'The Akhil Bharatiya Vidyarthi Parishad: An Introductory Study of Rightist Student Politics in India'. Paper prepared for the University of Wisconsin's College-Year-in-India Programme, The Delhi School of Social Work, 1968.

Azad, Abul Kalam. *India Wins Freedom: An Autobiographical Narrative*. Bombay: Orient Longman, 1959.

Badhe, G. S. and M. U. Rao, Bombay Civic Election of 1968. *Journal of the University of Bombay* 37 (October 1968), pp. 287–307.

Baker, D. E. U. *Changing Political Leadership in an Indian Province: The Central Province and Berar*, 1919–1939. Delhi: Oxford University Press, 1979.

Barlingay, S. S. *Poverty, Power, Progress*. New Delhi: Pansheel Prakashan, 1983.

Barnouw, Victor. 'The Changing Character of a Hindu Festival'. *American Anthropologist* 56 (February 1944), pp. 74–85.

Barnes, Samuel H. Ideology and the Organization of Conflict: On the Relationship between Political Thought and Political Action. *Journal of Politics* 28 (August 1966), pp. 513–30.

Barrier, Norman G. 'The Arya Samaj and Congress Politics in the Punjab, 1894-1904'. *The Journal of Asian Studies* 26 (May 1967), pp. 363–79.

Baxter, Craig. *District Voting Trends in India: A Research Tool*. New York: Columbia University Press, 1969.

Baxter, Craig. *The Jana Sangh: A Biography of an Indian Political Party*. Philadelphia: University of Pennsylvania Press, 1969.

Bayley, C. A. 'Local Control in Indian Towns—The Case of Allahabad, 1880–1920'. *Modern Asian Studies* 5 (October 1971), pp. 289–311.

Bedkihal, Kishore. *Rashtriya Swayamsevak Sangh*. Pune: M. Phule Samata Pratisthan Prakashan, 1982.

Bernier, Francois. *Travels in the Mogul Empire: A.D. 1656–1668*, 2nd ed., rev. Vincent A. Smith, trans. Archibald Constable. London: Oxford University Press, 1914.

Bharat Seva Samaj. *Slums of Old Delhi*. Delhi: Bharat Seva Samaj, 1948.

Bhargava, Kusum. 'Rajasthan Politics and Princely Rulers: An Analysis of Electoral Processes'. *Indian Journal of Political Science* 33 (October–December 1972), pp. 413–30.

Bondurant, Joan. *Conquest of Violence: The Gandhian Philosophy of Conflict*, rev. ed. Berkeley: University of California Press, 1967. Bose, Shankar and V. B. Singh. *Elections in India: Data Handbook on Lok Sabha Elections, 1952–1980*. New Delhi: Sage Publications, 1984.

Brass, Paul. *Factional Politics in an Indian State*. Berkeley: University of California Press, 1965.

Brecher, Michael. *Nehru: A Political Biography*, abridged ed. Boston: Beacon Press, 1962.

Brim, O. G. and Wheeler, S. *Socialization after Childhood*. New York: Wiley, 1966.

Broomfield, John. *Elite Conflict in a Plural Society: Twentieth Century Bengal*. Berkeley: University of California Press, 1968. Burway, Wamanrao. *The Struggle between the Mahrattas and Moghuls*. Bombay: n.p., 1914.

Campbell, A. et al. *The American Voter*. New York: Wiley, 1960. Carstairs, G. Morris. *The Twice Born: A Study of a Community of High Caste Hindus*. Bloomington: Indiana University Press, 1958.

Carter, A. T. 'Political Stratification and Unstable Alliances in Rural Maharashtra'. *Modern Asian Studies* 6 (October 1972), pp. 532–42. Cashman, Richard I. *The Myth of the Lokamanya*. Berkeley: University of California Press, 1975.

Chand, J. C. 'Mid-Term Poll in Punjab'. *Political Science Review* 10 (January–June 1971), pp. 1–29.

Chandidas, R.; Ward Morehouse, Leon Clark, and Richard Fontera, eds. *India Votes: A Source Book on Indian Elections*. New York: Humanities Press, 1968.

Clark, T. W. '*The Novel in India: Its Birth and Development*. Berkeley: University of California Press, 1970.

Clark, T. W. 'The Role of Bankimchandra in the Development of Nationalism'. *Historians of India, Pakistan and Ceylon*, ed. C. H. Philips. London: Oxford University Press, 1961.

Cohen, Stephen P. *The Indian Army: Its Contribution to the Development of a Nation*. Berkeley: University of California Press, 1971.

Cohn, Norman. 'Medieval Millenarism: Its Bearing on the Comparative Study of Millenarian Movements'. *Millenial Dreams in Action: Essays in Comparative Study*, ed. Sylvia L. Thrupp, pp. 31–43. The Hague: Moutan, 1962.

Converse, Philip and Georges Dupeux. 'Politicization of the Electorate in France and the United States'. *Public Opinion Quarterly* 26 (Spring 1962), pp. 23–30.

Cassirer, Ernst. *Language and Myth*, trans. Susanne K. Langer. New York: Dover Publishing, 1946.

Cassirer, Ernst. *Myth and the State*. New Haven: Yale University Press, 1973.

Curran, Jr. J. A. *Militant Hinduism in Indian Politics: A Study of the R.S.S.* New York: Institute of Pacific Relations, 1951.

Das, Durga, ed. *Sardar Patel's Correspondence: 1945–1950*, 10 vols. Ahmedabad: Navajivan Publishing House, 1973.

Das, J. I. 'Syamaprasad, The Uncompromising Patriot'. *Modern Review* 121 (June 1970), pp. 450–52.

Date, S. R. *Maharashtra Hindusabhachaya Karyacha Itihas*. Pune: S. R. Date, 1975.

Datta, Dhirendra Mohan. 'Some Philosophical Aspects of Indian Political, Legal and Economic Thought'. *The Indian Mind: Essentials of Indian Philosophy and Culture*, ed. Charles A. Moore, pp. 267–98. Honolulu: University of Hawaii Press, 1967.

Datta, V. N. *Madanlal Dhingra, Revolutionary Movement*. New Delhi: Vikas Publishing House, 1978.

Dennis, Jack and David Easton. 'The Child's Image of Government', *The Annals of the American Academy of Political and Social Science* 361 (September 1965), pp. 40–57.

Dharmadhikari, Dada. *Pakistanche Sankat*. Pune: Sulabha Rashtriya Granthmala, 1947.

DiBona, Joseph E. *Change and Conflict in the Indian University*. Durham, North Carolina: Duke University Press, 1969.

Dimock, Edward C., Jr. 'Doctrine and Practice Among the Vaishhavas of Bengal'. *Krishna: Myths, Rites and Attitudes, ed.*

Milton Singer, pp. 41–63. Chicago: University of Chicago Press, 1968.

Dhooria, Ram Lal. 'I Was a Swayamsevak–II: The Vilest Abortionists', *Secular Democracy* 2 (June 1969), pp. 21–23.

Dhooria, Ram Lai. 'I Was a Swayamsevak–III: Victims of an Idiotic Approach', *Secular Democracy* 2 (July 1969), pp. 12–14, 26.

Dobbin, Christine E. 'Competing Elites in Bombay City Politics in the Mid-Nineteenth Century (1852–1883)'. *Elites in South Asia*, eds Edmund Leach and S. N. Mukherjee, pp. 79–94. Cambridge: University Press, 1970.

Dobbin, Christine E. *Basic Documents in the Development of Modern India and Pakistan, 1935–1947*. London: Van Nostrand Reinhold, 1970.

Dubois, Abbe Jean Antoine. *Hindu Manners, Customs and Ceremonies*, ed. Henry K. Beauchamp, 3rd ed. Oxford: Clarendon Press, 1953.

Dumont, Louis. *Homo Hierarchicus: The Caste Systen and Its Implications*, eds. Julian Pitt-Rivers and Ernest Gellner, trans. Mark Sainsbury. Chicago: University of Chicago Press, 1970.

Easton, David. *A System Analysis of Political Life*. New York: Wiley, 1965.

Edelman, Murray. *Politics as Symbolic Action: Mass Arousal and Quiescence*. Chicago: Markham Publishing, 1972.

Edgerton, Franklin, trans., interpreter. *Bhagavad Gita*. New York: Harper and Row, 1964.

Eldersveld, Samuel J. *Political Parties: A Behavioral Analysis*. Chicago: Rand McNally, 1964.

Elenjimittan, Anthony. *Philosophy and Action of the RSS for Hind Swaraj*. Bombay: Laxmi Publications, 1951.

Erdman, Howard Lloyd. *The Swatantra Party and Indian Conservatism*. London: Cambridge University Press, 1967.

Erikson, Erik H. *Young Man Luther: A Study in Psychoanalysis and History*. New York: North and Co., 1956.

Erikson, Erik H. *Gandhi's Truth: On the Origins of Militant Non-violence*. New York: Norton and Co., 1969.

Etzioni, Amitai. *A Comparative Analysis of Complex Organizations*. New York: Free Press, 1961.

Farquhar, J. N. *Modern Religious Movements in India*. Delhi: Munshiram Manoharlal, 1967.

Gandhi, Mohandas Karamchand. *Autobiography*. Ahmedabad: Navjivan Publishing House, 1984.

Gandhi, Mohandas Karamchand. *On Hinduism*. Ahmedabad: Navjivan Publishing House, 1965.

Gangadharan, K. K. *Sociology of Revivalism: A Study of Indianisation, Sanskritisation and Golwalkarism*. New Delhi: Kalamkar Prakashan, 1970.

Geertz, Clifford. 'Ideology as a Cultural System'. *Ideology and Discontent*, ed. David E. Apter, pp. 45–56. Glencoe, Illinois: Free Press of Glencoe, 1964.

Geertz, Clifford. 'The Integrative Revolution: Primordial Sentiments and Civic Politics in the New States'. *Old Societies and New States: The Quest for Modernity in Asia and Africa*, ed. Clifford Geertz, pp. 105–157. Glencoe, Illinois: Free Press of Glencoe, 1963.

Geertz, Clifford. 'Religion as a Cultural System'. *Reader in Comparative Religion: An Anthropological* Approach, eds William Lessa and Evon Vogt, 3rd ed., pp. 1–46. New York: Harper and Row, 1972.

Ghose, Aurobindo. *The Doctrine of Passive Resistance*, 2nd ed. Pondicherry: Sri Aurobindo Ashram, 1952.

Ghose, Aurobindo. *Essays on the Gita*. Pondicherry: Sri Aurobindo Ashram, 1959.

Ghurye, Govind Sadashiv. *Social Tensions in India*. Bombay: Popular Prakashan, 1968.

Gilbert, Irene A. 'Autonomy and Consensus under the Raj: Presidency (Calcutta); Muir (Allahabad); M.A.O. (Aligarh)'. *Education and Politics in India*, eds Lloyd Rudolph and Susanne Hoeber Rudolph, pp. 172–206. Cambridge: Harvard University Press, 1972.

Godse, Nathuram. *May It Please Your Honour*. Pune: Vitasta Prakashan, 1978.

Gopal, Ram. *Indian Muslims: A Political History (1858–1947)*. Bombay: Asia Publishing House, 1959.

Gordon, Leonard A. *Bengal: The Nationalist Movement, 1876–1940*. New York: Columbia University Press, 1974.

Gordon, Richard. The Hindu Mahasabha and the Indian National Congress. *Modern Asian Studies* 9 (April 1975), pp. 145–203.

Goyal, D. R. *Rashtriya Swayamsevak Sangh*. New Delhi: Radhakrishna Prakashan, 1979.

Graham, Bruce. 'Shyama Prasad Mookerjee and the Communalist Alternative. *Soundings in South Asian History*, ed. D. A. Low, pp. 330–74. London: Weidenfeld and Nicholson, 1968.

Greenstein, Fred I. *Children and Politics*. New Haven: Yale University Press, 1965.

Grodzins, Morton. *The Loyal and the Disloyal: Social Boundaries of Patriotism and Treason*. Chicago: University of Chicago Press, 1956.

Gupta, Khadiya A. 'General Elections in a Small Town'. *Economic and Political Weekly* 6 (August 1971), pp. 1881–1886.

Haldar, Gopal. 'Revolutionary Terrorism'. *Studies in Bengal Renaissance*, ed. Atul Chandra Gupta. Jadavpur: National Council of Education, Bengal, 1958.

Hasan, K. Sarwar. *Transfer of Power*. Karachi: Pakistan Institute of International Affairs, 1966.

Heeger, Gerald A. Discipline versus Mobilization: Party Building and the Punjab Jana Sangh. *Asian Survey* 12 (October 1972), pp. 864–79.

Heimsath, Charles H. *Indian Nationalism and Hindu Social Reform*. *Princeton: Princeton University Press*, 1964.

Hess, Robert D. and Judith Torney. *The Development of Political Attitudes in Children*. Chicago: Aldine, 1967.

Hiriyanna, Mysore. *Outlines of Indian Philosophy*. London: George Allen and Unwin, 1932.

Hodson, Henry V. *Great Divide*. London: Hutchinson, 1969.

Hopkins, Thomas J. 'The Social Teaching of the Bhagavata Purana'. *Krishna: Myths, Rites and Attitudes*, ed. Milton Singer, pp. 3–22. Chicago: University of Chicago Press, 1968.

Ikram, Sheikh Mohmed. *Modem Muslim India and Birth of Pakistan: 1858–1951*. Lahore: Institute of Islamic Culture, 1977.

Inkeles, Alex. 'The Totalitarian Mystique: Sane Impressions of the Dynamics of Totalitarian Society'. *Totalitarianism: Proceedings of a Conference Held at the American Academy of Arts and Sciences, March 1953*, ed. Carl Joachim Friedrich, pp. 88–108. Cambridge, Mass.: Harvard University Press, 1954.

Janowitz, Morris. ''Social Stratification and the Comparative Analysis of Elites'. *Social Forces* 35 (October 1956), pp. 81–85.

Jaros, Dean. *Socialization to Politics*. New York: Praeger, 1973.

Javadekar, S. D. *Adhunik Bharat*. Pune: Rashtriya Grantha Prakashan, 1936.

Jayakar, M. R. *The Story of My Life*, 2 vols. Bombay: Asia Publishing House, 1958.

Jhangianai, Motilal A. *Jana Sangh and Swatantra*. Bombay: Manaktalas, 1967.

Jhari, K. D. 'I Was a Swayamsevak–V: Creating the Urge to Kill'. *Secular Democracy* 3 (July 1970), pp. 27–29.

Jhari, K. D. 'I Was a Swayamsevak–VII: Open Involvement in Politics'. *Secular Democracy* 3 (September 1970), pp. 9–10.

Johnson, Gordon. 'Chitpavin Brahmins and Politics in Western India in the Late Nineteenth and Early Twentieth Centuries'. *Elites in South Asia*, eds. Edmund Leach and S. N. Mukerjee, pp. 95–118. Cambridge, UK., Cambridge: University Press, 1970.

Johnson, Gordon. *Provincial Politics and Indian Nationalism: Bombay and the Indian National Congress, 1880–1915*. London: Cambridge University Press, 1973.

Jones, Kenneth. 'W. Communalism in the Punjab: The Arya Samaj Contribution'. *The Journal of Asian Studies* 28. (November 1968), pp. 39–54.

Joshi, Ram and Desai, Kirtidev. 'Dominance with a Difference: Strains and Challenges'. *Economic and Political Weekly* 7 (Annual Number 1973), pp. 189–196.

Kanter, Rosabeth Moss. *Commitment and Community: Communes and Utopias in Sociological Perspective*, 7th printing. Cambridge, Mass.: Harvard University Press, 1979.

Karve, Dinakar D., ed. and trans. *The New Brahmins: Five Maharashtrian Families*, ed. assistance Ellen E. McDonald. Berkeley: University of California Press, 1963.

Katzenstein, Mary. 'The Consequences of Migration: Nativism, Symbolic Politics and National Integration'. Presented at the American Political Science Association meeting in New Orleans, 1973.

Keer, Dhananjay. *Veer Savarkar*, 2nd ed. Bombay: Popular Prakashan, 1966.

Kelly, Harold H. and John W. Thibaut. *The Social Psychology of Groups*. New York: Wiley, 1959.

Keniston, Kenneth. Youth: A 'New' Stage of Life. *American Scholar* 39 (Autumn 1970), pp. 631–654.

Khare, N. B. *My Political Memoirs or Autobiography*. Nagpur: J. P. Joshi, 1959.

Khurshid, Abdus Salem, ed. *History of the Idea of Pakistan. Islamabad*: National Committee for Birth Centenary of Jinnah, 1977.

Kirtananda, Swami. *The Glory of the Divine Mother*. Calcutta: Ramakrishna Mission Institute of Culture, 1964.

Kishore, Mohammed Ali. *Jana Sangh Foreign Policy of India*. Delhi: Associated Publishing House, 1970.

Kochanek, Stanley. *The Congress Party of India: The Dynamics of a One-Party Democracy*. Princeton: Princeton University Press, 1963.

Kohn, Hans. *A History of Nationalism in the East*. New York: Harcourt, Brace, 1929.

Kothari, Rajni. 'The Congress System Revisited'. *Asian Survey* 14 (December 1974), pp. 1035–1054.

Kothari, Rajni. *Politics in India*. Boston: Little, Brown, 1970. Kubota, Akira and Ward, Robert E. Family Influence and Political Socialization in Japan. *Comparative Political Studies* 3 (July 1970), pp. 140–75.

Kurundkar, Narhar. *Jagar*. Pune: Deshmukh, 1969. Kurundkar, Narhar. *Shivratra*. Pune: Deshmukh, 1970. Lane, Robert E. *Political Man*. London: Free Press, 1972.

Langer, Susanne K. *Philosophy in a New Key: A Study in the Symbolism of Reason, Rite and Art*. Cambridge, Mass.: Harvard University Press, 1951.

Lasswell, Harold D. 'The Selective Effect of Personality on Political Participation'. *The Authoritarian Personality—Continuities in Social Research*, eds Richard Christie and Marie Jahoda, pp. 197–225. Glencoe, Illinois: Free Press, 1954.

Lenin, V. I. *What Is to Be Done?* New York: International Publishers, 1929.

Lipset, Seymour Martin and Stein Rokka. 'Cleavage Structures, Party Systems and Voter Alignments: An Introduction'. *Party Systems and Voter Alignments: Cross-National Perspectives*, eds. Seymour Martin Lipset and Stein Rokkan. New York: Free Press, 1967.

McCloskey, Herbert and Harold Dahlgren. 'Primary Group Influence on Party Loyalty'. *American Political Science Review* 53 (September 1959), pp. 762–770.

Madhok, Balraj. *Dr Shyama Prasad Mookerjee*. New Delhi: Deepak Prakashan, 1954.

Madhok, Balraj. *A Hindu Rashtra*. Delhi: Swastik Prakashan, 1955. Madhok, Balraj. *Indian Nationalism*. New Delhi: Bharatiya Sahitya Sadan, 1969.

Madhok, Balraj. *Indianisation? (What, Why and How)*. New Delhi: S. Chand, n.d.

Madhok, Balraj. *On India's Foreign Policy and National Affairs*. New Delhi: Bharatiya Sahitya Sadan, 1969.

Madhok, Balraj. *Portrait of a Martyr; Biography of Dr Shyama Prasad Mookerji*. Bombay: Jaico Publishing House, 1969.

Madhok, Balraj. *Sansad me Dilli*. Delhi: Navchetan Press, n.d.

Majumdar, R. C. *History of the Freedom Movement in India*, 3 vols. Calcutta: Firma K. L. Mukhopadhyay, 1963.

Malaviya, H. D. *The Danger of Right Reaction*. New Delhi: Socialist Congressman Publication, 1965.

Mayer, A. C. 'Caste and Local Politics in India'. *India and Ceylon: Unity and Diversity*, ed. Paul Mason, pp. 121–141. London: Oxford University Press, 1967.

Masani, Zareer. *Indira Gandhi: A Biography*. New York: Thomas Y. Cromwell, 1964.

Mead, George H. *Mind, Self and Society*, ed. Charles W. Morris. Chicago: Chicago University Press, 1954.

Menon, V. P. *Transfer of Power in India*. Princeton: Princeton University Press, 1957.

Michels, Robert. *Political Parties: A Sociological Study of the Oligarchical Tendencies of Modern Democracy*, trans. Eden and Cedar Paul. New York: Free Press, 1962.

Milbrath, Lester W. *Political Participation*. Chicago: Rand McNally, 1968.

Minault, Gail. *Khilafat Movement, Religious Symbolism and Political Mobilization in India*. New York: Columbia University Press, 1982.

Mishra, Dina Nath. *R.S.S.: Myth and Reality*. Ghaziabad: Vikas Publishing House, 1980.

Mishrawalla. *Delhi Diary*, Vol. 3. Delhi: Gyandeep Prakashan, 1978.

Misra, B. B. *The Indian Middle Classes: Their Growth in Modern Times*. London: Oxford University Press, 1961.

Mookerjee, Shyama Prasad. *A Phase of the Indian Struggle: How the Indian Constitution Works*. Calcutta: n.p., 1942.

Moon, Penderel. *Divide and Quit*. Berkeley: University of California Press, 1962.

Morris-Jones, W. H. *The Government and Politics of India*. London: Hutchinson University Library, 1964.

Morris-Jones, W. H. 'Political Recruitment and Political Development'. *Politics and Change in Developing Countries: Studies in the Theory and Practice of Development*, ed. Colin Leys, pp. 112–134. Cambridge,: Cambridge University Press, 1969.

Mosely, Leonard E. *The Last Days of the British Raj*. New York: Harcourt, Brace & World, 1961.

Muhammed, Shan. *Khaksar Movement in India*. Meerut: Meenakshi Prakashan, 1973.

Mukherjee, Haridas and Uma, Mukerjee. *'Bande Mataram' and Indian Nationalism*. Calcutta: Firma K. L. Mukhopadhyay, 1957.

Mullins, Willard. 'On the Concept of Ideology in Political Science'. *American Political Science Review* 66 (June 1972), pp. 498–510.

Murphy, A. and G. B, Murphy. *In the Minds of Men*. New York: Basic Books, 1953.

Mydeo, V. G. *A Catechism of Hinduism*. Pune: Sadhana Press, 1966. Nagarkar, V. V. *Genesis of Pakistan*. Bombay: Allied Publisher, 1975. Nandy, Ashis. 'The Culture of Indian Politics'. *The Journal of Asian Studies* 30 (November 1970), pp. 57–79.

Narayan, Jaiprakash. *Prison Diary*. Bombay: Popular Prakashan, 1977.

Nayar, Baldev Raj. 'Punjab'. *State Politics in India*, ed. Myron Weiner, pp. 435–502. Princeton: Princeton University Press, 1968.

Nayar, Pyarelal. *Last Phase*. Ahmedabad: Navjivan, 1958.

Nehru, Jawaharlal, comp. *A Bunch of Old Letters Written Mostly to Jawaharlal Nehru and Some Written by Him*, 2nd ed. Bombay: Asia Publishing House, 1960.

Nehru, Jawaharlal, comp. *Toward Freedom*. Boston: Beacon Press, 1958.

Olsen, Mancur, Jr. *The Logic of Collective Action: Public Goods and the Theory of Groups*. Cambridge, Mass: Harvard University Press, 1955.

Owen, Hugh. 'Negotiating the Lucknow Pact'. *The Journal of Asian Studies* 31 (May 1972), pp. 561–587.

Pandy, R. B. 'Hindu Sacraments'. *The Cultural Heritage of India*, eds Haridas Bhattacharya et al., 4 Vols., Calcutta: Ramakrishna Mission Institute of Culture, 1953–1962, Vol. 2, pp. 392–94.

Park, Richard L. 'The Rise of Militant Nationalism in Bengal: A Regional Study of Indian Nationalism'. Unpublished PhD dissertation, Harvard University, 1951.

Park, Richard and Tinker, Irene, eds. *Leadership and Political Institutions in India*. Princeton: Princeton University Press, 1959.

Patterson, Maureen L. P. 'A Preliminary Study of the Brahman vs. Non-Brahman Conflict in Maharashtra.' Unpublished master's thesis, University of Pennsylvania, 1952.

Phadke, Y. D. *Shodha Savarkarancha*. Pune: Sri Vidya Prakashan, 1984.

Piaget, Jean. *The Moral Judgment of the Child*, trans. Marjorie Gabain. London: Kegan, Paul, Trench, Trubner, 1932.

Punjabi, Kewalram L. *The Indomitable Sardar: A Political Biography of Sardar Vallabhbhai Patel*. Bombay: Bharatiya Vidya Bhavan, 1962.

Purani, A. B., ed. *The Life of Sri Aurobindo: A Source Book*. Pondicherry: Sri Aurobindo Ashram, 1964.

Puri, Balraj. 'Jammu and Kashmir'. *State Politics in India*, ed. Myron Weiner, pp. 215–243. Princeton: Princeton University Press, 1968.

Puri, Geeta. *Bharatiya Jana Sangh, Organisation and Ideology, Delhi: A Case Study*. New Delhi: Sterling, 1980.

Puri, Yogesh. 'An Analysis of Jammu and Kashmir Elections'. *Indian Political Science Review* 1 (April–September 1967), pp. 239–250.

Purohit, B. R. *Hindu Revivalism and Indian Nationalism*. Sagar: Sathi Prakashan, 1965.

Pye, Lucien W. and Sidney, Verba. *Political Culture and Political Development*. Princeton: Princeton University Press, 1969.

Qureshi, I. H. A Case Study of the Social Relations between the Muslims and the Hindus, 1935-1947. *The Partition of India*:

Policies and Perspectives, 1935-1947, eds. C. M. Philips and Mary Doreen Wainwright, pp. 360–368. Cambridge: M.I.T. Press, 1970.

Qureshi, I. H. *The Struggle for Pakistan*. Karachi: University of Karachi, 1965.

Rai, Satya. *Partition of the Punjab: A Study of Its Effects on the Politics and Administration of the Punjab* (I) 1947-1956. New York: Asia Publishing House, 1965.

Rajagopalan, C. *The Greater Bombay: A Study in Suburban Ecology*. Bombay: Popular Book Depot, 1962.

Raju, P. T. *The Idealistic Thought of India*. Cambridge, Mass: Harvard University Press, 1958.

Raju, P. T. *The Philosophical Traditions of India*. Pittsburg: University of Pittsburg Press, 1972.

Ramdas, Svami. *Dasbodha*. Bombay: Shabdaranjan, 1962.

Ranade, Eknath, comp. *Swami Vivekananda's Rousing Call to the Hindu Nation*. Calcutta: Swastik Prakashan, 1963.

Rosenthal, Donald. 'Factions and Alliances in Indian City Politics'. *Midwest Journal of Political Science* 10 (August 1966), pp. 320–349.

Rudolph, Lloyd I. and Susanne, Rudolph Hoeber. *The Modernity of Tradition: Political Development in India*. Chicago: University of Chicago Press, 1967.

Sahni, J. N. *The Lid Off New Delhi*. New Delhi: Allied Publishers, 1971.

Sartori, Giovanni. 'From the Sociology of Politics to Political Sociology'. *Politics and the Social Sciences*, ed. Seymour Martin Lipset, pp. 65–100. New York: Oxford University Press, 1969.

Sartori, Giovanni. 'Politics, Ideology and Belief Systems'. *American Political Science Review* 63 (June 1969), pp. 398–411.

Savarkar, Vinayak Damodar. *Hindutva, Who is Hindu?* Bombay: Veer Savarkar Prakashan, 1969.

Savarkar, Vinayak Damodar. *Samagra Savarkar Wangmaya: Hindu Rashtra Darshan,* 6 vols. Pune: Maharashtra Prantik Hindu Sabha, 1964.

Sayeed, Khalid B. *The Political System of Pakistan*. Boston: Houghton Mifflin, 1960.

Seal, Anil. *The Emergence of Indian Nationalism: Competition and Collaboration in the Later Nineteenth Century*, ed. John Gallagher. Cambridge: Cambridge University Press, 1968.

Seligman, Lester G. *Leadership in a New Nation: Development in Israel*. New York: Atherton, 1964.

Seligman, Lester G. 'Political Recruitment and Party Structure: A Case Study'. *American Political Science Review* 55 (March 1961), pp. 77–86.

Shils, Edward. *The Intellectual between Tradition and Modernity: The Indian Situation*. The Hague: Mouton and Co., 1961.

Shrader, Lawrence L. 'Rajasthan'. *State Politics in India,* ed. Myron Weiner, pp. 321–96. Princeton: Princeton University Press, 1968.

Singh, Harcharan. 'Mid-Term Elections in Punjab: Emerging Trends'. *Indian Political Science Review* 4 (April-September 1970), pp. 207–32.

Singh, Partap. Haryana State Assembly Polls of 1968 and 1972. *Indian Political Science Review* 7 (April–September 1973), pp. 143–64.

Sitaramayya, Pattabhi B. *History of the Indian National Congress,* 2 vols. Delhi: S. Chand, 1969.

Smelser, Neil J. *The Theory of Collective Behavior*. New York: Free Press, 1962.

Spratt, Philip. *Hindu Culture and Personality*. Bombay: Manaktalas, 1966.

Srinivas, M. N. *Social Change in Modern India*. Berkeley: University of California Press, 1969.

Stouffer, Samuel et al. *The American Soldier: Adjustment During Army Life*. Princeton: Princeton University Press, 1949.

Stouffer, Samuel et al. *The American Soldier: Combat and Its Aftermath*. Princeton: Princeton University Press, 1949.

Sutton, Francis X., Seymour E. Harris; Carl Kaysen and James Tobin. *The American Business Creed*. Cambridge, Mass.: Harvard University Press, 1956.

Talmon, Jacob L. *The Origins of Totalitarian Democracy.* New York: Praeger, 1960.

Tilak, Bal Gangadhar. *Gita Rahasya*, trans. Bhalchandra Sitaram Sukthankar, 2 vols. Pune: Tilak Brothers, 1936.

Tuker, Francis. *While Memory Serves.* London: Cassell, 1950.

Van Buitenen, J. A. B. 'On the Archaism of the Bhagavata Purana'. *Krishna: Myths, Rites and Attitudes*, ed. Milton Singer, pp. 23-40. Chicago: University of Chicago Press, 1968

Vivekananda, Swami. *The Complete Works of Swami Vivekananda*, 6th ed., 8 vols. Almora: Advaita Ashram, 1948.

Wainwright, Mary Doreen. 'Keeping the Peace in India: 1946-1947: The Role of Lieutenant Governor Sir Francis Tucker in the Eastern Command'. *The Partition of India: Politics and Perspectives 1935-1947*, eds. C. M. Philips and Mary Doreen Wainwright, pp. 127–47. Cambridge: M.I.T. Press, 1970.

Walker, Benjamin. *The Hindu World: An Encyclopedic Survey of Hinduism*, 2 vols. New York: Praeger, 1968.

Walzer, Michael. *The Revolution of the Saints: A Study of the Origins of Radical Politics.* London: Weidenfeld & Nicholson, 1966.

Weber, Eugen. *Varieties of Fascism: Doctrines of Revolution in the Twentieth Century*, ed. Louis L. Snyder. Princeton: D. Van Nostrand, 1964.

Weber, Max. Politics as a Vocation. Essays in Sociology, eds. Hans G. Gerth and C. Wright Mills, pp. 77–128. New York: Oxford University Press, 1958.

Weiner, Myron. *Party Building in a New Nation.* Chicago: University of Chicago Press, 1967.

Weiner, Myron. *Party Politics* in *India: The Development of a Multi-Party System.* Princeton: Princeton University Press, 1957.

Weiner, Myron. *The Politics of Scarcity.* Chicago: University of Chicago Press, 1962.

Weiner, Myron et al. *The Third General Elections: Studies in Voting Behavior.* Bombay: Newerk Printing Works, 1962.

White, James W. *The Sokagakkai and Mass Society.* Stanford: Stanford University Press, 1970.

Wilcox, Wayne. 'Madhya Pradesh'. *States Politics in India*, ed. Myron Weiner, pp. 127–74. Princeton: Princeton University Press, 1968.

Wolpert, Stanley A. *Tilak and Gokhale: Revolution and Reform in the Making of Modem India*. Berkeley: University of California Press, 1961.

Woodrooffe, John. *Sakti and Sakta: Essays and Addresses*, 7th ed. Madras: Ganesh, 1969.

Zimmer, Heinrich. *Philosophies of India*, ed. Joseph Campbell. New York: Pantheon Books, 1951.

Notes

Introduction

1. The English translation is the National Volunteer Corps.
2. For a discussion of the general issue of the social effects of rootlessness, see Robert A. Nisbet, *The Quest for Community* (New York: Oxford University Press, 1971); Ted Robert Gurr, *Why Men Rebel* (Princeton: Princeton University Press, 1970), pp. 46–50; and Hannah Arendt, *The Origins of Totalitarianism* (Cleveland: Meridian Books, 1962), pp. 227–43.
3. Hans Kohn analyses the revivalist roots of nationalism in his *History of Nationalism in the East* (New York: Harcourt, Brace and Company, 1929), Ch. 2.
4. The RSS sometimes refers to the most committed of the swayamsevaks, the RSS-trained full-time workers (the pracharaks), in the RSS itself and in the affiliates as the 'family.'
5. The Jana Sangh, established in 1951, developed into the political affiliate of the RSS. The Jana Sangh merged into the Janata Party in May 1977. The Jana Sangh group in the Janata Party along with some non-Jana Sangh allies bolted from the Janata party in April 1980 to form the Bharatiya Janata Party (BJP). RSS critics maintain that the BJP is the political front of the RSS and trace its roots to the Jana Sangh. In fact, as we

shall show, it is not yet clear if the BJP is a full member of the 'family', though early indications suggest that it is moving in that direction.

6. For a study of this psychological orientation in youth, see Kenneth Keniston, 'Youth: A "New" Stage of Life,' *American Scholar* 39 (Autumn 1970), pp. 631–54.

7. G. Morris Carstairs, *The Twice-Born: A Study of a Community of High Caste Hindus* (Bloomington: Indiana University Press, 1958). G.B. Murphy and A Murphy reach the same conclusion in *In the Minds of Men* (New York: Basic Books, 1953). A more poetic treatment of the proposition discussed in Philip Spratt, *Hindu Culture and Personality* (Bombay: Manaktalas, 1966).

8. For an analysis of the martial values of Maharashtrian brahmins, see Richard I. Cashman, *The Myth of the Lokamanya* (Berkeley: University of California Press, 1975), pp. 8–16. For example, Samarth Ramdas, the seventeenth century Maharashtrian religious figure, propagated a militant interpretation of the Bhagavadgita, a major Hindu religious text.

9. For a theoretical discussion of this proposition, see Giovanni Sartori, 'From the Sociology of Politics to Political Sociology,' in *Politics and the Social Sciences*, ed. by Seymour Martin Lipset (New York: Oxford University Press, 1969), pp. 65–100; and Samuel H. Barnes, 'Ideology and the Organization of Conflict: On the Relationship between Political Thought and Political Action', *Journal of Politics* 23 (August 1966), pp. 513–30. For the alternative proposition of the dependence of political ideology on political culture, see Seymour Martin Lipset and Stein Rokkan, 'Cleavage Structures, Party Systems and Voter Alignments: An Introduction', in *Party Systems and Voter Alignments: Cross-National Perspectives*, ed. by Seymour Martin Lipset and Stein Rokkan (New York: The Free Press, 1967), pp. 1–6; and Gabriel A. Almond and G. Bingham Powell, *Comparative Politics: A Developmental Approach* (Boston: Little Brown, 1966), pp. 110–112.

Chapter 1: Hindu Revivalism

1. For a discussion of the nationalist implications of the new education, see Anil Seal, *The Emergence of Indian Nationalism: Competition and Collaboration in the Later Nineteenth Century*, ed. by John Gallagher (Cambridge: Cambridge University Press, 1968), Ch. 1; and B. N. Javadekar, *Adhunik Bharat* (Pune: Rashtriya Grantha Prakashan, 1936), in Marathi.

2. Ibid., pp. 61, 87, 107.

3. For a discussion on political participation in the late nineteenth century, see Gordon Johnson, *Provincial Politics and Indian Nationalism: Bombay and the Indian National Congress 1880–1915* (London: Cambridge University Press, 1973), particularly Ch. 1.

4. For a discussion on the impact of Western norms on Indian culture, see Ashis Nandy's 'The Culture of Indian Politics', *The Journal of Asian Studies* 30 (November 1970), pp. 57–79.

5. Ibid., p. 59. Nandy uses 'restorationists' to describe what we call the revivalists. However, his term implies that the 'restorationists' sought to restore Hindu orthodoxy, which is misleading, for many of the changes that the 'restorationists' proposed were as radical as those proposed by the 'modernists'.

6. Ibid., pp. 59–60.

7. Lloyd I. Rudolph and Susanne Hoeber Rudolph, *The Modernity of Tradition: Political Development in India* (Chicago: University of Chicago Press, 1967), pp. 160–71.

8. See discussion in R. C. Majumdar, *History of the Freedom Movement in India*, Vol. 1 (Calcutta: Firma K. L. Mukhopadhay, 1963), pp. 320–28.

9. Guiseppe Mazzini, Johann Gottlieb Fichte, Conte Camillo Benzo di'Cavour and other nationalist writers were translated into Indian languages and their writings were widely read by the revivalists. Many revolutionary groups treated their works almost as catechisms of political action.

10. For a discussion of the groups which participated in the formation of the Indian National Congress in Seal, see *Indian Nationalism*, Ch. 1.

11. The British tended to blame almost every movement they disliked—nationalism, terrorism and communism—on the Western-educated class of Indians, who were typically portrayed as weak, effeminate and rather deceptive. In contrast, the heroic figures were the illiterate and martial tribesmen of the north-west who did not use Western political philosophy to challenge British political supremacy. The Bengali 'babu' was portrayed as an educated and politically conscious Indian who talked about Western values without understanding the essence of them and who was devoid of the fortitude and skill required to administer the institutions based on them. For critical portrayals of the 'babu,' see Rudyard Kipling's *The Enlightenment of Pagett M.P. and The Head of the District.*

12. For a theoretical discussion of the structural conduciveness necessary for the development and growth of social movements, see Neil Smelser, *Theory of Collective Behavior* (New York: Free Press, 1962), pp. 319–28. The three factors discussed here are derived from Smelser's treatment of structural conduciveness.

13. A.B. Purani (ed.), *The Life of Sri Aurobindo: A Source Book* (Pondicherry: Sri Aurobindo Ashram, 1964), p. 81. Ghose believed that national revival would not be achieved if Western models were employed. He asserted: 'If you try other and foreign methods, we shall either gain our end with tedious slowness, painfully and imperfectly, or we shall not attain it at all.' Ibid., p. 82.

14. Dhirendra Mohan Datta, 'Some Philosophical Aspects of Indian Political, Legal and Economic Thought', *The Indian Mind: Essentials of Indian Philosophy and Culture,* ed. by Charles A. Moore (Honolulu: University Press of Hawaii, 1967), pp. 274–75.

15. Ibid., pp. 277–78.

16. Many Hindu religious texts propose that the gunas (qualities that make up all matter) dispose a person to behave in a certain way and determine a person's varna, one of the fourfold functional divisions of Hindu society: (1) brahmin—priest and teacher, (2) kshatriya—political and military leader, (3) vaishya—producer and distributor of wealth, (4) sudra— manual worker, craftsman, and artisan. Theoretically, the gunas are independently determined by an individual's previous lives and not by the hereditary factor of birth into a particular caste. For a discussion on gunas, see Franklin Edgerton's translation and analysis in *Bhagavad Gita* (New York: Harper & Row, 1964), particularly Ch. 5.

17. Rajni Kothari, *Politics in India* (Boston: Little Brown & Co., 1970), p. 28.

18. P. T. Raju, *Idealistic Thought of India* (Cambridge: Harvard University Press, 1953), pp. 440–41.

19. Kothari, *Politics in India*, p. 34.

20. Norman Cohn, 'Medieval Millenarism: It's Bearing on the Comparative Study of Millenarian Movements,' *Millennial Dreams in Action: Essays in Comparative Study*, ed. by Sylvia L. Thrupp (The Hague: Mouton & Co., 1962), pp. 31–43.

21. The Bhagavadgita was theologically considered smriti (non-canonical) by orthodox Hindus. However, the revivalists tended to blur the distinction between noncanonical texts and the canonical shruti (the Vedas and Upanishads) and to treat both sets of texts as equally authoritative. Indeed, the less quietistic smriti texts were sometimes used to interpret the canonical texts.

22. This is Tilak's translation of karmayoga, the path of action. Bal Gangadhar Tilak's most systematic treatment of the subject is *Gita Rahasya*, 2 vols., trans. by Bhalchandra Sitaram Sukthankar (Pune: Tilak Bros., 1936). Also see Aurobindo Ghose, *Essays on the Gita* (Pondicherry: Sri Aurobindo Ashram, 1959); Swami Vivekananda, 'Thoughts on the Gita,'

The Complete Works of Swami Vivekananda, 6th ed., 8 vols. (Almora: Advaita Ashrama, 1948), Vol. 4, pp. 98–106.

23. *Gita Rahasya*, Vol. 1, p. xxiv.

24. Ibid., p. 29.

25. Ibid., pp. 30–31.

26. The text is composed of eighteen chapters inserted into the Mahabharata, one of the major epic texts of classical Hindu literature.

27. *Gita Rahasya*, Vol. 1, p. 37.

28. Ibid., p. 696.

29. Ibid., p. 697.

30. Ibid.

31. Charles H. Heimsath, *Indian Nationalism and Hindu Social Reform* (Princeton: Princeton University Press, 1964), pp. 323–27.

32. *The Complete Works of Swami Vivekananda*, trans. by Advaita Ashrama, Mayavati Memorial ed., 8 vols. (Almora: Advaita Ashrama, 1948–1955), Vol. 3, p. 379.

33. Vivekananda discusses the power potential in the context of *advaita*, ibid., pp. 366–84. Also Ghose speaks on the subject in very naturalist terms in *Bhavani Mandir*, a treatise written during the debate of the 1905 partition of Bengal. Presented in Purani, *Life of Sri Aurobindo*, pp. 75–86. For a general discussion of the doctrine, see John Woodroffe, *Sakti and Sakta: Essays and Addresses*, 7th ed. (Madras: Ganesh & Co., 1969); Swami Kirtanananda, *The Glory of the Divine Mother* (Calcutta: Ramakrishna Mission Institute of Culture, 1964).

34. According to Aurobindo, the Indian nation 'is a mighty Shakti, composed of Shaktis of all the millions of units that make up the nation . . . The Shakti we call India, Bhawani Bharati is the living unity of the Shaktis of three hundred million people . . .' Purani, *Life of Sri Aurobindo*, p. 79.

35. Majumdar, *Freedom Movement in India*, Vol. 1, pp. 329–37.

36. For a comprehensive study of the political impact of this anthem, see Haridas Mukherjee and Uma Mukherjee, '*Bande*

Mataram' and *Indian Nationalism* (Calcutta: Firma K. L. Mukhopadhyay, 1957).

37. Gopal Haldar, 'Revolutionary Terrorism,' *Studies in the Bengal Renaissance*, ed. by Atul Chandra Gupta (Jadavpur: National Council of Education, Bengal, 1958), pp. 224–57. For a study of revolutionary activity in Bengal, see Richard L. Park, 'The Rise of Militant Nationalism in Bengal: A Regional Study of Indian Nationalism'(Unpublished PhD dissertation, Harvard University, 1951).

38. In 1905, twelve years after the first Ganesh festival in Pune, the festival was celebrated in seventy-two other towns. Victor Barnouw, 'The Changing Character of a Hindu Festival', *American Anthropologist* 56 (February 1954), pp. 74–85. The festival drew fewer participants after 1910 in part because of government restrictions on it. Nevertheless, Tilak's experiment of combining religion and politics became a model for revivalist strategy. Richard Cashman discusses the political characteristics of this festival in *The Myth of the Lokamanya*, Ch. 4.

39. Dhananjay Keer discusses the revolutionary activities in Maharashtra in *Veer Savarkar*, 2nd ed. (Bombay: Popular Prakashan, 1966), Ch. 3.

40. For additional analyses of the Anushilan Samiti and the expansion of its activities after 1905, see Majumdar, *Freedom Movement in India*, Vol. 2, pp. 267–98. Leonard A. Gordon discusses this revolutionary society in *Bengal: The Nationalist Movement, 1876–1940* (New York: Columbia University Press, 1974), Ch. 5.

41. Its success in heightening a sense of Hindu identity discussed in Kenneth W. Jones, 'Communalism in the Punjab: The Arya Samaj Contribution', *The Journal of Asian Studies* 28 (November 1968), pp. 39–54. Also see his book, *Arya Dharma, Hindu Consciousness in Nineteenth Century Punjab* (Berkeley: University of California Press, 1976).

42. N. Gerald Barrier, 'Arya Samaj and Congress Politics in Punjab, 1894-1904', *The Journal of Asian Studies* 26 (May 1967), p. 364.

43. Rudolph and Rudolph, *Modernity of Tradition*, Pt. 2; Erik Erikson, *Gandhi's Truth: On the Origins of Militant Non-Violence* (New York: Norton & Co., 1969), pp. 395–409.

44. Edgerton, *Bhagavad Gita*, pp. 127–31.

45. Benjamin Walker, *The Hindu.eWorld: Tin Encyclopedic Survey of Hinduism*, 2 vols (New York: Praeger Publishers, 1968), Vol. 1, pp. 78–80.

46. Rudolph and Rudolph, *Modernity of Tradition*, pp. 196–200.

47. For an analysis of Gandhi's use of satyagraha, see Joan Bondurant, *Conquest of Violence: The Gandhian Philosophy of Conflict*, rev. ed. (Berkeley: University of California Press, 1967), Ch. 2.

48. For reference to the practice, see Balkrishna Govind Gokhale, 'Gandhi and History,' *History and Theory, Studies in the Philosophy of History* 11, No. 2 (1972), p. 221.

49. Tilak, *Gita Rahasya*, pp. 43–44. Aurobindo Ghose argues along similar lines in *The Doctrine of Passive Resistance*, 2nd ed. (Pondicherry: Sri Aurobindo Ashram, 1952), pp. 87–8.

50. Tilak, *Gita Rahasya*, p. 36.

51. *Mahratta* (Pune), 29 October 1922.

Chapter 2: Formation and Development of the Rashtriya Swayamsevak Sangh

1. The British in 1909 introduced constitutional reforms which permitted some Council members to be elected. The reforms conceded separate electorates for the Muslims. This action touched off Hindu opposition and was one of the factors which led Hindus to organize. For a discussion of the Lucknow Pact, see Hugh Owen, 'Negotiating the Lucknow Pact', *The Journal of Asian Studies* 31 (May 1972), pp. 561–87).

2. Pattabhai Bhogaraju Sitaramayya, *History of the Indian National Congress,* 2 vols (Delhi: S. Chand, 1969), vol. 1, p. 200; Mukund Ramarao Jayakar, *The Story of My Life*, 2 vols. (Bombay: Asia Publishing House, 1958), Vol. 1, pp. 390–403. For a discussion of the Khilafat movement, see Gail Minault, *Khilafat Movement, Religious Symbolism and Political Mobilization in India* (New York: Columbia University Press, 1982).

3. Sitaramayya, *Indian National Congress*, Vol. 1, p. 205.

4. For a history of tension between the two communities, see Govind Sadashiv Ghurye, *Social Tensions in India* (Bombay: Popular Prakashan, 1968), particularly Ch. 10.

5. Inder Malhotra, in a perceptive analysis of the May 1973 communal riots in Pune, points out that events and personalities from the distant past may contribute to the memory bank which can spark a communal riot. He notes that, 'The Jagmohan Reddy Commission recorded . . . that the attack on the Jagannath temple in Ahmedabad [during 1969] inflamed the local Hindus because it reminded them of the sack of Somnath by Ghazni [a Muslim commander who seized this Hindu religious centre several hundred years ago]. In Pune, communal fires were stoked by an attack on a youth immediately after he had played the role of Shivaji in a tableau.' 'A Recurring Nightmare: After Poona, What?', *Times of India* (Bombay), 31 May 1973, p. 6.

6. Ram Gopal, *Indian Muslims: A Political History (1858–1947)* (Bombay: Asia Publishing House, 1959), pp. 154–58; and Khalid B. Sayeed, *The Political System of Pakistan* (Boston: Houghton Mifflin, 1967), pp. 25–26.

7. Sitaramayya, *Indian National Congress*, Vol. 1, p. 220.

8. *Mahratta* (Pune), 23 June, 1922.

9. *Leader* (Allahabad), 1 May 1922.

10. Ibid., 12 November 1921.

11. For an analysis of the Hindu Mahasabha's formation and early development, see Richard Gordon, 'The Hindu Mahasabha

and the Indian National Congress, 1915 to 1926,' *Modern Asian Studies* 9 (April 1975), pp. 145–203.

12. The formation of these centres or sabhas, as they were called, in August 1923, is reported in ibid., pp. 17–18. Following the Benares session, the Mahasabha was reorganized. A working committee was established with headquarters at Banaras Hindu University; the country was divided into twenty-three linguistic provinces (as in the Congress). However, Gordon notes that in 1924 there were only nine provincial branches and 362 local branches, 80 per cent in Punjab, United Provinces and Bihar. Richard Gordon, 'The Hindu Mahasabha', p. 173.

13. *Leader* (Allahabad), 23 July 1923.

14. Ibid., 23 August 1923.

15. Ibid., 22 August 1923.

16. An acrimonious debate between the revivalist reformers and the orthodox occurred at the 1926 Hindu Mahasabha session on these issues. An account of the proceedings is reported in ibid., 15, 17, 18 March 1926.

17. Ibid., 13 April 1925.

18. Ibid.

19. Government of India, Home Political File (I) No. 18-21/25, 1925.

20. Experimental research in social psychology suggests that, when groups which feel deprived succeed in overcoming the obstacles that are perceived as preventing them from sharing in the benefits enjoyed by a 'favoured' group, the 'deprived' will experience a marked increase in aggressiveness towards the 'favoured.' For a discussion of the general principle, see John W. Thibaut and Harold H. Kelley, *The Social Psychology of Groups* (New York: John Wiley & Sons, 1959), pp. 181–84.

21. The most comprehensive and authentic biography of Hedgewar was written by Narayan Hari Palkar. The book, *Dr K. B. Hedgewar* (Pune: Hari Vinayak Datye, 1964), was published in Marathi and has since been published in other

Indian languages. We have relied primarily on the original Marathi edition, although we have also gone through the later Hindi translation. Not only did Palkar have access to RSS documents, but he was personally acquainted with many of Hedgewar's closest colleagues. There is now an English language biography, *Dr Hedgewar: The Epoch Maker*, compiled by B. V. Deshpande & S. R. Ramaswamy, ed. by H. V. Seshadri (Bangalore: Sahitya Sindhu, 1981).

22. Palkar, Dr *K. B. Hedgewar*, p. 7.

23. Ibid., p. 10.

24. RSS pamphlet, *Hamare Hedgewar* (Lucknow: Rashtradharm Pustak Prakashan, n.d.), pp. 9–11, in Hindi.

25. Palkar, *Dr K. B. Hedgewar*, p. 14.

26. Appaji Joshi, perhaps Hedgewar's closest confidant, discusses their relationship in an article in *Tarun Bharat* (Pune), 4–5 May 1970 (in Marathi).

27. Palkar, *Dr K. B. Hedgewar*, pp. 36–37. R. C. Majumdar outlines the organizational structure of the Samiti in *History of the Freedom Movement in India*, Vol. 2, pp. 282–86.

28. *Maharashtra State Gazetteers: Nagpur District* (Bombay: Government Printing and Stationery, 1966), p. 118.

29. Ibid.

30. Palkar, *Dr K. B. Hedgewar*, p. 66.

31. Ibid., p. 70.

32. Ibid., p. 78–79.

33. M. R. Jayakar, one of Tilak's closest associates, reports the dismay among Tilak's Maharashtrian followers when prominent allies such as Lajpat Rai and C. R. Das supported Gandhi at the Nagpur session. *The Story of My Life*, Vol. 1, p. 420. Indeed, some of Tilak's own Maharashtrian supporters were converted to Gandhi's programme. Discussion in Richard Cashman, *The Myth of the Lokamanya*, pp. 206–7.

34. Palkar, *Dr K. B. Hedgewar*, p. 78.

35. Ibid., p. 90.

36. This letter to Motilal Nehru was written on 19 February 1922, shortly after the non-cooperation movement was cancelled. The letter is published in Jawaharlal Nehru, comp., *A Bunch of Old Letters Written Mostly to Jawaharlal Nehru and Some Written by Him*, 2nd ed. (Bombay: Asia Publishing House, 1960), p. 23.

37. Hedgewar was a member of the All-India Congress Committee in 1928 and attended the 1928 Congress session at Calcutta. For a discussion of these activities, see Palkar, *Dr K. B. Hedgewar*, p. 198. After 1928, his time was devoted almost exclusively to building the RSS. He did, however, participate in one more major Congress activity, the 1930–31 satyagraha. In the Central Provinces, this satyagraha took the form of a protest against the restricted use of government-controlled forest lands. Hedgewar informed his RSS colleagues that his participation did not commit the RSS to the movement. An account of his participation can be seen in Palkar, *Hedgewar*, Ch. 17. Individual swayamsevaks could and did participate in politics, but only with the approval of RSS officials. RSS officers for their part were not permitted to engage in any political activity. Generally, Hedgewar tried to portray the RSS as apolitical. He may have been concerned that the educational objectives of the RSS would be undermined if the participants were drawn into the intense factional infighting of Nagpur's Congress organization. More importantly, he probably feared that the young organization might be banned if it appeared to have political objectives.

38. Ibid., p. 115.

39. Ibid., p. 116.

40. *Mahratta* (Pune), 18 November 1922.

41. Palkar, *Dr K. B. Hedgewar*, p. 117.

42. Ibid., p. 126.

43. *Mahratta* (Pune), 18 January 1925.

44. Quoted in Palkar, *Dr K. B. Hedgewar*, p. 129.

45. Ibid., p. 120. Vinayak Damodar Savarkar was a militant Hindu nationalist. While a college student at Pune, he formed with the revolutionary Abhinava Mela. In 1906, he left for England on a scholarship which required that he swear never to work in any way for the British. During his study in England, he recruited Indian students into an underground unit which smuggled anti-British literature manuals on the manufacture of explosives, guns, and nationalist books into India. For a discussion of these activities, see Keer, *Veer Savarkar*, Chapters 2 and 3. In 1910, Savarkar was tried and convicted as a co-conspirator in the murder of a British official in India, and was sentenced to life imprisonment on the Andaman Islands. In 1921, he was removed to a prison in India. While at the Ratnagiri jail in 1922, he wrote *Hindutva*. Copies of this tract were reproduced by hand and distributed among Maharashtrian nationalists. Hedgewar read one of these handwritten copies. The work was eventually published in English, which can be found in Vinayak Damodar Savarkar, *Samagra Savarkar Wangmaya: Hindu Rashtra Darshan*, 6 vols. (Pune: Maharashtra Prantik Hindusabha, 1964), Vol. 6, pp. 1–91.

46. Ibid., pp. 7–9, 28–46.

47. Palkar, *Dr K. B. Hedgewar*, Ch. 1; Madhav Sadashiv Golwalkar, *Bunch of Thoughts* (Bangalore: Vikrama Prakashan, 1966), pp. 331–32.

48. At about this time, Jawaharlal Nehru also expressed dismay over the lack of a well-organized cadre of young men which the Congress could mobilize for its various activities. Jawaharlal Nehru, *Toward Freedom* (Boston: Beacon Press, 1958), pp. 120–21.

49. This Hindu festival occurs on the tenth day of the waxing lunar fortnight of the Hindu month of Ashwina (September–October). The festival has particular martial significance in Maharashtra for this was the date on which Shivaji's

armies crossed the frontiers to fight the enemy, an event called *simolanghan* in Marathi. The elder brother of Vinayak Damodar Savarkar, G. D. (alias Babarao) Savarkar, designed the RSS's flag, the *bhagva dhwaj*, and it was displayed on the day Hedgewar launched the RSS. See D. N. Gokhale, *Krantiveer Babarao Savarkar*, 2nd printing (Pune: Sri Vidya Prakashan, 1979) in Marathi, p. 275. Some RSS informants also claim that G. D. Savarkar wrote the first oath, which was used up to 1947. (There is some debate over whether he authored the oath.)

50. Palkar, *Dr K. B. Hedgewar*, p. 135.

51. Ibid. For a testimonial on the character-building potential of akharas, see Dinakar Dhondo Karve, ed. and trans., *The New Brahmins: Five Maharashtrian Families*, with editorial assistance of Ellen E. McDonald (Berkeley: University of California Press, 1963), pp. 180–81.

52. *Census of India, 1931, Vol. 12: Central Provinces and Berar, pt. 1—Report,* by W. H. Shoobert (Nagpur: Government Printing, 1933), p. 296.

53. Palkar, *Dr K. B. Hedgewar*, pp. 138–39. B. K. Kelkar, a swayamsevak, wrote in his diary in February 1943 that Hedgewar asserted that an understanding of his philosophy required a thorough study of the writings of Ramdas. (Unpublished diary of B. K. Kelkar.)

54. Ibid., pp. 136–39.

55. The uniform was the same as that worn by the Bharat Sevak Samaj, the volunteer force Hedgewar organized during the 1920 Congress session in Nagpur. It consisted of white shirt, khaki shorts and a black khaki cap. In choosing a name, Hedgewar rejected putting Hindu in the title because that would suggest that Hindus were but one community among many. Rather, Hindus were, in his view, the nation. He also rejected names that emphasized the Maharashtrian origins of the RSS. For discussion on this, see C. P. Bhishikar, *Bhayyaji Dani* (Pune: Bharatiya Vichar Sadhana, 1983) in Marathi.

56. The account emphasizes the bitterness of the brahmin priests who denounced Hedgewar for disrupting their lucrative business.

57. Ibid., pp. 141–42. Lathi training was a part of traditional training in the akharas of Maharashtra, and elsewhere. Its introduction was the suggestion of Anna Sohani, a former revolutionary who was close to Hedgewar. Sohani was later to introduce instruction in still other martial arts.

58. Ibid., pp. 145–46.

59. Ibid., p. 161.

60. See report of this incident in H. V. Seshadri, *Dr Hedgewar, the Epoch Maker* (Bangalore: Sahitya Sindhu, 1981), pp. 95–97.

61. Palkar, Dr *K. B. Hedgewar*, pp. 202–03.

62. Palkar describes a speech Hardikar gave in Nagpur in which he denounced the nonpolitical nature of the RSS and a number of other associates. Ibid., p. 204.

63. D. V. Kelkar, 'The R.S.S.', *Economic Weekly* (4 February 1950): 132, quoted in J. A. Curran Jr, *Militant Hinduism in Indian Politics: A Study of the R.S.S.* (New York: Institute of Pacific Relations, 1951), pp. 12–13.

64. Information in this paragraph from K. R. Malkani, *RSS Story* (New Delhi: Impex India, 1980), pp. 21, 28; and interview with Malharrao Kale, RSS general secretary 1943–1945, on 30 June 1983 at Nagpur.

65. Palkar, *Dr K. B. Hedgewar*, pp. 202–210.

66. As will be explained in the next chapter, the RSS banner is considered the 'guru' and RSS members are careful to employ the term only to the banner.

67. For an explanation of the relationship between a Hindu teacher and his student, see Abbe Jean Antoine Dubois, *Hindu Manners, Customs and Ceremonies,* trans. and ed. by Henry K. Beauchamp, 3rd ed. (Oxford: Clarendon Press, 1953), Ch. 10.

68. RSS Pamphlet, *Guruji: Rashtriya Swayam Sevak ke Sarsanghchalak* (Delhi: n.p., n.d.), p. 43, in Hindi.

69. Palkar, Dr *K. B. Hedgewar*, pp. 160–65.

70. Ibid., p. 329.

71. The Khaskars were formed in 1930 in Punjab to unite all Muslims in South Asia into a common political front. In 1939 the organization claimed 400,000 members, chiefly in Punjab, Hyderabad, Sind, and the North-West Frontier Province. For a description of the organization, see Shan Muhammed, *Khaksar Movement in India* (Meerut: Meenakshi Prakashan, 1973).

72. Government of India, Home Political File (I), No. 18.

73. Palkar, *Dr K. B. Hedgewar*, p. 255, and Ch. 21.

74. Ibid., Ch. 28. The membership figures for 1939 were mentioned by Golwalkar in a speech he gave at an RSS ceremony in Nagpur. *Mahratta* (Pune), 25 August 1939.

75. Palkar, *Dr K. B. Hedgewar*, Ch 23.

76. In his work on the RSS, Curran Jr describes the Rashtra Sevika Samiti. He writes that Hedgewar was against a women's branch because 'the leaders of the Sangh had taken a vow of "Brahmacharya" (which obliged them to avoid all temptations such as that of association with women).' Curran Jr, *Militant Hinduism*, p. 81. We believe his explanation is wrong. Many of the early leaders of the RSS did not take any vow of sexual abstinence and there have always been married pracharaks (full-time workers). P. B. Dani, a former general secretary of the RSS, for example, was married, as were other members of the RSS central executive. As far as we know, no swayamsevak or pracharak is required to take any vows of sexual abstinence. At the time the Rashtra Sevika Samiti was formed, it would have been unacceptable for an organization like the RSS to accept women participants. In fact, many RSS members indicated to us that it would still be socially unacceptable for the two to unite.

77. Palkar notes that most of the early participants in Nagpur and the surrounding region were largely from the 'middle

classes'. The frequent reference both in RSS correspondence and Palkar's biography to swayamsevaks going to high school and college further indicates the middle-class composition of the RSS.

78.   Palkar, *Dr K. B. Hedgewar*, p. 270.

79.   Ibid.

80.   Ibid., pp. 181–82.

81.   As early as 1929, Mahasabha leaders approached Hedgewar with the proposal that the RSS become an affiliate of the Mahasabha. He rejected the notion. See D. E. V. Baker, *Changing Political Leadership in an Indian Province: The Central Province and Berar 1919–1939* (Delhi: Oxford University Press, 1979), p. 106. Hedgewar bluntly told Munje in 1938 that the RSS was not the youth wing of the Mahasabha. After that, Munje was not invited to deliver special lectures (*baudhik*) at RSS functions. Interview with Malharrao Kale, general secretary of the RSS from 1943 to 1945, in Nagpur on 30 June 1983.

82.   For a discussion of the relationship between the RSS and the Hindu Mahasabha both before and after Hedgewar's death, see Walter K. Andersen, 'The Rashtriya Swayamsevak Sangh,' *Economic and Political Weekly* (7, 11, 18, 25 March and 1 April 1972).

83.   From a mimeographed statement read by Godse to the court on the day he was convicted, p. 11. Copy of the statement was given us by Gopal Godse, brother of Nathuram.

84.   Letter from Vinayak Damodar Savarkar to S. L. Mishra, 3 March 1943. Savarkar Files, Bombay.

85.   There was considerable speculation both within and outside the RSS over whether Golwalkar was, in fact, Hedgewar's choice for the position. Some argue that Hedgewar would not choose a person with the religious and ascetic orientation of Golwalkar. Even more important, Golwalkar had no revolutionary or political experience, and he was only recently

promoted in the RSS hierarchy before Hedgewar's death. Others expected V. D. Savarkar or preferred his younger brother revolutionary, staunch Hindu nationalist freedom fighter, Dr Narayan Damodar alias Bal Savarkar would be chosen as Hedgewar's successor. Palkar writes that Dr L. B. Paranjpe, Babasaheb Apte and Appaji Joshi were other names considered by Hedgewar but he never discussed them publicly (Palkar, *Dr K. B. Hedgewar*, p. 385). Of these possibilities, Appaji Joshi was considered the most likely choice. Since the formation of the RSS he had been close to Hedgewar; he was perhaps the most successful of the RSS organizers, and he was its senior-most official. After Hedgewar's death, Joshi did not believe the announcement; moreover, he did not think Golwalkar had the requisite political sophistication to lead the RSS. Joshi, a 'good RSS soldier', eventually put his grudge aside and continued his work in the RSS. He frequently defended Golwalkar against those who charged that Golwalkar had abandoned the objectives laid out by Hedgewar. He served as RSS general secretary from 1943–1946. In the 4 and 5 May 1970 issues of *Tarun Bharat* (Pune), he strongly denied any fundamental differences between Golwalkar and Hedgewar.

86. *Organiser*, 14 July 1973.

87. Peerhaps the two best accounts of his youth are in the RSS publications, *Shri Guruji, the Man, and His Mission: On the Occasion of His 51st Birthday* (New Delhi: Bharat Prakashan, 1955), in English and *Guruji: Rashtriya Swayamsevak Sangh ke Sarsanghchalak*, in Hindi.

88. An account of their early acquaintance can be found in Palkar, *Dr K. B. Hedgewar*, Chapters 22 and 23. Hedgewar was attracted to young intellectuals. Prior to grooming Golwalkar for a career in the RSS, Hedgewar had shown a great interest in G. M. Huddar, a scholarly young man from Nagpur who was selected the first general secretary of the RSS (1928–1931).

89. *Shri Guruji, the Man and His Mission,* p. 6.

90. Palkar, *Dr K. B. Hedgewar,* pp. 360–61.

91. RSS Pamphlet, *Justice on Trial: A Collection of the Historic Letters Between Sri Guruji and the Government* (Mangalore: Sharada Press, 1968), p. 96.

92. All RSS teachers are expected to attend three Officers' Training Camps, two at the state level and the third at the all-India Camp at Nagpur. Each of these camps are held for four to six weeks in the summer. The curriculum includes exercises, the martial arts (lathi, sword, dagger), games, songs and political philosophy. The RSS leadership is able to observe the trainees at close quarters and to evaluate their leadership potential.

93. Palkar, *Dr K. B. Hedgewar,* p. 378.

94. Martandrao Jog, head of the military department of the RSS, wanted the RSS to take a more militant line towards the British. When his advice was rejected, he resigned. Information from an interview with Malharao Kale, RSS general secretary from 1940 to 1943, on 30 June 1983 at Nagpur.

95. V. D. Savarkar and Munje, as well as other Maharashtrian Hindu nationalists, were the most active spokesmen in this drive. They felt that Hindus would have to fight for control of India at the conclusion of World War II. Control of the military and training in the martial arts would be critical in this engagement. The major role played by Maharashtrians, who formed the prime source of recruitment into the military services in this drive, may derive from the British policy of excluding most Maharashtrians from the 'martial races'. This exclusion not only limited job opportunities, but also challenged the martial traditions of Maharashtra's dominant castes. See discussion of British recruitment policy in Stephen Cohen, *The Indian Army, Its Contribution to the Development of a Nation* (Berkeley: University of California Press, 1971), particularly Pt. 3.

96. Limaye resigned in 1943, and he returned to the RSS in 1945.

97. Interview with his brother, Gopal Godse, in Pune on 3 July 1969.

98. Government of India, Home Political File (I), No. 28/3/43. In 1940, the government, under the power given it by Defense of India Rule 56 (I), required all paramilitary groups to apply for a license before permitting them to have parades or conduct camps. Defence of India Rules 58 (I) and 59 (I) covered drill and uniforms, respectively, and gave the government the power to limit their use during national emergencies.

99. Ibid. The Home Department advised all provinces that government servants, under GSC Rule 23, should not take part in a 'political' organization like the RSS. RSS materials and the Home Department files both indicate that the RSS continued to recruit many civil servants.

100. Ibid.

101. Ibid. Participation in shakha may have been even higher. One source notes that there were at this time some 600 shakhas attended by 100,000 people. See S. R. Date, *Maharashtra Hindusabhachaya Karyacha Itihas* (Pune: S. R. Date, 1975), in Marathi.

102. While interviewing in an area of Delhi with a large Scheduled Caste population, we met many swayamsevaks from the lower and scheduled castes. They mentioned several reasons for joining the RSS and remaining with it: the opportunity to play games; the social acceptance accorded them by high-caste shakha mates; its respect for Hinduism. An explanation that ran through almost all the interviews concerned the 'respectability' they earned through participation in the RSS. Many stated that they learned 'proper behaviour' (i.e., cleanliness, hard work, discipline, knowledge of India's 'great history and traditions') according to norms accepted by the highest castes. The RSS, for them, is a 'Sanskritizing'

institution which opens up the prospect of social mobility. A similar appeal for the Jana Sangh among many Scheduled Caste voters was noted in a study of municipal elections in Delhi. See Mahender Kumar Saini and Walter K. Andersen, 'The Basti Julahan Bye-Election,' *The Indian Journal of Political Science*, Vol. 30 (July–September, 1969), pp. 260–76.

103. Leonard E. Mosley, *The Last Days of the British Raj* (New York: Harcourt, Brace & World, 1961), p. 11.

104. Mary Doreen Wainwright, 'Keeping the Peace in India, 1946-1947: The Role of Lieutenant General Sir Francis Tucker in the Eastern Command,' *The Partition of India: Politics and Perspectives 1935–1947* eds C.M. Philips and Mary Doreen Wainwright (Cambridge, Mass.: MIT. Press, 1970), p. 131.

105. Ibid., pp. 138–39.

106. The following provide accounts of that election: Satya M. Rai, *Partition of the Punjab: A Study of Its Effects on the Politics and Administration of the Punjab* (I) 1947–1956 (New York: Asia Publishing House, 1965), pp. 39–46; Chaudhri Muhammad Ali, *The Emergence of Pakistan* (New York: Columbia University Press, 1967); and Penderel Moon, *Divide and Quit* (Berkeley: University of California Press, 1962), pp. 71–96.

107. Chaudhri Muhammad Ali, *Emergence of Pakistan* (New York: Columbia University Press, 1967), p. 101. As a matter of fact, Sikh paramilitary units were also banned.

108. *Leader* (Allahabad), 9 March 1947.

109. Moon, *Divide and Quit*, p. 95. Moon relates that the Muslim police in Bahawalpur state were very unreliable protectors of the Sikh and Hindu minorities. In fact, they sometimes participated in the violence and actively participated in the attempt to rid the state of its minorities as quickly as possible.

110. Michael Brecher, *Nehru: A Political Biography*, abridged ed. (Boston: Beacon Press, 1962), pp. 143–45.

111. Accurate figures of the refugee flow are difficult to determine. V. P. Menon, adviser to Lord Mountbatten, estimates that about 5,500,000 Hindus and Sikhs were brought from West Punjab to India by 1948. See his *Transfer of Power in India* (Princeton: Princeton University Press, 1957), p. 431. Rai, in *Partition of the Punjab*, also reports that India established over 160 refugee camps which accomodated some 1,250,000 people. This does not include camps established by private groups like the RSS. Ibid., p. 108.

112. Moon, *Divide and Quit*, p. 217.

113. Interview with Chaman Lal in Delhi on 5 September 1969. Before the 1975–1977 Emergency, Chaman Lal was office secretary of the Delhi karyalay and the person responsible for maintaining contact with swayamsevaks and RSS-related activities outside of India.

114. K. D. Jhari, 'I was a Swayamsevak: Creating the Urge to Kill', *Secular Democracy* 3 (July 1970), pp. 27–29.

115. Golwalkar, in conversations with us, during the interview in Nagpur on 19 April 1969, expressed considerable bitterness over the criticism of the RSS for its involvement in the violence during the partition period. He noted that the government supplied the RSS with weapons (as it did other groups) to protect Hindu refugees, and, at the time, expressed its gratitude for the 'protective' activities of the RSS. However, in the milieu of hate that existed at the time, it was difficult to demarcate what was 'aggressive' from what was 'defensive'. There are numerous accounts of RSS members who did initiate violence against Muslims. For example, see I. H. Qureshi, 'A Case Study of the Social Relations between the Muslims and the Hindus, 1935-1947', Philips and Wainwright eds *Partition of India: Policies and Perspectives, 1935-1947*, pp. 360–368.

116. *R.S.S. in Punjab* (Lahore: Government Printing Press, 1948).

117. For an account of Gandhi's visit to the RSS shakhas in Delhi, see Pyarelal Nayar, *Mahatma Gandhi: The Last Phase*, Vol. 2

(Ahmedabad: Navjivan Publishing House, 1958), pp. 439–41; and Mishrawala, *Delhi Diary*, Vol. 3 (Delhi: Gyandeep Prakashan, 1987), pp. 257, 264–7.

118. See *Sixty Years of the RSS* (Delhi: Suruchi Prakashan, 1985), p. 22; and *Rashtriya Punaruttanchya Aghadivar,* RSS (Pune: Bharatiya Vichar Sadhana, 1985), p. 19, in Marathi.

119. D. R. Goyal, *R.S.S.: Poisonous Tree* (Delhi: Kamleshwar Prakashan, 1979), p. 98.

120. K. R. Malkani, *The RSS Story* (New Delhi: Impex India, 1980), p. 50.

121. When the RSS stages one of its public functions, its practice is to invite a locally prominent person to preside, even though the person may have no affiliation with the RSS.

122. For a survey of RSS relief activities, see *Organiser*, 21 August 1947.

123. Interview with Madhukar Dattatreya Deoras (invariably referred to in RSS publications by his alias, Balasaheb—an alias we shall use hereafter), then general secretary of the RSS, in Nagpur, on 21 April 1969.

124. This meeting is reported in *Leader* (Allahabad), 5 February 1948.

125. 'Sardar Patel on Indian Problem', cited by Kewalram Lalchand Punjabi, *The Indomitable Sardar: A Political Biography of Sardar Vallabhbhai Patel* (Bombay: Bharatiya Vidya Bhavan, 1962), p. 131.

126. For an excellent account of the conditions leading up to Gandhi's fast, see Abul Kalam Azad, *India Wins Freedom*: An Autobiographical Narrative (Bombay: Orient Longman, 1959), pp. 213–22. Azad also points out that anti-Muslim sentiment 'was not confined to the refugees or even to the general public. Even the areas where only government servants lived were involved. When the reports of massacres in the West Punjab reached Delhi, Muslims in the city were attacked by mobs of unruly men. Some Sikhs took a leading

part in organizing these murderous attacks in Delhi [sic].' Ibid., p. 201.

127. Interview with Gopal Godse in Pune on 13 May 1969.

128. Nathuram Godse had ceased to participate in RSS activities prior to World War II.

129. This newspaper was widely considered an advocate of Savarkar's philosophy. For example, Savarkar's secretary wrote to a Jabalpur editor, 'If you request some ten Hindu Sabha workers there to subscribe [to *Agrany*, Godse's newspaper] ... you will be able to read the day-to-day thoughts [of Savarkar] as seen through our ideology.' Letter to N. R. Shukla, 20 April 1944, in Savarkar Files, Bombay.

130. Figures reported in an RSS pamphlet, *Shri Guruji, The Man and His Mission: On the Occasion of His 51st Birthday*, p. 37.

131. In response to a letter from Nehru suggesting that Gandhi's murder was 'a part of a much wider campaign organized chiefly by the RSS', Home Minister Patel, in charge of the investigation, responded: 'It ... clearly emerges that ... the RSS was not involved at all. It was a fanatical wing of the Hindu Mahasabha directly under Savarkar that [hatched] the conspiracy and saw it through.' Patel's letter of 27 February 1948, responding to Nehru's 26 February letter in Durga Das, ed. *Sarder Patel's Correspondence: 1945–1950*, ten vols (Ahmedabad: Navajivan Publishing House, 1973), vol. 6, pp. 56–58.

132. Restrictions noted in RSS pamphlet, *Justice on Trial*, pp. 69–70.

133. Ibid.

134. Ibid., pp. 8–9 (letter dated 24 September 1948).

135. Ibid., pp. 23–26 (letter dated 24 September 1948).

136. Ibid., pp. 16–17 (letter dated 10 November 1948).

137. Ibid., pp. 17–20 (letter dated 12 November 1948).

138. Ibid., pp. 26–28 (letter dated 11 September 1948).

139. Ibid., pp. 70–82.

140. Ibid., pp. 85–87.

141. Because P. B. Dani was arrested, the leadership of the RSS passed to Eknath Ranade and Madhavrao Mule who directed the RSS protest movement (which it refers to as satyagraha).

142. In recalling the ban and the protest movement, RSS members who participated in the events find a number of 'anti-national' reasons that motivated the leadership to continue the ban even after no evidence showed up on an RSS connection with the assassination of Gandhi. The more frequently mentioned were 'fear' (1) that the RSS would transform itself into a political party, (2) that some foreign 'design' would prevent India from becoming strong and united, (c) of Nehru's 'pro-Muslim' bias, (d) of an attempt on the part of the 'vested interests' to 'keep the people down'. One recollection which came up in almost all the interviews was the shock the members experienced at being labelled 'murderers', 'hooligans', and 'criminals', and the pressure to denounce the RSS, the abandoned friends, lost jobs, and expulsions from college. Almost all those interviewed recall that their commitment to the RSS was strengthened during the ban period.

143. Interview with Eknath Ranade in Kanyakumari on 29 December 1969.

144. RSS literature draws a sharp distinction between Nehru and Patel. The latter is portrayed as a practical Hindu, and the former as an impractical visionary. In seeking to identify themselves with Patel, RSS writers exaggerate Patel's pro-RSS sympathies. No doubt, he respected their help to the refugees. But the record seems to indicate that he thought they sometimes acted intolerantly towards the Muslims. Nehru did not, as far as the records indicate, interfere in Patel's handling of the ban issue. Patel did not exactly deal gently with the RSS during the ban period and exacted some hard terms from them before he agreed to lift the ban. Patel did support RSS entry into the Congress. One could argue against

the conventional RSS wisdom about why he wanted them in. He might only have wanted to exploit the disciplined cadre to build the organizational infrastructure of the Congress. In a letter to Rajendra Prasad in 1948, Shankarrao Deo claims that Patel was upset over the deplorable state of the Congress organization. Referred to in Stanley Kochanek, *The Congress Party of India: The Dynamics of a One-Party Democracy* (Princeton: Princeton University Press, 1968), p. 15. It could well be that Patel planned to delegate the hard 'leg work' to the swayamsevaks. He could hardly have expected them to be a major asset in his opposition to Nehru, for at the time, the RSS leaders had almost no experience at practical politics. He very likely foresaw little possibility of the politically unsophisticated swayamsevaks influencing the ideology of the Congress or playing a major role in its factional struggles.

145. *Justice on Trial*, pp. 40–44 (letter dated 3 May 1949).

146. Ibid., pp. 44–49 (letter dated 17 May 1949).

147. Copy of letter published in the *Times of India* (Delhi), 11 June 1970, and discussion of it in the *Times of India* (Delhi), 12 June 1970. There was considerable interest in this issue of succession at the time because there were rumours that the government was again considering a move to place restrictions on RSS activities. The letter of clarification to Sharma was given to D. P. Mishra, home minister of the Central Provinces. Mishra immediately forwarded it to Patel, who was convalescing at Dehra Dun. Patel consulted with Nehru to get his approval of an order to lift the ban, satisfied that Golwalkar intended to implement democratic reforms within the RSS. It is believed that the letter of clarification influenced Patel's decision to support lifting the ban.

148. *Justice on Trial*, pp. 50–52 (letter dated 24 May 1949).

149. Ibid., p. 102 (Appendix 15).

150. Ibid., pp. 102–03 (Appendix 16). At least one prominent government figure, Morarji Desai, home minister of Bombay

in 1949, stated on the floor of the provincial assembly that the ban on the RSS was lifted unconditionally. *Bombay State Legislative Assembly Debates*, Vol. 15 (Bombay: Government of Bombay Press, 1949), p. 2126.

151. Mahratta Chamber of Commerce, Industries and Agriculture (MCCIA), Pune, 18 November 1949.

152. In November 1947 RSS full-time workers met in Bombay to discuss the role of the RSS in an independent India. (Interview with Yeshwantrao Kelkar, 14 July 1983 in Bombay.)

Chapter 3: RSS: Ideology, Organization and Training

1. The two approaches most frequently employed to analyse the social determinants of belief systems (or ideologies) are interest theory and strain theory. In the former, a belief system is perceived in terms of the struggle for advantage through the pursuit of power; in the latter, socio-psychological stresses create ideological responses. The latter, as Geertz notes, allows a more systematic presentation of motivation and the social context in which the ideology develops. He points out that interest theory 'turns attention away from the role that ideologies play in defining (or obscuring) social categories, stabilizing (or upsetting) social expectation, maintaining (or undermining) social norms, strengthening (or weakening) social consensus, relieving (or exacerbating) social tensions'. Clifford Geertz, 'Ideology as a Cultural System,' *Ideology and Discontent*, ed. by David E. Apter (Glencoe, Illinois: Free Press, 1964), p. 53. Also see Francis X. Sutton et al., *The American Business Creed* (Cambridge, Mass.: Harvard University Press, 1956), pp. 303–10.

2. Willard Mullins, 'On the Concept of Ideology in Political Science', *American Political Science Review* 66 (June 1972): p. 509.

3.   Giovanni Sartori, 'Politics, Ideology, and Belief Systems,' *American Political Science Review* 63 (June, 1969): p. 401.

4.   Clifford Geertz, 'Religion as a Cultural System', *Reader in Comparative Religion: An Anthropological Approach*, ed. by William A. Lessa and Evan Z. Vogt, 3rd ed. (New York: Harper & Row, 1972), pp. 1–46.

5.   For a discussion of Cassirer's explanation of myth, see Ernst Cassirer's *Language and Myth*, trans. by Susanne K. Langer (New York: Yale University Press, 1946), and *The Myth of the State* (New Haven: Yale University Press, 1973). For a discussion of the elements of symbolic formulation, see Susanne K. Langer, *Philosophy in a* New *Key: A Study in the Symbolism of Reason, Rite, and Art* (Cambridge, Mass.: Harvard University Press, 1961), Chapters 2 and 3.

6.   This passage is taken from *Bhawani Mandir* which Ghose wrote during the first partition of Bengal. Quoted in Purani, *Sri Aurobindo*, p. 82.

7.   The four social divisions are brahmin (mouth), kshatriya (arms), vaishya (thighs), and sudra (feet).

8.   This passage, explaining the origin of the caste system, is found in the twelfth verse of the nineteenth hymn of Mandala 10 of the Rig Veda.

9.   See Michael Walzer's discussion of a similar political purpose of the organic image in the English puritan movement in *The Revolution of the Saints: A Study of the Origins of Radical Politics* (London: Weidenfeld & Nicholson, 1966), pp. 171–83.

10.   For a rather lengthy discussion of the concept, see Golwalkar, *Bunch of Thoughts*, Ch. 3.

11.   For a discussion of the function of out-groups in belief systems, see Murray Edelman, *Politics as Symbolic Action: Mass Arousal and Quiescence* (Chicago: Markham Publishing Co., 1972), pp. 77–78. The organic conception of society is conducive to the identification of the 'disrupters' of the social order, and RSS spokesmen have frequently utilized the metaphor to point

out those groups which 'weaken' the Hindu nation through undermining the sensitive organic fabric which holds society together. Any movement which aims to create a cultural identity separate from the Hindu mainstream is considered particularly dangerous, for its fruits, RSS writers allege, are various forms of political separatism.

12. *Organiser* (Delhi), 3 September 1963.

13. Shripaty Sastry, *A Retrospect, Christianity in India* (*An Exposition of the RSS Views on the Relevance of Christianity in India Today*) (Pune: Bharatiya Vichar Sadhana, 1984), p. 8.

14. Golwalkar, *Bunch of Thoughts*, p. 128.

15. Deendayal Upadhyaya, *Integral Humanism* (Delhi: Navchetan Press, 1968).

16. Golwalkar, *Bunch of Thoughts*, p. 16.

17. Ibid., p. 19.

18. Ibid.

19. Ibid., pp. 40–45.

20. D.B. Thengadi, G. S. Gokhale, and M. P. Mehta, *Labour Policy*, 4 vols. (Nagpur: Bharatiya Mazdoor Sangh, 1967–1968), Vol. 1, p. 276.

21. Mysore Hiriyanna, *Outlines of Indian Philosophy* (London: George Allen & Unwin, 1932), pp. 51–64.

22. Ibid., pp. 339–80.

23. For a comprehensive discussion of this doctrine, see Heinrich Zimmer, *Philosophies of India*, ed. by Joseph Campbell (New York: Pantheon Books, 1951), pp. 209–63; P. T. Raju, *The Philosophical Traditions of India* (Pittsburgh: University of Pittsburgh Press, 1972), Ch. 2.

24. Hiriyanna, *Indian Philosophy*, pp. 378–79. Hiriyanna explains that there are two stages in the acquisition of knowledge. The first stage takes place during the period when the individual is expected to perform his social obligations; the objective of the training at this stage is to cultivate a spirit of detachment. When the RSS speaks of character building, it is referring to

activities during this first stage. Its goal is to train people to live in the world according to the principles enunciated in its belief system. It does not offer instruction which aims at the more advanced stage of knowledge. Because of this conception of its function, it does not claim to be a religious organization, though it does consider its activities of a 'spiritual' nature, training men in the first stage of knowledge. It prefers to call itself a cultural organization. Its 'cultural' orientation is demonstrated by the fact that the full-time workers wear no religious garb; meditation and devotional worship are not part of the discipline of the full-time workers; they do not conduct the traditional samskars (rituals) of Hinduism.

25. Edgerton, *Bhagavad Gita*, Vol. 2, p. 47.

26. See Edgerton's discussion of the doctrine, ibid., pp. 139–45.

27. In two places, Krishna explicitly enjoins people to abide by their caste duties. The Bhagavadgita, Ch. 2, Shlokas 31–38, Ch. 18, Shlokas 41–47. Hiriyanna explains that the writers had no need to be explicit because 'in the relatively simple organization of the society when the teaching was formulated, the duties of the several classes were known fairly clearly'. Hiriyanna, *Indian Philosophy*, p. 124.

28. Edgerton translates the Sanskrit term for the elements (guna) as 'strands'. Edgerton, *Bhagavad Gita*, p. 141.

29. Golwalkar, *Bunch of Thoughts*, p. 24.

30. Ibid., pp. 24–25; Ch. 7, Pts 1–2; Ch. 8. Various terms are employed to name the Nation-God: Jagan Mata (mother of the world), Adishakti (original force), Mahamaya (great illusion), Mahadurga (great goddess of power), Mathrubhumi (motherland), Dharmabhumi (land of religion), Devabhumi (God's land), Mokshabhumi (land of salvation).

31. Ibid., p. 84.

32. Upadhyaya, *Integral Humanism*, p. 52.

33. Ibid., pp. 54–55.

34. Golwalkar, *Bunch of Thoughts*, p. 102.

35. Ibid., p. 115.

36. Ibid., p. 112.

37. Thengadi, Gokhale, and Mehta, *Labour Policy*, Ch. 20.

38. Ibid., p. 350.

39. See discussion of concept in Hiriyanna, *Indian Philosophy*, pp. 381–82; Zimmer, *Philosophies of India*, pp. 441–55.

40. Hiriyanna outlines the two stages. *Indian Philosophy*, pp. 379–81.

41. Zimmer, *Philosophies of India*, pp. 353–63.

42. Soon after assuming his position as sarsanghchalak, Golwalkar identified Hedgewar as an avatar (incarnation of the divine) thus signifying that he was a jivan mukta. RSS pamphlet, *Guruji: Rashtriya Swayamsevak Sangh ke Sarsanghchalak*, p. 43. In an RSS pamphlet on his life, it was noted that Golwalkar's yoga training 'had brought to him the realization of 'self' which is the sine qua non for knowledge of the eternal and ultimate truth.' RSS pamphlet, *Shri Guruji, the Man and His Mission*, p. 6.

43. Ibid., p. 15.

44. Ibid., p. 32.

45. A monograph on the RSS, published in India, summarizes many of the arguments directed against the RSS. In this critical analysis of the RSS, the author portrays it as an organization committed to brahmin supremacy in India. K. K. Gangadharan, *Sociology of Revivalism: A Study of Indianisation, Sanskritisation, and Golwalkarism* (New Delhi: Kalamkar Prakashan, 1970). In her study of the non-brahmin movement in Maharashtra, Maureen Patterson claims that the RSS represented brahmin interests in that controversy. 'A Preliminary Study of the Brahman vs Non-Brahman Conflict in Maharashtra' (unpublished master's thesis, University of Pennsylvania, 1952), pp. 61–62. Gangadharan also claims that the RSS supports the orthodox varna system (pp. 11–12) and defends almost all the 'outmoded customs' of Hinduism

such as female infanticide and sati (p. 91), and favours a restoration of the Hindu monarchical system (p. 81), and defends the privileged position of the 'rich class of landlords and industrialists', (pp. 92–94).

46. On the basis of his fieldwork on the RSS soon after India's independence, Curran concluded that RSS members were disposed to favour a socialist solution to India's developmental problems, *Militant Hinduism*, p. 51. In an analysis of the economic policy of the Jana Sangh, Howard Lloyd Erdman concludes that 'it would appear that on balance large-scale property in industry and land receives no principled endorsement and that the Sangh would not be adverse to attacking it'. *The Swatantra Party and Indian Conservatism* (London: Cambridge University Press, 1967), pp. 54–5. Also see Myron Weiner, *Party Politics in India: The Development of a Multi-Party System* (Princeton: Princeton University Press, 1957), pp. 174–75, 210–13.

47. Golwalkar, *Bunch of Thoughts*, p. 107.

48. Ibid., p. 401.

49. This proposal was first adopted at a meeting of the Jana Sangh Working Committee at Indore in 1954. The committee passed a resolution advocating a minimum income of 100 rupees per month and a maximum of 2,000 rupees per month. It is an interesting footnote to this meeting that a conservative business-oriented faction of the Jana Sangh leadership bolted the party on the grounds that it had been captured by the RSS. *Organiser*, 13 September 1954.

50. In 1969, Atal Bihari Vajpayee, then the Jana Sangh president, informed the party's working committee that the party had been unfairly tarred as a conservative reactionary party; he instructed all units to educate the public that it was neither 'rightist' nor 'leftist', but a party that takes the 'common man's approach to economic problems'. *Statesman* (Calcutta), 3 September 1969. In one of the party's first systematic analyses

of India's economic situation, the Jana Sangh Working Committee in 1954 resolved: 'As a general rule production of consumer goods should be confined to cottage industry and only big and capital good may be reserved for large-scale industry.' The resolution further proposed profit sharing and labour participation in management. In the agricultural sector, the party advocated the total abolition of 'landlordism' and it proposed that no compensation be provided the former landlords, except for those with no alternative source of income. See report of working committee resolutions in *Organiser*, 13 September 1954.

51. L. K. Advani, in his 1973 presidential address to the Eighteenth Annual Jana Sangh Session at Kanpur, stated that luxury consumption should be severely curtailed, and he proposed a direct consumption tax on expenditures of incomes above Rs 2500/month for each household unit. *Organiser*, 17 February 1963.

52. Golwalkar, *Bunch of Thoughts*, pp. 116–117.

53. See Jacob Leib Talmon's discussion of left and right totalitarianism where he makes this distinction. *The Origins of Totalitarian Democracy* (New York: Praeger Publishers, 1960), pp. 6–8.

54. See discussion of elements of fascism in Eugene Weber, *Varieties of Fascism: Doctrines of Revolution in the Twentieth Century*, ed. by Louis L. Snyder (Princeton: D. Van Nostrand, 1964), Chapters 1–4.

55. *Organiser*, 14 July 1973.

56. Palkar, *Dr K. B. Hedgewar*, p. 61. Hedgewar's participation in Bengal's faction-ridden revolutionary movement, where the death or defection of a leader often resulted in the disintegration of his faction, might have convinced him of the need to emphasize organizational loyalty. For a discussion of organization deficiencies in Bengal's revolutionary organizations, see Gordon, *Bengal: The Nationalism Movement*, pp. 155–6.

57. This suggests that Max Weber's evolutionary assumptions on charisma were necessarily one-directional. Occupants of bureaucratic positions might use their positions in such a way as to develop considerable charisma, as Golwalkar and Deoras appear to have done.

58. Alex Inkeles, 'The Totalitarian Mystique: Some Impressions of the Dynamics of Totalitarian Society', *Totalitarianism: Proceedings of a Conference Held at the American Academy of Arts and Sciences, March 1953*, ed. by Carl Joachim Friedrich (Cambridge, Mass.: Harvard University Press, 1954), pp. 99–101. The RSS does not make total claims on society. The members are not encouraged to overthrow or replace the government. Their claims are partial, and they demand primacy only in the character-building area. It has infrequently challenged government authority. When it did so, the actions were limited, and lasted only until the specific grievances were resolved. These examples were acts of civil disobedience, not revolution. Perhaps, the revolutionary impulse was negated by the ability of India's political system to accommodate newly politicized social classes.

59. *Organiser*, 26 August 1972.

60. See an excellent discussion of samskaras in R. B. Pandy, 'Hindu Sacrament', *The Cultural Heritage of India*, ed. by Haridas Bhattacharyya et al., 4 vols. (Calcutta: Ramakrishna Mission Institute of Culture, 1953–1962), Vol. 2, pp. 392–94.

61. Ibid., pp. 402–06.

62. J. A. Curran Jr, *Militant Hinduism*, p. 50. In our field notes, we estimated that one-half to three-fourths of the participants were between 10 and 25.

63. Most shishu and bal meet in the evening, and taruna and proudh in the morning. The choice of times varies according to the type of neighbourhood in which the shakha is located.

64. Interview with Madhavrao Mule in Delhi, on 3 July 1968. He later became general secretary of the RSS.

65. For a discussion of group cohesion and conformity, see Etzioni, *Comparative Analysis of Complex Organizations* (New York: Free Press, 1961), pp. 189–90.

66. Ram Lal Dhooria, 'I Was a Swayamsevak–II: The Vilest Abortionists', *Secular Democracy* (June 1969): p. 22.

67. To vote, a swayamsevak must be over eighteen and a regular participant in RSS activities for one year or more. RSS Constitution, art. 16 (c) (Mimeo).

68. Ibid., Art. 19 (b), i, ii, iii.

69. Ibid., Art. 16 (b).

70. Ibid., Art. 15 (b) i, ii, iii.

71. Ibid., Art. 15 (e).

72. Interview with Eknath Ranade at Kanyakumari on 1 January 1970.

73. The 'typical' RSS pracharak was not deduced from any scientific sample survey. We base our remarks on some twenty which we interviewed.

74. Those pracharaks from Maharashtra and south India were largely from brahmin castes while those from north India tended to come from vaishya (i.e., business) and kayastha (i.e., writer) castes. We did not meet any pracharaks from the scheduled castes or tribes, though we were told that there are a few.

75. RSS Constitution, Art. 17 (a) ii.

76. Interview with Madhukar Dattatreya Deoras, then RSS general secretary, at Nagpur, on 21 April 1969.

77. The RSS constitution states that the 'sarsanghchalak will nominate his successor, as and when the necessity arises, with the consent of the then *kendriya karyakari mandal*'. However, Deoras was selected without such consent. Neither Golwalkar nor Hedgewar chose their successor until shortly before their deaths. Unless the RSS abandons the *guru-model* of authority, it is unlikely that they will submit the position to any real scrutiny by the kendriya karyakari mandal.

78. RSS Constitution, Art. 12.

79. Interview with Madhav Sadashiv Golwalkar at Nagpur, on 16 April 1969.

80. RSS leaders have stated that Golwalkar's opposition to the Jana Sangh participating in coalition governments with communists was a rare incident of involvement in policy making.

81. For the complete speech, see *Organiser*, 21 July 1973.

82. Because of public criticism that they were a paramilitary group, the RSS during 1970–71 opened shakhas in half circles rather than in rows in some places (e.g., Delhi).

83. Until 1940, simulated gun practice (i.e., use of a wooden rifle) was a regular feature of the shakha, but it was eliminated from the 'curriculum' when the British government prohibited such military drills during World War II.

84. Dhooria, 'I Was a Swayamsevak–III: Victims of an Idiotic Approach', *Secular Democracy* 2 (July 1969): p. 12–1 4, 26.

85. Ibid., p. 12.

86. Dhooria comments that when enforcing such discipline, 'there was … never any rancour malice, for Bhaiji … was always loving and affectionate', ibid.

87. Baudhik sessions have recently been explicitly reoriented to cover current political and economic issues.

88. Golwalkar, *Bunch of Thoughts*, pp. 335–6.

89. It is traditional Hindu practice for jatis (subcaste) to perform puja (worship) of the implements connected with hereditary jati occupation.

90. The costs to the participant are kept to a minimum. For example, in 1969, participants from Allahabad (in Uttar Pradesh) who joined a winter camp in Lucknow paid 10 rupees for round-trip transportation and 10 rupees for camp fees. If they did not already have a uniform (and most have it), they were required to spend another 40 rupees to cover the cost of footwear, half pants, cap, shirt, lathi, boots, socks. The RSS itself sells these

items at a minimal profit margin. This was an ITC, and fees for an OTC (Officers' Training Camp) would be approximately three times those charged for the ITC. The district branch of the Allahabad RSS paid fees, round-trip transportation cost, and the cost of uniforms for those who could not afford them. Interview with Dr Krishna Bahadur in Allahabad, 16 January 1970.

91. These overseas affiliates have begun in two ways. Either emigrating swayamsevaks begin RSS work in their new country, or overseas Indians themselves will initiate the work. In some African and Asian countries, there are organizations which function very much like the RSS in India. In other countries, the swayamsevaks agree to support various Hindu cultural organizations. In the United States, for example, the RSS members actively support the work of the Ramakrishna Mission, as well as the Vishwa Hindu Parishad, a Hindu umbrella religious organization linked to the RSS. The Delhi office keeps extensive records of all swayamsevaks who leave the country and endeavours to remain in communication with them. This is particularly the case with students who intend to return to India.

92. Reported in *Organiser*, 14 July 1973.

93. These notes are translated from Marathi and were a part of the diary of a swayamsevak attending a 1971 Maharashtra state Officers' Training Camp.

94. We have several diaries which note themes similar to those mentioned here.

95. These questions were given to participants at an Officers' Training Camp run for swayamsevaks from Jammu and Kashmir, Punjab, Haryana, Delhi, and Himachal Pradesh in 1969.

96. The RSS pracharak at Allahabad mentioned that only about 40 per cent of those who regularly attend ever take the pratigya (oath). He mentioned that he (and other pracharaks)

were very careful regarding who could take the oath. In most cases, the oath is administered only after a person has proven himself through several years of active RSS work. It is a kind of confirmation ceremony indicating that one is an ideal swayamsevak.

Chapter 4: The RSS 'Family Takes Shape

1. These terms are somewhat arbitrary. The attitudes of the pracharaks vary along a continuum between the activist and traditionalist poles.

2. Much of the information we have regarding the activist stirrings in the 1940s comes from interviews with three men who were active in the RSS in the 1940s: B. K. Kelkar, 2 August 1983, at New Delhi; Madhukar Deval, on 12 July 1983, at Pune; D. V. Gokhale, on 26 May 1983, at Bombay.

3. The lack of such support led some activists to suspect that the RSS leadership had pro-Congress political leanings. See S. R. Date, *Maharashtra Hindusabhechya Karyacha Itihas* (Pune: S. R. Date, 1975), pp. 210–13, in Marathi.

4. One sign of this high standing was the increased attendance at shakha in Punjab during the first half of 1947. According to Punjab government figures, attendance increased from 47,000 in January 1947, to almost 50,000 in June 1947. Statistics from *The R.S.S. in Punjab* (Lahore: Government Printing Press, 1948).

5. Golwalkar spelled out his justification in a speech to senior pracharaks in October 1949 at Nagpur. See his speech in *Sri Guruji Samagra Darshan*, Vol. 2 (Nagpur: Bharatiya Vichar Sadhana, 1979), pp. 110–147, in Marathi.

6. Material regarding the internal tensions resulting from differing views on the activities of the RSS are drawn from *Samagra Guruji Darshan*, Vol. 2 (Nagpur: Bharatiya Vichar Sadhana, 1978), pp. 110–147, in Marathi; Gangadhar Indurkar,

Rashtriya Swayamsevak Sangh: Kal, Aaj, Aani Udya (Pune: Sri Vidya Prakashan, 1983), pp. 141–49, in Marathi; and Swarnalata Bhishikar, *Samarpit Ek Adyam Utkat Chaitanya, Dr V. V. Pendse* (Pune: n.p., n.d.), pp. 27–63, in Marathi. Also interviews with Madhukar Mahajan, 21–22 May 1983, at Bombay; and D. V. Gokhale, 26 May 1983, at Bombay. Both were activist pracharaks at the time.

7. Golwalkar's speech on 'positive Hinduism' reprinted in *Shri Guruji Samagra Darshan*, Vol. 3 (Nagpur: Bharatiya Vichar Sadhana, 1978), pp. 1–38, in Marathi.

8. Interview with Madhukar Mahajan on 21–22 May 1983, at Bombay.

9. Letter from K. B. Hedgewar to Appaji Mular on 13 February 1932, in Hedgewar files, translated from Marathi.

10. Letter from K. B. Hedgewar to Vasant Krishna Oke on 11 December 1936, in Hedgewar files, translated from Marathi.

11. There is an excellent description of the methods employed to sell shares, in Dr K. D. Jhari, 'I Was a Swayamsevak–VII: Open Involvement in Politics', *Secular Democracy* 3 (September 1970), pp. 9–10.

12. The source for most of the information on trusts is an interview with K. R. Malkani, editor of *Organiser*, in Delhi, on 25 June 1969.

13. The former was published from Lucknow and the latter from Nagpur. The editors of both were RSS pracharaks. Atal Bihari Vajpayee, the first editor of *Panchjanya*, later became president of the Jana Sangh. C. P. Bhishikar, editor of *Rashtra Shakti*, new is editor of *Tarun Bharat*, a Marathi daily published in Pune and managed by an affiliated RSS trust.

14. By 1971, RSS-affiliated newspapers and journals were published in Hindi (nine weeklies, ten dailies), Marathi (two weeklies, one monthly, one daily), Telugu (two weeklies), Gujarati (two weeklies), Assamese (one weekly, two monthlies), Kannada (one weekly, one monthly), Sindhi (one weekly), Urdu (one

weekly), Malayalam (one weekly). RSS-affiliated trusts also control one English and one Hindi national journal. Over the following decade the number of affiliates in the print media remained stable, though the circulation increased significantly.

15. These figures were provided by S. S. Apte, the manager of the Bombay office of the *Hindustan Samachar*, on 11 January 1969.

16. *Motherland* was one of the few RSS-affiliated newspapers which did not reopen after the Emergency. The financial costs of reviving it were considered prohibitive.

17. The government quickly recognized that RSS members were forming a number of front organizations; and Nehru, during the ban on the RSS, suggested to the home minister that the police watch these developments very carefully. Letter from Jawaharlal Nehru to Sardar Vallabhbhai Patel dated 28 February 1948, published in Durga Das, ed., *Sardar Patel's Correspondence: 1945–1950*, ten vols (Ahmedabad: Navajivan Publishing House, 1973), Vol. 6, pp. 55–56.

18. The All-India Students' Federation was formed in 1926 with the support of the Congress, and it included a mix of Gandhians, socialists, communists, and other nationalist students.

19. Philip Altbach has a good description of the radicalization and disillusionment of Indian students during World War II. See his *Student Politics in Bombay* (Bombay: Asia Publishing House, 1968), pp. 85–96.

20. This argument was developed by Datta Devidas Didolkar, one of the early organizers of the Vidyarthi Parishad, during an interview with him at Nagpur, on 20 April 1969. Didolkar was himself a participant in the AISC-sponsored Quit India movement and recalls many RSS participants in that movement.

21. This argument was developed by professor Yeshwantrao Kelkar in an interview on 14 January 1969. Professor Kelkar was a former Vidyarthi Parishad president and also a participant in the Quit-India movement.

22. Madhok mentioned this to Reuben Auspitz. Auspitz wrote what is still the best study of the Vidyarthi Parishad, 'The Akhil Bharatiya Vidyarthi Parishad: An Introductory Study of Rightist Student Politics in India', an unpublished paper completed for the University of Wisconsin's College-Year-in-India Programme (The Delhi School of Social Work, 1968), pp. 45–47.

23. Interview with Ved Prakash Nanda on 7 September 1969, in Delhi. Nanda was one of those swayamsevaks assigned by the RSS to work for the Vidyarthi Parishad.

24. This is an estimate provided by Giriraj Kishore, the organizing secretary of the Vidyarthi Parishad, at an interview with him on 31 July 1969, in Delhi.

25. Professor Yeshwantrao Kelkar claims that the reversal on campus politics was a reaction to the atmosphere of violence created by other student groups and that the Parishad's new approach to student strikes was a response to the intransigent attitude of college administrators towards the legitimate needs of students. Interview with him on 14 January 1969, in Bombay.

26. Some of the more dramatic examples of the Vidyarthi Parishad's success were its victories at Delhi University. After years of domination by the Congress or the communist student affiliates, the Vidyarthi Parishad gained control of the students union in 1972, and repeated its victory in 1973. In the 1973 election, the union president was, for the first time, directly elected. The Parishad candidate won 15,053 votes, and his nearest rival 3,677. It also won all four of the union's executive positions, and 26 of the 37 union presidents in the affiliated undergraduate colleges belonged to the Parishad. Reported in *Organiser*, 18 September 1973. The Parishad reasserted its dominance of Delhi University after the lifting of the Emergency.

27. The topics at a 1969 All-India Students and Teachers workshop provide a clue to the types of topics considered by

the Study Circles. Delegates were asked to prepare themselves on the following subjects: 'Prophecy of regionalism—a suicidal loyalty', 'Naxalbari—a challenge to democracy', 'Future for imperialism—red and white', 'Centres of the 3rd world war', 'Remedies to end untouchability.' The delegates were told that formal lectures would be given on 'Students participation in university affairs', 'Students' unrest: diagnosis and cure', 'Education unemployment problem', 'Young leadership in nation-building activities'.

28. We were informed that these two programmes are best organized at the Bombay University unit.

29. Taken from a brochure prepared by the Bombay University unit of the Parishad, printed in 1968.

30. Ibid. Since the programme was launched in 1966, the Parishad has placed up to 400 young tribals each year in various university programmes.

31. Taken from the pamphlet, 'General Secretary's Report to the 23rd National Conference, Varanasi, 4–6 November 1977', p. 3. RSS informants estimate that only about one-third of the Vidyarthi Parishad members have ever taken part in any RSS activities and that an even smaller percentage are RSS members.

32. Information regarding these discussions from ibid., p. 4.

33. Ibid., p. 2.

34. He was president of the Delhi University Students Union.

35. Information on the underground activities from an interview with Professor Yeshwantrao Kelkar, on 14 July 1983, at Bombay.

36. Information from an interview with Professor Om Prakash Kohli, national president of the Vidyarthi Parishad, at Bombay on 7 May 1983; and from the General Secretary's Report, 23rd Session, p. 11.

37. The Bharatiya Yuva Sangh, the youth group of the Jana Sangh element in the Janata Party, also attended, but the Yuva Sangh

was not included on the steering committee on the ground that the Vidyarthi Parishad was the Jana Sangh's 'representative.' This incident underscored a dilemma faced by the Parishad. In fact, it was not the youth wing of the Jana Sangh; but the common links of the Jana Sangh group and the Parishad to the RSS tended to blur the distinction between them and the general public.

38. Information on the Vidyarthi Parishad's walkout is from an interview with K. N. Govindan, organizing secretary of the Parishad's south zone, at New Delhi on 31 July 1983. Other amalgamation efforts can be found in Ashok Tandon, 'Janata party ke Yuva Sanghatano ke Tutne ka Atut Silsila,' in *Rashtriya Chhatra Shakti* (February–March 1980), pp. 51–61, in Hindi.

39. In contrast to the Vidyarthi Parishad, other pro-Janata Party groups permitted their members to contest in elections. Information in this paragraph from an interview with Professor Om Prakash Kohli, op. cit.

40. Interview with Professor Yeshwantrao Kelkar, op. cit.

41. *Organiser*, 18 June 1978.

42. For example, in Bombay according to Professor Yeshwantrao Kelkar, over three-fourths of the Parishad members are non-RSS.

43. The Parishad as well as other members of the RSS 'family' did not totally agree with the objectives of the All-Assam Students Union. For example, the Parishad does not consider the Hindu immigrant from Bangladesh illegal, and the Parishad is willing to accept a later cut-off date to determine who is an illegal immigrant.

44. From a press interview with Golwalkar, published in *Organiser*, 23 October 1948.

45. The press statement was released on 2 November 1948, and is published in *Justice on Trial*, pp. 78–79.

46. For discussion of the negotiations between Mookerjee and the RSS, see Craig Baxter, *The Jana Sangh: A Biography of* an

Indian Political Party (Philadelphia: University of Pennsylvania Press, 1969), Ch. 4; Myron Weiner, *Party Politics in India: The Development of a Multiparty System* (Princeton: Princeton University Press, 1957), pp. 181–94; Bruce Graham, 'Shyama Prasad Mookerjee and the Communalist Alternative', in D. A. Low, ed., *Soundings in South Asian History* (London: Weidenfeld and Nicholson, 1968); pp. 330–74.

47. *Organiser*, 25 June 1956.

48. For a comprehensive biographical sketch of Mookerjee, see J. I. Das, 'Syamaprasad: The Uncompromising Patriot', *Modern Review* 121 (June 1970): p. 318.

49. As Bengal's Muslim community became more politically articulate, Mookerjee began to exhibit a Hindu revivalist urge to unite the Hindu castes to protect Hindu interests in Bengal, a province with a Muslim majority. Fazlul Haq, leader of the Krishak Praja Party, a party which drew most of its support from rural Muslim constituencies, organized the first ministry in Bengal under the 1935 Government of India Act. The ministry's policy of extending government control over educational institutions, of increasing the percentage of Muslims employed in government services, and of supporting the interests of landless labour and tenant farmers were viewed by Mookerjee as thinly veiled attempts to diminish the influence of the Hindu community.

50. Reported in the *Statesman* (Calcutta), 7 February 1948.

51. Resolution 7 of 14–15 February 1948 working committee meeting in New Delhi. Taken from the minutes of that meeting.

52. Resolution 4 of 8–9 August 1948 working committee meeting in New Delhi. Taken from the minutes of that meeting.

53. Resolution 10 of the meeting defined a Hindu: 'A Hindu means a person who declares that he is a Hindu and regards this land of Bharatvarsha from Sindhu to the Seas as his Fatherland and his Holy-land.' This definition is an almost direct quotation

from Savarkar's definition of Hindu in *Hindutva*, a book he wrote to describe the shape of the future Hindu nation. It indicates the powerful intellectual influence he still exerted over the Mahasabha.

54. In a rare display of solidarity with the RSS, the delegates at this meeting requested the government to lift the ban on the RSS. L. B. Bhopatkar, the Mahasabha's president, prepared a lengthy statement full of effusive praise for the RSS. The leadership was well aware of the fact that the RSS possessed resources that were politically valuable. It had a large committed cadre; it had pracharaks who could help organize party units; it had widespread sympathy among Hindus because of its refugee relief work. Mahasabha informants relate that Dr N. B. Khare was chosen president of the Mahasabha in 1949 largely because he had close connections with the RSS leadership and might be able to arrange some kind of cooperation between the two Hindu groups. However, Golwalkar had no intention of supporting a party with so little prospect of political success. Moreover, the RSS leadership was still uncertain about what political role to assume. The RSS dramatically signaled its non-support of the Mahasabha with minimal help during its 1949 all-India meeting at Calcutta.

55. See Graham, 'Shyama Prasad Mookerjee', p. 338.

56. N. B. Khare, *My Political Memoirs or Autobiography* (Nagpur: J. P. Joshi, 1959), pp. 427–28.

57. Interview with Appaji Joshi on 21 December 1968 at Chandrapur, Maharashtra.

58. Reported in a biographical sketch of Dani in *Organiser*, 31 May 1965.

59. Graham comes to the same conclusion. See his discussion in 'Shyama Prasad Mookerjee', pp. 346–52.

60. Patel died on 15 December 1950, and Nehru, who had previously left organizational matters to him, began to take an active interest in the party's organization. Three months

before Patel's death, Purushottam Das Tandon, a supporter of Patel, was elected Congress president. Nehru resigned from the Congress Working Committee on 6 August 1951, claiming that he could not work with people who had 'the wrong kind of ideas', clearly referring to Tandon's more Hindu nationalist orientation. On 8 September the All-India Congress Committee (AICC) accepted Tandon's resignation and elected Nehru president. This gave Nehru unprecedented power within the Congress, controlling both its ministerial and organizational wings.

61. Golwalkar discusses his talks in *Organiser*, 25 June 1956. While sorting out the terms of cooperation with Mookerjee, RSS activists were mounting a campaign to involve the RSS in the political process. *Organiser* was one forum for their views. The editor of *Organiser*, writing under the pen name 'Kamal', wrote four articles which analysed the role which the RSS should play in politics. He defended RSS involvement by arguing that politicians had their 'hand on the pulse of the Nation', and could facilitate the acceptance of 'natural cultural trends'. He advised the RSS leadership that they would not be faithful to their civic duty if they left nation building to political parties who had little respect for Indian culture (obviously referring to the Congress). In the last of four articles, he wrote that the RSS must enter politics to protect itself from future political attack, an argument which figured prominently in the leadership's decision to support Mookerjee's party. These articles published in *Organiser*, 23 November, 30 November, 7 December and 14 December 1949, written before Mookerjee's resignation from the cabinet, summarize the arguments which the activists used to support their case.

62. Balraj Madhok, *Portrait of a Martyr: Biography of Dr Shyama Prasad Mookerji* (Bombay: Jaico Publishing House, 1969), p. 98. Madhok, who played a key role in forming the party, writes: 'R.S.S. leadership was not yet clear in its mind about the shape

and character of the political party to which it could lend its support, and the role it would have to play in bringing it into existence. There was no unanimity even about the advisability of having such a political organization.' In addition, Madhok writes that the RSS leaders feared that politics 'would corrode idealism and spirit of selfless service to society in the R.S.S. and create an unhealthy rivalry between the R.S.S. workers working in different fields'. Ibid., p. 97.

63.   See Golwalkar's article on Mookerjee in *Organiser* (25 June 1956).

64.   The preparations for this meeting had begun in January 1951 when prominent RSS citizens, including Hans Raj Gupta, RSS *sanghchalak* for Delhi and Punjab, met to draw up plans for a new party in Punjab, PEPSU (Patiala and East Punjab States Union), Himachal Pradesh and Delhi. Mookerjee attended the meeting to inform the group of his own plans to form a party in Bengal and to propose that an all-India party should be considered to link the non-Congress nationalist parties. For discussion, see Madhok, *Portrait of a Martyr*, pp. 99–102.

65.   An organization was hastily created in the first week of January 1952, shortly before the general elections were held. The reason for this delay was that Bombay Pradesh Congress committee president, S. K. Patil, a follower of Deputy Prime Minister Vallabhbhai Patel, wanted RSS support in the first general elections and was willing to offer assembly seats to swayamsevaks in exchange, according to RSS sources. However, the talks collapsed. Interview with Madhukar Mahajan, former Jana Sangh organizing secretary, 21–22 May 1983, at Bombay.

66.   The text of that speech was printed in *Mahratta* (Pune), 22 June 1951.

67.   Madhok, *Portrait of a* Martyr, p. 121.

68.   Thengadi, a graduate of Nagpur's law college and an RSS pracharak, served as an RSS organizer between 1942 and

1948. He was one of the organizers of the Vidyarthi Parishad. Prior to forming the Bharatiya Mazdoor Sangh, Thengadi had worked as an organizing secretary in INTUC, the labour movement affiliated with the Congress. His uncle, Dhundiraj Thengadi, was one of India's pioneer trade unionists.

69. For a report of the meeting, see *Organiser*, 19 September 1955. It was claimed that the delegates represented 56,000 workers. According to BMS leader G. S. Gokhale, this figure is very much inflated. Interview with him in Bombay, on 14 January 1969.

70. For an analysis of its geographic distribution, see *Organiser*, 4 September 1971.

71. The best sources for Bharatiya Mazdoor Sangh theory are: G. S. Gokhale, M. P. Mehta and D. B. Thengadi, *Labour Policy* (Nagpur: Bharatiya Mazdoor Sangh, 1967–1968); D. B. Thengadi, *Focus on the Socio-Economic Problems* (New Delhi: Suruchi Sahitya, 1972); and D. B. Thengadi, *Why Bharatiya Sangh?* (Pune: V. R. Shingre, 1959).

72. *Why Bharatiya Sangh?* pp. 1–34.

73. Ibid., p. 63.

74. Interview with G.S. Gokhale on 22 November 1969, at Bombay.

75. The slogan of the Mazdoor Sangh is, '1. Nationalize Labour; 2. Labourize the Industry; and 3. Industrialize the Nation.'

76. For a good discussion of the theory, see Gokhale at al., *Labour Policy*, pp. 344–56.

77. Interview with Gokhale on 22 November 1969 in Bombay.

78. On most labour issues the Jana Sangh relied heavily on the advice of the Bharatiya Mazdoor Sangh, and the Jana Sangh consistently defended labour's right to strike and to bargain collectively. While the Jana Sangh supported 'labourizing' industry, the party opposed extending the principle to agriculture on grounds that it was impractical and that it would increase social tension in rural India and would enable an

exploitive government bureaucracy to become more powerful. To underscore Jana Sangh opposition to cooperative farming, the party organized an anti-cooperative conference in Bombay in 1959. Reported in *Organiser*, 21 December 1959.

79. *Organiser*, May 1982.

80. Thengadi, *Why Bharatiya Sangh*, pp. 81–83.

81. Ibid., p. 46.

82. An alternative name for the god is Twashta.

83. For details of the BMS role in the 1974 railway strike, see D. B. Thengadi, *Railway Karmachariyon ki Hartal* (Nagpur: Bharatiya Mazdoor Sangh, 1974), in Hindi. According to Gajanan Gokhale, a senior BMS official at the time of the railway strike, the BMS drafted the unions' negotiating document. Interview with him on 26 April 1983, at Pune.

84. He was selected general secretary of the Lok Sangarsh Samiti in November 1976, after the arrest of Ravindra Verma who had in turn replaced Nana Deshmukh when Deshmukh was arrested.

85. For details of the merger negotiations, see D. B. Thengadi, *Vichar Sutra* (Pune: BMS Research Institute, 1980), in Hindi.

86. There was total agreement on the independence of the projected united union, and a consensus on replacing 'class struggle' with 'struggle against injustice and exploitation', and on observing both Vishwakarma Day and May Day. Ibid., p. 123.

87. *Organiser*, 12 April 1980.

88. Bharatiya Mazdoor Sangh, *BMS Souvenir* (New Delhi: BMS, 1980), p. 14.

89. These goals are noted in the 'General Secretary's Report', in the *Souvenir Volume* published on the occasion of the Vishwa Hindu Parishad's annual meeting at Allahabad in late January 1966, pp. vii–viii.

90. *Hindu Vishwa* 5 (March 1970), p. 43.

91. Ibid.

92. Ibid., December 1969/January 1970, p. 63.
93. Later in 1977, the VHP turned over its work among tribals to the Bharatiya Vanavasi Kalyan Ashram, a national coordinating body established in 1977 to coordinate work among tribals.
94. *Hindu Vishwa* (November 1981), pp. 11, 33, 36.
95. The VHP collected the money in about four months. Interview with Lala Har Mohan, general secretary of the Parishad, on 23 May 1983, at New Delhi.
96. *Hindu Vishwa* (July 1981), p. 3.
97. *Hindu Chetana* (April 1986), p. 27, in Hindi.
98. Some 3 crore rupees (30 million) was raised according to *India Today* (30 November 1983), p. 34.
99. Statistics from *Sangh Sandesh* (8 April 1984), the official organ of the Hindu Swayamsevak Sangh in England.
100. *India Today*, International edition (28 February 1986), p. 66.
101. *Hindu Chetana* (April 1986), p. 6, in Hindi.
102. *India Today* (31 March 1986), pp. 30–39.
103. *Dharma Sansad* (New Delhi: Vishwa Hindu Parishad, 1982), p. 14, in Hindi.
104. Ibid., pp. 36–63.
105. Interview with Mahesh Mehta, general secretary of the Vishwa Hindu Parishad of America, on 10 September 1985, at Chicago.
106. *Hindu Chetana* (April 1986), p. 7, in Hindi.
107. There are VHP branches in Canada, England and several East African countries. The information on its activities in the United States is taken from a brochure published by the American branch.
108. Interview with Mahesh Mehta on 18 July 1986 at Boston, Massachusetts.
109. The VHP is the only affiliate in which the chief of the RSS is a trustee. Because of ill health, Moropant Pingale, a member of the RSS national executive and one of the most respected

pracharaks, was appointed by Deoras as an additional trustee to represent RSS interests.

110. The book is *Swami Vivekananda's Rousing Call to the Indian Nation* (Calcutta: Swastik Prakashan, 1963). This book contains a number of aphorisms used frequently in the RSS.

111. The events leading up to the formation of the Vivekananda Lay Order were provided by Eknath Ranade in an extensive interview with him on 1 January 1970 at Kanyakumari.

112. The village has a Christian majority; most of its inhabitants are Roman Catholic fishermen.

113. The total cost for the elaborate memorial was approximately 12 million rupees (approximately $1.5 million) most of which was collected by the time the memorial was dedicated in 1970. A general body, consisting of some of India's leading politicians, businessmen, educators and journalists, set the general policy. In fact, it was controlled by Ranade and a small group of full-time workers, most of whom were swayamsevaks. RSS members (and others) are encouraged to visit the site, which consists of a large structure housing the statue of Vivekananda, prayer rooms, and an assembly hall, as well as a separate structure housing the footprint of the Devi Kumari.

114. The curriculum of the six-month training includes a mix of religious philosophy, classical languages, social science theory and history.

115. The Kendra set the goal of 20 million rupees (approximately $2.5 million) to launch the order, and the first class of fourteen trainees assembled at Kanyakumari on 30 August 1973. The trainees were selected from some 700 applicants and came from eight Indian states and Union territories. All were unmarried and below thirty. They were all college graduates and none had family commitments. The first class had twelve men and two women.

116. Interview with G. Vasudevan, organizing secretary of the Kendra, on 27 June 1983, at Delhi.

117. The General Secretary's Report for 1982 (p. 3) noted that it had received 3.2 million rupees in 1982–83.

118. Relief work is not new for the RSS. It has been engaged in relief work since the 1930s. What was unique about the projects begun in late 1977 in Andhra Pradesh was the incorporation of economic development.

119. See report in *Organiser*, 19 December 1979.

120. For a description of its original objects, see J. P. Mathur, ed., *Jana Deep Souvenir* (Delhi: Rakesh Press, 1971), pp. 13–14.

121. See report of the DRI's development activities in Andhra Pradesh in *Organiser*, 5 November 1978.

122. Information taken from pamphlet *Bharatiya Vanavasi Kalyan Ashram* (Bombay: Kalyan Ashram, 1984).

123. For information on the BVKA's aggressive outreach programme, see *Sangh Sandesh* (January 1985), the newsletter of the RSS affiliate in England.

124. *Organiser*, 28 October 1979.

125. See report of this new missionary venture in *Organiser*, 1 August 1982.

126. Information from an interview with Har Mohan Lal, VHP general secretary, on 23 May 1983, at New Delhi.

127. *Organiser*, 12 April 1983.

128. In previous years, only senior pracharaks had met together at the national level in Nagpur at the time of the annual Akhil Bharatiya Pratinidhi Sabha meetings.

129. Senior Jana Sangh figures, however, continued to meet on an ad hoc basis with RSS leaders. Information regarding the samanvaya samitis in an interview with Murli Manohar Joshi, all-India secretary of the Bharatiya Janata Party on 9 August 1983 in Delhi.

130. Deendayal Upadhyaya represented the Jana Sangh at the annual Nagpur meetings until his death in 1968. After him, Nana Deshmukh and Sunder Singh Bhandari attended. Interview with J. P. Mathur, BJP member of the Rajya Sabha, on 26 July 1983, at New Delhi.

131. For example, senior BJP figures in Maharashtra attended a state level samanvaya samiti meeting at Pune in June 1985. See Divakar Deshmukh, 'Maharashtra Kuthe Chalaya', in *Dharmabhaskar* (15 July 1985), pp. 44–46, in Marathi.

Chapter 5: The RSS in Politics

1. While Bhai Mahavir had little practical experience in politics, he came from a politically active family. His father, Bhai Parmanand, had participated in revolutionary activities during his youth and had become a leading spokesman of the Arya Samaj in Punjab. Parmanand also played an active role in the Hindu Mahasabha.

2. For a very good discussion of this manifesto, see Baxter, *Jana Sangh*, pp. 83–9.

3. The concept of a unitary state, which was not mentioned in this manifesto, later became a central plank in Jana Sangh manifestos. In the place of the existing states, the party proposed the creation of smaller janapads as regional administrative units exercising powers delegated to them by the Central government. This proposal was to receive considerable attention after the decision was made by the government to reorganize the states on a linguistic basis in the mid-1950s. Both the RSS and the Jana Sangh opposed unilateral states, claiming they would undermine national integration by encouraging regional sub-nationalism and political separatism.

4. The cow, as a symbol of the divine mother, evokes a powerful emotional response from members of the RSS. Those who would do damage to this symbol are considered enemies of Indian culture. Both the Jana Sangh and the RSS have periodically participated in agitations aimed at forcing the government to ban cow slaughter. The largest single RSS effort was a nationwide cow protection campaign in late 1952. It was

reported that sane 54,000 RSS swayamsevaks visited 85,000 villages to generate support for the movement. The RSS organized a conference in November 1953 to mobilize political support behind the campaign. Mauli Chandra Sharma, the Jana Sangh president, and several other prominent Jana Sangh leaders took an active role in that conference. See report in *Organiser*, 2 November 1953.

5. By receiving 3.06 per cent of the vote, the party was entitled to the exclusive use of a particular symbol. It used the deepak (the traditional lamp) as its symbol after the first general election.

6. Mookerjee won from the South-east Calcutta constituency, and Durga Charan Banerji, the second Jana Sangh member from West Bengal, won the Midnapur seat. The party's third member of parliament was Umashankar Muljibhai Trivedi, who won the Chittor seat in Rajasthan. Trivedi was to play a leading role in the early development of the Jana Sangh.

7. *Organiser*, 25 February 1952.

8. See Baxter, *Jana Sangh*, pp. 107–16.

9. Deendayal Upadhyaya, an RSS pracharak, had been the joint organizing secretary of Uttar Pradesh RSS when Golwalkar loaned him to the Jana Sangh. He was appointed secretary of the Uttar Pradesh Jana Sangh. At the Kanpur annual session he was appointed one of the two general secretaries, a position he held until 1967 when he became party president.

10. This proposition was suggested to us by Vasantrao Krishna Oke in an interview with him on 4 September 1969 in Delhi.

11. How seriously Chatterjee was considered is not clear. Some Jana Sangh informants claim that Chatterjee was not a serious candidate. Indeed, some claim that he was never even offered the position.

12. Interview with N. C. Chatterjee on 29 May 1969 at Calcutta. Much of the material in the discussion of a new party president is taken from that interview.

13. Myron Weiner interviewed Chatterjee soon after the talks, and he reports that Chatterjee told him of a meeting in his New Delhi home in which Jana Sangh and Mahasabha leaders discussed four options: The first proposed that the three Hindu-oriented parties (the Jana Sangh, the Hindu Mahasabha, and the Ram Rajya Parishad) disband and reorganize as a single party. The second proposed a merger of the three, but with the provision that the Mahasabha continue to exist as a purely cultural organization. Another proposed an electoral alliance between the Mahasabha and the Jana Sangh, with each retaining its own organizational structure. The fourth proposed the amalgamation of the Jana Sangh and the Hindu Mahasabha into a new political body. See discussion in Myron Weiner, *Party Politics in India: The Development* of *a Multi-Party System* (Princeton: Princeton University Press, 1957), p. 206. In our interview with him, Chatterjee claimed that he personally supported the second option.

14. If as Chatterjee asserts the second option of the four discussed was the one he personally favoured, V. D. Savarkar had good cause to doubt if the Hindu Mahasabha could exert influence within the proposed political arrangement. The RSS would surely have had far more influence. Considering his views towards the RSS, Savarkar could not have relished the prospect of the Mahasabha operating in the shadow of the RSS.

15. *Organiser*, 8 February 1954. The previous August, Madhok wrote in *Organiser*, that 'the successor of Dr Mookerjee must have that quality of carrying the workers with him ... that demands perfect coordination between the Jana Sangh and the RSS. There can be persons who may like to disturb this coordination in the name of self-aggrandizement. Such people will be the worst enemies of these organizations and they will be betraying the sacred trust of Dr Mookerjee.' Ibid., 16 August 1953. Considering subsequent events, it is clear that

Madhok used this forum to advise Sharma to take the RSS cadre into his confidence.

16. Interview with Mauli Chandra Sharma on 18 August 1969 at Delhi.

17. Interview with Vasantrao Krishna Oke on 4 September 1969 at Delhi.

18. Interview with Eknath Ranade on 29 December 1969 at Kanyakumari.

19. Interview with Sharma on 18 August 1969 at Delhi.

20. The usual RSS interpretation of Oke's rebellion is that he lost the 'egoless' qualities necessary for a worthy swayamsevak. Oke has since recanted and the RSS has again given him work.

21. Interview with Sharma on 18 August 1969 at Delhi. Sharma claims that he tried to raise money 'to put the party on a sound financial footing'.

22. Oke realized the cause was doomed, and according to informants, he said nothing during the proceedings to defend his views.

23. The Jana Sangh constitution did not give the organizing secretaries the right to interfere in the party's decision making, but their influence among the swayamsevak participants provided them the de facto power to exert significant influence over the cadre. Indeed, the Jana Sangh constitution did not even describe their duties, specifying only that they would be appointed by state working committees, and that their duties would be established by these committees. Jana Sangh constitution (amended by All-India General Council session, Bhagalpur, 5–7 May 1972), Art. 13, para. 6.

24. This factional struggle in the Delhi Jana Sangh reported extensively in *Hindustan Times* (Delhi), 4–5 November 1954.

25. These manouevres are reported in *Organiser*, 8 November 1954.

26. Ibid.

27. The next plenary session of the party was held at Jodhpur in late December 1954, and the party leaders selected Prem Nath Dogra president. Dogra, a former RSS sanghchalak in J&K and founder of the Praja Parishad, could be relied upon to cooperate in purging the party of its 'undisciplined' elements. Few of the legislative members of the new Jana Sangh were RSS members, and many deserted it during the struggle for control of the party. Most of its legislators in Delhi, Uttar Pradesh, West Bengal and Rajasthan were either expelled or switched party allegiances. A group of Jana Sangh dissidents in Delhi organized the National Democratic Front. This group, sometimes referred to as the Democratic Jana Sangh, also received some scattered support in Uttar Pradesh and Punjab. However, the new party could generate little enthusiasm and, as the 1957 elections approached, many of its active participants drifted into other parties. A discussion on this splinter party, see H. D. Malaviya, *The Danger of Right Reaction* (New Delhi: Socialist Congressman Publication, 1965).

28. Even the Jana Sangh constitution stipulated that the president would choose the general secretary, this 'selection' was never in doubt after 1954. Upadhyaya was annually 'chosen', and he was recognized as the de facto leader of the party.

29. This manifesto is discussed in Baxter, *Jana Sangh*, pp. 141–42.

30. Loyalty to party principles played more of a role in candidate selection than in 1952. Consequently, few candidates chosen in 1952 were again nominated in 1957 and a larger number of RSS members were awarded tickets.

31. Of the assembly constituencies Baxter defines as rural, the Jana Sangh contested 334 seats in the 1957 elections in Uttar Pradesh, receiving 15.5 per cent of the vote, though this still did not measure up to the 22.69 per cent of the vote it won in the 34 urban constituencies it contested. He also pointed out that its 'rural' vote increased 78 per cent between 1957 and

1962, while the 'urban' vote increased only 26 per cent. Baxter, *Jana Sangh*, pp. 235–36.

32. Those cities are Agra, Allahabad, Benares, Kanpur and Lucknow. Figures from *Organiser*, 9 November 1959.

33. See Wayne Wilcox's discussion of Madhya Bharat in '*Madhya Pradesh*,' in Weiner ed., *State Politics in India* (Princeton: Princeton University Press, 1968), pp. 132–37.

34. Prabhakar Balwant Dani, one of the most successful RSS organizers, established RSS work in Madhya Bharat in the 1930s. After serving there, he was chosen the RSS general secretary in 1946, a post he held until 1956. He also served as general secretary between 1962 and 1965. Biographical data on Dani in *Organiser*, 31 May 1965.

35. Lawrence L. Shrader discusses these elections in 'Rajasthan' in Weiner, *State Politics*, pp. 329–37.

36. In the first three elections, the Jana Sangh won assembly seats in eleven districts of the state, all but one in the eastern districts.

37. We are referring here only to those districts included within the present state of Punjab. The party has received rural support in the Hindi-speaking districts of the southern part of Punjab, which are now included in Haryana.

38. The Jana Sangh's opposition to Maha Delhi (greater Delhi) was linked to its opposition to the division of Punjab. The Congress unit in Delhi, until 1967, had consistently advocated the creation of an expanded Delhi state that would include the Hindi-speaking districts of southern Punjab. The Jana Sangh in Delhi vehemently opposed the idea. An expanded Delhi might lead to a dilution of its support in Delhi as well as in Punjab.

39. See discussion in Baldev Raj Nayar, 'Punjab', in Weiner, *State Politics*, pp. 449–56.

40. *Ambala Tribune* (Ambala), 3 November 1960 reported Golwalkar's comments.

41. Ibid., 20 October 1960.

42. *Times of India* (Delhi), 9 November 1961.

43. Balraj Madhok won a seat in the New Delhi constituency in a 1961 bye-election. This seat was lost the following year in the 1962 general elections.

44. For a discussion of that factional conflict, see Mahender Kumar Saini and Walter Andersen, 'The Congress Split in Delhi: The Effect of Factionalism on Organizational Performance and System-Level Interactions', *Asian Survey* 9 (November 1971): 1084–110.

45. Puri, Balraj. 'Jammu and Kashmir'. *State Politics in India*, ed. Myron Weiner, pp. 224–38. Princeton: Princeton University Press, 1968.

46. The Parishad's percentage of the total vote in the two elections was a respectable 28.44 per cent in 1957 and 24.45 per cent in 1962.

47. The Jana Sangh general secretary reported that party membership in Maharashtra had fallen off considerably between 1957 and 1960, declining from 45,000 to 10,000. Reported in *Organiser*, 1 February 1960.

48. RSS leaders opposed the creation of linguistic states, arguing that unilingual states were likely to create separatist sentiment. Despite this, the Jana Sangh organization in Maharashtra and Gujarat joined electoral alliances whose major objective was the division of Bombay state on a linguistic basis.

49. For a discussion of her Congress party critics, see Zareer Masani, *Indira Gandhi: A Biography* (New York: Thomas Y. Cromwell, 1964), pp. 154–76.

50. For a critical account of the RSS participation, see D. R. Goyal, *Rashtriya Swayamsevak Sangh* (New Delhi: Radhakrishna Prakashan, 1979), p. 106.

51. Senior party leaders had met in the late 1950s to consider an ideological statement, but the party remained without one

until Deendayal Upadhyaya formulated his views on Integral Humanism.

52. Upadhyaya, Deendayal, *Integral Humanism* (Bombay: Bharatiya Jana Sangh, n.d.).

53. Quoted in Walter K. Andersen, 'Political Philosophy of Deendayal Upadhyaya', in Raje Sudhakar, ed., *Destination* (Delhi: Deendayal Research Institute, 1978), p. 47.

54. These resolutions printed in Bharatiya Jana Sangh: Resolutions passed by the Bharatiya Karya Samiti at the Twelfth Session, a Jana Sangh pamphlet.

55. Resolution passed at 15 January 1966 Kanpur session of the working committee.

56. Resolution passed at 30 April, 1 May 1966 working committee session at Jalandhar.

57. Resolution passed at 12–13 July 1966 working committee meeting at Lucknow.

58. Deendayal Upadhyaya, who remained general secretary, was still the dominant figure in the central executive. Madhok was a logical choice as president because he had a reputation as a dynamic articulate politician. Atal Bihari Vajpayee, a skilful parliamentarian and orator, remained leader of the Jana Sangh parliamentary group.

59. *Organiser*, 8 May 1966.

60. The analysis of the Jana Sangh's urban vote is taken from the Ministry of Information and Broadcasting's *Fourth General Elections: An Analysis* (Faridabad: Thompson Press, 1967), p. 251.

61. Yogesh Puri, 'An Analysis of Jammu and Kashmir Elections', *Indian Political Science Review* 1 (April–September 1967), pp. 239–50.

62. See Baxter's analysis of the urban vote, *Jana Sangh*, pp. 288–89.

63. Four of the winning parliamentary candidates were, in fact, members of the Scindia Rajmata's group and did not formally register themselves as Jana Sangh members in parliament.

64. *Fourth General Elections*, p. 179.

65. Interview with Golwalkar on 26 February 1969 at Delhi.

66. *Hindustan Times* (Delhi), 23 April 1967.

67. *Organiser*, 9 April 1967.

68. Ibid., 21 September 1967.

69. Many Jana Sangh critics interpreted the party's shift as more a rhetorical than a real commitment to a radical change in policies. However, the pressure of the party's delegates on the leadership to change the party's policies do indicate real popular support from the cadre for its new policies and tactics.

70. Upadhyaya, during his fourteen years as general secretary, had remained in the background, devoting his efforts to building the organizational structure of the party. He began to prepare for his new and more public role by running unsuccessfully for the Jaunpur parliamentary seat (in Uttar Pradesh) in 1964.

71. The working committee at its 7–8 September 1969 meeting at Indore supported the strike. The Bharatiya Mazdoor Sangh helped organize that strike.

72. See reports of the conflict in *Hindustan Times* (Delhi), 21 and 26 September 1968

73. *Indian Express* (Delhi), 10 September 1969.

74. *Statesman* (Delhi), 3 September 1969.

75. Ibid.

76. Reported in *Northern India Patrika* (Allahabad), 1 March 1967.

77. Reported in *Statesman* (Delhi), 30 January 1967.

78. *Statesman* (Delhi), 2 September 1969.

79. A summary of the talks in *Hindustan Times* (Delhi), 30 May 1969.

80. Reported in *Times of India* (Delhi), 17 September 1969.

81. Ibid., a good summary of events leading up to agreement, 26 January 1971.

82. In recognition of the importance of the Scindia family's influence in Madhya Pradesh, the Jana Sangh included Madhavrao Scindia on its working committee in 1971.

His mother, Vijaya Raje Scindia, the politically astute head of the family, formally joined the Jana Sangh in October 1972. Madhavrao and his mother have fallen out politically. Madhavrao left the Jana Sangh during the 1975–77 Emergency; he joined Mrs Gandhi's Congress party. His mother remained a senior figure in the Jana Sangh and now in the BJP, serving as vice president from 1980 to 1986.

83. Results reported in *Organiser*, 7 November 1970.

84. One month after the general elections, Delhi had municipal corporation elections. The Congress in Delhi was deeply divided and the Jana Sangh retained control of the corporation with an even larger majority than in 1967.

85. Reports of the criticism in *Organiser*, 17 July 1971 and *Hindustan Times* (Delhi), 4 July 1971.

86. Reported in *Jana Deep Souvenir*, ed. by J. P. Mathur (Delhi: Rakesh Press, 1971), p. 3. Vajpayee did not need much convincing because he already believed that the party should portray itself as a representative of the 'common man.'

87. For a study of the political influence of Rajasthan's princely order, see Kusum Bhargava, 'Rajasthan Politics and Princely Rulers: An Analysis of Electoral Processes', *Indian Journal of Political Science* 33 (October–December 1972), pp. 413–20.

88. *Organiser* printed a surprisingly frank report, indicating the depth of feeling among the cadre. *Organiser*, 12 May 1972.

89. The Rajya Sabha is India's Upper House of parliament, somewhat analogous to the British House of Lords.

90. The party had already moved to implement this decision in 1971 by selecting Sheikh Abdul Rahman to its working committee, the first Muslim to be chosen to it. Sheikh Rahman was the most prominent party activist from the Muslim community in Jammu and Kashmir. He bolted the party in 1974 to join the Bharatiya Kranti Dal.

91. Quoted from a party pamphlet reporting his speech to the Bhagalpur annual session held during 5–7 May 1972.

92.   Advani served as secretary of the Rajasthan Jana Sangh, 1952–57; secretary of the Delhi Pradesh Jana Sangh, 1958–62; vice-president of the Delhi state unit, 1965–67; assistant editor of *Organiser*, 1960–67. Before joining the party, he served as an RSS pracharak; among other offices, he was a secretary of the RSS unit in Karchi and an organizing secretary in Rajasthan. Vajpayee continued to serve as leader of the parliamentary wing of the party. Party informants suggest that Vajpayee himself wanted to reduce the scope of his duties, preferring to concentrate on legislative activities.

93.   The party's 1967 election manifesto also stated that Rs 2000 per month was the maximum expendable income, but it did not specify if this was family or individual income.

94.   Parts of that speech printed in *Organiser*, 17 February 1973.

95.   Reported ibid., 23 April 1973.

96.   The first significant example of agitation employed by the Jana Sangh was its participation in Jaya Prakash Narayan's anti-corruption drive in Bihar. Both the Jana Sangh and the RSS supplied cadre to this movement, which emerged in early 1974 from a student-led protest against inadequate university facilities and quickly escalated into a major confrontation with the government of Prime Minister Indira Gandhi.

97.   Madhok, in proposing such changes, misread the mood of the grass-roots cadre. Events were to show that they did not favour his conservative approach.

98.   Reported in *Indian Express* (Delhi), 14 March 1973.

99.   Reported ibid., 30 March 1973.

100. Vajpayee took his MA in political science from the D. A. V. College in Kanpur where he was actively involved in the communist-affiliated Students' Federation. He later joined the RSS as a pracharak. Vajpayee was assigned to serve as private secretary to Shyama Prasad Mookerjee and was involved in the party's organizational work until his election to parliament in 1957. Biographical material from a Jana Sangh pamphlet

brought out on the occasion of the fifteenth annual Jana Sangh session at Bombay in April 1969.

101. After leaving the Jana Sangh, Madhok established the Lok Tantrik Jana Sangh, which merged with the Bharatiya Lok Dal in 1974. Refused a ticket by the Janata alliance in the 1977 election, he established his own Jana Sangh party.

102. The RSS also loaned workers to Narayan's movement in Bihar.

103. Vajpayee and other Jana Sangh national leaders advocated closer cooperation among the opposition parties for the sixth general elections scheduled for early 1976. They proposed that the parties jointly run candidates under a common electoral symbol.

104. The Jana Sangh won 18 of the 40 seats assigned to it by the Lok Sangharsh Samiti, though it received about the same percentage of the vote as in the 1972 elections (approximately 9 per cent).

105. This data was collected during 1968–1971 by Walter Andersen and included in his unpublished doctoral dissertation submitted in 1975 to the University of Chicago, 'The Jana Sangh: Ideology and Organization in Party Behavior'. In one of the three parliamentary constituencies included in this study, the zilla level was above the nagar in the party hierarchy, and we have taken this into account in preparing the tables.

106. Amitai Etzioni, for example, notes that strong personal bonds between leaders and followers is likely to generate congruency between the views of followers and leaders, resulting in stronger group cohesiveness. See his *Comparative Analysis of Complex Organizations*, pp. 187–89. In a study of small groups in the military, Shils and Janowitz discovered that commitment to Nazi ideology was higher in those units where officers with Nazi beliefs developed strong personal relations with the enlisted men, regardless of group cohesiveness among the enlisted men themselves. E. A. Shils and M. Janowitz, 'Cohesion and Disintegration in the Wehrmacht in World

War II', *Public Opinion Quarterly* 12 (1948), pp. 280–315. Similar conclusions on group cohesion and loyalty were found in studies of American soldiers. See Samuel Stouffer et al., *The American Soldier: Adjustment During Army Life* (Princeton: Princeton University Press, 1949), pp. 414–20; Samuel Stouffer et al., *The American Soldier: Combat and Its Aftermath* (Princeton: Princeton University Press, 1949), pp. 324–61.

107. Even when an individual swayamsevak has no great conviction about RSS goals, loyalty to the RSS organization is likely to remain strong if the small subunits of the shakha are able to stimulate group loyalty among the participants. The influence of small groups on larger group loyalties is discussed in Morton Grodzins, *The Loyal and the Disloyal: Social Boundaries of Patriotism and Treason* (Chicago: University of Chicago Press, 1956), pp. 43–47.

108. The Jana Sangh had annual party elections for organizational positions.

109. Etzioni, *Comparative Analysis of Complex Organizations*, p. 182.

110. The Jana Sangh favoured a system of proportional representation as one means of overcoming its mobilization problems. Because it had difficulty in accumulating enough support in a single constituency to win elections, the party's percentage of seats at both the state and Central level was consistently lower than its percentage of vote.

111. See his discussion of this proposition in Myron Weiner, *The Politics of Scarcity* (Chicago: University of Chicago Press, 1962), pp. 26–30.

Chapter 6: The Triumph of Activism

1. As the generation of swayamsevaks trained during the period of Hedgewar passes from the scene, the ranks of the traditional element within the RSS are being depleted. The younger generation tends to be on the activist side.

2. Deoras' address mentioned in an 8 January 1979 interview with Guru Vaid Dutt, former member of Jana Sangh national executive, reported in Geeta Puri, *Bharatiya Jana Sangh, Organization, and Ideology, Delhi: A Case Study* (New Delhi: Sterling, 1980), pp. 46–47.

3. *Organiser*, 9 April 1967.

4. Madhok was not opposed to alliances per se, but to alliances with parties of the left. Regarding alliances, the united fronts both at the state and national levels between 1967 and 1971 convinced many Jana Sangh workers that alliances could not be sustained unless the participants first agreed on a common ideological framework. For example, see article on the subject by J. P. Mathur, the all-India secretary of the Jana Sangh, in *Organiser*, 20 October 1973. The question of alliances has remained a controversial one in the Jana Sangh and remains so in its successor, the Bharatiya Janata Party. Many Jana Sangh workers doubted that an alliance strategy could ever work because other politicians did not share the political culture of the Jana Sangh. The Jana Sangh cadre thought of themselves as members of a community, and they were so largely because of their common RSS background. On the other hand, the party is not large enough in most places to assume power on its own and can aspire to a governing position only if it works with other parties.

5. See *Why Emergency*? (New Delhi: Government of India, 1975).

6. From an editorial in *Organiser*, 21 September 1974, commenting on a Jana Sangh study camp.

7. *Organiser*, 7 December 1974.

8. See a discussion sympathetic to the RSS' reaction to Narayan's Total Revolution in Dina Nath Mishra, *R.S.S.: Myth and Reality* (Ghaziabad: Vikas Publishing House, 1980), p. 43.

9. *Organiser*, 15 March 1975.

10. *Organiser*, 24 May 1975.

11. For a comprehensive chronology of the events leading up to the Emergency of 26 June 1975, see *Why Emergency?*, Ch. 10.

12. Madhavrao Mule, the general secretary of the RSS, became acting head of the RSS following the arrest of Deoras. This follows the precedent of the 1948–49 ban when Prabhakar Balwant Dani, the RSS general secretary, became acting chief in the wake of Golwalkar's arrest.

13. However, none of the RSS-affiliates was banned.

14. Most of the information regarding the reaction of the RSS to the ban is taken from an interview with Rajendra Singh, general secretary of the RSS, on 16 July 1982 at Chicago, Illinois.

15. Ranade was given a similar responsibility during the first ban in 1948–49.

16. Statement of then general secretary, Madhavrao Mule, reported in *Organiser*, 4 June 1977. See a description of the RSS activities in *The Economist* (London), 4 December 1976, pp. 67–68.

17. Quoted in *Organiser*, 28 May 1977.

18. Ibid. The RSS claims that over 100,000 of its members participated in the satyagraha. The 'family' of organizations was expected to contribute participants to the satyagraha as well. For example, the Vidyarthi Parishad contributed 12,000 and the Bharatiya Mazdoor Sangh some 10,000. Interview with Yeshwantrao Kelkar, former president of the Vidyarthi Parishad, on 14 July 1983 at Bombay. Dina Nath Mishra points out that many swayamsevaks argued that only violent methods would convince the government to change its policies, but that no national RSS leaders supported such a move and that the satyagraha was a visible sign of their commitment to non-violence. Mishra, *R.S.S.: Myth and Reality*, p. 46.

19. *Organiser*, 28 May 1977.

20. The talks broke down, according to Moghe, when the government failed to agree to such RSS conditions as the full release of all RSS prisoners and the return of all RSS property.

Organiser, 8 August 1977. When news of such talks became known, critics of the RSS inside the Janata Party charged that the RSS was more concerned with protecting itself than with assisting the underground effort. To buttress the argument, they pointed out that Deoras himself had written two letters in November 1975 to Prime Minister Gandhi, requesting a removal of the ban on the RSS. Deoras admits to writing the letters, but he argues that they were intended only to open a dialogue. *Organiser*, 25 March 1979. Dina Nath Mishra claims that the letters 'were written with the specific purpose of replying to the criticism of the Sangh by the government . . .' Mishra, *R.S.S.: Myth and Reality*, p. 50

21. In 1971 the Jana Sangh campaigning alone won 22 seats, and in the 1967 national elections it won 35 seats. The Janata Party partners in 1977 were the Congress (0), the Socialist Party, the Bharatiya Lok Dal, and the Jana Sangh. The four merged on 1 May 1977. A fifth group, Jagjivan Ram's Congress for Democracy, which worked closely with the alliance during the 1977 campaign, merged with the Janata Party on 5 May 1977.

22. *Indian Express* (Delhi), 12 April 1977.

23. *Organiser*, 5 March 1978. There is some discrepancy in reports on the number of shakhas. *Organiser*, 2 April 1979, gives a figure of 9500 in 1975.

24. *Organiser*, 29 March 1979.

25. *Organiser*, 5 April 1981.

26. *Organiser*, 31 January 1982.

27. The RSS general secretary in 1982 reported that there were 5600 *shakhas* in these four states: Karnataka, 1500; Kerala, 2500; Tamil Nadu, 400; and Andhra Pradesh, 1200. *Organiser*, 14 February 1982.

28. *India Today*, 11 May 1977, p. 34.

29. Reported in Kuldip Nayar, 'Mistrust of RSS Could Split the Opposition', in *India Abroad* (New York City), 18 June 1982, p. 2.

30. *Organiser*, 12 April 1980.

31. Interview with Professor Om Prakash Kohli, national president of the Vidyarthi Parishad, on 7 May 1983 at Bombay.

32. This was admitted in an interview with Nana Deshmukh on 16 April 1983 in Pune. Deshmukh, however, was careful to emphasize that no RSS instructions to the Jana Sangh were given during such talks.

33. *Organiser*, 29 August 1977. The proposal that the RSS merge with one of the youth groups affiliated to the Janata Party revealed a complete misunderstanding of the traditional RSS perception of its role. The RSS has never defined itself as the political adjunct of any political organization, even though Vinayak Damodar Savarkar tried unsuccessfully to use it as the volunteer front of his Hindu Mahasabha in the 1930s, and Sardar Vallabhbhai Patel in 1949 envisaged a similar role for it vis-à-vis the Congress party. Rather, the RSS has always conceived of itself as a character-building organization training young men who would reform society in their own 'perfected' image.

34. Janata Party Constitution, Article 5, Section a (i).

35. See report of these manoeuvres in *The Hindu* (Madras), 12 March 1979.

36. For a Jana Sangh interpretation of its problems with Charan Singh, see Nana Deshmukh, *R.S.S.: Victim of Slander* (New Delhi: Vision Books, 1979), pp. 50–63. Deshmukh writes that Singh offered to drop his criticism of the Jana Sangh on the dual-membership issue if it supported his bid to become prime minister.

37. Prime Minister Desai, who depended on the Jana Sangh group, did not back the demand that Jana Sangh legislators sever their links to the RSS.

38. Vajpayee, in what the press reported to be a highly emotional speech, made these remarks at a party meeting called in early April 1979 to discuss the RSS question. See *The Hindu* (Madras), 3 April 1979.

39. *Indian Express* (Delhi), 7 July 1979.
40. *Indian Express* (Delhi), 13 July 1979.
41. *Indian Express* (Delhi), 14 July 1979.
42. *Indian Express* (Delhi), 17 July 1979.
43. *Indian Express* (Delhi), 25 July 1979.
44. Ibid. The RSS constitution states that anyone holding an office in a political party could not simultaneously hold any post in the RSS.
45. Indian Express (Delhi), 30 July 1979.
46. Ibid.
47. Indian Express (Delhi), 5 August 1979.
48. Indian Express (Delhi), 2 August 1979.
49. For example, D. P. Thengadi, now the chief theoretician of the RSS, noted at the time that Vajpayee resorted to this publicly critical stance towards the RSS to preserve his national political stature. Interview with him on 10 September 1979 at Chicago.
50. Vajpayee and Advani, according to Nana Deshmukh, were given responsibility 'to decide anything and everything' regarding which Jana Sangh members would go into the government or work in the organization. Interview with Nana Deshmukh on 16 April 1983 at Pune.
51. This is not to say that there was no grumbling from within the Jana Sangh ranks regarding the leadership's non-assertive role. There was. This was pointed out to us by Nana Deshmukh in an interview with him on 16 April 1983; the same point was made by J. P. Mathur, a Janata Party member of parliament from the Jana Sangh group, in an interview on 26 July 1983 at Delhi.
52. One indication of this consideration is a reported letter of Madhavrao Mule, acting chief of the RSS during the Emergency, to a Janata alliance spokesman assuring him that the RSS intended to make it a more inclusive organization. See *Times of India* (Bombay), 14 March 1977.
53. *Organiser*, 28 May 1977.

54. Interview with Balasaheb Deoras on 29 July 1983 at Nagpur.

55. Narayan's 13 September 1977 letter on this matter is reported in *Organiser*, 3 October 1977.

56. RSS leaders were indeed talking with their counterparts in the Jama' at-i-Islami. Statement reported in *Organiser*, 3 October 1977.

57. *Organiser*, 12 September 1977.

58. *Organiser*, 19 November 1977.

59. Reported in *Organiser*, October 1979.

60. For a discussion of the importance of membership and ritual on community commitment, see Rosabeth Moss Kanter, *Commitment and Community: Communes and Utopias in Sociological Perspective* (Cambridge: Harvard University Press, 1972), pp. 93–94.

61. The Janata Party's popular percentage of the vote dropped from 43.2 per cent in 1977 to 28.3 per cent in 1980. Because the opposition was divided in India's winner-take-all system, the Janata Party's parliamentary percentage did not reflect its popular standing.

62. It fought the election under the name of Janata Party (Secular).

63. See *India Today*, 1 March 1980, for a description of the discontent in the ranks of the Jana Sangh group.

64. *Times of India* (Bombay), 8 March 1980.

65. *Times of India* (Bombay), 23 March 1980.

66. *Organiser*, 2 March 1980.

67. *Organiser*, 16 March 1980.

68. See discussion of Muslim voting in Myron Weiner, *India at the Polls: 1980: A Study of the Parliamentary Elections* (Washington, DC: American Enterprise Institute, 1983), pp. 120–24.

69. Newspaper reports as late as mid-March 1980 note that senior Jana Sangh figures believed that the general assembly of the RSS would adopt a resolution barring its members from active politics. For example, see *Times of India* (Bombay), 17 March 1980.

70. The wording of the parliamentary board's formula would also have prevented Janata Party members from participating in the activities of the labour and student affiliates of the RSS. The advisory proposal stated: 'No legislator or office bearer of the Janata Party shall participate in the day-to-day activities of the RSS. No members of the Janata party shall work for any front organization which functions in competition with the one sponsored by the Janata party.' *Times of India* (Bombay), 20 March 1980.

71. For the RSS view of developments, see *Organiser*, 30 March 1980.

72. General Secretary Rajendra Singh stated in an interview on 25 July 1982 at Bethesda, Maryland, that there was a large number of central assembly delegates opposed to making RSS members 'second class' persons in politics.

73. In the vote, Desai and three other non-Jana Sangh members voted against the hard-line stand.

74. For a description of the proceedings of the gathering, see *Times of India* (Bombay), 7 April 1980.

75. *Organiser*, 15 May 1980.

76. Interview with Rajendra Singh on 25 July 1982 at Bethesda, Maryland.

77. *Organiser*, 16 April 1980.

78. *Times of India* (Bombay), 27 December 1980.

79. Ibid.

80. See a summary of his speech in *Election Archives* (June 1981), pp. 675–87.

81. *Times of India* (Bombay), 31 December 1980.

82. The Congress party, however, formed the government because it was able to lure independents to its side.

83. *Organiser*, 28 February 1982.

84. Ibid.

85. *Times of India* (New Delhi), 31 August 1982.

86. *Organiser*, 10 October 1982.

87. *Organiser*, 21 November 1982.

88. *Organiser*, 23 May 1982. The Vidyarthi Parishad was under great pressure from its own ranks to revoke the 1977 decision, which many thought would over the long run undermine the Vidyarthi Parishad's appeal in the student community.

89. The election was unusual in other ways. The Congress did very well in traditionally Jana Sangh, Hindu, Punjabi-speaking neighbourhoods, while the BJP picked up unexpected support among Muslims and among voters in outlying suburban areas, which in the past had supported the Congress. One plausible reason for the loss of support among RSS cadre might be the backing of Punjabi Hindus—and the RSS cadre in Delhi is largely Punjabi Hindu—for Prime Minister Gandhi's tough stand towards the growing Sikh demand for an autonomous Punjab.

90. *Organiser*, 24 April 1983. Also see *Times of India* (Bombay), 24 April 1983.

91. For a discussion on the controversy generated by Vajpayee's proposal, see *Times of India* (Bombay), 18 April 1983.

92. Despite the dismal parliamentary showing, the BJP did secure about 7.7 per cent of the total vote, suggesting sufficient support to rebuild the party's legislative representation at the state and national levels. Indeed, only the Congress party polled a larger percentage of voters. In fact, the Jana Sangh had only once before performed better—in the 1967 elections when it polled 9.4 per cent of the vote.

93. The Communist Party of India (Marxist) criticized Rajiv Gandhi and his party for not making the RSS an issue. See *India Abroad* (New York City), 4 January 1985, p. 14.

94. *India Abroad* (New York City), 11 January 1985.

95. L. K. Advani, BJP general secretary, notes that the BJP from its inception in 1980 has recruited RSS pracharaks for party work. He argues that this recruitment demonstrates that the

RSS itself has not turned its back on politics. Interview with him on 15 September 1985 at Potomac, Maryland.

96. Vajpayee reportedly stated that the shift was only 'a change in terminology and not in content'. *The Telegraph* (Calcutta), 23 July 1985. This decision was ratified by the party executive in early October 1985.

97. See reports of the six-day conference in *Times of India* (Bombay), 9, 14, 16 October 1985.

98. For a comprehensive review of proceedings, see *Indian Express* (Delhi), 13 May 1986.

99. Atal Bihari Vajpayee, the former president of the BJP, is an exception, but even he is careful not to distance himself from the pracharak network that exercises a powerful voice in party affairs.

Conclusion

1. Movements comparable to the RSS are discussed in Michael Walzer, *The Revolution of the Saints: A Study of the Origins of Radical Politics* (London: Weidenfeld & Nicholson, 1966), a study of the puritan movement in England; and James W. White, *The Sokagakkai and Mass Society* (Stanford: Stanford University Press, 1970), the study of a Japanese religious organization and its political affiliate, the Komeito. Also see Rosabeth Moss Kanter's study of American communes in *Commitment and Community: Communes and Utopias in Sociological Perspective*, (7th printing) (Cambridge, Mass.: Harvard University Press, 1981).

2. For a discussion of the two ethical standards, see Max Weber, 'Politics as a Vocation,' in Hans H. Gerth, C. Wright Mills, eds., *From Max Weber: Essays in Sociology* (New York: Oxford University Press, 1958), pp. 77–128.

3. This is not an uncommon reaction of normative groups to politics. Amitai Etzioni, for example, points out that leaders in

normative organizations, in order to build moral commitment to themselves, seek to avoid instrumental activities and positions. Etzioni, *A Comparative Analysis of Complex Organizations*, pp. 217–18.

4. A theoretical discussion of 'significant audiences' in George H. Mead, *Mind, Self and Society*, ed. by Charles W. Morris (Chicago: University of Chicago Press, 1954), pp. 149–ff.

5. According to Leon Festinger and J. Merrill Carl-Smith, the more it 'costs' a person to do something, the more 'valuable' he will consider it, in order to justify the psychic 'expenses' required. See their article on the process in 'Cognitive Consequence of Forced Compliance', *Journal of Abnormal and Social Psychology*, 58 (March 1959), pp. 203–10.

6. For a discussion regarding the importance of social homogeneity on group cohesiveness, see Rosabeth Moss Kanter, *Commitment and Community*, pp. 93–94.

Index